On Ancient Warfare

Other Books By Richard A. Gabriel

Great Generals of the Ancient World (2017)
God's Generals: Military Lives of Moses, Buddha, and Muhammad (2016)
The Madness of Alexander the Great (2015)
Between Flesh and Steel: Military Medicine from the
Middle Ages to the War in Afghanistan (2013)
Man and Wound in the Ancient World (2012)
Hannibal: The Military Biography of Rome's Greatest Enemy (2011)
Philip II of Macedonia: Greater Than Alexander (2010)
Thutmose III: Egypt's Greatest Warrior King (2009)
Scipio Africanus: Rome's Greatest General (2008)
Muhammad: Islam's First Great General (2007)
The Warrior's Way: A Treatise on Military Ethics (2006)
Soldiers' Lives: Military Life and War in Antiquity:
4000 BCE to 1453 AD (2006)
Jesus The Egyptian: The Origins of Christianity
and the Psychology of Christ (2005)
Ancient Empires at War, 3 vols (2005)
Subotai The Valiant: Genghis Khan's Greatest General (2004)
Lion of the Sun (2003)
The Military History of Ancient Israel (2003)
Great Armies of Antiquity (2002)
Sebastian's Cross (2002)
Gods of Our Fathers: The Memory of Egypt in Judaism and Christianity (2001)
Warrior Pharaoh (2001)
Great Captains of Antiquity (2000)
Great Battles of Antiquity (1994)
A Short History of War: Evolution of Warfare and Weapons (1994)
History of Military Medicine: Ancient Times to the Middle Ages (1992)
History of Military Medicine: Renaissance to the Present (1992)
From Sumer to Rome: The Military Capabilities of Ancient Armies (1991)
The Culture of War: Invention and Early Development (1990)
The Painful Field: Psychiatric Dimensions of Modern War (1988)
No More Heroes: Madness and Psychiatry in War (1987)
The Last Centurion (French, 1987)
Military Psychiatry: A Comparative Perspective (1986)
Soviet Military Psychiatry (1986)
Military Incompetence: Why the US Military Doesn't Win (1985)
Operation Peace for Galilee: The Israeli-PLO War in Lebanon (1985)
The Antagonists: An Assessment of the Soviet and American Soldier (1984)
The Mind of the Soviet Fighting Man (1984)
Fighting Armies: NATO and the Warsaw Pact (1983)
Fighting Armies: Antagonists of the Middle East (1983)
Fighting Armies: Armies of the Third World (1983)
To Serve With Honor: A Treatise on Military Ethics (1982)
The New Red Legions: An Attitudinal Portrait of the Soviet Soldier (1980)
The New Red Legions: A Survey Data Sourcebook (1980)
Managers and Gladiators: Directions of Change in the Army (1978)
Crisis in Command: Mismanagement in the Army (1978)
Ethnic Groups in America (1978)
Program Evaluation: A Social Science Approach (1978)
The Ethnic Factor in the Urban Polity (1973)
The Environment: Critical Factors in Strategy Development (1973)

On Ancient Warfare

Perspectives on Aspects of War in Antiquity 4000 BC to AD 637

by

Richard A. Gabriel

Pen & Sword
MILITARY

AN IMPRINT OF PEN & SWORD BOOKS LTD.
YORKSHIRE – PHILADELPHIA

First published in Great Britain in 2018 by
Pen & Sword Military
An imprint of
Pen & Sword Books Ltd
Yorkshire – Philadelphia

ISBN 978 1 52671 8 457

A CIP catalogue record for this book is
available from the British Library.

Printed and bound in England by TJ International Ltd, Padstow, Cornwall

Pen & Sword Books Limited incorporates the imprints of Atlas, Archaeology, Aviation, Discovery, Family History, Fiction, History, Maritime, Military, Military Classics, Politics, Select, Transport, True Crime, Air World, Frontline Publishing, Leo Cooper, Remember When, Seaforth Publishing, The Praetorian Press, Wharncliffe Local History, Wharncliffe Transport, Wharncliffe True Crime and White Owl.

For a complete list of Pen & Sword titles please contact

PEN & SWORD BOOKS LIMITED
47 Church Street, Barnsley, South Yorkshire, S70 2AS, England
E-mail: enquiries@pen-and-sword.co.uk
Website: www.pen-and-sword.co.uk

Or
PEN AND SWORD BOOKS
1950 Lawrence Rd, Havertown, PA 19083, USA
E-mail: Uspen-and-sword@casematepublishers.com
Website: www.penandswordbooks.com

Table of Contents

Introduction

This book attempts to acquaint the reader with an understanding of the nature and conduct of war that emerged as a defining characteristic of human society during the period historians call 'antiquity'. 'Antiquity' can be defined as that time period beginning around 4000 BC with the near simultaneous establishment of Sumer and Egypt as national states, and ending with the Arab conquests in the fifth century AD. In antiquity, humans brought into being for the first time genuine cities, the complex social structures to govern them, written languages, bureaucracies, large-scale irrigation systems, the domestication of animals, organized religions, written moral codes, ships, navies and the first professional armies. The period was among the most inventive in human history, and witnessed the invention and development of the prototype of every major social institution upon which modern society is built. The development of these institutions made the conduct of war possible for the first time in human history.

These innovations were the result of the invention of efficient large-scale agriculture and animal domestication that produced the resources adequate to sustain large populations in place. The stability of large human populations made increasingly large and complex societies possible. Thus, the early Mesopotamian and Egyptian urban societies produced the first state-governing institutions in human history. Centralization required the creation of an administrative apparatus to direct large-scale social and economic resources toward national goals. By 3000 BC, such an apparatus was evident in Egypt, India and throughout the states of Mesopotamia. Central state institutions and a supporting governmental administrative apparatus inevitably gave form and stability to military structures. The standing army emerged as a permanent part of a new societal structure, the national state.

These developments would not have succeeded unless accompanied by profound changes in the psychological basis of human social relationships. The aggregation of large numbers of people in these complex societies required that those living within them refocus their allegiances away from the extended family, clan and tribe toward a larger social entity, the state. This psychological change was facilitated by the emergence of religious castes that gave meaning to the individual's life beyond a parochial context that demanded loyalty to its rulers. Organized belief systems were integrated into the social order and given institutional expression through public rituals that linked religious worship to national identity, political loyalty and to military objectives national in scope. Thus, the Egyptian pharaoh became divine and Mesopotamian kings the personification of their respective national divinities. The military achievements of national leaders were perceived as divinely ordained, and the propulsive power of religion was placed at the service of the state and its armies.

These changes had profound consequences, for this same period was seminal to the development of war and its instrumentalities. By 3000 BC, war had become an important social institution in major cultures of the ancient world. As a mechanism of cultural development, war became a legitimate and indispensable function of the national state, supported by an extensive institutional infrastructure. Properly understood, war is a level of organized conflict involving forces of significant size rooted in the larger society's organizational and resource structure, applying a killing technology with some degree of organization and expertise. Without these conditions, one finds murder, small-scale scuffles, raids, ambushes, executions, etc., but not war *per se*. War requires the systematic, organized societal application of orchestrated violence on a significant scale. This period saw the introduction of a range of social, political, economic, psychological and military technologies that served to make the conduct of war a possible and normal part of human social existence. In less than 1,500 years, humans went from a condition in which war was relatively rare and largely ritualistic, to one in which death and destruction were achieved on a modern scale. It is no exaggeration to say that war is among the most important legacies the ancient world bequeathed to the modern one.

It may be argued that the ancient period was the most creative period in human development. If this seems too strong a claim, it may be wise to remember when assessing the legacy of the ancients that it is always easier to improve upon or modify an existing structure, practice, technology or institution than it is to invent it in the first place. Thus, computers can do remarkable things, but they are ultimately only variations on the twin innovations of writing and mathematics, both invented by the ancients. In many areas of human endeavour, the ancients were truly inventors, and the greatness of the ancient world lies even more in its social inventiveness than in its technical refinements, which were often revolutionary in any case.

The period's great contribution was to bring into existence original paradigms that had never before existed, and to bequeath them to the future. There is no denying the creativity of the modern period, itself less than 200 years old. But when compared to the ancient period in terms of the nature, scope, breadth, longevity and depth of innovation, the modern period, as remarkable as it is, has yet to attain similar dimensions. One need only consider what the modern world would look like had not some ancient genius attempted to portray human expression first in pictographs, and then later in written script.

The emphasis that modern society places upon change and technological innovation risks devaluing history, especially ancient history, as a subject of worthwhile consideration, as if the tension and resistance to social change evident in today's societies somehow did not exist in ancient societies. One consequence is that the ability of the past to provide context for the present becomes lost. The future becomes all, the past of no value; thus, Henry Ford's comment that 'history is bunk'. Of equal concern is that those who inhabit the enticing present, itself so seemingly different from the ancient world, risk coming to believe that the difficulties we face are occurring for the first time in human experience. It is but a short step from there to the view that we must be different in nature and intellect from those who lived so long ago. And so we conclude that we have little to learn from an understanding of the past.

One therefore ought to enrich oneself by learning about the world of antiquity and the conduct of war during this time. But the very complexity and vastness of the period (4000 BC–632 AD) makes this a very difficult task indeed. The study of war in antiquity requires the military historian to be familiar with the armies and practices (recruitment, training, tactics, logistics, weapons, animals, staff structures, battles, sieges, etc.) of the major armies of the period. These armies include those employed by Egyptians, Sumerians, Hyksos, Aryans, Canaanites, Israelites, Hittites, Mitanni, Assyrians, Persians, Carthaginians, Classical Greeks, Imperial Greeks, the Successor Greeks, Republican Romans, Imperial Romans, the eastern tribal invaders and the armies of the Muslim Conquest, to mention only the major armed forces of the period. It hardly needs mentioning that to adequately understand war in antiquity, the military historian requires a working knowledge of the national cultures that produced and sustained these armies. It is not difficult to imagine that one might well spend one's entire academic career in the study of the ancient world and its wars. Even so, a complete study of ancient warfare would likely remain beyond the capacity of any single historian to achieve.

The purpose of this book, then, is to offer a collection of essays on various relevant topics pertaining to the evolution and conduct of war in the ancient period that the general reader, student of history, military buff, professional soldier, academic and amateur historian will find interesting and enlightening. There is no claim that the collection offers anything but a partial foray into the subject, and it is, to some extent, arbitrary in that I have chosen subjects for presentation that I believe will spark the reader's interest by exposing him or her to something that they did not know. It may be useful for the reader to begin with an examination of the timeline at the beginning of the book to obtain some temporal and historical context into which to fit the additional articles. I have packed each chapter with footnotes to point the way to any further reading the reader may wish to undertake on a subject that he or she finds of greater interest. I hope this makes up for not including a bibliography which, given the scope and complexity of the subjects it would have to address, would have been enormous. My hope is that my readers will find the world of antiquity as intriguing as I have.

Timeline

500,000 BC	*Homo erectus* produces the first stone tools
100,000 BC	*Homo sapiens* invents the first long-range weapon, the fire-hardened, wooden-tipped spear
10,000 BC	Humans learn how to herd wild animals
9000 BC	Sheep become the first pastoral animal to be domesticated by humans
8300 BC	First archaeological evidence of planting of wild cereals in Mureybet, Syria; the earliest town founded at Jericho
7500 BC	First use of pressure flaking, making it possible to fashion longer one-piece knives, leading to the invention of reaping and skinning knives that led eventually to the dagger
6500 BC	First evidence of organized violence among humans occurs at Jean Sahara in the Sudan; first rock painting of humans killing humans found in the Transcaucasus
6000 BC	Cattle, goats, and dogs are domesticated; first evidence of harvesting of wild grains in Byblos
5500 BC	First large-scale irrigation to support agriculture occurs at Catal Huyuk in Anatolia
5000 BC	First evidence of settled agriculture; planting of domesticated cereal grains; humans stabilize their food supply, bringing an end to the hunter-gatherer way of life they have practised for 800,000 years; first cities are now possible
4500 BC	Sling invented at Catal Huyuk in Anatolia
4000 BC	Beginning of the Bronze Age in the Middle East and south-eastern Europe; first fortified towns appear; sling, dagger, mace and bow have become common weapons; emergence of the first large urban societies in Egypt, Mesopotamia and the Indus River valley in India
4000–3000 BC	War has now become an important social institution characteristic of all major human cultures of the world
3500–2200 BC	Empire of Sumer and Akkad in Mesopotamia established; first Sumerian war between Lagash and Umma in 2525 BC

3200 BC	Upper and Lower Egypt unified by force by Namer; the first dynastic period in Egypt begins and lasts 700 years; Egypt establishes the largest irrigation system in the world to support its large population
2750 BC	Babylonians are the first people to diagnose mental illness in soldiers as caused by a curse from the gods
2686 BC	Period of the Old Kingdom in Egypt; age of the pyramids; first evidence of military staffs
2500 BC	First evidence of soldiers wearing helmets found in Death Pits of Ur; Sumerians introduce the primitive chariot, the first military use of the wheel; the chariot, composite bow, sickle-sword, penetrating axe, body armour, helmet, neck collars, battering ram and scaling ladder are all invented in Mesopotamia, increasing the killing power of weaponry
2500 BC	Sumerians invent the first military medical corps
2500 BC	Hittites migrate from the lower Danube to Anatolia
2325–?	Sargon the Great of Akkad conquers Sumer and establishes an empire; his grandson, Nara-Sin (2254–2218 BC) introduces the composite bow to warfare
2200–1750 BC	Period of the Xia Dynasty in China
2158–2000 BC	The world's first military medical text is produced by the Third Dynasty of Ur
2050–1786 BC	Egyptian Middle Kingdom period; borders expanded before country collapses into civil war; Hyksos invade Egypt in 1750 BC and occupy the country for almost 200 years; the invaders introduce the chariot to Egypt
2000 BC	First evidence of the field pack in Egypt
1850 BC	The Kahn Papyrus, the oldest Egyptian medical text, is written down
1728–1686 BC	The reign of Hammurabi of Babylon
1700 BC	First evidence of the military field boot introduced by the Aryan invaders of India
1600 BC	Mitanni establish themselves as a new kingdom in Syria; first to exploit the horse as an instrument of war and introduce the horse-drawn, spoked-wheel chariot; introduced the *maryannu* socio-military system of warfare throughout the Middle East
1600 BC	Indo-European migration from central Asian steppes begins
1580–960 BC	Period of the New Kingdom in Egypt; Hyksos driven out; Eighteenth Dynasty established by Amenhotep I (1570–1546 BC); imperial expansion completed under Thutmose III

1500–1200 BC	Archaic Age of Greece; siege of Troy; *Iliad* as an oral poem first performed
1500–900 BC	Emergence of the Canaanites on the Palestinian land bridge; adoption of the *maryannu* military system of the Mitanni
1497 BC	Thutmose III of Egypt defeats a Mitanni-Canaanite coalition at Megiddo, military history's first battle for which there is substantial evidence
1450–1180 BC	Rise of the Hittite empire under Suppiluliumas and his son Muwatallis
1400 BC	First weapons fashioned of iron appear in India
1300 BC	The Kizwadana people of Armenia are the first to make iron implements in the West
1275 BC	Ramses II of Egypt introduces the ox-cart as a military logistics vehicle; defeats the Hittite at the Battle of Kadesh
1275–1225 BC	Israelite exodus from Egypt
1225–1200 BC	Successful Israelite invasion of Canaan under Joshua
1225–1177 BC	The Bronze Age ends in the collapse of all the major cities of the Levant; probably caused by a half-century of earthquakes, storms, drought, famine, disease and malnutrition; attacks by Sea Peoples finished off the depleted populations
1177 BC	Ramses III defeats a coalition of Sea Peoples and Philistines that attack Egypt; first evidence of iron sword in the West; introduction of the Argive shield and grip to Greek warfare
1200–1000 BC	Invasion by unknown peoples destroy Archaic Greece
1200–1050 BC	Period of the Judges in Israel
1200–700 BC	Indo-European invasion of India; the *Rig Veda* and the *Mahabharata* are written; chariot introduced to Indian warfare; first evidence in India of the use of prosthetic limbs for the wounded
1150–1100 BC	Period of the Shang Dynasty in China
1100–256 BC	Period of the Zhou Dynasty in China
1053 BC	Philistines defeat Israelites at Aphek and take control of most of Canaan; Philistines are defeated by Solomon in 960 BC
1005–961 BC	David establishes Kingdom of Israel
1000 BC	Beginning of the Iron Age in the West; iron weapons do not become common until 800 BC
961–921 BC	Kingdom of Solomon in Israel; military recruitment and logistics are rationalized; new chariot armies created
921–587 BC	Period of the Hebrew kings; ends with deportation of Israelite religious elites and Philistines

890–612 BC	Rise of the Assyrian Empire; King Tukulti-Ninurta II introduces mounted cavalry teams for the first time; single mounted horsemen appear fifty years later
853 BC	Battle of Qarqar; first use of horse cavalry in battle; first use of camel cavalry by Gingibu the Arab in the same battle; later the Assyrians are the first to use the chariot as a platform for mounted infantry
814 BC	Rise of Carthage
771–464 BC	Spring and Autumn period in China; civil wars among seven states; first use of the bronze sword, crossbow and laminar armour in Chinese warfare
700 BC	Vedic social order in India collapses; replaced by sixteen states constantly at war with one another
612 BC	Assyrian Empire destroyed by the Persians
600 BC	Elephant used for the first time as an instrument of warfare in India; the elephant replaces the chariot
600–338 BC	Age of Classical Greece; Peloponnesian War; Persian invasion; bronze cuirass replaced by linen armour
546–323 BC	Rise of the Persian Empire; Cyrus II the Great comes to the throne of Persia; introduces universal military training for all Persians; introduces the scythed chariot and mobile siege towers; first use of naphtha throwers; Cyrus dies in battle in 529 BC
544–496 BC	Sun Tzu writes *The Art of War* in China
525 BC	Cambyses defeats the Egyptians at the Battle of Pelusium
500 BC	First appearance of mounted cavalry in China; cavalry does not become common for another 200 years
500 BC	Indians introduce the Wootz process for making steel
500–28 BC	The period of the Roman Republic
483–400 BC	Lifetime of Buddha
481 BC	Xerxes attempts to invade Greece; fails
464–221 BC	Period of the Warring States in China
400 BC	Iron working for military purposes introduced in China; iron swords used for the first time at the Battle of Guiling in 353 BC
394–386 BC	The Corinthian War rages
390 BC	Iphicrates introduces *peltast* light infantry to Greek warfare
382–336 BC	Philip II of Macedon unites Greece by conquest; introduces the fortified camp, artillery and cavalry as the combat arm of decision to Greek warfare; improves logistics using horses to replace the ox-cart

357 BC	Stymphalian Aenas writes the first comprehensive work in the West on military theory
356–323 BC	The period of Imperial Greece created by Philip II of Macedon and led later by Alexander the Great
340–290 BC	Roman wars against the Samnites; Romans acquire the *pilum*, the *scutum* shield and the military sandal from the Samnites
334 BC	Alexander crosses the Hellespont to invade Persia
331 BC	Alexander defeats Darius at Arbela; all Persia falls to Alexander
323–280 BC	Alexander dies in Babylon; Wars of the Successors break out; Antagonids rule in Greece, Ptolemies rule Egypt and the Seleucids rule south-west Asia
323–168 BC	Reign of the Successors
321 BC	Chandragupta Maurya establishes the Mauryan Empire in India
300 BC	The Age of Steel begins; Roman Army adopts chain mail from the Celts
281–275 BC	Pyrrhus' wars with Romans; introduction of the elephant as an element in war in the West by the Carthaginians
264–241 BC	First Punic War; Rome vs Carthage
222 BC	Pyrrhus introduces the double and articulated phalanx to Greek warfare at the Battle of Sellasia
220–206 BC	Rule of the Han Empire in China
218–201 BC	Second Punic War; Hannibal invades Italy
216 BC	Battle of Cannae; Hannibal defeats the Romans
204 BC	Romans replace the maniple with the cohort; adopt the *gladius* as the main weapon of infantry
202 BC	Scipio Africanus defeats Hannibal at Zama, bringing the Second Punic War to an end
197 BC	Rome invades Greece; defeats Pyrrhus at the Battle of Cynoscephalae
149–146 BC	Third Punic War; Carthage defeated and the city destroyed
100 BC	Gaius Marius reforms the Roman army; military training introduced and logistics improved
63 BC–AD	Gaius Julius Caesar Octavianus, known to history as Caesar Augustus, defeats Mark Antony in the civil war and founds the Roman Empire
58–52 BC	Julius Caesar conquers Gaul and invades Britain

48 BC	Civil war between Caesar and Pompey; Pompey defeated at the Battle of Pharsalus
44 BC	Caesar assassinated; civil war begins
AD 9	Romans defeated by Arminius at the Battle of the Teutoburg Forest, forcing Roman influence back across the Rhine
AD 9–450	Period of Imperial Rome; *lorica segmenta* introduced as new armour; Roman medical corps invents the surgical clamp and the tourniquet
AD 235–297	Rome suffers through sixty years of civil strife, during which 16 emperors are assassinated
AD 284–305	Emperor Diocletian divides the Roman Empire into two administrative districts; Constantine establishes Byzantium as the eastern imperial centre
AD 378	The Goths defeat the Romans at the Battle of Adrianople; open a breach in the eastern frontier through which various tribes enter Roman imperial territory
AD 410	Goths capture and sack Rome; first time in its history
AD 450	Rome defeats Attila the Hun at the Battle of Chalons; Roman armies are by now completely barbarized; for all practical purposes, the Western Roman Empire ceases to exist
AD 464–484	Rise of the Sassanid Empire of Persia
AD 475	Odoacer deposes Romulus Augustulus, the last Roman emperor; this is the date usually accepted as marking the end of the Roman state established more than a millennium earlier; imperial power shifts east to Constantinople
AD 474–524	The Eastern Roman Empire is on the defensive against numerous Persian and tribal attacks
AD 476–600	The former Western Empire shattered into a number of kingdoms ruled by barbarian peoples i.e., Ostrogoths, Angles and Saxons, Visigoths, Franks and Burgundians, Vandals, Lombards, Bulgars and Slavs, and Avars
AD 527–565	Justinian's wars; defeats Persia and attempts to re-establish the empire in the West; Belisarius attacks Italy and recaptures Rome; a series of battles fought with Goths; Belisarius recalled to Constantinople and Goths reoccupy Rome and most of Italy
AD 546–553	Rise of the Turks; they overthrow the Avar Empire and establish themselves as the most powerful force in northern and central Asia; they begin a career of military conquest that has profound impact upon the West, leading ultimately to the establishment of the Ottoman Empire

Chapter 1

The Invention of War

War is the legacy that the ancient world bequeathed to the modern one. There is little evidence of war before the emergence of the world's first complex human societies. War is a social invention that required specific conditions to bring about. But because war has been omnipresent from the very beginning of man's recorded history, about 3500 BC, it is assumed by some that war must have been present even before that.[1] But when war as a social institution is placed in historical perspective, it is obvious that it is among the most recent of man's social inventions.

The first evidence of a hominid culture that used tools emerged 500,000 years ago in the Olduvai Gorge stone culture in Africa. The honour of initiating the Stone Age with the first use of tools goes to *Homo erectus*, our direct though not most immediate ancestor. Four hundred thousand years later, *Homo sapiens* and his now extinct cousin, Neanderthal man, created a more advanced stone culture with a wider range of tools, including the first long-range weapon, the spear. It is this later period that serves as a baseline from which to study the emergence of warfare. Otherwise, we would have to admit that for more than 98.8 per cent of its time on this planet, the human species lived without any evidence of war whatsoever.

Using the Stone Age cultures of *Homo sapiens* and Neanderthal man as a starting point, some remarkable facts emerge about the development of war. Humans required 30,000 years to learn how to use fire, and another 20,000 years to invent the fire-hardened, wooden-tipped spear; spear points came much later. Sixty thousand years later, humans invented the bow and arrow. It required another 30,000 years for humans to learn how to herd wild animals, and another 4,000 years to domesticate goats, sheep, cattle and the dog. At about the same time, there is the first evidence for the harvesting of wild grains, but it took another 2,000 years for humans to transplant wild grains to fixed campsites, and another 2,000 years to learn how to plant domesticated strains of cereal grain. It is only after these developments, around 4000 BC, that warfare made its appearance as a major human social institution.[2] Seen in historical perspective, mankind has known war for only about 6 per cent of the time since the *Homo sapiens* Stone Age began.[3]

Once warfare became established, however, it is difficult to find any other social institution that developed as quickly. In less than 1,000 years, humans brought forth the sword, sling, dagger, mace, bronze and copper weapons, as well as fortified towns. The next 1,000 years saw the emergence of iron weapons, the chariot, the standing professional army, military academies, general staffs, military training, permanent arms industries, written texts on tactics, military procurement, logistics systems, conscription and military pay. By 2000 BC, war had become an important social institution in all major cultures of the world.[4]

War is properly defined as a level of organized conflict involving forces of significant size rooted in the larger society's organizational structure, applying a killing technology with some degree of organization and expertise. War also requires the systematic, organized societal application of orchestrated violence on a significant scale.[5] Without these conditions, one might find murder, small-scale scuffles, raids, ambushes, executions and even cannibalism, but not war.[6] Accordingly, for the first 95,000 years after the *Homo sapiens* Stone Age began, there is only limited evidence that humans engaged in organized conflict on any level, let alone one requiring organized group violence.[7]

The first evidence of truly organized violence on some scale occurs sometime around 6500 BC at Jebal Sahaba in the Sudan. The skeletal remains of fifty-nine people, including women and children, suggest that they were killed by repeated arrow wounds and spear thrusts.[8] It is unclear if these people were killed in a raid or ambush, or simply executed. About half the skeletons had arrow points embedded in them, and it appears that the bodies may have been deposited in smaller groups over time. What is certain is that an organized force of some size was necessary to

Neolithic war. Pictorial evidence of man fighting against man is as old as the Neolithic Age, as this painting from Spain reveals. Note that the 'army of four' is attempting to direct flanking fire against the 'army of three' in what may be the earliest evidence of 'envelopment' in battle.

From Arther Ferrill, *The Origins of War* (London: Thames and Hudson, 1985).

Figure 1: Neolithic Rock Painting

carry out the killing. A Neolithic site in the Transcaucasus reveals the first rock painting of the period that seems to show a small armed squad attacking and killing other men with bows and arrows. While it required another 1500 years for humans to reach a level of organized violence that could be unequivocally identified as war, it seems clear that by 6000 BC humans had already learned to use organized groups to kill other humans. Still, for most of the Stone Age humans lived without even small-scale organization for killing other humans. This is hardly surprising considering how humans lived for all but the last few hundred years of the period.

For all but the last 10,000 years, humans lived as hunter-gathers organized into small groups of twenty to fifty people. Most of the members of these groups were related by blood or marriage, much like an extended family. These groups travelled constantly in small migratory bands following the seasonal migration of the game, and assembled as clans on a seasonal basis as the normal migration of the wild herds brought them together. It is unlikely that these clan groups had any social organization of any kind. They had certainly not yet evolved into tribes. Under these conditions, organized conflict of any sort was a rare occurrence. The small size of the groups alone would have mitigated against it. The average hunter-gatherer group had within it not more than six or seven armed adult males, and the need to hunt and feed their families would have made it impossible for them to serve primarily as warriors. The constant movement of the group also made it unlikely that they would come into contact with other groups, except on rare occasions.[9] The only weapon capable of being used in war at this time was the spear, and there is no evidence that humans ever used it to kill other humans during this period.[10]

For humans to abandon seasonal migrations required an expansion and stability of their food supply and a more certain way to obtain migratory game. The expansion of the food supply came first. At Mureybet in Syria around 8300 BC, there appears the first archaeological evidence of the planting of wild cereals.[11] Later, humans moved from harvesting wild grains to transplanting them to more stable home camps. Humans were on the threshold of creating the tribe. Mureybet appears as the first stable small village made possible by the rudimentary cultivation of cereal grains. At about the same time (8350 BC), the 'earliest town in the world' came into being at Jericho in Palestine, the world's first large-scale permanent human settlement. The people of Jericho had mastered the secret of seed corn and the technology of irrigation to plant and grow it, supporting a population of about 2,500 people.[12]

The first evidence of humans' ability to domesticate animals on some scale also appears around 7000 BC. Byblos offers the first evidence of the domestication of sheep, goats and cattle, and using the trained dog as a helper.[13] Five hundred years later, at Catal Huyuk in Anatolia, we find the first large-scale irrigation to support agriculture. The number of dwellings within the town, about 1,000, suggests that the population of Catal Huyuk was about 6,000 people, twice the size of Jericho.[14] By 5,000 BC, humans had succeeded in stabilizing and expanding their food supply to a degree that could support human groupings in the thousands, with agriculture bringing to an end the hunter-gatherer way of life that humans had known for more than 800,000 years. Large stable populations permanently tied to specific places made possible the evolution of the tribe. Tribal societies with their larger populations, adequate food supply and the corresponding de-emphasis on hunting were able to produce a class of hunters that evolved into a new class of warriors, whose claim to social role and status was based less upon their hunting prowess than their ability to fight and kill other warriors in defence of the tribe. For the first time in human experience, there arose a social group whose specific function and justification was its ability to kill other human beings.[15]

Once a warrior caste came into being, it would have been a matter of only a few generations before no one could remember when there had been no warriors at all. Within a short time, the new social institution would have seemed as normal a part of society as cattle herders and farmers. Once the military technology became available, these new warriors and the tribal social orders that created them were able to fight wars of much greater scope and lethality than had previously been the case. But the presence of a warrior caste by itself did not mean that it would have had to develop into an organized force for large-scale warfare. Most early war was highly ritualized, with low levels of death and injury, much as combat between other species of animals is. To move from ritualized combat to genuine killing required a change in human psychology. When and how Neolithic tribes transitioned from ritual to real warfare is unknown. What is certain, however, is that they did make the journey.

War, then, seems a social invention brought into being as a consequence of previous human social developments. Certain kinds of behaviour (war) require certain structures to initiate and sustain that behaviour. From this perspective, warfare on a large scale requires at least the following social developments: (1) a stable population of a size large enough to produce a surplus population freed from traditional economic roles to serve as a source of military manpower; (2) a territorial attachment specific enough to change the psychology of the group so that it thinks of itself as both special and singular, i.e. territoriality of some sort, ethnic, religious, land, etc.; (3) a warrior class with social influence in the decision-making process; (4) a technology of war, i.e. weapons; (5) a complex, role-differentiated social order, a political and administrative structure; (6) a larger mental vision of human activity that stimulates the generation of artificial reasons for engaging in behaviour, often religiously or culturally based.[16]

The late Neolithic age (6000–5000 BC) witnessed an advance in the development of new weapons that was, until then, unparalleled in human history. It was but a short time before these weapons were used in large-scale warfare. The major weapons of this period were the bow and arrow, the mace, spear, dagger and sling.[17] The fire-hardened spear had been around for thousands of years. Its major improvement in the Neolithic period was the use of stone, flint and obsidian spear points. Flint and obsidian spear points require pressure-flaking when chipping the point from the larger stone. Pressure-flaking makes possible spear and arrow points that are flat on two sides, reducing weight and increasing penetration. Pressure-flaking also made possible longer one-piece blades, an innovation first applied to reaping and skinning knives before giving rise to the dagger. This new technology first appeared between 7500–6800 BC at Cayonu in Syria,[18] and spread widely and rapidly throughout the Middle East.[19]

The dagger made an excellent short-range weapon, and as soon as man developed metals technology to increase the length of the blade, the sword followed. The mace with a stone head affixed to a wooden handle could easily cave in a man's skull. The handle also increased the accuracy and striking momentum of the weapon when thrown. The bow had been in existence for millennia, but aside from the use of flat arrow heads, there appear to have been no improvements in its composition or strength until much later, when the Sumerians introduced the composite bow. The bow was easy to fashion and use, and could kill from a distance, capabilities which probably made it the basic killing weapon of the Neolithic warrior.

An important innovation was the sling.[20] Evidence for its existence appears at Catal Huyuk between 5500–4500 BC. Here we also find the first evidence of shot made from sun-baked clay, the first human attempt to make a specific type of expendable ammunition. The sling represented a great leap in killing technology. Even an average slinger can throw shot to a range of 200 yards. Small shot can be delivered on a trajectory almost parallel with the ground over ranges of 100–200 yards, while larger stones can be fired howitzer-like over greater ranges.[21] All these weapons except the sling have developmental histories that point to their original invention as weapons of the hunt. The sling may have been the first weapon designed primarily to kill humans, since its hunting function is marginal at best.

But weapons are useless without tactics to direct their employment in battle. The most basic tactics are the line and column, and the ability to approach in column and move into line. Tactics, of course, require commanders, which implies at least some rudimentary military organization. The importance of tactics in the development of war is suggested by H. Turney-High, who argues that evidence of simple tactical formations is the definitive characteristic that constitutes a 'military horizon' separating fighting from genuine war.[22] While the Neolithic period may have witnessed the first use of tactics in fighting among humans at war, it is likely that they were originally developed long before as techniques of the hunt.

Just prior to 4000 BC, there appears the first evidence of fortified towns. The classic and much earlier example is Jericho. While other towns of the period show some degree of fortification, mostly ditches and mud walls or, as at Catal Huyuk, houses abutting one another so that the outside walls of the dwellings constitute a wall around the whole settlement, only Jericho reflects a type of architecture that would be readily recognizable as military architecture. Jericho's walls enclosed an area of 10 acres and ran to a length of 765 yards. The walls were 10ft thick and 30ft high. A 28ft tower with a base 35ft in diameter enclosing a doorway in its middle was its most striking feature. A population of 2,500 people could field about 600 adults to defend the wall, or one soldier per yard of wall.[23] Jericho's walls seem to have been built in stages sometime between 8000–7000 BC. The emergence of fortified sites in the late Neolithic period seems evidence enough of warfare conducted on some significant scale.

The connection between the development of agriculture and warfare has been long noted by scholars such as Quincy Wright in his study of 633 cultures. Wright notes that even before the establishment of agriculture as the dominant form of economic and social organization, peoples who were partially agriculturized demonstrated a greater tendency toward war, while the higher agriculturalists were the most warlike of all.[24] The post-Neolithic period or Bronze Age saw a great explosion in the spread of these large-scale agricultural societies, and with it the spread of warfare conducted on a large scale.

The spread of agriculture set the stage for the emergence of large urban societies. The first of these societies appeared almost simultaneously around 4000 BC in Egypt, Mesopotamia and the Indus River valley in India. This period saw the development of new weapons – the chariot, composite bow, sword, axe, penetrating axe, mail armour, helmet, battering ram, scaling ladder and stronger fortifications – that increased the scale and lethality of war. Supporting social and psychological structures struck deep roots, so that within a mere thousand years the humans of the Bronze Age could not imagine a way of life without warriors, armies and war. The expectation of war made possible the large conscript armies that came to characterize the period. Military service, warrior kings and large armies became routine aspects of life when only a millennium earlier they were unimaginable. Increased agricultural efficiency produced an explosion in population, providing the raw human material for war on a large scale. Humans stood on the brink of yet another revolution, this one in the area of metals technology. As humans entered the Bronze Age, it is unlikely that they realized that they had given birth to yet another great social invention, one that they bequeathed to every generation since then. Humans had invented war.

Chapter 2

Armies of the Ancient World

How large were the armies of the ancient world? While the armies of the Late Bronze Age (2000–1500 BC) were significantly larger than those which emerged at the beginning of the Early Bronze Age (3000–2500 BC), they were small compared to the armies that fought in the Iron Age (1250 BC). The Persians, for example, routinely deployed field armies that were ten times larger than anything seen in the Bronze Age. A Chinese field army that fought at the Battle of Chengpu (632 BC) comprised 700 chariots supported by 52,000 infantry.[1] Two centuries later, a unified China could put one million soldiers in the field in a supreme national effort.[2] During the Early Bronze Age, Sargon I of Akkad could mobilize an army perhaps as large as 5,400 soldiers. But an army of this size required a major national effort on the part of all Sargon's vassals, and could not be deployed in the field for very long.[3]

Even the smaller states of the Late Bronze Age could field armies much larger than Sargon's. The Hittites and Mitanni, both major states of the period, could deploy only comparatively small armies. The Hittites, for example, could only deploy 17,000 soldiers at the Battle of Kadesh in 1275 BC, and this included almost all of their allies.[4] It is unlikely that the king of Hatti could have put more than 10,000–12,000 men in the field by himself. While the size of the fully deployed army of the Mitanni (1480–1335 BC) is unknown, a reasonable guess would place it somewhere around 10,000 men. By the Late Bronze Age, however, armies were growing much larger.

Two factors restricted the size of Early Bronze Age armies. The first was the lack of national administrative mechanisms of political and social control. By the Iron Age, these had been developed almost to modern levels of efficiency, so that larger numbers of recruits could be called to military service with considerably less disruption of the domestic economy. The second factor was the replacement of bronze with iron as the basic metal for war. Bronze is a combination of copper and tin, and was very expensive to manufacture because tin was very rare in the Middle East. Archaeological evidence shows that tin could only be found in significant quantities in Bavaria, Afghanistan and Cornwall, from where it had to be imported at great expense. The cost of bronze weapons was a significant limitation upon the number of troops that could be armed with them by a state. The discovery and utilization of iron, a metal commonly available almost everywhere, reduced the cost of weapons considerably so that more soldiers could be equipped at reasonable cost. The result was an increase in the size of Iron Age armies.

Examples of Iron Age armies are instructive. The Egyptian army in the time of Ramses II (1279–1212 BC) numbered over 100,000 men when the garrisons of military fortresses are included.[5] The army was comprised largely of conscripts, with one-in-ten adult males being called to some kind of national service, including corvee labour. An Egyptian field army was organized into divisions of 5,000 men each, and could be deployed individually or as a combined force of several divisions.[6] At the Battle of Kadesh between the Hittites and Egyptians, the first ancient battle for which we have reliable manpower figures, the Egyptians deployed a four-division force of 20,000 men against the Hittite army of 17,000.[7]

The Assyrian army of the eighth century BC was comprised of 150,000–200,000 soldiers, the largest standing military force the Middle East had witnessed to this time.[8] An Assyrian combat field army numbered approximately 50,000 men with various mixes of infantry, chariots and cavalry.[9] The Assyrian army was equal in size to five modern American army divisions or eight Russian army field divisions. When arrayed for battle, the Assyrian army occupied an area 2,500 yards across and 100 yards deep. It was also the first army of the ancient world to be entirely equipped with iron weapons. There were weapons armouries strategically placed throughout the empire in which iron weapons and other equipment were stored. The armoury at Dur-Sharrukin (Fort Sargon) alone contained 200 tons of iron weapons, helmets and armour.[10]

Figure 2: Ramses II Army Camp at Kadesh

As large as the Assyrian army was for its day, it was surpassed by the national army of Persia that appeared 300 years later. Darius' army in the Scythian campaign numbered 200,000 soldiers, and the force deployed by Xerxes against the Greeks comprised 300,00 men and 60,000 horsemen.[11] One analysis of Xerxes' army suggests that when support troops are included, the army included more than a million men.[12] Even at the end of the empire, the Persians could deploy very large forces. In 331 BC, just before Alexander destroyed it at the Battle of Arbela, the Persian army under Darius fielded 300,000 infantry, 40,000 cavalry, 250 chariots and fifty elephants.[13]

Philip of Macedon had bequeathed his son, Alexander, a professional army of 32,000 soldiers organized into four divisions of 8,192 soldiers each, a military instrument far too small to achieve Alexander's dream of empire. Alexander quickly expanded the old army to 60,000, and during his campaign in India, at the Battle of Jhelum (Hydaspes River) in 326 BC, his army had grown to 120,000 infantry and 50,000 cavalry through the enlistment of entire tribes of Central Asian soldiers.[14]

During the Roman Republic, Rome could put armies into the field that exceeded 80,000 men, although this required a supreme effort, such as in the war against Hannibal. At the Battle of Cannae (216 BC), Hannibal destroyed the Roman army, killing 78,000 men. The Roman response was to raise another army. The imperium that replaced the Roman Republic in the first century AD had a standing army of 350,000 soldiers, all full-time professionals, augmented by almost as many tribal allies and militias brought into Roman military service for various periods of time. Rome could routinely field armies of 40,000 men with little effort.

The barbarian armies – Gauls, Germans and Goths – that fought the Romans during Caesar's time and the early days of the empire often produced very large armies. In Caesar's day, the population of Gaul was between fifteen and twenty million, divided into 300 or so tribes.[15] In 58 BC, Caesar attacked the Helvetii and killed 238,000 men, women and children. Two years later, he trapped a German tribe at the junction of the Moselle and Rhine rivers, killing 430,000 Germans.[16] The habit of these tribes of bringing their families with them to the battlefield, thus exposing them to slaughter, accounts for these horrendous casualty figures. Nonetheless, even if only one third of the casualties were soldiers, the figures still suggest a very large tribal army.

German tribes also could deploy large armies. The average German tribe comprised about 35,000–40,000 people, and there were twenty-three different tribes living in the area between the Rhine and Elbe rivers.[17] An individual tribe could, on average, raise 5,000–7,000 warriors. When assembled in coalition, the German armies easily could exceed 60,000 men. If we are to believe Eunapius, the army of Goths that crossed the Danube in 376 BC prior to the Battle of Adrianople consisted of 200,000 warriors. This is surely an exaggeration. But if the number of people in the tribe was this large, then at least 50,000–60,000 of them were warriors.[18]

Probably the largest armies in the ancient world during the Iron Age were those of China during the fifth–fourth centuries BC, and the armies of India during the Magadha state ascendancy (fifth–fourth centuries BC) and the period of Chandragupta (324–300 BC) which came after it. With the entire agricultural and urban populations of China organized down to the clan level for corvee labour, it was an easy task for Chinese rulers during the Warring States period to mobilize armies of 400,000 men. Documents of the time tell of armies approaching one million men, although this number is certainly somewhat exaggerated.

We can be more certain of the size of the Indian armies. After the Battle of the Jhelum River (Hydaspes) in 326 BC, Alexander advanced inland and attempted to cross the Ganga River. When Alexander's scouts reported the size of the Indian force awaiting him on the opposite bank, his army mutinied and refused to cross. As recorded by Plutarch, the combined Indian armies of the kings of Gandaritai and Praisai awaiting Alexander comprised 80,000 cavalry, 8,000 war chariots, 6,000 fighting elephants and 200,000 infantry.[19] During the Mauryan period, Megasthenes, the Greek ambassador at the court of Chandragupta, recorded the strengths of the armies of some of the states comprising the Mauryan realm. His figures appear below in Table 1.[20] In times of national crisis, the Mauryan king could call upon the military resources of any or all of the states of the imperial realm. Armies of the size that China and India could deploy during the Iron Age were not seen again in the West until at least the time of the American Civil War.

Only in both Bronze Age and Iron Age Greece do we find armies that remained relatively small. In the *Iliad*, the poet never tells us the size of the Mycenaean army besieging Troy, but the often quoted figure of 10,000 men is surely inaccurate. More likely the army numbered less than 5,000 men, if that.[21] Mycenaean society

Table 1: Military Strength of Maurayn States

State	Elephants	Cavalry	Infantry
Mauryan	8–9,000	30,000	600,000
Calingas (Kalinga)	700	1,000	60,000
Modubae	400	4,000	50,000
Andrae (Andhra)	1,000	2,000	100,000
Magallae	500	–	–
Chrysei	300	800	30,000
Odomoboerae	16,000	5,000	150,000
Pandae	500	–	150,000
Gangaridae (Vanga)	700	1,000	60,000

was comprised of warrior clans in which individual combats, not engagements of masses of troops, were the practice. It is likely that few of the clans could put as many as 2,000 warriors in the field at any time, and an assembly of the clans would hardly produce an army of 12,000–14,000 at the maximum. It would, however, have been impossible for the Bronze Age Greeks to logistically sustain an army of this size in the field, since Mycenaean armies seem to have had no quartermasters or sutlers to supply the army on a regular basis.[22]

The Iron Age armies of Classical Greece were products of relatively small city-states whose populations, even at maximum use, could not produce very many soldiers. Even Israel under Ahab at the Battle of Ai could put 30,000 men into the field, while at the Battle of Marathon the Greeks were able to field only 10,000 men against the Persians. Thucydides recorded that at the start of the Peloponnesian War in 431 BC, Athens had a population of 100,000 free men and 140,000 slaves and aliens,[23] but could only raise 13,000 hoplites, 16,000 older garrison soldiers, 1,200 mounted men and 1,600 archers in a maximum effort in which the survival of the country was at stake.[24] When the security situation stabilized a decade later, Thucydides reported that Athens returned to her usual military practices and could only muster 1,300 hoplites and 1,000 horsemen. In addition, it could draw upon 1,400 recruits. Most of the Athenian army in 420 BC were not Athenians at all, but metics and aliens.[25] Battles between the city-states of the Greek classical period usually involved no more than 20,000 men on both sides and, more often, involved combined forces of less than 10,000 soldiers. As products of their respective social orders, warrior clans and city-states, the armies of both Bronze and Iron Age Greece never reached the size or level of military sophistication and capability of other armies of these periods.

The growth in the size of armies in the Iron Age was almost exponential when compared to the armies of the previous era. What made this growth possible? First, the populations of Iron Age states were generally much larger than during the Bronze Age, perhaps as a function of more productive agricultural techniques that allowed more and better nutrition, and thus a healthier population. Second, the ability of government to organize and control the social order grew in scope and sophistication, and permitted greater governmental control over all aspects of social life, including recruitment for corvee labour and military service. States had developed the bureaucratic mechanisms to govern territory of imperial dimension, and to do it efficiently. Third, the introduction of iron weapons greatly reduced the cost of equipping a soldier, so that even small states could afford to maintain larger armies. While iron seems to have made its appearance in the Middle East sometime around 1200 BC, and perhaps even earlier in India, bronze remained the primary metal for military weapons until 900 BC or so, when iron replaced it on a large scale.[26] Fourth, the professional officer corps of the major states of the

Iron Age had acquired the experience and ability to command and control larger military establishments, so that larger armies could be employed and supplied effectively. As a consequence of these factors, the armies of the Iron Age were of greater size than anything the world had seen to that point.

Napoleon is supposed to have remarked that, 'in war, quantity conveys a quality all its own.' The armies of the Iron Age were truly modern with respect to their size. With the collapse of the Roman imperium and its large armies in the fourth century AD, only a few states were able to maintain large military establishments until well into the nineteenth century, and none of them were in the West. The composite armies of Islam were quite large, as were the armies of China and India. In the West, it was Napoleon who reintroduced the large conscript army. But even this was an exception. With Napoleon's defeat, Europe returned to the practice of retaining relatively small standing armies buttressed by large conscript reserve forces that could be called to service to meet a national emergency, a pattern which survived into the beginning of the twenty-first century.

Chapter 3

Life of the Common Soldier

There is a tendency among people in the modern world to regard themselves as unique. That is because their lives are happening to them for the first time. The claim to historical uniqueness is, of course, false. Human beings have been unchanged in their essentials for more than 100,000 years. Those who lived in the ancient world loved and feared the same things we do, especially when it came to the organized violence that was war itself. The brain structures required for conceptual thought, language and cultural learning had already been in place at least 100,000 years before the beginning of the age of antiquity, and they have not changed since. Humans have been humans for a very long time. And anyone who thinks of those who have preceded us as less intellectually agile and creative need only gaze upon the pyramids or the Roman road network to know how false that idea is.

The inhabitants of the ancient world were physically smaller than we are, but psychologically identical. The average age of death was about 44 years, an age that remained unchanged in the West from the beginning of the Bronze Age to the introduction of antibiotics in the middle of the twentieth century.[1] About a third of their children in the ancient world died before age 5, a mortality rate that also remained mostly unchanged until very modern times, even in the industrial West.[2] The health of individuals would, of course, vary from place to place depending upon a number of variables. People in ancient times suffered from many of the same ills as their descendants. Anaemia, tuberculosis of the bone and lung, syphilis, cancer and poor dentition are all in evidence among ancient corpses. Various forms of malaria and other diseases caused by water-borne parasites were also present, as they still are today in much of the Middle East and Asia.[3] In ancient times, virulent outbreaks of diseases – plague, smallpox, measles – sometimes reduced whole sections of countries to uninhabited wastelands. And yet in the midst of all this, there arose some of the greatest civilizations – Sumer, Egypt, India, China, Hatti, Israel, Persia, Greece and Rome – ever fashioned by human effort. War, too, had its place, along with its practitioner, the ancient soldier.

The ancient soldier was shorter and weighed less than his modern counterpart, varying in average height from 5ft 5in to 5ft 9in,[4] or about the same height as the average adult male in the nineteenth-century industrial West. The primary determinant of height in humans is nutrition. Averages, however, hide interesting variations. We learn from Caesar that the average Gaul was 7in taller than the Roman soldier, and that Tacitus was impressed by the 'large frames' of the Germans.[5] Thutmose III, the Napoleon of Egypt, was taller than the average Egyptian, while his son, Amenhotep II, was taller still, more than 6ft.[6] Battles in the ancient world involved mostly close combat, where physical size and strength provided an advantage. Gilgamesh of Sumer and Goliath of the Philistines are both portrayed as taller, broader and stronger than average. But the Talmudic *Midrash* of the Israelites tells of instances where Jewish recruits were rejected by the Roman army as being too short.[7] If we may believe Vegetius, the Roman army had a minimum height requirement for its legionnaires, so that the average Roman soldier of the Imperial period (first–fourth century AD) was taller than the average Roman civilian.[8] In antiquity, a medium-framed soldier of 5ft 9in weighed about 145lb, an almost ideal height and weight to make maximum use of the calorific content of his diet.

The age of military service varied somewhat among the armies of antiquity for which we have evidence. In the Israelite and Egyptian armies, the age at which a male became eligible for military service was 20 years. This is interesting in that in both societies, the age at which a male became a full member of the community was considerably less. In Egypt, a male was considered an adult at 13 years, women even younger. The average age of first pregnancy onset for Egyptian women in antiquity was only 13 years.[9] Hittite and Mycennaean males became warriors at 17 years of age, and the age at which males were eligible to serve in the army of the Roman Republic was also 17. During the Roman imperium, the eligible age was 18, although many recruits seem to have been at least 20. It was not, however, uncommon for officers and warrior kings to take their sons with them on campaign at earlier ages. We find Cornelius Scipio on campaign with his father at 16, and Hannibal with his father in Spain at age 10. Assyrian kings usually took their young sons with them on military campaigns, befitting the experience required of a future warrior king.

With the average lifespan in antiquity being only 44 years, taking males into military service in late adolescence provided a soldier who was at the peak of his physical strength and endurance, elements important to surviving military life. How long a person served in the military varied considerably from country to country. Egyptian conscripts under the Old Kingdom served only when there was a campaign to be fought, the army being mostly a feudal levy. By the New Kingdom, however, Egypt's army was a large, conscript force commanded by a professional officer corps. In these circumstances, one in every ten men was drafted into military service in both peacetime and war, where they served for two years. Soldiers of the legions of Republican Rome were called to the colours as required, serving until the need had passed. During the imperial period, all Roman soldiers were professionals who enlisted for six-year terms. In Sumer, Hatti, China and India, most soldiers were conscripts brought to service as the need arose, remaining there until no longer needed.

By contrast, most armies of the ancient period possessed officer corps of professional quality, many of whom served for most of their active lives. The professionalism of these cadres was a consequence of their high social status in warrior societies. In Egypt, the officer corps was a professional cadre created by and commanded by Pharaoh in his role as warrior king. In Sumer, all kings were warriors first, as were their nobles. The same was true in Assyria, Hatti and Mycenaean Greece. The Mitanni and Vedic Indians were professional warrior nobilities that imposed themselves on native cultures, where their continued ability to rule depended upon their military prowess. Rome's centurionate, although technically not officers but non-commissioned officers, was a thoroughly professional military elite, although it lacked any status as nobility.

The armies of antiquity were mostly led by experienced and talented officers, whose ability to devise and execute sophisticated tactical designs and command large formations of troops stands as proof of their professional skills. That the ancient soldier could execute these designs with effective results also speaks of the quality of the ancient soldier in applying his trade. The battle tactics of ancient armies were as sophisticated and demanded as much discipline under stress as do modern tactics, if not more given the inability of commanders to communicate with their troops once engaged. The soldiers of conscript armies like India, China and Egypt often performed superbly on the battlefield.[10] The notion that ancient armies, officers and soldiers were somehow primitive is false, and probably derives from the Western experience with primitive armies and commanders in the Middle Ages, lasting until at least the turn of the nineteenth century.[11]

The officer corps of ancient armies was drawn from the aristocracy, and we might correctly assume that its members were at least as educated and literate as the general social elite from which they came. Many of the military histories of the ancient world that have come down to us were written by soldiers – Polybius, Xenophon, Appian and Josephus, to name but a few of the most famous. Literacy and the ability to do basic mathematics were absolute requirements for commerce in ancient times, and were even more important to armies. Most officers and non-commissioned officers of the period were functionally literate. In Roman times, only literate recruits were accepted into the army. Where literacy was lacking, it was supplied by professional scribes assigned to the army by the king. The armies of Egypt, India, China and Assyria all had professional corps of scribes that acted as record keepers and administrators.

Most ancient kings were taught to read and write at a young age, if only to be able to conduct their civic and religious functions. Some, like Thutmose III of Egypt, wrote poetry, while others, like Sargon II of Assyria, were genuine scholars. Sargon spoke and wrote Akadian and ancient Sumerian, the latter learned so that he might study the texts of ancient battles to which he often appended commentaries.

The association of illiteracy with military service is probably once more a result of the West's experience with the kings and generals of the Middle Ages who, indeed, often were illiterate. Charlemagne, for example, was illiterate and could barely write his name, surviving samples of which more resemble a child's drawing than the genuine signature of a literate hand.[12]

Because the ancient soldier was psychologically identical to today's soldier, he was subject to the same fears and sufferings that have always accompanied military life in whatever age. He reacted to his environment in the way soldiers always have. He felt the physiological arousal and stress of his experiences, especially the sights and sounds of battle, and, like today's soldier, was subject to psychiatric collapse. A soldier's life in antiquity was a hard one, and the lack of sleep, physical exhaustion, insufficient nutrition and the impact of the elements – heat, freezing cold, bone-soaking rain, the terror of the dark and the general discomfort of living outdoors, often with poor equipment – all took their toll on the ancient soldier's body and mind.

Life in the ancient world was harsh, and the ancient soldier was exposed to sickness and death as a matter of common occurrence from his earliest childhood. A third of all live births were dead by age 6. By age 16, almost 60 per cent of all live births would have already died. By age 26, that number would have increased to 75 per cent, while by age 44, 90 per cent of all live births would have died. Very few, perhaps not more than 3 per cent, would live to see age 60.[13] There were no hospitals in antiquity, and families witnessed the deaths of their relatives, parents, children and siblings as a matter of course.

Military service in the ancient world could quickly turn harsh and even deadly if the soldier ran afoul of military authorities. Like modern armies, ancient armies had codes of discipline that set out penalties for infractions of laws governing military life. These rules and regulations addressed such issues as desertion, being absent without leave, failure to obey superiors, proper care of equipment and sleeping on guard duty. Other more serious offences – rape, looting, murder, mutiny – were also addressed by these codes. The expected rules of behaviour were the subject of official military education. In India, for example, soldiers were instructed in the proper code of military ethics, and held strictly accountable for its provisions.[14] The Hittite *Oath of the Soldier* is very specific as to what is expected of the soldier, and spells out the punishments that might befall the soldier who breaks his oath.[15]

The punishments for infractions of military rules might strike the modern reader as draconian, and in some cases they were indeed. Many modern armies, however, retain similar elements in their provisions for the death penalty for desertion, cowardice and mutiny. It is interesting to examine the punishments that were inflicted by ancient armies upon the soldier who violated military regulations. A Hittite soldier who violated his oath of service could be deafened, blinded or slain.[16] The Code of Hammurabi (1728–1686 BC) levied a punishment of death upon any soldier who was ordered on campaign and refused to go. Beating seems to have been the most common punishment in the armies of Egypt. In a letter written sometime in the thirteenth century BC, an Egyptian soldier wonders why he and his comrades (conscripts) are always being beaten.[17] A letter written two centuries later describes the lot of a typical conscript upon arriving in the military camp:

> He is brought while a child [20 years old was the age of military service in Egypt] to be confined in the camp. A searing beating is given his body, an open wound inflicted on his eyebrows. His head is split open with a wound. He is laid down and he is beaten like papyrus.[18]

This is a description of a conscript's initiation into military life, or 'boot camp'. Pharaoh Horemheb (1323–1295 BC) punished troops who were stealing hides from the local population by 'beating him a hundred blows, opening five wounds, and taking from him by force the hides which he took'.[19] The 'opening of wounds' probably refers to cutting of the skin so that the soldier would suffer additional pain for some time after the beating. In order to keep soldiers from stealing from the royal estates, Seti I (1294–1279 BC) ordered that anyone caught would have his ears cut off.[20] Ramses II was furious at the chariot commanders who had abandoned him during the Battle of Kadesh, almost costing him his life. He ordered the cowardly officers brought before him and personally beheaded them in full view of the assembled army.[21] The laws of warfare in India called for punishments ranging from social ostracism to death. A soldier who deserted his comrades in battle 'should be done to death with sticks or stones. Or he might be rolled in a mat of dry grass and burnt to death.'[22]

Xenophon served as a mercenary soldier in the army of the Persian king, Cyrus the Great, and described the punishments employed by both Persian and Greek commanders in their armies. Xenophon himself once ordered a man to be beaten who had refused to carry his wounded comrade and had attempted to bury him alive to avoid having to do so. What is interesting is that the man was first given a hearing and permitted to offer a defence. Xenophon tells us that Cyrus himself was a strict disciplinarian, and that 'his punishments were exceptionally severe'.[23] Cyrus' punishments included blinding, amputation of hands and feet, and beheading.[24]

During the classical period (500–350 BC), Greek city-states with their hoplite citizen militia armies used a much different system. The civilian system of justice that guaranteed the accused a hearing before an assembly of citizens, the presentation of evidence and a secret ballot to determine guilt or innocence was the same as used by the military. Greek soldiers were drawn from the politically enfranchised classes, and fought short wars led by elected commanders, conditions that made a separate and different system of justice for Greek citizen-armies unlikely.

Rome also valued its civilian traditions of law and legal institutions, and found them too valuable to abandon, even when the citizen armies of the Roman Republic were replaced by the armies of the imperium, armies mostly filled by non-Romans. Soldiers charged with crimes were entitled to a hearing to defend themselves against the charge. Serious charges were heard by senior officers or tribunes, elected officers part of whose responsibility was to look after the welfare of the troops.[25] Punishments in the Roman army included fines, extra work details, confinement to camp, being forced to eat barley instead of wheat for rations and forced to bivouac beyond the protective walls of the camp. The most feared Roman military punishment was the *fustuarium*. Reserved for the most serious offences, a soldier found guilty by court martial was led before his comrades and touched with a cudgel by a centurion, at which point his comrades commenced to beat the guilty man to death. When an entire unit of soldiers performed in a cowardly manner, they were subject to decimation. The tribunes assembled the legion and led forward those guilty of leaving the ranks. The accused were lined up, and 10 per cent of the unit was selected at random to be stoned or beaten to death.[26] By way of a harsher comparison, Carthaginian officers who performed poorly in battle were crucified in front of their troops; senior officers were executed in this manner in Carthage's public square.[27]

The brutality of the political establishments in antiquity was often publicly displayed. During Hammurabi's reign in Babylon, the great law-giver could gaze from his palace window and see corpses floating down the Tigris. Assyria made a fetish of public displays of brutality, sometimes skinning people alive or impaling them at public gatherings. Egyptian reliefs portray the Pharaohs bashing in the skulls of their enemies; so commonly did they do this that one of pharaoh's official titles was 'Smasher of Foreheads'. Among the Israelites, the Old Testament tells of one slaughter after another of the population of whole towns by Joshua and Phineas. The punishment for withholding loot in the Israelite army was burning alive.[28]

In all armies of antiquity, the slaughter of innocent populations was commonplace. In his campaign against the Germans in 55 BC, Caesar slaughtered an entire people, some 430,000 human beings, in an act of calculated political butchery. Even the Romans were appalled. One senator called the slaughter, 'unquestionably the most atrocious act of which any civilized man has ever been guilty'.[29] The ancient soldier was exposed to death and slaughter to a degree rarely seen in modern times, with the exception of the genocides carried out by the Nazis, Turks, Rwandans and, most recently, Isis.

Chapter 4

Killing Technology:
Weapons and Armour in Antiquity

The first evidence of metals technology in war appeared in Anatolia and Mesopotamia around 4000 BC when the technique of combining melted copper with 10–12 per cent tin to make bronze was invented. The impact of the new technology on warfare varied widely, however. In Mesopotamia, where warfare between city-states was endemic, metal weapons assumed an immediate importance and accounted for a large number of weapons innovations introduced by the Mesopotamian states of this period. Elsewhere, in Egypt for instance, where conflict was less endemic, metals technology had only a marginal impact, and the rate of weapons innovation was slow.

Bronze manufacture was expensive. Copper was relatively available and cheap, but tin was scarce and expensive. The supply of tin was never adequate for large-scale weapons production, and the cost of metal and manufacture was high. These factors placed major limitations on the size of the armies that could be economically equipped with bronze weapons. It was the Iron Age that marked the first true revolution in metal weapons technology. There is substantial evidence that iron-making occurred in central India in the fourteenth century BC,[1] and that the Indians made iron weapons in the form of double-edged daggers, socketed axe-heads, flat axes, spear heads and arrow heads at this early date.[2] Whenever iron was first manufactured in the Near East, it was not widely used for weapons until around 900 BC, bronze remaining the preferred metal for weapons because it was much easier to smelt and cast.[3] It is not until Sargon II of Assyria (721–705 BC) that we encounter an army that was mostly equipped with iron rather than bronze weapons.[4]

The military advantage of iron did not lie in its physical properties. Iron weapons are much more difficult to manufacture, requiring repeated heating and hammering to fashion the required shape. Iron rusts, dulling the edge and weakening the weapon's strength. The importance of iron to ancient warfare lies in the fact that it was available almost everywhere. The plentiful supply of iron ore made it possible to produce large numbers of weapons at low cost. Iron weapons required fewer specialized tools, expensive moulds and technical expertise to manufacture, resulting in the decentralization of manufacturing from out of the palaces to the general society. Almost anyone could learn the skills and obtain the tools to manufacture iron weapons. No longer was it only the largest and wealthiest states that could afford sufficient weapons to equip a large army. The consequence was a dramatic increase in the size of armies and the scale of warfare.

Weapons fashioned of steel made their way into Europe and the Near East sometime around 200 BC. Steel requires higher melting temperatures than bronze or iron. These temperatures were now made possible by the introduction of the funnel bellows to force air over the heated ore, drawing off more carbon from the molten metal. This process, too, appears to have originated in India sometime around the fifth century BC,[5] and may have made its way to the Near East and West as a consequence of Alexander's campaigns.[6] By the Second Punic War (218–202 BC), the armies of Rome and Carthage were equipped with steel weapons. Steel has remained the metal of choice for weapons ever since.[7]

The Mace

The oldest weapon for which we have archaeological evidence is the mace. Originating in the Neolithic period as an improvement upon the simple club, the mace remained the most commonly used close-range battlefield weapon from 4000–2500 BC. The most common mace used a stone head with a hollow cut in the base into which a handle could be inserted. The head was further secured by leather wrappings. The mace disappeared from the battlefields of Sumer around 2500 BC, when the Sumerians invented the helmet. Constructed of 2mm of copper worn over 4mm of leather or woolen cap underneath, the Sumerian helmet was sufficient to neutralize the mace as a killing weapon. To fracture a human skull under a helmet of this sort requires a force of 810 foot-pounds. A mace weighing 1.8lb can only be swung at a speed of 60ft per second by a human arm, generating only 101 foot-pounds of energy on impact, insufficient to fracture the skull or even render the soldier unconscious.[8] The Egyptians continued to fight without the helmet for another millennium, with the result that Egyptian military physicians became expert at treating head fractures.[9]

The Spear

The fire-hardened tipped spear had its origins in the pre-Neolithic age as a weapon of the hunt. But it was not until the introduction of the cast bronze socket spear blade affixed to the shaft with rivets that the spear became a reliable combat weapon. The socketed spear blade probably made its first appearance in Sumer sometime around 2250 BC. This spear became the primary weapon of ancient armies, and remained so until around 200 BC, when the legions of Republican

Rome adopted the steel sword (*gladius*) and became the first army in antiquity to use the sword as its primary weapon.

The dominance of the spear for more than 2,000 years shaped the tactical deployment of ancient armies. If soldiers armed with the spear were to fight effectively, they had to arrange themselves in close-order formation, giving rise to the infantry phalanx. The first recorded instance of a phalanx of spear infantry appears in Sumer in 2500 BC.[10] The unwieldy nature of the spear in meeting an attack from any other direction than the front forced soldiers to fight in closely packed formations. The spear thus produced the phalanx, which remained the basic infantry formation in all armies of antiquity for more than two millennia.

The spear had various tactical functions. The short spear or javelin was meant to be thrown, and found wide use among Alexandrian, Persian and Numidian cavalry. Indian, Chinese and Assyrian cavalrymen used both the javelin and the lance, a long spear used for stabbing. The Macedonian *sarissa* was 13ft long, and had to be wielded with two hands. It was specifically designed to be used in a packed phalanx. The Roman legions carried the *pilum*, a short weighted spear with a thin pointed metal rod extending from a wooden shaft. The *pilum* was hurled just before the sword-wielding legionnaires closed on the enemy. When the *pilum* struck the enemy shield, its metal rod bent, making it impossible to remove and the shield difficult to use against the Roman sword attack. Greek *hoplite* infantry used 7ft spears (*dory*) for stabbing at close range. Homeric, Indian and Mycenaean wars saw individual combats between spear-bearing warriors rather than group fighting.[11] Achaean warriors carried one long spear and one shorter one. The latter was initially thrown at one's opponent. If it missed, the combat continued with the long spears.[12]

The Battle Axe

The axe was the most effective close-order weapon of ancient armies, and its evolution over 1,500 years of warfare offers an excellent example of the search for a new weapon to deal with the advances in body and head armour. The Sumerians invented the socket-axe with a bronze socket and blade cast in one piece. The oldest image of the socket-axe appears on the Stele of Vultures around 2200 BC, and early Sumerian kings are portrayed holding the new weapon.[13] The Egyptians did not adopt the socket axe until its introduction by the Hyksos in their invasion and occupation of Upper Egypt in the seventeenth century BC. The socket axe appeared in India around 1400 BC.[14]

The old style axes worked well enough against troops not equipped with armour. But by the dawn of the second millennium, effective body armour was becoming standard equipment among most armies of the ancient world, Egypt and India being exceptions. Both the size and shape of the older types of axe blades worked

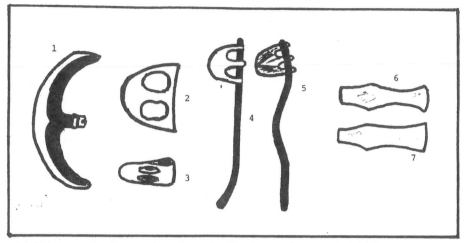

Note: Various types of battle-axes used in ancient armies: (1) epsilon axe, (2) eye axe, (3) duck-bill axe, (4) tang axe, (5) socket axe, and (6,7) two types of lugged axeheads.

Figure 3: Development of the Battle Axe

to distribute the force of the blow over too wide an area, reducing the power of the blade to penetrate. The Sumerians hit upon the solution of making the axe heavier and narrowing the blade to reduce the impact area to less than ½in and the wound area to 1¾in. The result was the socketed penetrating axe, one of the most devastating close-combat weapons of the Bronze and Iron ages.[15] The new axe could generate 77.5 foot-pounds of impact energy against existing body armour that required only 66 foot-pounds to penetrate.[16] For 2,000 years it remained the only close-combat weapon that could defeat body armour, and afforded an enormous advantage to the armies that possessed it.

The Sickle-Sword

The sickle-sword was invented by the Sumerians around 2500 BC.[17] The length of the weapon as portrayed on the Stele of Vultures is relatively short, suggesting that its most primitive origins may have been the common agricultural sickle used to harvest grain. In Sumer, the sickle-sword quickly gave way to the more effective penetrating socket axe, while in Egypt it remained a major weapon until the dawn of the Iron Age. The Egyptian sickle-sword grew longer and heavier over time and became a basic weapon for all the armies of the Near East, including the Israelites and Canaanites. When the Bible speaks of someone being 'smited by the edge of the sword', the reference is to the sickle-sword.

The sword was not a major weapon of ancient armies, however. The problem of affixing the blade securely to the handle, the success of the penetrating axe and the pre-eminence of the spear utilized in packed formations all worked against the development of the sword as an effective weapon. Dense formations afforded little room for the individual sword infantryman to manoeuvre. All ancient armies after the seventeenth century BC carried the sword, but in none was it a major infantry weapon. It was used when the soldier's primary weapons were lost or broken, forcing the soldier to use the sword as a last resort.

For the sword to emerge as a major infantry weapon required a change in battle formations from the densely packed phalanx to a looser formation with built-in spaces that allowed the soldier adequate room to wield his sword. The Roman army introduced the first open infantry formation, the famous *maniple* (literally, 'handful') formation arranged in checkerboard (*quincunx*) fashion. With the change in tactics, Rome abandoned the spear and produced the first soldier in history whose primary weapon was the sword. The *gladius* was introduced to the Roman army as a result of its experience in Spain during the Second Punic War. Although its origins were Spanish, by the first century BC the *gladius* had undergone enough changes at Roman hands to make it a new weapon.[18]

Forged from high-grade steel, the *gladius* was slightly less than 2ft long, with a blade 3in wide rising to a slight spine in the middle and weighing just under 2lb. The weapon was meant to be a stabbing weapon. Stabbing permits the soldier to strike while keeping his body mostly covered with his shield, whereas raising the arm to chop or slash exposes the soldier's body to a greater degree. The *gladius* was the deadliest of all weapons employed by ancient armies, killing more soldiers than any other weapon until the invention of the firearm.[19]

Of interest is the sword used by the Sherden, one of the Sea Peoples that attacked Egypt in the eleventh century BC, only to be defeated and settled in Palestine where they became known to history as the Philistines. The Sherden sword was 38in long and very narrow, its raised spine blade ending in a sharp needle-like point. The sword's design suggests that it was used for the specific purpose of killing charioteers in close combat. The sword's length gave the Sherden warrior superior 'reach' while on foot and below the enemy charioteer. Striking from below, the needle-like point could slip upward until finding a seam or slide under the overlapping scales of the charioteer's scale-armour coat, delivering a lethal blow.

Bow and Sling

The primary long-range weapons of ancient armies were the bow and sling. The bow underwent three stages of development, beginning with the simple bow, followed by the compound bow and culminating in the composite bow. The bow remained a primary instrument of war among most armies of antiquity. The range, rate of fire and penetrating power of the composite bow easily outperformed the rifle until Napoleonic times.

The simple bow was constructed of a single piece of wood powered with a gut or leather bowstring. A simple bow of the fourth millennium required 30–40lb to draw to full length, and could fire an arrow between 100–150 yards that would easily penetrate an unprotected body. Evidence from an Egyptian graveyard of 2000 BC revealed the remains of soldiers shot through the skull with ebony-tipped arrows fired by the simple bow.[20]

Ancient armourers attempted to increase the killing power of the bow by varying its shape. The double convex bow appeared in Egypt around the middle of the third millennium. Constructed of a single piece of wood, the double convex bow was shaped like Cupid's upper lip, an arrangement that brought the ends of the bow closer to the centre to increase its pull weight. It was constructed of two pieces of wood glued or bound with hide at the centre and shaped like a double convex bow or a triangle. The compound bow increased the pull weight of the weapon by 10 per cent.[21]

The first evidence of the composite bow appears on the victory stele of Naram Sin (2254–2218 BC) in Sumer. The composite bow was constructed of wood, horn and the tendons of oxen, all carefully laminated together. The laminated layers gave the bow greater strength and recoil power, and its recurved shape positioned the ends as close to its centre as possible when at full extension. The weapon was a mixed military blessing, however. It could easily outrange the simple and compound bows and deliver long-range fire, but could not usually penetrate the armour of the day. It was smaller and could be more easily carried, but was a very expensive weapon, requiring nine months to manufacture. Its composition made the weapon susceptible to moisture and humidity, which rendered it useless. Egyptian tombs show portrayals of bowmen carrying their fragile bows in what look like violin cases.[22]

Strength and endurance were important for the archer of the composite bow. Modern archery experts note that fatigue is a great factor affecting range and accuracy. After ten to twelve arrows fired at maximum pull, even a professional archer can no longer perform well.[23] The most common use of the bow was as a weapon of indirect fire in support of infantry. Large groups of archers positioned behind the main bodies of contesting armies fired in salvo to rain down a hail of arrows upon the enemy. It was common to have either a large shield standing on the ground from behind which the archer fired, or a shield-bearer holding the shield to protect the archer.

How effective was archery fire? A composite bow can fire a 553-grain arrow 250 yards at a 30–35° angle in about 5.8 seconds into a crosswind of less than eight miles an hour. At that range, an experienced archer can place almost 100 per cent of his arrows within a 50x20 yard target box. At 300 yards, however, accuracy drops off to where only 50 per cent of the arrows fall within the target box. As the infantry phalanx closes from 200 to 100 yards, accuracy remains at about 50 per cent. But the angle of the plunging arrow is severely acute, almost vertical, so that the number of hits upon enemy soldiers drops off drastically.[24] Still, these accuracy rates were much higher than those for the muzzle-loading musket of the eighteenth century. Field tests of these muskets conducted by the armies of the time showed that, on average, of 200 rounds fired at a 50ft wooden square from 250 yards, only 16 per cent would hit anywhere in the target area. Of these, only 1.5 per cent would actually hit a soldier.[25]

The sling is among the oldest weapons used by ancient armies, appearing sometime in the seventh millennium BC.[26] A sling could hurl a variety of lead and clay shot, varying in weight from 1–10oz, and in size from a small plumb to a tennis ball.[27] Heavier shot could be lobbed into enemy formations at distances up to 200 yards; smaller shot could be fired along an almost flat trajectory like a bullet at ranges up to 75 yards. Short-range shot was made of lead or clay, cast in the shape of a plumb to increase its penetrating power. The wide head and tapered tail allowed the tissue of the wound to close behind the missile, making extraction from the body difficult. Vegetius tells us that the Roman standard for certifying a slinger as combat-qualified was his ability to hit a man-sized target at 600ft, a feat he suggests could be accomplished with regularity.[28]

As a combat weapon, however, the sling was not very effective. Slinger units had to be deployed in mass, which increased their own vulnerability to sling and archery counterfire. They had no defensive weapons with which to protect themselves from close attack by chariots, infantry or cavalry. Finally, slinger units were usually much smaller in relation to the other combat arms deployed on the battlefield, and were never decisive to the battle's outcome.

Body Armour

The most militarily significant impact of metals technology on war in antiquity was its contribution to personal defensive systems: the armour, helmets, shields, neck collars, greaves and other defensive equipment worn by the soldier for protection. These protective systems had an enormous impact on warfare and tactics, and the development of new metal weapons during this period was stimulated mostly by the search for ways to overcome the effectiveness of armour. The inherent dynamic of weapons development operated then as now, but in reverse. In modern times we are prone to see the advent of a new offensive weapon, which provokes a defence against it. In the Bronze Age, the more significant military revolution was in defensive systems, which then stimulated a search for new weapons to overcome them.

The major protective devices of the ancient soldier were the helmet, neck collar, body armour and shield. The leather collar was another Mesopotamian invention. Between 1–2in thick, the collar was constructed of sewn leather layers that sometimes had thin bronze or iron plates sewn between them to afford more resistance to penetration.[29] The leather collar could easily withstand a blow from a sword blade, and was impervious to arrows. By the time of Mycenaean Greece and Etruscan Rome, bronze greaves to protect the shins and forearms of the soldier were standard items of military equipment.

The first recorded use of body armour is found on the Stele of Vultures in ancient Sumer (circa 2500 BC) which shows Eannatum's soldiers wearing leather cloaks on which a number of spined metal disks are sewn.[30] By 2100 BC, the victory stele of Naram Sin shows metal scale armour, and it is likely that such armour had already been in use for a few hundred years. Certainly by 1700 BC, the Hyksos possessed scale armour and, once introduced to Egypt by the Hyksos invaders, metal scale armour became standard throughout the Near East. Scale armour was constructed of thin bronze plates sewn to an about ¼in thick leather shirt. The plates themselves were less than a tenth of an inch thick, and had slightly raised spines to allow them to overlap and hang correctly.[31] This type of armour became the standard protection of the Egyptian heavy spear infantry and charioteers of

SUMER (2500 BC)   EGYPT (1700 BC)   ASSYRIA (900 BC)

GREECE (400 BC)   CELTIC CHAIN MAIL (200 BC)   ROME (100 AD)

Figure 4: Development of Body Armour

the New Kingdom. In the eighth century BC, Assyria introduced a more effective form of body armour called lamellar armour. Lamellar armour was comprised of a shirt constructed of laminated layers of leather or linen sewn or glued together. To the outer surface of this coat were attached fitted iron plates, each plate joined to the next at the edge with no overlap and held in place by stitching or gluing. It weighed about 30–35lb.[32]

By 600 BC the Greeks and Romans introduced the bell muscular cuirass made of cast bronze. Cast in two halves, front and back, the cuirass was joined at the side with hinges and locks or belts. The bell cuirass weighed about 25lb, was hot and uncomfortable, and slowed the soldier's movement, factors which worked against its wide use or adoption by other armies.[33] By the third century BC, the bell cuirass had given way in Greece to the linen cuirass. Constructed of strips of linen glued and sewn together in laminated fashion, it was cheaper and more flexible than the bell cuirass. When outfitted with exterior metal plates, it weighed about 15lb. The origin of the linen cuirass is obscure, but in all probability it was an Egyptian innovation that made its way to Greece during the reign of Philip II of Macedonia.[34] Both Greek and Roman varieties of this linen armour were around ½in thick.

Early Mycenaean and Minoan charioteers wore the Dendra panoply, an arrangement of bronze armour that fully enclosed the soldier. The bronze plates were assembled to form front and back halves backed with linen or leather, loosely fastened together by leather thongs. The corslet was called a *torake* (literally thorax). The design of the Dendra armour was clearly intended to deflect spear thrusts encountered in individual combats. The armour of the Chinese Shang Period (1700–1100 BC) consisted of breastplates fashioned of bronze or leather. A thousand years later, during the Spring and Autumn Era (771–464 BC), the heavy bronze and iron cuirass was replaced by lighter, more flexible laminar armour made of overlapping rows of hard, lacquered leather plates.[35] Chinese armour for lower ranks was usually made of quilted cloth stuffed with raw cotton. A similar type of armour is found among the Aztecs of South America circa AD 1500. The Aztec armour, *ichcahuipilli*, was constructed of unspun brine-saturated raw cotton quilted between layers of cloth made into a sleeveless jacket that was 2in thick. The principle of using a thick fibre inside a 'sandwich' of cloth to 'trap' the projectile is the same one used today in Kevlar body armour. The Aztec armour was lighter and cooler, and afforded such good protection that the Spanish invaders (Conquistadors) abandoned their metal cuirass and adopted the cotton armour.[36]

The third century BC saw the introduction of iron chain mail invented by the Celts.[37] Chain mail was constructed of thousands of small iron circles linked together to form an iron-mesh shirt. The shirt weighed about 32lb, but its close fit distributed the weight proportionally over the soldier's body and permitted adequate mobility. The mail shirt remained the basic armour of the Roman infantryman until the first century AD, when the Roman army was equipped with laminated leather armour that provided sufficient protection against the tribal armies that they now mostly encountered. Perhaps the ultimate in body armour, the *lorica segmentata*, appeared at the same time. The *segmentata* was constructed of thin sheet steel plates riveted to leather blanks held together by straps, buckles and locks. It weighed about 20lb, considerably lighter than the 30lb mail shirt it replaced.[38]

The Helmet

The earliest evidence for the helmet is found in Sumer at the Death Pits of Ur dating from 2500 BC. The Sumerian helmet was a cap of hammered copper approximately a tenth of an inch thick fitted over a leather or wool cap approximately a seventh of an inch thick, providing a total protective thickness of ¼in. Once the helmet made its appearance, it became a standard item of military equipment until the seventeenth century AD. The bronze helmet is mentioned in the Vedic sagas in India dating to 1600 BC.[39] Indian troops also wore helmets made of hide or thick cloth reinforced with some hard substance, like animal hooves.[40] Achaean and Mycenaean soldiers wore helmets fashioned from slivers of horn cut from boars' tusks bound by thongs to a leather cap. In the *Iliad*, Hector's helmet was made of three layers of leather with boars' teeth strung on the outside.[41] The Mitanni charioteers wore a leather cap onto which several layers of overlapping bronze plates were sewn.[42] The Mitanni infantryman wore a leather helmet fashioned from goatskins cut into triangles and sewn together at the seams. The helmet of the Hittite guardsmen was very similar to the Mitanni helmet, but had a chin strap.[43] The chin strap was probably introduced by the Sea Peoples while in their military service in Egypt during the New Kingdom. Different Sea Peoples wore different types of helmets. The Sherden wore bronze helmets with horns sticking out from the sides, while the Peleset helmet was a circle of reeds, stiffened hair, horsehair, linen or leather strips held in place by a fillet and chin strap.[44] Chinese helmets of the Shang Period were bronze with a rounded crown, with sides and back that came down over the ears and protected the nape of the neck.[45]

The Assyrians wore an iron helmet shaped at an acute angle so the top came almost to a point, an effective design for reducing the target area and deflecting blows.[46] The Assyrian helmet required an inner cap of wool or leather to absorb the energy of a blow and dissipate heat. It also had a chin strap. Greek helmets of the classical and imperial periods were constructed of bronze and had cheek and face plates. Face plates came to characterize later Roman helmets as well, but were never a major feature of helmets in the Near East, probably because they made the

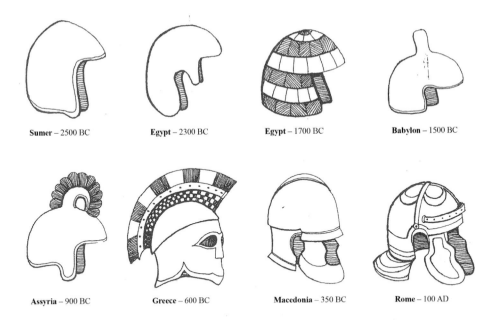

Sumer – 2500 BC   **Egypt** – 2300 BC   **Egypt** – 1700 BC   **Babylon** – 1500 BC

Assyria – 900 BC   **Greece** – 600 BC   **Macedonia** – 350 BC   **Rome** – 100 AD

Figure 5: Development of the Helmet

head too hot. The Romans were the first to mass-produce bronze helmets in state arms industries, a practice that led to frequent complaints from soldiers that the helmets didn't fit.[47]

Shields

The shields carried by soldiers of ancient armies were usually made of laminated wood covered with cowhide, beaten bronze and even sheet iron. Early Egyptian and Sumerian shields were fabricated of bull, oxen and cowhide stretched over a wooden frame. These had to be oiled regularly with animal fat to keep them from drying out and cracking. Other shields were made of woven reeds. Shields came in a variety of shapes: square, rectangle, figure-eight, keyhole shaped and round. Since even the earliest shields afforded good protection against any type of deadly penetration by hand-wielded weapons, the most important considerations were weight, which affected the ability of the soldier to manoeuvre and protect himself in close combat, and size, which provided him with protection against hails of arrows fired in concert by archers. For the most part, the ancient shield offered good protection against close combat weapons and archery fire.

Almost all the portrayals of shields discovered by archaeologists show a single hand-grip in the centre of the shield. These grips were either a leather strap or a carved wooden handle. Held in this manner, the shield required considerable strength to raise, and was difficult to press against an opponent with much force. Other shield grips, like those of the Achaeans, Mycenaeans and early Greek city-states, were constructed of a collection of tethers that met at a ring in the centre.[48] The difficulty in using the Greek tether shield-grip was that it required a great deal of strength and training to use effectively, factors that restricted military service in Greece to the nobility. In the sixth century BC, this grip was replaced by the Argive grip, a single loop through which the forearm could pass with another loop at the shield's rim held by the hand in a strong grip. This considerably reduced the strength and training required for use, so that the average citizen could now easily master the use of the shield.[49] Mass production of these shields also made them cheaper. These developments made it possible to enrol the common citizenry for war. Very quickly the practice of war shifted from the exclusive domain of the nobility to battles between disciplined groups of militia heavy infantry, bringing into being the famous Greek *hoplite*.[50]

The body armour, helmet and shield of the ancient soldier afforded him good protection against the weapons of the day, indeed much better protection than was available to the modern soldier until recent times. The introduction of the firearm that could pierce the plate armour of the knight led armies to abandon the search for personal protection, and body armour and the helmet began to disappear from the battlefield. This was a tragic mistake. The protective devices of the ancient soldier would have provided excellent protection against firearms well past the time of Napoleon. When the dispersion of battle formations, inaccuracy of firearms and slow rates of fire are factored in, the ancient soldier would have been safer on the battlefields of the nineteenth century than he was on his own.

From the seventeenth to the nineteenth century AD, no army wore helmets or body armour, even though this period saw the introduction of long-range artillery and exploding shells, both of which produced shrapnel at alarming rates. Infantrymen up to the early days of the First World War went into battle with no protective headgear as a storm of steel crashed around them. The bronze shields of the ancient Greeks would easily have repulsed the gunfire of a Napoleonic rifle, and the angled helmet of the Assyrians would have made penetration difficult even by a Civil War musket. During the First World War, the French discovered that units of firemen had very low rates of head wounds precisely because they had brought their fire helmets with them to the war. The French rushed this style helmet into production to equip their troops with protective headgear. Body armour made a return to the battlefield during the Vietnam War, and is now used by most armies.

Chapter 5

Death, Wounds, Infection, Disease and Injury in Ancient Armies

A n ancient army on the march was a medical disaster. An army of 10,000 could expect to lose 400 men to heatstroke or exhaustion and another 1,700 to routine injuries, falls, fractures, sprains, foot injuries, etc., moving even a short distance to the battlefield. As the army moved along, soldiers endured chronic discomfort. Dust choked their lungs, dried out their sinuses and brought on chronic coughing, blinding headaches and nosebleeds. Blisters from the leather thongs on the sandals or from ill-fitting boots often caused crippling pain, forcing soldiers to fall out of the column and be left on the side of the road. In desert or mountain climates, soldiers died of extreme heat or cold. The soldier endured all this before battle was joined, where, if the army was victorious, it could still expect to lose another 10 per cent of its men killed and wounded. If it suffered defeat, 70 per cent of its men would be casualties. Above it all lurked the spectre of disease that sometimes caused more death than battle itself. Then, as now, military life was dangerous to the soldier's health.

With the exception of the Roman army that fought in an open formation and could manoeuvre in all directions, the armies of antiquity fought in some form of packed, largely immobile infantry phalanx. Under pressure from the flanks or rear, the phalanx could come apart, its soldiers taking flight as the once cohesive fighting formation dissolved into a mob of terrified humanity trying to escape death. For more than 2,000 years, soldiers could rely upon flight to save them, as the victor's exhausted troops could pursue no more rapidly than the vanquished could run. The introduction of the Egyptian chariot and mounted archer and Assyrian spear and archer horse cavalry changed all that. Fleeing soldiers now became vulnerable targets, easily overtaken and slain. The pursuit, once a rare event on the battlefields of antiquity, now became the primary means of destroying a defeated army.

Killed in Action

The table below presents strength and death ratios for fourteen battles between 2250–45 BC, and includes battles involving the armies of Sumer, Persia, Classical Greece, Imperial Greece, Rome and tribal engagements in both the Bronze and

Iron Age.[1] The number of dead suffered by a defeated army was, on average, 37.7 per cent, or more than one third its combat force. Death rates for victorious armies were only 5.5 per cent of combat force. The disparity in the number of casualties suffered by defeated and victorious armies suggests that most of the killing occurred after one side's infantry formations broke apart, leaving soldiers to be hunted down and slain with comparative ease, or else surrounded and killed in a packed mass. Close-range killing is nasty business, and it required several bloodletting hours to destroy a vanquished army. At Cannae, Hannibal's army required four hours to slaughter 70,000 Romans.[2]

The difference in kill rates was evident whenever a technically and tactically superior army fought an inferior one. At the battles of Issus, Arbela, Granicus, Cynoscephalae, Pydna and Aix-en-Provence, the superior army killed on average 42.6 per cent of the inferior force, inflicting 5 per cent more casualties than would have been expected had the armies been equal. These higher kill rates were inflicted over a shorter period of time, a fact reflected in the lower death rates suffered by the victorious armies. Alexander's armies suffered only a 0.5 per cent average casualty rate in three battles against the Persians, and the Romans only 1.3 per cent against the Macedonians and Teutones. Armies relatively equal in combat

Table 2: Combat Death Rates of Ancient Armies

Date/ BC	Battle	Adversaries		Troops		Killed		% Defeated
		Victor	Defeated	Victor	Defeated	Victor	Defeated	KIA
2250	***	King of Akkad	Ur	5,400	13,500	***	8,040	59.5%
334	Granicus	Alexander	Memnon	36,000	40,000	125	10,000	25.0%
333	Issus	Alexander	Darius III	36,000	150,000	200	50,000	33.0%
331	Arbela	Alexander	Darius III	40,000	340,000	300	100,000	29.4%
237	Mactaris	Hamilcar Barcas	Mercenaries	10,000	25,000	***	6,000	24.0%
218	Trebia	Hannibal	Sempronius	50,000	40,000	Few	20–30,000	50.0%
216	Cannae	Hannibal	Varro	50,000	80,000	5,500	70,000	87.5%
202	Zama	Scipio Africanus	Hannibal	50,000	50,000	2,000	20,000	40.0%
197	Cynoscephalae	Flamininus	Philip V	20,000	23,000	700	8,000	34.7%
168	Pydna	Aemilius Paullus	Perseus	30,000	44,000	***	20,000	45.4%
102	Aix	Marius	The Teutons	40,000	100,000	300	90,000	90.0%
86	Chaeronea	Sulla	Archelaus	30,000	110,000	14	100,000	90.9%
48	Pharsalus	Caesar	Pompey	22,000	45,000	300	15,000	33.0%
45	Munda	Caesar	Pompey	48,000	80,000	1,000	33,000	41.2%

strength could expect to lose 5.5 per cent of their forces killed in action. Tactically and technically superior armies suffered, on average, only 2.2 per cent of their forces killed in action, a force multiplier of more than 100 per cent. A defeated army could expect to lose 35.4 per cent of its force to serious wounds. When the wounded are added to the number of soldiers killed, no less than 73 per cent of the defeated force could expect to be killed or wounded. The victors could expect to lose approximately one man in ten killed or wounded to enemy arms.[3]

Wounded

Literary accounts of ancient battles usually do not record the number of wounded. However, captured soldiers were booty that could later be sold as slaves or ransomed. If we deduct the number of soldiers killed and taken prisoner from the strength of the total force, we are left with a rough approximation of the number of wounded. The table below presents data on the number of soldiers killed, wounded and taken prisoner for the six battles for which the information was available in classical texts. On average, approximately 35.4 per cent of a defeated army could expect to be wounded.[4] We might surmise that most of these wounds were serious, since those with only slight wounds would have been taken prisoner for later sale or use as slaves.

There is no certain way to estimate the number of wounded for the victor's army. If the proportion holds, the ratio suggests a wound rate for the victorious army of 5.8 per cent. Engels' analysis of Alexander's armies shows that the Macedonians suffered roughly five wounded for every soldier killed in action.[5] Thus, the average Killed in Action rate suffered by the Macedonians at Issus, Granicus and Arbela of 0.5 per cent produced a wound rate of no more than 2.5 per cent. The Roman army medical system planned for a wounded casualty rate of 6 per cent.[6]

The *Iliad* provides the oldest Western account of battle wounds suffered in antiquity.[7] Of the 147 wounds recorded by Homer, 114, or 77.7 per cent, were

Table 3: Calculation of Wounded in Ancient Battles

Battle	Total Force	Killed	PoW	Wounded	% Wounded
Granicus	40,000	10,000	20,000	10,000	25.0%
Mactaris	25,000	6,000	2,000	17,000	68.0%
Zama	50,000	20,000	20,000	10,000	20.0%
Cynoscephalae	23,000	8,000	5,000	10,000	43.4%
Pydna	44,000	20,000	5,000	19,000	43.2%
Pharsalus	45,000	15,000	24,000	6,000	13.3%

fatal. The areas of greatest lethality were the head and chest, areas that still account for most battle wound fatalities in the modern era. Arrows accounted for less than 10 per cent of the wounds. The mortality rate from arrows was 42 per cent, the lowest of all the weapons examined. Arrows from a composite bow would usually not penetrate body armour to sufficient depth to kill. Blood loss and shock killed most men on the ancient battlefield. The most lethal weapon of the ancient Greeks was the spear, responsible for 106 of the 147 wounds recorded by Homer. Later, the Roman *gladius* became the most lethal weapon in antiquity. The most common wound suffered by the ancient soldier was a broken bone, because it was so easy to inflict. There is very little difference in the amount of force required to fracture any of the bones in the human body. Only 67.7 foot-pounds of impact energy will produce a fracture to any bone except the skull.[8] Any of the ancient weapons could easily cause a fracture.

The *Iliad* provides the only glimpse into the wound profile suffered by the ancient soldier available to us. The information provides only a rough baseline of measurement, since it is clear that the frequency and type of wounds varied considerably in light of the weapons, armour and battle tactics employed by armies at different periods of antiquity. But any army at any time in history that lost its cohesion in battle was defenceless to any type of attack. Under these circumstances, the ancient soldier was at great risk indeed.

Infection

Tetanus

The threat to the ancient soldier of dying from an infected wound from the beginning of the Bronze Age until the early days of the First World War was about the same. The wounded soldier of ancient times was at risk of wound infection from three microbiological causes: tetanus, gas gangrene and septicemia. The most common was tetanus. Tetanus is caused by an anaerobic bacterium called *Clostridium tetani* that enters the body through deep breaks in the skin and viscera, the deep puncture wound of exactly the type caused by ancient weapons. A description of tetanus symptoms appears in the *Aphorisms* of Hippocrates, evidence that the Greeks were aware of the condition.[9]

Tetanus is found mainly in the richly manured soil typical of the agricultural societies and battlefields of the ancient world. It is common where sanitation is poor, and where human waste is present. If a wound was not thoroughly cleansed or if it was sutured or bandaged too quickly, tetanus infection was almost a certainty. Military physicians of ancient Egypt, Assyria, Rome and India knew enough to leave certain wounds open for several days before bandaging, a procedure that was likely to result in fewer tetanus infections.[10] Military physicians only rediscovered this technique during the First World War. There was no means of preventing tetanus infection until the introduction of immunization in the First World War. It is likely that the rates of tetanus infection in ancient armies were about the same as the rates for the five wars of the modern era: 5.6 per cent, with a mortality of 80 per cent.[11]

Gangrene

Gas gangrene is caused by six species of bacteria generically named *Clostridium perfingens*. Like tetanus, these bacteria are anaerobic and found in common soil. Until the middle years of the First World War, the average rate of incidence of gangrene infection among the wounded was 5 per cent. With treatment, the survival rate among British forces was 28 per cent. We may safely assume, however, that in ancient armies gangrenous wounds produced almost 100 per cent mortality.[12] Until the Boer War, British doctors routinely bandaged or sutured wounds immediately. This permitted necrotic tissue to remain in the wound, increasing the onset of gangrene. By the middle years of the First World War, British physicians began leaving the wounds open for several days, cleansing it several times before finally closing it with stitches or bandages. The rediscovery of this ancient method of treating wounds resulted in a decline in the gangrene mortality rate from 28 per cent to just 1 per cent.[13]

Septicemia

Septicemia, or blood poisoning, occurs when the common body bacteria, *Staphylococcus bacteri*, enter the blood stream. If a blood vessel is punctured or the accompanying wound permitted to fester by infection, the infection can spread to the sterile blood stream. Wounds to arteries and veins presented an increased risk of blood poisoning. The rate of such wounds in antiquity was approximately 1.7 per cent. Until very modern times when antibiotics made it possible to combat a blood stream infection, septicemia was fatal, as it frequently still is. Until late in the Second World War, any soldier with a septicemic infection usually died.

If the data on wound mortality and infection are combined, it is possible to produce a statistical profile of the causes of death for wounded soldiers in ancient armies. Of 100 soldiers wounded in action, 13.8 per cent would likely die of shock and bleeding within two to six hours of being wounded. Another 6 per cent would likely contract tetanus infections, and 80 per cent of them would die within three to six days. Another 5 per cent would see their wounds become gangrenous, and 80–100 per cent of these would die within a week. A septicemic infection from arterial or venous wounds would be contracted by 1.7 per cent of the wounded, and 83–100 per cent of them would die within six to ten days.[14] On average, one in every four wounded soldiers, 24.4 per cent, would die of their wounds within seven to ten days. These same four causes remained the major causes of death among the wounded, as did the rates at which the wounded succumbed to them, at least until the closing years of the First World War.

Disease

Until the Russo-Japanese War of 1905, which saw the first systematic use of preventive military medicine in modern times, more soldiers met their deaths from disease than from the effects of enemy weapons.[15] The descriptions of diseases in the ancient world that have come down to us are often insufficiently precise to permit their identification with certainty. Modern medical writers cannot agree, for example, if the great plague described by Thucydides that killed a quarter of the Athenian army during the Peloponnesian War was caused by typhus. And while the descriptions of the Antonine plague which decimated the population of Rome in the second century AD suggest an outbreak of smallpox, diagnosticians cannot be certain. Some diseases, such as cholera and bubonic plague, have relatively recent origins, and can be safely omitted from the list of diseases that afflicted ancient armies. Others, like dysentery, typhus, typhoid and smallpox, can be asserted with confidence to have afflicted ancient armies.

Dysentery

Dysentery has been the most common disease among soldiers throughout human history. Usually called 'campaign fever', the first description of it occurs in an Egyptian medical text, the *Ebers Papyrus*, around 1550 BC.[16] Dysentery is also described in Hippocrates' writings, and Roman medical texts outline procedures for preventing its occurrence. It has been called the 'most dangerous and pervasive disease in human history'.[17] Some variants of the disease have a mortality rate of 50 per cent, but the usual rate is 5 per cent.[18] The disease can immobilize an entire army for three weeks. Even marginal care of the sick requires additional manpower drained from the combat force. Some idea of the magnitude of the impact of dysentery on an army can be obtained from the fact that while 81,360 men of the Union Army during the American Civil War and its prelude (1860–1865) died from dysentery, a mortality rate of about 5 per cent, 1,627,000 soldiers, or twenty times as many, contracted the disease at one time or another.[19] The number who contracted dysentery was almost four-fifths of the entire Union Army of 2,100,000 men.

Typhoid

Typhoid is caused by the bacterium *Salmonella typhi* that lives in the human digestive tract and is transported by human faeces. The disease is contracted by ingesting contaminated food and water, the same factors that cause dysentery. An army caught in the midst of a typhoid outbreak was quickly rendered useless as a combat force. The disease's mortality rate was between 10–13 per cent, and required four weeks of pain and delirium fever to run its course, during which time the soldier was completely helpless.[20] In the Napoleonic Wars, 270 of every 1,000 men who succumbed to disease did so from typhoid.[21] In the Crimean War, it was a more common cause of death than enemy fire. During the Boer War, the British lost 13,000 men to typhoid, while an additional 64,000 cases were invalided home with the disease. Only 8,000 British soldiers were lost to hostile fire.[22] Ninety per cent of American units deployed to Cuba during the Spanish American War suffered outbreaks of typhoid, and 20 per cent of the entire American force contracted the disease.[23] In ancient times, it is likely that the disease was endemic to Southern Europe and the Near East rather than epidemic.

Typhus

Typhus is among the most common and deadly of diseases associated with armies throughout history. It is caused by an organism midway between a bacterium and a virus that lives in the blood of various animals, including, but not limited to, rats. It is transmitted by several insect vectors, the most common of which is *Pediculus humanus*, the human body louse living in the clothes and hair of the individual. The mortality rate of the disease is between 10–40 per cent, but it has been known to kill entire armies.[24] Typhus decimated the French army during Napoleon's Russian campaign. On the retreat from Moscow, Napoleon abandoned 30,000 soldiers suffering from typhus in the town of Vilna in Lithuania. Almost all died.[25] Typhus is a disease of temperate zones, and the armies of Greece, Rome, India and China were familiar with it. The armies of Egypt and Babylon, operating in hotter and less humid climates and having a tendency to wear fewer clothes, may have suffered a lower incidence of the disease. The great plague that struck down the Athenian army during the Peloponnesian War was probably typhus.

Smallpox

Smallpox outbreaks were probably fairly common in the ancient world, although we cannot be certain.[26] Surviving texts suggest that smallpox was among the most feared diseases because of its propensity to blind, cripple and severely scar the victim. It is also likely that many accounts of outbreaks of leprosy were really epidemics of smallpox. The Antonine plague that decimated Rome in the second century AD was probably smallpox carried by the legions returning from the eastern provinces.[27] Smallpox has several variants, some of which produce mortality rates of 90 per cent. The more common *variola* strain causes a mortality of between 20–40 per cent.[28] Ancient armies were always subject to sudden and devastating epidemics that could kill thousands of soldiers and operationally cripple the army as a combat force. The outbreak of one disease did not preclude the simultaneous outbreak of another after the first onslaught had reduced the soldier's resistance.

Injuries

An army in the field suffered considerable manpower loss through injury. In the First World War, the manpower loss for Allied armies on the Western Front was almost 6,000 men a month from accidents, falls, accidental wounds, frostbite, trenchfoot and heat stroke. In antiquity, an army on the march could expect to lose a considerable percentage of its combat force to injuries in simply moving to the battlefield. Alexander's army of 65,000 men and 6,000 cavalry arranged in column ten-abreast stretched for 16½ miles, not counting baggage animals and pack-trains.[29] The air breathed by the men in the centre of the column was putrid. The dust choked their nostrils, eyes became irritated and lungs congested. In only a single day, nosebleeds, eye irritation and respiratory problems would cause injury of such severity that men would fall out of the columns to be left behind.

Modern armies estimate that an average soldier carrying a moderate load for eight hours of walking requires 3,402 calories and 70 grams of protein a day.[30] In desert or semi-arid climates with high temperature and low humidity, the soldier requires a minimum of nine pints of water per day. These requirements are minimums, and will keep the soldier functioning for the first few days. If nutritional requirements are kept at this minimal level over a march of ten days, by the end of that time most soldiers would be unable to function. The ancient soldier carried an average load of 60lb on his back. Carrying 60lb amid conditions of high temperature and low humidity, aggravated by dust and putrid air, caused the soldier to succumb to heat exhaustion and dehydration. Almost the entire army that Aelius Gallus, the Roman governor of Egypt in 24 BC, led into Arabia died of heatstroke and thirst. Many of the survivors suffered permanent damage, and had to be discharged from military service.[31]

Some idea of the loss rates experienced by armies in antiquity can be obtained from the results of a Navy/Marine experiment conducted at the Twenty-Nine Palms desert training area in California in 1984.[32] Although the troops in the exercise were provided with the best nutrition, clothing and shelter, more than sufficient water, frequent rest periods and precise instructions on how to conserve body energy, 110 men had to be hospitalized for heat exhaustion over a fifteen-day period. Another fifty-three suffered debilitating headaches induced by heat, thirty-one were hospitalized for severe body cramps and nausea, forty-six suffered nosebleeds from the dust and another forty-six were hospitalized for eye irritations.[33] In all, 286 men were lost to heat-related illness alone, even though the exercise required no sustained marching.[34]

Ancient armies suffered the same injuries that plague modern armies, including accidents, falls, contusions, cuts, bruises, sprains and broken bones. In the Twenty-Nine Palms study, 1,101 men suffered some injury serious enough to require attention at the battalion aid station or evacuation to the rear.[35] Two hundred and twenty-eight soldiers suffered from blisters, lacerations and abrasions. Another 169 suffered general trauma serious enough to take them out of the field, while 152 soldiers had irritations of the nose and throat. The generous category of 'other' injuries listed 377 soldiers requiring medical treatment. Seventeen per cent of the total force required medical treatment or hospitalization for injuries after only fifteen days. We might surmise that the large number of animals and wagons that accompanied ancient armies, as well as the poor quality of military footwear, probably resulted in an even higher rate of injuries to the feet and ankles of soldiers in ancient armies.

Ancient armies often fought in cold climates. The Assyrian incursions into Armenia and Kurdistan required fighting in snow, rain and freezing temperatures. Roman armies fought in Germany, the Alps, Eastern Europe and the mountains of Spain, all of which have climates that challenged the survivability of soldiers in the years up to and including the Second World War. Cold weather could cause tremendous casualties. Alexander crossed the Hindu Kush with 100,000 men to arrive on the other side thirteen days later with only 64,000, a loss rate of 36 per cent. Hannibal crossed the Alps at terrible cost. His army of 38,000 infantry and 8,000 cavalry lost 18,000 infantry and 2,000 cavalry by the time he reached Italy. Studies of cold casualties in the Second World War demonstrate that only 15 per cent of soldiers injured by cold can be returned to service, suggesting that most cold injuries then and now were serious indeed.[36]

As difficult as the life of the soldier in antiquity was, it was often better than the life of most people, many of whom were slaves and most of whom led lives of hard labour in the fields. Many young men entered military service precisely to avoid the back-breaking agricultural labour that would have otherwise been their lot. The soldier was usually better fed than the average person, and had access to some medical care. Military camps were often less crowded and more hygienic than the urban centres, and for all its horrors, battle was not a constant occurrence. Most of the soldier's time was spent in peacetime garrison or training. He often lived longer. Under the Roman Empire, the soldier lived an average of five years longer than the Roman citizen. Still, war and military service was risky business indeed.

Chapter 6

Logistics: The Invisible Art in Ancient Warfare

T he records of war are filled with praise for great generals. But one can search in vain for praise of the logistics officers who made their victories possible. Even in modern times, logistics officers and their contributions to victory remain largely invisible in the reports of military success. Supporting an army hundreds of miles from its base for extended periods was no easy task. The logistics officers who made possible the victories of the great commanders of antiquity are the invisible heroes in the history of warfare.

By the Iron Age, the size of armies had grown enormously, along with the scale of their battles and campaigns. Ancient armies had to master the task of supporting these large armies in the field over greater distances and for longer periods of time. The logistical feats of ancient armies were often more difficult and achieved more proficiently than those accomplished by the armies of the nineteenth century, when the railroad, mass production of supplies, mechanical manufacture, standard packaging and tinned and condensed food made the problem of supply considerably less difficult. Of all the achievements of the armies of antiquity, those in the area of logistics remain the most unappreciated by students of military history.

Food and Water Supplies

The most important supplies were, of course, food and water for the soldiers and animals. In hot climates like the Near East, India and parts of China, the nutritional and water requirements of man and beast were much higher than in moderate climates. The ancient soldier was issued about 3lb of wheat a day as his basic ration, and he required nine pints of water a day to remain effective. An ancient army of 65,000 men (about the size of Alexander's field army) required 195,000lb of grain a day to meet minimum nutritional requirements. To sustain the army's cavalry, baggage and transport animals required 375,000lb of forage per day.[1] Horses and other pack animals required 30–60 quarts of water a day.[2] To meet the needs of an army of 40,000 soldiers required 21,000 gallons of water per day. An additional 158,000 gallons was needed for the animals.[3] Soldiers carried canteens, but these were for use between the springs and rivers that provided the major source of an army's water.

Water supply in the Near and Far East is highly dependent upon weather. In summer, wells, streams and springs dry up, so logistics officers had to be aware of the locations of water sources and their rates of flow. Without sufficient water, the army's animals would die within days, so providing them with water was as important, if not more so, as the troops. Campaigns in desert environments required armies to carry water with them. The Roman general, Pompey, campaigning against the Albanians in the Caspian Sea region, ordered 10,000 water skins to permit his army to cross the desert waste.[4]

The number of animals in the baggage trains of ancient armies was substantial. A Roman legion of 4,800 men had 1,400 mules,[5] or one animal for 3.4 men. This number of mules equalled the carrying capacity of 350 wagons.[6] By comparison, an American army of 10,000 men during the Mexican War (1844–1846) required 3,000 mules and 800 wagons.[7] General Sherman's army (1864) of 100,000 men during the American Civil War had 32,600 pack-mules and 5,180 wagons.[8] The number of pack animals to be fed and watered does not include cavalry horses and chariot horses that also had to be cared for in ancient armies. The number of these animals was substantial. An Indian field army during the *Mahabharata* period (400 BC) had 6,561 chariot horses and 19,683 cavalry horses.[9] At Arbela, Darius III put 40,000 cavalry in the field,[10] and Alexander at the Battle of the Hydaspes (326 BC) fielded 13,000 Macedonian cavalry.[11]

Fodder for the animals was the largest logistical requirement of any army of the ancient period. In the American Civil War, daily forage requirements were three times as great in weight as subsistence requirements for soldiers.[12] Fodder may be either rough fodder, grasses and hay cut from fields or grazed by the animals themselves, or hard or dry fodder, a grain, usually barley or oats.[13] Ten thousand animals required 247 acres of land per day to obtain sufficient fodder,[14] and an army would quickly consume its supply of fodder in a few days if it didn't move. Livy tells us that armies often waited 'until there was an abundance of pasture in the fields' before undertaking a campaign.[15] One of the reasons why ancient armies broke off campaigns in winter was that there was insufficient fodder to feed the animals.[16] Dry fodder (oats, barley) could be carried with the army in sufficient quantities to sustain the animals for a few days across desert or rocky terrain. But no army could carry sufficient grain to feed its troops and animals, so that finding enough fodder was an important concern in planning the route of march. Table 1 summarizes the logistics requirements for a typical Iron Age army, in this case the army of Alexander the Great.

Ancient armies had to transport more than food and weapons, both of which could be carried by the soldier himself. The advances in military technology since 1800 BC had begun to make armies far more complex, with a resulting increase in their logistical burdens. The development of the chariot, for example, required

Table 4: The Logistics Requirements for the Army of Alexander the Great

	Numbers	Ration	Weight (lb.)
Personnel	65,000	3 lb. grain	195,000
		1/2 gal. (5 lbs.) water	325,000
Cavalry horses	6,100	20 lb. grain & forage	122,000
		8 gal. (80 lb.) water	488,000
Baggage animals	1,300	20 lb. grain & forage average	26,000
		8 gal. (80 lb.) water average	104,000
Animals carrying provisions	8,400	20 lb. grain & forage average	168,000
		8 gal. (80 lb.) water average	672,000

Source: Donald W. Engels, *Alexander the Great and the Logistics of the Macedonian Army* (Berkeley: University of California Press, 1978), Table 7, p. 153.

ancient armies to maintain repair depots and special mobile repair battalions to keep the vehicles combat-ready.[17] Chariots were disassembled for transport, requiring ox-carts or donkeys to transport the wheels, while human porters carried the chariot bodies. More animals and humans had to be fed and watered as a result.

The introduction of cavalry squadrons after 850 BC brought into existence special logistics units whose task was to obtain and train the horses as cavalry mounts. Greater numbers of horses now had to be watered and fed on the march. The *musarkisus* was the Assyrian army's horse logistics branch. It obtained and processed 3,000 horses a month for military training and use,[18] a feat not repeated in the West until the time of Napoleon. The integration of chariots with cavalry forced ancient armies to sustain two types of military 'vehicles' at the same time. The armies of India had to supply three types of combat vehicles – cavalry, chariots and elephants. Elephants required large numbers of attendants to feed, wash and tend the animals, in addition to the *mahouts* (mounted 'drivers'), combat archers and spearmen who rode the animal into battle. Unlike horses, elephants will not breed in captivity. Each animal had to be captured in the wild and trained, requiring a corps of elephant trappers and trainers.

Other technological advances increased logistical burdens. Advances in siegecraft required armies to transport siege equipment as they moved through hostile territory. Without siege equipment to reduce enemy cities, an army risked leaving hostile garrisons across its line of supply and communication. Ropes, picks, levers, scaling ladders, shovels for tunnelling and covered battering rams with heavy metal heads all had to move with the army. The Persians moved huge siege towers on wheels pulled by teams of sixteen oxen. Xenophon tells us that these towers weighed 13,920lb.[19]

The use of artillery, introduced by the Greeks and brought to perfection by the Romans and Chinese, added another requirement to transport catapults and shot. Indian siege machines were enormous, and were transported by elephants. Although some of the siege machines of the ancient armies could be dismantled for transport, they required many more pack and baggage animals to carry the parts. Roman armies sometimes carried construction materials with them in anticipation of having to build bridges. The need to repair tools and weapons brought into existence the military blacksmith with his travelling forge. Livy tells us that a Roman army of eight legions (approximately 40,000 men) required 1,600 smiths and craftsmen (*fabri*) to keep its equipment ready for battle.

Much of the new technology of war was too heavy or oddly shaped to be carried by pack animals, forcing ancient armies to use the wagon in ever greater numbers. Wagons, of course, also needed animals to pull them, as well as repairmen and extra parts to keep the wagons operational. Wagons came to make up 20–30 per cent of the supply train relative to pack-animals.[20]

Bases and Depots

Even a well-supplied and logistically sophisticated army could not carry all the supplies it required to sustain itself for very long. All armies had to 'live off the land' to some extent. At the minimum, this meant finding sufficient daily supplies of water and fodder for the animals and firewood for cooking, light and warmth for the troops. 'Living off the land' meant foraging, requisitioning and plundering. Foraging required sending units of soldiers to find certain items like fodder or firewood. Requisitioning involved obtaining supplies from friendly authorities or individuals, often by paying for them, other times simply taking them with a promise to pay. Plundering involved seizing provisions or property from the owners without compensation.

Of the three logistical activities, foraging was by far the most difficult and dangerous work. Foraging parties were always subject to attack, and sufficient security forces usually had to be sent with them to provide protection. Mowing and hauling hay for the animals, cutting firewood or digging wells was hard work, precisely the kind of agricultural labour that many soldiers had joined the legions to avoid. The *Iliad* tells us that after the Greeks had established themselves before Troy, a great number of soldiers were kept busy pillaging the countryside and 'turning the soil' (ploughing and planting crops) to feed the army.[21] Foraging parties gathered only as much as the army's supply train could reasonably carry, usually not more than four or five days' provisions at a time.[22] Foraging took time and slowed the army's rate of advance.

As long as the army was moving within the borders of its own country or imperial realm, it could supply itself from stocks of food and supplies pre-positioned at supply depots and forts along its route. Once beyond the borders, however, the problem of supply became more pressing. Almost all armies of antiquity used a system of operational bases, tactical bases and depots to keep their armies supplied in foreign territory. The armies of Classical Greece, by contrast, usually fought no more than a few days' march from their homelands, and supplied their armies by having each soldier and his attendants provide and carry supplies for themselves. There was no military logistical system in Classical Greece until Philip of Macedon introduced one for his army.

An operational base might be a port or a large city located in or close to enemy territory that could be used to collect and store large amounts of food and supplies. Livy described the Carthaginian operational base at New Carthage as 'a citadel, treasury, arsenal, and storehouse for everything'.[23] When Thutmose III captured the coastal cities in northern Palestine, he did so to turn them into operational bases for use in the war with the Syrians. The advantage of a port over an inland city was that larger amounts of supplies could be moved faster and more cheaply by ship than overland. The most common transport ship of the Roman period could carry about 80–90 tons of cargo, and make 7–9 knots on the open sea. A troop transport could hold about 380 soldiers. Configured as a horse transport, it could hold fifty horses. As a supply ship, it could accommodate 120,000lb of grain. Water transport during Roman times was forty times less expensive than overland transport.[24] It was for this reason that when Titus planned his attack on Jerusalem in 70 AD, he assembled his army at Caesarea, a seaport, rather than at Joppa, or another city closer to Jerusalem itself.

The tactical base served as the main resupply facility when the army was close to or in contact with the enemy. The army would move from its operational base and establish a tactical base, usually a fortified position like the Roman camp. The forward tactical base advanced with the army, and previous tactical bases were converted into depots.[25] Supplies were then moved from the operational base to a series of depots positioned behind the army's line of march. Supplies were shuttled forward to the army over a series of intermediate supply storage depots by series of alternating animal pack trains and wagon convoys used repeatedly, while travelling only relatively short distances, perhaps 20 miles between depots.[26] If the army was forced to retreat, it could do so along its previous line of communication, finding supplies at each of the depots to replenish itself and maintain its integrity. This system made it possible for ancient armies to project force over long distances. This or some minor variation in the supply system of bases, depots and pack convoys was found among all the armies of the Near East throughout antiquity, and in India and China as well.[27]

Animal Transport

The primary means of moving supplies in antiquity was the animal pack train comprised of donkeys, mules, horses, oxen, camels and elephants in some appropriate mix. These animals were used either as draught animals (load-pullers) or pack animals (load-bearers). Ramses II revolutionized Egyptian logistics by introducing the ox-drawn cart to Egyptian logistics. For centuries the Egyptians had used donkeys and donkey-drawn carts. Ramses probably got the idea for ox-drawn carts from his experience with the Sea Peoples who, like the Hittites, used the ox-cart as a standard means of military transport. Although ox-drawn and mule-drawn wagons can move larger loads, pack animals can move both on and off prepared roads, go further per day and travel faster and for longer periods than wagons.[28] They are also less expensive and take up less space in camp. The ox-cart slowed military movement to a crawl, however.[29] One reason was that the animal collar pressed upon the animals' windpipes, choking them and increasing their rate of physical exhaustion.[30] Oxen move more slowly than mule-drawn wagons, usually no more than 9 miles a day,[31] while a mule-drawn wagon can make 19 miles a day.[32] Regardless of the animal, damaged hooves were a major source of lameness in pack animals. Logistics trains were further burdened by having to take along spare animals or finding some way to acquire them along the way. Ancient armies used 'hipposandals', a leather or cloth bag tied over the animal's hooves to reduce damage to their feet.[33]

With the introduction of cavalry and chariots, the horse became a fixture in ancient armies. Although some use was made of the horse as a draught animal (Assyrians, Romans and Indians), horses were used almost exclusively as cavalry mounts and usually not in the logistics train. Unlike mules or donkeys, horses are fragile creatures whose health fails quickly if forced to live on rough fodder or remain uncovered in the cold or wet. Nonetheless, when outfitted with panniers to carry cargo, horses were comparatively efficient when compared to the ox-cart. An ox-cart could move a 1,000lb load 9 miles per day, while five horses could carry the same load 32 miles a day at twice the speed on half the forage.[34] The use of the horse as a prominent animal in a logistics train occurred first in the Persian army, and was quickly adopted by Philip of Macedon.[35]

The donkey was the most common transporter of goods in the civilian and military economies of the ancient period. Properly equipped with pack saddles, panniers or wooden frames, a donkey can carry a 220lb load.[36] Mules are stronger and more sure-footed than donkeys, and cheaper to feed than the horse.[37] They were, however, more expensive than donkeys. A mule can easily carry 300lb. Although a relatively slow traveller, 4–5 miles per hour, the mule has incredible endurance and can march continuously for ten to twelve hours.[38] A mule can easily travel 40 miles a day. In the nineteenth century, US Army mule trains could make 80–100 miles a day under forced march conditions.[39] The expense and slow speed of the ox-cart led Philip of Macedon to remove them from his army, an innovation that tripled the army's rate of movement and increased its ability to move over rough terrain.[40]

The camel was first domesticated around 1000 BC and quickly became a common logistics animal in the armies of the ancient Near East. A camel can carry between 400–600lb,[41] usually in panniers. Camels are more difficult to control than mules and have softer feet, which makes them unsuitable for mountainous or rocky terrain. The ability of the camel to go long periods without water, however, makes them ideal for desert campaigns. In India, the elephant was considered the best animal with which to transport goods. It could carry very heavy loads and did double duty as a fighting animal.[42] Ox-drawn wagons were also used by the armies of later antiquity to carry heavy and bulky loads. The lack of brakes, a pivoting front axle and axle bearings significantly reduced the wagon's efficiency on the march, however. Still, wagons were the basic form of transport for most tribal armies in the West, and could be quickly turned to military advantage by forming them into a *laager* for defensive purposes.

Human Transport

Hired or conscripted human porters and the soldiers themselves were an important part of the carrying capacity of the logistics train. Alexander, the Romans, Indians and Chinese made extensive use of porters, and Alexander and the Romans made maximum use of the carrying capacity of their own soldiers. Both the Greek and Roman soldier carried 60–70lb on his back; in an emergency, the soldier could carry 100lb.[43] The ability of the soldier to carry his own load drastically reduced the overall logistical burden of the army. With soldiers carrying only one-third the load that would normally have been hauled by animals, an army of 50,000 men required 6,000 fewer pack animals and 240 fewer additional animals to haul feed for the others.[44] Armies sometimes drove large cattle and sheep herds with them to provide meat for the troops. Livy tells us that Hannibal had more than 2,000 head of cattle with his army of 30,000 men.[45]

Roads and Bridges

The speed and ease of movement of supplies could be increased by improvements to the logistical infrastructure. By the time of the Persian Empire, states had begun to construct regular roads for logistical and military purposes. The Persian, Chinese and Roman empires all built extensive road networks. In Persia, these roads were mostly unpaved packed dirt tracks sufficiently wide to permit the movement of wheeled siege towers towed by oxen harnessed eight abreast. A system of bridges made crossing streams and other terrain obstacles easier, greatly increasing rates of movement. The most famous of the Persian roads ran from Sardis on the Mediterranean to the Persian capital of Susa, a distance of 1,500 miles. A horse messenger could travel the distance in fifteen days. Without the road, the journey would have taken three months.[46] The most amazing system of roads in the ancient world was that of the Romans. The Romans constructed 250,000 miles of roads, including 50,000 miles of paved roads, throughout the empire.[47] The effect on the movement of armies and supplies was dramatic. On dry unpaved roads, a Roman legion could move no more than 8 miles a day.[48] In wet weather, movement was almost impossible at any speed. On paved roads, however, a legion could make 20 miles a day in all kinds of weather. The Roman road system revolutionized logistics and transport.

The need to increase the armies' rates of movement while keeping them supplied led to the use of tactical engineering units that travelled with the armies. These units kept the supply trains moving by cutting roads, building bridges and floating supplies across rivers. Assyrian engineers invented the world's first military pontoon bridges made from palm wood, planks and reeds called *keleks*.[49] Persian engineers became skilled at the construction of bridges with vertical sides so that horses could cross steep ravines without the fear that often caused the horses to bolt.[50] While Egypt and India had used small coastal vessels from time immemorial to supply their armies, the Persians were the first to introduce a regular navy to support ground operations.[51] Using the ship-building and maritime skills of the peoples of their coastal provinces, the Persians commissioned special ships to transport horses, infantry and supplies, including shallow-draught vessels for use on rivers. Herodotus tells us that Xerxes' expedition against the Greek states in 481 BC deployed 3,000 transport ships to supply the army.[52] The Roman army also made extensive use of water transport by constructing a network of canals in Gaul and Germany to supply their armies.

Money

Another important means of supplying ancient armies was the suttler or military contractor that came into wide practice during the Persian Empire. Darius I was the first monarch to coin money on a national scale.[53] Backed by enormous Persian gold reserves, the 130 grain gold *daric* became the only gold currency of the early ancient world and could be spent anywhere. The use of currency led to the establishment of uniform weights and measures that allowed logistical planners to obtain military supplies in precise amounts. One result of this type of purchasing was the emergence of merchants whose business was the provision of supplies to the army, the first military contractors. A special kind of military-civilian supplier went along with the army on the march, setting up shop in the evening to sell the soldiers everything from food to oil.[54]

The logistical apparatus of ancient armies was remarkable for what it could accomplish in an age without mechanical transport. It is worth remembering that no army of the modern period equalled or exceeded the rates of movement of the armies of the ancient period until the American Civil War, when the railroad made faster troop movement possible.[55] Supported by an efficient logistical train, ancient armies could routinely conduct operations 50–60 miles beyond their last tactical base, and remain well-supplied.[56] It was only in the era of mechanical transport that armies have been able to better this performance.

Chapter 7

Siegecraft and Artillery

Siegecraft and artillery came into existence in order to deal with one of the most powerful defensive systems produced by the Iron Age, the fortified city. The first fortified city to appear in the Middle East was at Jericho, although it is by no means clear that the walls of this city were originally built for military reasons.[1] Undisputed fortified cities are found almost a millennium earlier, around 2000 BC, in India, where they were constructed by the Indus Valley civilization.[2] These cities, located on hills and surrounded by brick walls, may have been originally constructed to protect against floods.[3] By the Bronze Age, there was unambiguous evidence of fortifications constructed for purely military purposes. The first undisputed example of a fortified city in antiquity was Urak in Iraq, dating from 2700 BC. Its walls enclosed an urban population of 3,000–5,000 people.[4] Within 200 years, fortification of urban areas had become the norm.

The fortifications of the Bronze Age were remarkable. The fortress at Buhun built by the Egyptians in the Sudan around 2200 BC was 180 yards square and surrounded by a mud-brick wall 15ft thick and 30ft high. The wall had firing bastions every 18ft. Outside the wall was a second wall serving as a steep revetment, with its own set of firing enclosures every 30ft. A moat 26ft across and 18ft deep surrounded the outer wall with yet another steep glacis on the inner slope. The gate complex was 45ft high and stretched from the inner wall across the moat, allowing archers to cover the parallel approaches with arrow fire.[5] Fortified cities in India had even more extensive towers and gates, with walls often extending 4 miles in circumference.[6] The Israelite fortress at Hazor had walls that ran 1,000 metres by 7,000 metres.[7] The city of Qatna had walls 4 miles long, and the Hittite capital of Boghazkoy was surrounded by walls 6 miles in length. The entire wall of Boghazkoy and its supporting strongpoints were made of solid rock and fired brick.[8] So important were fortifications to the ancient armies that the need to secure adequate stone and wood to construct them led both Egypt and Assyria to occupy Syria repeatedly in their attempts to obtain these strategic materials.

Fortified cities put field armies at grave risk. Safe behind the city's walls, defending armies could provision themselves for long periods while attacking armies were forced to live off the land until hunger, thirst and disease ravaged them. An army bent on conquest could not force a strategic decision as long as the defender refused to give battle. An army that chose to bypass fortified cities and garrisons placed itself at risk of attack from the rear and across its line of supply and communication. If an army was to achieve its strategic objectives, it had little choice but to find a way to subdue enemy fortifications. Alexander learned this lesson after the Battle of Issus when he attempted to subdue the fortified cities along the Phoenician coast. The ability to overcome fortifications was a capability that no successful Bronze or Iron Age army could afford to be without.

There are five ways for an attacking force to overcome a fortified city: an assault over the walls, penetration through the walls, tunnelling below the walls, gaining access to the city by trickery or ruse and prolonged siege.[9] All other things being equal, the advantage usually lay with the attacker, whose army had the advantage of numbers. Most cities of antiquity, at least up to the Middle Iron Age, were relatively small in population, with about 240 people per urban acre, enclosed by the walls.[10] Thus, a city like Jerusalem in David's time (1050 BC) enclosed 16 acres with a wall 1,540 yards long. Its population was about 4,000 people.[11] Approximately a quarter of a city's population could be employed in its defence,[12] or about 1,000 soldiers in this case, each soldier defending 1.5 metres of wall. An attacking army could easily deploy four or five soldiers against each metre of wall. Joshua's army at Jericho was sufficiently large to encircle the city with ranks of soldiers six-men deep.[13] Moreover, the attacker could mount assaults at several places at once along the wall, forcing the defenders to shift forces from place to place, leaving other sections of the wall undefended. For reasons of simple mathematics, most assaults on fortified cities were successful.[14]

Military engineers invented the techniques for overcoming the defences of fortified cities. One of the earliest inventions was the battering ram, which dates from at least 2500 BC.[15] By 2000 BC, the battering ram was found in almost all armies of the ancient world. The Egyptians also invented the technique of securing a large metal blade to a heavy pole and using it to pry bricks and stones from the walls to create a breach. The Hittites used the technique of building an earthen ramp to a low spot in the wall, and then rolling large covered battering rams up to the wall to attack it at its thinnest point. Assyrians and Persians constructed massive siege towers that were taller than the defensive walls, using archers to provide covering fire for the battering ram crews working below. Persian siege towers were set on wheels and moved with the army.

The scaling ladder was one of the earliest siegecraft devices. Egyptian texts tell of soldiers strapping their shields on their backs to have both hands free to climb the ladders. The shields acted like a turtle's shell protecting the soldiers from stones and arrows thrown down upon them by the defenders. The Assyrians sometimes used a short scaling ladder to mount soldiers with axes and levers to dislodge stones mid-way up the wall, while tunnellers weakened it from below. Longer ladders were used by all armies to insert combat forces over the walls.

Figure 6: Egyptian Siege Lever Team, 2300 BC

If an army was to preserve the offensive, it had to subdue fortifications quickly. The absolute masters of rapid assault on cities were the Assyrian armies of the seventh century BC. The key to success was to coordinate several different types of assaults on the walls at the same time, but at different places. Mobile battering rams supported by siege towers were first brought into position at several points along the wall. Scaling ladders with lever crews were simultaneously deployed at other places. At the same time, sappers and tunnellers worked to gain entry from beneath the wall by weakening and collapsing a section of the foundation. This worked very well if the walls were casement walls. Casement walls are really two walls filled with rubble between them. By weakening the outer wall, the weight of the rubble itself pressing out against the weakened wall would cause it to collapse. At the appropriate time, long scaling ladders were used to mount attacks over the walls at several points to force the defender to disperse his forces.[16]

The armies of Classical Greece were hopelessly primitive in the arts of siegecraft, as were the tribal armies of Gaul and Germany. Carthaginian armies also lacked siege trains. After the Battle of Cannae, Hannibal failed to attack Rome supposedly because he lacked the siege equipment to do so.[17] Greek armies relied primarily upon blockade and starvation to subdue a city, methods far too slow to be used by an army trying to force a strategic decision. It was not until the late Classical period that the citizen armies of Greece made a few rudimentary attempts at using siege engines. In 440 BC, Artmon used siege towers against Samos, but failed to take the city.[18] In 424 BC, the Boeotians may have used a primitive flamethrower – a hollow wooden tube that held a cauldron of burning sulphur, charcoal and pitch at one end – against the wooden walls of Delium.[19] In 397 BC, Dionysius successfully employed siege towers and rudimentary catapults in the attack on Motya.[20]

Greek armies did not begin to approach the siegecraft capabilities of the armies of the Near East until the reigns of Philip of Macedon and Alexander. Philip realized that the new Macedonian army would remain a force fit only for obtaining limited objectives if it was not provided with the capability for rapidly reducing cities. Alexander's victories would also have been impossible without this ability. Philip introduced sophisticated siegecraft capabilities into his army, copying many of the techniques used by the Assyrians and passed to him by the Persians. Both Philip's and Alexander's armies made regular use of siege towers, battering rams, fire arrows and the *testudo*.[21]

Alexander's campaigns against the Indian republics after the Battle of the Hydaspes River (326 BC) provide a glimpse into the nature of Indian fortifications, and Alexander's methods of reducing them. Curtius tells us that although most Indian towns had walls, probably erected to protect against bandits, most were only made of mud and wattle or wood, and were easy targets. Others were more difficult because they took advantage of terrain characteristics, such as building on a hill or steep cliff.[22] Important towns, however, displayed impressive fortifications. Curtius described Massaga as being defended by:

> an army of 38,000 infantry ... a city that was strongly fortified by both nature and art. For, on the east an impetuous mountain stream with steep banks on both sides barred approach to the city, while to the south and west nature, as if designing to form a rampart, had piled up gigantic rocks, at the base of which lay sloughs and yawning chasms hollowed in the course of ages to vast depths, while a ditch of mighty labour drawn from their extremity continued the line of defence. The city was surrounded by a wall 35 *stadia* [6.2km or around 3¾ miles] in circumference which had a basis of stonework supporting a superstructure of unburnt, sundried bricks. The brickwork was bound into a solid fabric by means of stones ... Strong beams had been laid upon these supporting wooden floors which covered the walls and afforded passage among them.[23]

To overcome these defences, Alexander had his troops demolish the houses outside the walls to make a platform of the debris. Depressions in the ground were filled in with stones and trees to make a level platform. On the levelled ground, Alexander had his men construct several mobile wooden siege towers, and placed his *balistae* on their tops. The *balistae* then hurled stones down on the defenders, shattering their walls.[24] Curtius says that the defenders were awed by the *balistae*, implying that they might have been unknown in India at this time. The texts describing

Indian siege techniques do not describe *balistae*, and focus mostly on defensive measures, such as fire pots thrown from the walls or *satghanis*, a large wooden log with metal spikes that could be dropped from the walls to crush attackers below.[25] Another weapon, the *yantra*, may refer to a device for hurling stones and missiles at the enemy, but we have no information as to its design. We might reasonably conclude that both fortifications and the techniques for demolishing them were not as highly developed in India as they were in the Near East, at least during Alexander's time.

Military fortification seems to have come late to China, at least on any large scale. It is only with the dawn of the Warring States Period (464–221 BC) that we begin to find the regular fortification of cities and towns for military purposes. Chinese military architecture, including the Great Wall, is credited with a major innovation in construction. By mixing mortar with rice milk instead of water, Chinese engineers invented a new kind of mortar that was relatively impervious to rain and moisture. When dry, its strength permitted the laying of bricks at very steep angles without having the structural load of the bricks pull the structure apart. The introduction of extensive fortifications led to developments in siegecraft, including the use of specialized equipment such as chariots with large shields to protect workers, wheeled towers and rams, movable ladders, catapults and powerful crossbows that could discharge several large bolts at once. On campaign, it was customary for armies to construct fortified camps with walls of rammed earth.[26]

The Roman ability to reduce fortifications was probably the best in the ancient world, but it relied primarily upon organization and application rather than upon engineering innovation. Roman siege engines were mostly improved versions of the old Greek and Persian machines. The Romans used armoured siege towers, some as high as 24 metres, massive iron battering rams far larger and heavier than any predecessor, large iron hooks to dislodge stones, covered platforms to protect miners and assault teams, bridges, drawbridges and elevators mounted on towers to swing assault teams over the walls.[27] Most important, Roman siegecraft depended upon manpower, organization, discipline and determination. Once the Romans were committed to a siege, the results were inevitable, no matter how long it took to succeed.

The Romans raised the art of circumvallation and countervallation to new heights. At Masada in Judea, they constructed a stone wall around the entire mountain. Manned at regular intervals with soldiers, the purpose of the wall was to prevent anyone from escaping the besieged fortress. When there was a threat from a relieving army, circumvallation was supplemented by countervallation, where another wall was built so that the troops could defend against an attack from outside. Caesar did this at the siege of Alesia in 52 BC.[28] Constructing these walls took considerable time. In the case of Masada, the Romans laid siege to the mountaintop fortress for three years. In the process they constructed a 3 mile-long sloping earthen ramp to the top of the mountain, along which they moved siege machinery and troops for the final assault.

It was Philip of Macedon who first organized a special group of engineers within his army to design and construct catapults. Philip's and later Alexander's use of catapults allowed Greek science and engineering to contribute to the art of war. By the time of Demetrios I (305 BC), known to history as *Poliorcetes* (the Besieger), Greek inventiveness in military engineering was probably the best in the ancient world.[29] It fell to Alexander's engineers to develop a number of new ideas. Diades invented a hook mounted on a lever suspended from a high vertical frame that was used to knock down the upper parapets of a wall. Diades also invented the *telenon*, a large box that could hold a number of armed men. Suspended from a tall mast, the *telenon* could be raised and lowered on tackle like an elevator to hoist men over the walls.[30] To this day, the military art of siege warfare is called 'poliocretics', in honour of the Greek contributions to the art.

The Invention of Artillery

The most important contribution of Greek military engineering of this period was the invention of artillery, the earliest of which took the form of catapults and torsion-fired missiles. The earliest example dates from the fourth century BC and was called a *gastraphetes*, literally 'belly shooter'.[31] It was a primitive crossbow that fired a wooden bolt on a flat trajectory along a slot in the aiming rod. Later, weapons fired by torsion bars powered by horsehair and ox tendon could fire arrows, stones and pots of burning pitch along a parabolic arc. Some of these machines were quite large, and were mounted on wheels to improve tactical mobility. One of these machines, the *palintonon*, could fire an 8lb stone over 300 yards, a range about equal to Napoleonic cannon.[32] All these weapons were used by Philip in his sieges. It fell to Alexander, however, to use them in a completely new way – as covering artillery. Alexander's army carried smaller prefabricated catapults weighing only 85lb. The larger machines were dismantled and carried along in wagons.[33]

Roman advances in the design, mobility and firepower of artillery produced the largest, longest-ranged and most rapid-firing artillery pieces of the ancient world. The rate of fire of Roman field artillery was not surpassed until the invention of the breach-loading artillery gun firing fixed ammunition at the end of the American Civil War. Roman catapults were much larger than the old Greek models, and were powered by torsion devices and springs made of sinew kept supple when stored in canisters of oil. Josephus recorded in his account of the Roman siege of Jerusalem that the largest Roman artillery pieces were the *onagi*, or 'wild ass', so called because of its recoil kick. According to Josephus, an *onager* could hurl a 100lb stone over 400 yards.[34] Vegetius tells us that each legion had ten *onagi*, one per cohort, organic to its organization.[35] Smaller versions of these machines, such as the scorpion and *ballista*, were sufficiently compact to be transported disassembled by horse or mule. These machines could fire a 7–10lb stone over 300 yards.[36] Caesar required that each legion carry thirty of these smaller guns, giving the legion a mobile, organic artillery capability.

Smaller machines fired iron-tipped bolts. Designed much like the crossbow but mounted on small platforms or legs, these machines required a two-man crew to operate, and were used as rapid-fire field guns against enemy formations. They could fire a 26in bolt over a range of almost 300 yards.[37] Larger versions mounted on wheeled frames were called *carroballistae*, and required a ten-man crew. These larger machines could fire three or four bolts a minute, and were used to lay down a barrage of fire against enemy troop concentrations.[38] They were the world's first rapid-fire field artillery guns.

The development of siegecraft as a requirement of Iron Age armies represented a major innovation in warfare. Without the ability to reduce cities and fortified strongpoints, no army on the march in hostile territory could hope to force a strategic decision with any rapidity. Under these circumstances, the very idea of empire would have been unthinkable, in much the same way as it was for the armies of Classical Greece, which had no siegecraft capability at all. The search for more

Figure 7: Roman *Onager* Catapult

effective ways to destroy fortifications produced the new combat arm of artillery. While Alexander was the first to use this new arm of war, it was the Romans who gave birth to the idea of using artillery as an anti-personnel weapon. Both siege engines and artillery represent the emergence of major new ideas in warfare, ideas that came to fruition with the introduction of gunpowder 1,000 years later.

Chapter 8

Iron Rations: The Soldier's Diet

The night before the Battle of Badr (AD 624), the Prophet Muhammad had a problem. He knew the enemy was waiting in the darkness, but did not know how large a force he was facing. During a break in the interrogation of a captured soldier, Muhammad asked, 'How many camels did they slaughter every day?' The prisoner answered nine or ten. As an experienced caravanner, Muhammad knew that the meat from a single camel was enough to feed 90–100 men. Now he knew he was facing a force of 900–1,000 men.[1]

What an army eats is an important factor in its military capability. The armies of the Arab Conquests survived on dates, water and porridge (sa'alik) that each soldier carried with him. Their camels ate almost anything – brush, thorn bushes, scrub, leaves – so rations and forage did not have to be carried in the supply train. The result was armies that could move 60–70 miles a day on horse and camel back. Mongol soldiers put slabs of meat under their saddles. The horse's sweat turned the meat to jerky, that the soldier then sliced off a piece at a time and ate. This led some observers to believe Mongols ate the flesh of their live horses. Mongol soldiers did drink their horses' blood, however, mixing it with kumis, fermented mare's milk. The hardy Mongol Przhevalsky horse could survive on leaves and brush, and dig through the snow for forage, something most horses could not do. Mongol armies could move 100 miles a day.[2] Tacitus says the Gallic tribal contingents in Hannibal's army were 'eaters of meat and drinkers of milk', a diet that required animal herds to accompany the army. The herds reduced Hannibal's rate of movement to only 9 miles a day, much slower than the unencumbered Roman army that was fed on bacon and pre-baked biscuits (buccelatum), and could easily make 20 miles a day.[3]

The field rations of some ancient armies are recorded in historical texts. There is the complaint of Egyptian soldiers on campaign in Canaan (1475 BC) that all they were given to eat was 'sour milk, salted fish, and hard bread'. Higher-ranking soldiers were provided with better fare. One text from Old Kingdom Egypt (2200 BC) instructs that officers receive 'good bread, ox meat, wine, sweet oil, olives, fat, honey, figs, fish, and vegetables'.[4] Avidius Cassius, a Roman officer during the reign of Marcus Aurelius (AD 175), ordered his troops to carry nothing on the march except 'laridum ac buccellatum atque acetum', or 'bacon fat, hard biscuit and sour wine'.[5] A surviving Indian text (1000 BC) lists the supplies needed to resist a siege. These include 'great stores of grass, wood, water, rice, and wheat, sesame, beans, vetches, and cereals and medicines, including *ghee*, fresh butter, oil, honey, sugar and salt'.[6]

Roman sources record the military diets of some tribal peoples. Livy notes that when Perseus the Macedonian provided rations for his Gallic auxiliaries, he gave them wine and grain, but they demanded 'animals' because they ate mostly meat.[7] The Roman historian Appian tells us that the Germans and Numidians 'lived on herbs or grass' and that the Numidians drank only water, not wine.[8] Caesar says that the British diet was mostly meat and dairy products.[9] Boudicca, queen of the Britons, tells us that:

> The Romans cannot bear up under hunger and thirst as we can … they require kneaded bread and wine and oil, and if any of these things fail them, they perish; for us, on the other hand, any grass or root serves as bread, the juice of any plant as oil, any water as wine.[10]

The Romans ate hard tack biscuits (*buccelatum*) as field rations, as well as *cibaria cocta*, or 'cooked rations', usually dried meat, vegetables and fruit. Prepared rations eliminated the need for cooking, reducing the time to gather firewood and for eating, thus increasing the time on the march. The Roman soldier carried a canteen of *posca*, a sour wine turned almost to vinegar (*acetum*) mixed with water. *Posca* was an excellent ration in that the *acetum* provided vitamin C, and reduced the bad taste of local water supplies. The highly acidic *acetum* also killed harmful water-borne bacteria. Unlike the peoples of the Middle East, who preferred sweet wines, the Romans preferred strong, harsh wines. The New Testament records the story of the Roman legionnaire at the foot of the cross giving Jesus 'vinegar on a sponge' to quench his thirst. The story says that the soldier was tormenting the victim. In fact, the soldier was trying to comfort Jesus. In response to Jesus' cry for water, the legionnaire offered him a sponge soaked in *posca* from his own canteen. But to the Middle East palate, the *posca* tasted like vinegar, leading to the false impression that the legionnaire was being cruel.[11]

The *Iliad* provides a description of the Mycenaean diet of the Homeric warriors laying siege to Troy. They ate cattle and goat meat roasted on a spit, served in round, pita-like unleavened flat bread made from parched barleycorn and cooked on an iron plate.[12] The first mention of leavened bread in Greek literature is in Xenophon's *Anabasis* (401 BC),[13] but leavened bread is found 2,000 years earlier in Old Kingdom Egypt (2200 BC). The Greeks ate beans, chickpeas, cheese and goat's milk. Cow's milk was considered unhealthy, and not consumed. Cattle were eaten as soon as they were slaughtered. There is no mention of any preserved rations in the *Iliad*.[14]

A typical military diet in antiquity included: (1) grain prepared as bread, porridge, biscuit or hardtack; (2) meat, including pork, mutton and beef (pork was the most commonly consumed meat in the form of salt pork or bacon, long-lasting items ideal for military field rations); (3) vegetables such as beans, peas and lentils, usually boiled, but sometimes crushed into a flour to make soup; (4) milk from goats and cows, including cheese and butter or *ghee*; (5) oil, including olive, sesame, sunflower and linseed oil; (6) salt on a daily basis for health and flavouring; (7) liquids, usually water, wine or beer. A litre of wine with 12 per cent alcohol provides 700 calories and is anti-scorbutic, that is, prevents scurvy. Beer is high in B-complex vitamins, and is a good source of carbohydrates.[15] These foods were available to the soldier mostly in garrison. In the field, the soldier's diet changed considerably, and was not nearly as extensive or healthy.

The standard grain ration in ancient armies was 2–3lb of raw grain per soldier per day. Ground into flour and mixed with water and salt, it produced just over 1¾lb of bread that provided 1,950 calories, or two-thirds of the soldier's daily calorie requirement.[16] By contrast, flour heated and ground by machine during the American Civil War required the removal of the grain kernel, the primary source of calories, so that the flour provided only 650 calories per pound.[17] The caloric content remains the same whether grain is prepared as bread, porridge or biscuits. Meat is particularly high in calories. Three ounces of mutton produces 317 calories; of salt pork, 400 calories; of roasted beef, 245 calories; of pork, 340 calories; of chicken, 200 calories; and of goose flesh, 175 calories. The American soldier of the Civil War was given either 20oz of beef per day or 12oz of salt pork.[18]

The caloric demands of the human body vary with the soldier's age and weight. Caloric requirements peak in late adolescence, decline dramatically and remain constant until middle age.[19] Most soldiers in antiquity entered military service around age 20, when their caloric needs were already reduced, and most left service before their caloric needs increased again. The average soldier in antiquity was about 5ft 7in in height and weighed about 145lb, and required approximately 3,000 calories a day to stay healthy, or about 25 per cent less than the 3,500–4,000 calories the American military estimates is required for the modern soldier.[20]

Quartermasters of ancient armies were experts at food preservation. After the collapse of the ancient world, knowledge of food preservation was largely lost and not rediscovered until the eighteenth century.[21] Cereal grains, the main ration of most armies through all periods of antiquity, could be stored for as long as ten years, if kept in sacks stacked in a manner to permit air to circulate around the bundles.[22] Grain could also be stored loosely if kept dry and turned regularly. Exposure to rain or extreme humidity, however, could cause deadly fungi to contaminate the grain. Carried as loose grain in the packs of the soldier, however, cereals kept for the duration of any campaign. Baked into bread, grain lasted for about a week. Baked into biscuits or hardtack, it lasted for months.

Smoked meat and fish kept for months, and pork and beef jerky for years. A favourite ration of the Egyptian army was smoked goose flesh. It was the Egyptians who probably discovered the secret of salt preservation; salting preserved meat for as long as two years.[23] But salted meat had to be soaked in water before it could be cooked and eaten, and soaking drew the nutrients out of the meat. Moreover, its use as food required an adequate local supply of water, something not always available in some climates. While boiled salt beef filled the soldier's stomach, it provided little in the way of nutrients or calories.[24] It did, however, provide salt. A soldier requires a ½oz of salt a day for his body to maintain its electrolyte balance. In high temperature, low humidity climates, a lack of salt can be fatal.

The first references to pickling are found in Sumer (3000 BC), where ox-joints were pickled for transport and sale.[25] Vegetables could also be pickled, and olives, beets and carrots (bulb vegetables) were commonly preserved in this manner. Pickling was done with vinegar and salt. Vinegar is an excellent source of vitamin C and eight important amino acids,[26] and is an anti-scorbutic. In modern times, German and Russian naval crews were fed *sauerkraut*, sliced cabbage in vinegar, to prevent scurvy. The pulse vegetables – beans, lentils, peas – were easily preserved by drying, lasted for years and could be ground into a thick flour to make soup. Onions and garlic kept for months without any preservation, while leafy green vegetables could not be preserved, and were foraged in the field when they were to be had.

Fruits were easily preserved by drying. Dried fruit was pressed into large blocks for easier transport or pressed around a string that could be hung from the soldier's belt.[27] Pressing fruit required removal of the kernels or stones that were then used as a source of fuel when firewood was scarce. The ancient soldier supplemented his diet with various vegetable and animal oils. Vegetable oils – olive, sesame, sunflower, balsam, radish or linseed – could be stored for long periods without spoiling. An Indian oil, *ghee*, made by skimming off the oil from melted butter while leaving the solids behind, kept for very long periods, even in the warmest and most humid climates.[28] Oils could also be used as fuel for lamps and cleansing the skin after bathing.[29] Two staple military rations of the ancient armies were wine and beer. Sealed properly in jars or wooden casks, wine could be kept for years. Even when transported in leather skins, wine still keeps for weeks. Beer, on the other hand, tends to spoil quickly, often within a few days, so it was not usually transported in the supply train, but made on the spot whenever the army was encamped for more than a few days.

The most widely consumed foods of the ancient world were cereal grains: wheat, barley, emmer, rye, oats, and millet.[30] It was only late in the ancient period that rice was imported from India and China, where it had been a staple for centuries.

In the West and Middle East, wheat, barley and emmer were the most commonly used grains for making bread, and were the primary source of carbohydrates in the ancient soldier's diet. The pulse crops – beans, peas, lentils and soybean – provided the primary source of protein. The major sources of vitamins were fruits and green vegetables. The Sumerians invented shade gardening, where small gardens were shaded by date palms to lessen the heat of the sun and break the force of the wind.[31] This technique made it possible to grow leafy green vegetables in the hostile climates of the Middle East and India. The oils extracted from these plants were a valuable source of vitamins. A variety of fruits – olives, grapes, figs, sycamore figs, pomegranates, dates, apples, pears, plums and cherries – were widely cultivated, and were an important part of the ancient military diet. Cereals and plants constituted 90 per cent of the soldier's diet; the remaining 10 per cent came from the meat of animals and products derived from them, like milk, cheese, *ghee* and eggs.[32]

Sheep were the most common meat resource during all periods of antiquity.[33] Next came goats, and around the sixth millennium BC, cattle were domesticated in Anatolia. The pig was domesticated soon after, and remained a major source of meat until the Late Bronze Age. During the Iron Age, pork was the major meat ration of the Roman army. The chicken was first domesticated in China during the Neolithic period, but did not become a major food source until circa 600 BC.[34] The goose was also widely available, and smoked goose flesh was a staple of the Egyptian soldier's diet.[35]

Protein is needed to sustain tissue, create body fluids and balance the nitrogen levels of the body. Salt is needed to retain fluids. The water requirement for troops in desert conditions of high temperature and low humidity is estimated by the US Army to be 9 pints a day. Trained soldiers can get along on less, perhaps 6 pints a day. If we are to believe the Persians, they got along on just 2 pints a day.[36] In cooler climates, it is not unreasonable to expect a soldier to consume only 2–3 pints of water daily.

Vegetables were more important for providing vitamins than calories. Eight ounces of beans or lentils a day provided 350 calories. The American Civil War soldier was issued three times that amount of vegetables for his daily vegetable ration. Two ounces of cheese provided ninety calories, 8oz of goat's or cow's milk 160 calories and 1½ oz of olive oil 350 calories. A half-litre of wine or beer provided 350 calories. Dried fruits greatly enhanced the soldier's diet. A dried fig provided fifty calories, a date twenty-five calories and an apple 150 calories.[37] It is likely that the ancient soldier consumed somewhat greater quantities than the minimum amounts calculated here whenever he had opportunity to do so.

The soldier's diet in antiquity provided more calories per day than the diet of an American soldier serving in the Civil War. The mandated ration for a Federal soldier included 20oz of fresh or salted beef, or 12oz of salted pork, 1lb of white flour, a vegetable (usually dried beans) and a ration of coffee (sometimes four pints a day), sugar, vinegar and salt.[38] A pound of white flour provides about 650 calories, 12oz of salt pork 1,020 calories and 20oz of salted beef 1,400 calories, or a total of 1,800–2,000 calories a day. Although ancient quartermasters had no scientific knowledge of nutrition, military diets in antiquity provided sufficient quantities of all the nutritional components of which we are aware today. It is telling that, on average, the Roman soldier lived five years longer than the Roman civilian, a fact that can be attributed in part to his better diet.[39] No army from the Middle Ages to the Second World War provided their troops with rations as nutritionally sufficient as did the armies of the ancient world.

Chapter 9

Medical Care in Ancient Armies

The armies of the ancient world invented the first military medical services, and were the first to stress the pragmatic aspects of medicine over the theoretical. The history of empirical medicine is at least 2,500 years older (Egypt and Sumer) than in Classical Greece, and sophisticated surgery of the head can be found almost 8,000 years before it was attempted in the modern era. It seems apparent that the general level of medical care available to the Sumerian (2500 BC), Egyptian (1700 BC) and Assyrian (900 BC) soldier was superior to that which attended the hoplite warrior of Classical Greece. The apex of military medical care was reached under the Romans during the imperial period, and declined continually after that, only reaching the previous Roman level of care during the First World War. The ancient soldier often had a better chance of surviving a battlefield injury or wound than did his counterpart in the nineteenth century.[1]

Ancient physicians attending the wounded on the battlefield would not have encountered wounds that were remarkably different from those they routinely encountered in civilian practice. The cuts, bruises, fractures and gaping flesh wounds produced by ancient weapons driven only by muscle power would have appeared commonplace. Fractures of the arms, legs, wrists and skull, for example, were familiar to Egyptian doctors who served a population that often suffered fractures of the extremities from slipping on rocks on the Nile riverbank. Archaeological evidence indicates that the most common fractures in ancient Egypt were fractures of the wrist and arm.[2] It is no accident that the first evidence for the splint is found in ancient Egypt.[3] Skull, chest, pelvis and lower leg fractures suffered by soldiers in siege operations were familiar to Egyptian physicians who attended workers constructing the tombs, pyramids and other public works. Even gaping flesh wounds caused by a hacking sword had a more familiar counterpart in civilian medical practice: crocodile bites.

While most armies of the ancient world had physicians attending the wounded, the regular presence of military physicians, that is, something akin to an organized military medical service, was more evident in some armies than others. The major difficulty in providing medical care to the wounded soldier in antiquity was not so much a lack of practical medical knowledge as the inability of armies to bring this knowledge to bear on the battlefield in an institutionalized and consistent manner. So, for example, despite a high level of empirical medical knowledge in both countries, the Greeks did little to establish a medical service for their armies, while the Romans established a military medical service that was truly modern by any standard, and not surpassed until the Russo-Japanese War of 1905.

Sumer

It was the Sumerians who produced the world's oldest military medical texts and developed the first code of medical ethics more than 1,000 years before Hippocrates introduced a similar code in Greece.[4] The Sumerian text dates from the Third Dynasty of Ur (2158–2000 BC), and is almost 300 years older than the oldest surviving Egyptian medical text, the Kahun Papyrus written in 1850 BC.[5] The Sumerian military doctor was the *Asu*, and a surviving document tells us that Sumerian physicians were routinely posted to military garrisons.[6] Many of these physicians seem to have been full-time military personnel rather than conscripted for military service only in wartime. If so, this is the first evidence of a military medical corps in the armies of the ancient world. The Stele of Vultures (2500 BC) provides a glimpse into the role of physicians in the Sumerian army. The stele shows the wounded being assembled in a single place after the battle for examination and treatment. It also shows trenches being prepared to bury the dead.[7] Assembling the wounded and burying the dead remain two major functions of a military medical service to this day.

Egypt

In Egypt, the practice of medicine remained strongly under the control of the priesthood. Even so, there is evidence of the presence of empirical medical practitioners (*Swnw*) in military service. Documents tell of the presence of physicians at outlying military posts, and Egyptian physicians were regularly employed to care for the health and injuries of the workers on the great construction projects. Egyptian medical literature refers commonly to the type of wounds received on the battlefield, with the result that Egyptian military physicians became highly pragmatic students of wounds and wound treatment. It was the Egyptians who first developed the splint, and were the first to use adhesive bandages.[8] To counteract the shock and bleeding that was the most common cause of death on the battlefield, Egyptian physicians were the first to use the heated knife to cauterize wounds.[9] They were the first to use the extract of the poppy and distilled opium as painkillers, and invented the use of wild honey as a treatment for infection.[10] Modern tests demonstrate that wild honey was the most effective bacteria-killing compound until the discovery of penicillin.[11] Egyptian military physicians were expert at surgical procedures for treating linear and depressed fractures of the skull, an injury that must have been common in an army whose primary weapon for centuries was the mace, and which for 2,300 years did not use the helmet. Figure 8 details the Egyptian method of closing a head wound with adhesive bandages (top) and wrapping the skull.

Also portrayed is the procedure for washing a wound, filling it with honey-soaked lint and suturing the wound with a needle made from the thorn of the acacia tree. Other Egyptian innovations include the roller bandage for immobilizing arm and shoulder fractures, and the use of exotic mixed chemical compounds to treat various conditions. The Egyptians passed this practice to the Greeks. The root of the word chemistry, from the Greek *chemi* meaning black, is a reference to Egypt, known to the Greeks as the 'Black Land', from which the Greeks first obtained their knowledge of chemical compounds.

Although Egyptian medicine remained strongly empirical, it remained under the control of the religious priesthood, a dominance that seems to have prevented the emergence of a military medical service that was as organizationally sophisticated as in Sumer. Unlike Sumer, the Egyptians never clearly placed the responsibility for providing medical care to the army in the person of the king. As a result, Egyptian military medical care never reached the degree of institutional regularity that it did elsewhere. Yet Egyptian medical literature is replete with references to treating wounds and injuries of soldiers, references that hint strongly at a medical presence on the battlefield.

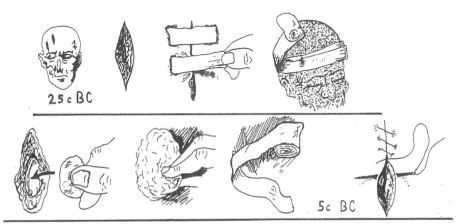

These techniques are described as early as 2000 BC in Egyptian medical literature.
Artwork by Tara Badessa.

Figure 8: Egyptian Techniques for Treating Head Wounds

Assyria

Assyria's military medical service was the most advanced in the ancient world prior to the coming of the Romans. The heir to the 2,000-year-old Sumerian tradition of empirical medicine, the Assyrians possessed the most complete collection of empirical medical practices and remedies in the ancient world.[12] The military surgeon was a product of the secular military state, and was a career medical professional. It was in Assyria for the first time that we find a surgeon whose profession was military medicine.[13] Assyrian military garrisons had full-time physicians stationed there, and they attended the army on the march and the battlefield.

Assyrian military physicians were also employed to oversee the health and treatment of populations that the Assyrians deported from their homelands.[14] It is likely that when the Assyrians deported the Israelite populations in the ninth and fifth centuries BC, it was Assyrian military physicians who treated them on the march. The appearance of the professional military surgeon may be regarded as one of the more important innovations in military history. Unfortunately, the institution died with the destruction of the Assyrian state in the fifth century BC, and did not reappear until the Romans created the most modern and effective military medical service in the ancient world.

Greece

One reason why military medicine in Greece never reached the level found in earlier states of the ancient world was that the overall level of Greek social and institutional development never reached much beyond the tribe. The result was that Greece never developed a military medical service, and what medical aid there was evident on the battlefield depended upon the few civilian physicians who could be hired, coaxed or forced to attend the militia army at war. We find these physicians in the *Iliad*, and Xenophon recorded the presence of eight surgeons accompanying the army of Ten Thousand that met its fate at Cunaxa.[15] The presence of physicians with the army does not indicate the presence of a military medical corps, however. Rather, it demonstrates the nature of the citizen armies of the period. The medical profession in Greece remained a private, civilian enterprise that accompanied the army on an *ad hoc* basis. Even in Alexander's professional armies this was the case, although the presence of medical services can be seen as a much more integral part of the military force than had ever appeared before in Greece. Alexander also made special provisions for the use of wagons as ambulances.[16] In Greece, the training and employment of physicians remained a private enterprise, and the citizen militia armies assumed no responsibility for it.

The one significant Greek innovation in military medicine was its recognition and treatment of psychiatric casualties. The Greeks were aware of mental illness, and were the first to practise a sophisticated psychiatry and to connect psychiatric syndromes to battle stress.[17] Greek literature is filled with accounts of soldiers driven mad by war. Ajax's slaying of sheep in the belief they were enemy soldiers is but the most well known. It was Greek society that invented the mythos of military heroism, and it should come as no surprise that Greek physicians were acutely aware of the failure of nerve that often afflicts soldiers in battle.

Rome

The great advance of Roman military medicine was its incorporation of a professional medical service for delivering care to the soldier in a regular and organized manner, something that the armies of the ancient world had not seen since the demise of Assyria. From the founding of Rome until the start of the imperial period in 24 BC, Roman military medicine was largely indistinguishable from the Greek; that is, it employed civilian physicians on an *ad hoc* basis and relied primarily upon the ability of the soldiers themselves to care for each other's wounds. With the rise of Augustus came the professional army, and with it a professional military medical service. Roman military physicians were recruited and trained by the army itself, a development that no other army in the world undertook until 1865, and spent a career within military service.[18] The military produced its own medical manuals. Roman military surgeons, the *immunes*, were supported by surgical assistants, orderlies and a corps of combat field medics whose task was to treat victims of shock and wounds on the battlefield before evacuating the soldier to a legion aid station located close behind the battle line. This was the principle of proximity of treatment, and no army in the West practised it again until the First World War.

Each legion post had its full complement of medical personnel who were responsible for maintaining the health of the legion. Their duties included overseeing the procurement, storage and preparation of food, locating and securing safe water supplies, constructing latrines and sewers, and ensuring that the soldiers bathed regularly and practised other sanitation habits such as hand washing after toileting. They also trained medical personnel and staffed the legion hospital. Each legion fort had its own hospital, that surpassed anything any army of the world used until the American Civil War. The hospital was usually located in the quietest part of the camp to avoid disturbing the sick and wounded. Within its four wings were contained an entrance hall that could be pressed into service as a triage centre, a well-lit surgical centre, a kitchen, heating plant, storage rooms, latrines and baths.

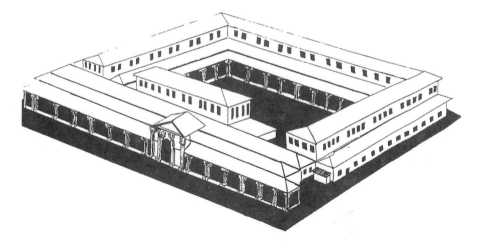

Figure 9: Roman Military Hospital, Vetera, Germany

Vetera Germany, Second Century AD

Figure 9 portrays a typical Roman legion camp hospital. To minimize noise, wards were designed so that a corridor separated the rooms from the general hospital. The roof was constructed so as to allow adequate cooling and ventilation. The large central courtyard was a source of quiet, fresh air and light to be enjoyed by the recuperating patients. Each hospital was constructed to accommodate 6–8 per cent of the legion's strength as casualties.[19]

Roman medical practice was the most effective in the late ancient world, and was not duplicated by any army until the First World War. The level of Roman surgical skill was not achieved again until the sixteenth century of the modern era. Roman operating rooms came complete with a beehive oven in which water was heated to sterilize surgical instruments. Roman surgical instruments included disposable scalpels, hemostats, chest separators, forceps, probes and needles. The Romans were the first to solve the old problem of arrow wounds by inventing the first surgical tool to extract arrows without causing further damage to the wound. They were the first in the West to perform amputation regularly, and used henbane and opium to lessen the pain of surgery. Roman physicians invented the surgical clamp that allowed the surgeon to tie off severed arteries without stopping the entire blood flow to the affected limb, reducing the prospect of gangrene and shock. The surgical clamp disappeared from medical knowledge after the fourth century until it was reinvented by Ambroise Pare in the 1600s.

Using ligatures and another Roman innovation, the tourniquet, doctors could stop the massive blood loss that produced shock and most often caused death. Roman physicians were expert at wound cleansing, suturing, bandaging, splinting broken bones and even used prosthetic devices to replace missing arms and legs. Their plastic surgery was as good as that found in India, and the old Etruscan art of artificial dentistry was also practised. The excellence of Roman military medical care is demonstrated by the fact that even though the Roman soldier was exposed to war, on average he lived five years longer than his civilian counterpart.[20]

India

The almost constant warfare between the Indian principalities of the Epic Age, the period between 1000–600 BC, and the central role of the warrior caste in Indian society inevitably brought into existence a corps of physicians to care for wounded warriors. One of the oldest Indian texts, the *Rig Veda*, contains accounts of battles, weapons and wounds, complete with a list of medical treatments used to treat battle wounds.[21] Early Vedic texts testify to the presence of military doctors in war. The importance of warfare as a formative force in Indian medicine is reflected in the fact that a physician who specialized in surgery was called the *shalyahara*. The word *shalya* means arrow, sword or lance, while the word *hara* means extractor or remover.[22] The concern for military medicine is evident in other texts. The king is urged to learn not only the methods of war, but also the diseases and injuries that can afflict his troops. A king is always to take proper care to see that drugs and medicines were stockpiled in advance, and that sufficient surgeons were available to the army.[23] Military physicians were used to inspect camp sites and to ensure the cleanliness of food and water.[24] Other texts note that doctors were in attendance while the army was on the march.

The *Arthashastra* describes a military ambulance corps whose wagons were drawn by horses and elephants. Instructions were given to ensure an adequate number of physicians were present, and that drugs and bandages were in good supply. The text tells of women in the medical service who provided food and beverages to the wounded, perhaps the first evidence of a woman's nursing corps. The medical tent is always to be placed near the commander's tent, and is to fly a flag to mark its location to minimize delay in finding where the wounded could be treated.[25] The king was to accompany the physician on visits to the wounded to lift their spirits and praise their bravery.[26] Nowhere in the early ancient world do we find a military medical service so organized and integrated into the military structure as in Vedic India. One is left with the impression that a great deal of empirical clinical medicine in India was produced by military physicians in their efforts to treat the thousands of casualties that resulted from the incessant wars.

Indian physicians were required to memorize two basic medical texts: the 1,700-page *Shusruta* and the *Charaka*, which was twice as long. These texts show a remarkable medical knowledge. Indian physicians were expert in cleansing, suturing and bandaging wounds, showing an awareness of infection and how to prevent it. No wound was to be stitched or bandaged 'as long as the least bit of morbid matter or pus remains inside it'.[27]

Surgical techniques available to Indian military physicians of this period included incising abscesses, lancing infected wounds, venesection, the use of probes to locate missiles that had penetrated the body, extracting missiles, suturing, bandaging, injections with syringes (the world's first), cautery, hemostasis and even amputation.[28] The *Rig Veda* includes descriptions of legs that were amputated and replaced by iron substitutes.[29] No physician had more treatment techniques at his disposal than Indian military physicians until the First World War.

Nowhere in the early ancient world do we encounter a medical tradition that is more empirically and pragmatically orientated than the Indian tradition. It far surpasses anything that came before it, and in most major aspects – empirical description of clinical traditions, treatment of infection, surgical skill, hemostasis, drugs and amputation – surpassed any level of medical practice until the Romans. No military medical service except the Romans surpassed the skills of the military physicians of the armies of India.

Chapter 10

War and Madness

The battles of antiquity in which the ancient soldier took part were different from modern battles in one very important respect: the distance at which killing was done. Since the practical use of gunpowder in the seventeenth century, killing in most battles has been accomplished at a considerable distance from the victim. Modern rifles easily kill at 500 yards, a range at which one cannot clearly see the effects of the bullets striking the body. Except for the recoil of the rifle against one's shoulder and the sound of the discharge, there is no physical contact with the victim. Of course infantrymen are armed with the bayonet, but in modern wars, instances of hand-to-hand combat are very rare indeed.[1] In ancient battles, by contrast, the soldier was always in close physical contact with the person he killed. Richard Heckler, in his book *In Search of the Warrior Spirit*, describes the killing experience of the ancient soldier correctly when he says, 'The ancient warrior met his foe in direct struggle of sinew, muscle, and spirit. If flesh was torn or bone broken, he felt it give way under his hand … he felt the pulse of life and the nearness of death under his fingers. He also had to live his days remembering the man's eyes whose skull he crushed.'[2]

The impact of battle was felt directly upon the physical senses of the ancient soldier to a much greater degree than battle usually is experienced by the modern combatant. Engaged in violent hand-to-hand combat, the ancient soldier could hear the pitiful screams of the wounded and dying; smell the stench of blood, entrails and gore even as he tried to gain purchase on earth made slippery with blood, urine and faeces, the latter secreted by soldiers' bodies seized with fear; feel the blade of his sword or spear push through his opponent's flesh, and suddenly stop as it struck bone; hear the sound of air rushing from the body cavity as the weapon was withdrawn; taste the salt of his own sweat as it ran down his face into his eyes and mingled with the taste of the bits of sticky blood and flesh that struck him whenever he opened a wound in his adversary; and see the terrible results of the slaughter around him, in which he was an integral participant. Sometimes, when a town was sacked or a civilian population put to the sword, or an enemy army slain to a man where it had surrendered, the assault on the ancient soldier's senses went on for hours at a time. At Cannae, Carthaginian troops massacred more than 70,000 Roman soldiers packed so tightly together that they could not raise their weapons in defence. The slaughter went on for five hours before the last Roman was slain. The ancient soldier was affected by the sensory slaughter of battle to a degree mostly unknown in the modern world.

Livy provides us with a description of the aftermath of the battlefield at Cannae that adequately captures the horror of the ancient battlefield:

> On the following day, as soon as it dawned, they set about gathering the spoils and viewing the carnage, which was shocking, even to enemies. So many thousands of Romans were lying, foot and horse promiscuously, according as accident had brought them together, either in battle or flight. Some, whom their wounds, pinched by the morning cold, had roused, as they were rousing up, covered with blood, from the midst of the heaps of the slain, were overpowered by the enemy.
>
> Some too they found alive with their thighs and hams cut, laying bare their necks and throats, bid them drain the blood that remained in them. Some were found with their heads plunged into the earth, which they had excavated; having thus, as it appeared, made pits for themselves, and having suffocated themselves by overwhelming their faces with the earth which they threw over them.
>
> A living Numidian, with lacerated nose and ears, stretched beneath a lifeless Roman who lay upon him, principally attracted the attention of all; for when the Roman's hands were powerless to grasp his weapon, turning from rage to madness, he had died in the act of tearing his antagonist with his teeth.[3]

It is not surprising, then, that the ancient soldier was as subject to psychiatric collapse from his war experience as is the modern soldier who, for the most part, fights under far less stressful conditions. Even so, rates of psychiatric casualties in modern wars are amazingly high. In every war in the twentieth century, the chances of a soldier becoming a psychiatric casualty were greater than the chances of being killed by enemy fire.[4] The American Army in the First World War admitted 158,994 soldiers to hospital who were unable to continue in service due to psychiatric reasons.[5] In the Second World War, 1,393,000 US Army soldiers suffered psychiatric symptoms serious enough to debilitate them for some period of time.[6] Some 504,000 of these in the US Army alone were permanently lost to the fighting effort.[7] In Vietnam, 12.6 per cent of the combat force suffered psychiatric symptoms serious enough to remove them from their units for some period.[8] In the 1982 invasion of Lebanon, the Israeli Defense Force suffered a psychiatric casualty rate 150 per cent greater than its killed in action rate.[9] And in Iraq (2005), the American psychiatric casualty rate was almost twice that of the rate at which American soldiers were killed in action.

The long-term psychological consequences of exposure to intense battle can be gauged further from the fact that more than 1.5 million soldiers who served in Vietnam suffered from some degree of Post-Traumatic Stress Disorder.[10] One can only imagine what psychological effects exposure to intense hand-to-hand combat had upon the ancient soldier. It is clear from surviving accounts, however, that the ancients were well aware of psychiatric collapse due to the stress of battle. The earliest explanation for mental illness is found in Babylon in 2750 BC, where madness was seen as a punishment from the gods.[11] The Old Testament attributes madness to divine sanction. The oldest example of applied military psychiatry is found in the Bible, in Deuteronomy 20:5–9, where Israelite troop commanders are instructed to remove from the fighting ranks those soldiers that might break in battle. This is the first report of psychiatric screening in history.[12] The Greeks of the Classical Age (700–500 BC) were the first to attribute mental illness to physical and emotional causes, and invent the dualism that characterizes psychiatry to this day.[13] This awareness prompted the Greeks to develop the one area of medical practice that the modern world owes exclusively to them, the practice of military psychiatry.[14] Greek physicians were aware of mental illness caused by the trauma of war, and were the first to practice a sophisticated form of psychiatry.[15] They were also the first to link psychiatric symptoms to the stress of battle.[16]

Greek literature is filled with accounts of soldiers driven mad by their experience in war. Aristodemus and Pantities, two Spartan soldiers, had to be removed from the line at Thermopylae when overtaken by fear. Herodotus tells us that Leonidas, the Spartan commander, 'dismissed them when he realized that they had no heart for the fight and were unwilling to take their share of the danger'. Reviled as cowards, Pantities hanged himself and Aristodemus, called 'the trembler', lived a life of isolation.[17] Herodotus tells us (9.71) that a year later at the Battle of Plataea, Aristodemus 'rushed forward with the fury of a madman in his desire to be killed before his comrades' eyes'.[18] This was not an attempt to retrieve his lost honour, but out of his sense of guilt at having survived the earlier battle at Thermopylae. Aristodemus was trying to redeem himself with one last suicidal act of bravery.[19]

Sophocles' play, *Ajax*, is probably the best-known illustration in Greek literature of this phenomenon. After fighting at Troy for months, Ajax is 'seized with madness in the night'. Entering in to a fugue state, Ajax sets out to kill Odysseus and the other Greek soldiers who denied him his rightful share of glory. In a dream-like state, he attacks and brutalizes the cattle and other animals, believing them to be the soldiers themselves: 'Some he beheaded; of some he cut the back-bent throat or cleft the chine; others he tormented in their bonds as though they were men, with onslaughts on the cattle.' When Ajax comes out of the dream-like state and 'by slow painful steps regained his reason', he becomes concerned about how he will be thought of. Unable to bear the shame and guilt, he commits suicide.[20]

Herodotus recorded the symptoms of the first clinical case of psychiatric collapse in battle. In his account of the Battle of Marathon (490 BC), Herodotus tells us that soldiers along the battle line steadied themselves for the attack. Up and down the line, men shook with fear, vomited and lost control of their bladders and bowels. Suddenly, a projectile struck one of the soldiers squarely in the face, sending a shower of blood and brain over Epizelus, the man next to him: 'And then Epizelus, the son of Cuphagoras, an Athenian soldier, suddenly lost the sight of both eyes, though nothing had touched him anywhere – neither sword, spear, nor missile. From that moment he continued blind as long as he lived.'[21]

Xenophon also described a case of psychosomatically induced illness due to fear of death on the battlefield.[22] At Marathon, one of the Spartan soldiers, Aristodemus, 'finding his heart failed him', remained in the rear and did not join the fight. Plutarch notes that in the Roman siege of Syracuse in 211 BC, a number of the soldiers defending the city 'were struck dumb with terror', an example of a psychiatric condition called surdo–mutism.[23] Polybius, the Greek historian and Roman general, records that some Roman soldiers injured themselves (self-inflicted wounds) so as not to have to fight. That war drove some soldiers mad was further evident in their behaviour when the psychiatrically damaged soldiers returned to their towns and villages.

Alexander the Great offers a classic case of cumulative combat stress that destroyed his sanity. Although there was nothing clinically remarkable about Alexander's personality as a youth, he ended his life a paranoid, megalomaniacal alcoholic given to violent rages in which he killed some of his closest friends. He grew more cruel with each passing year, taking pleasure in witnessing torture and killing helpless civilians. He once led his army in a two–week campaign of slaughter against a harmless tribe, killing every man, woman and child in a prolonged fit of rage to relieve his depression over the death of Hephaestion, his homosexual lover. What gradually drove Alexander to madness was his exposure to thirteen years of war and slaughter. A survey of historical and psychiatric literature reveals that the conditions brought on by battle stress encountered by modern soldiers are identical to those that have afflicted soldiers since ancient times. Perhaps psychiatric reactions to war are only the normal reactions of sane minds to insane circumstances.[24]

The physically and mentally wounded soldiers of ancient times often sought help at the temples of Asclepios, the most important healer god of antiquity. There, patients drank of the 'water of forgetfulness', and underwent deep drug-induced sleep as a form of incubation therapy that represented a very modern and sophisticated abreaction treatment for psychiatric reactions to combat.[25] The *asclepieion* at Epidaurus was the most celebrated healing centre of the Greek-Hellenic world. Seventy case histories of patients have been preserved on *stelae* found at the centre. Among them are a number of cases involving combat veterans suffering from physical conditions, including battle wounds to the jaw, lungs and legs. Other soldiers were afflicted with battle-induced psychiatric conditions, including hysterical paralysis, blindness, headaches and nightmares.[26]

Some of the *stelae* inscriptions are illuminating. There was Timon, 'wounded by a spear below his eye. This man, sleeping here, saw a dream. It seemed to him the god ground up a herb and poured it into his eye, and he became well.' Another veteran, Antikrates of Knidos,

> had been struck with a spear through both his eyes in some battle, and he became blind and carried around the spearhead with him, inside his face. Sleeping here, he saw a vision. It seemed to him the god pulled out the dart and fitted the so-called girls [pupils of the eyes] back into his eyelids. When day came he left well.

Another veteran, Gorgias of Herakleia,

> was wounded in the lung by an arrow in some battle, and for a year and six months it was festering so badly, that it filled sixty-seven bowls of pus. When he was sleeping here, he saw a vision. It seemed to him the god drew out the barb from his lung. When day came he left well, carrying the barb in his hands.[27]

Greek physicians also recommended that veterans suffering from mental problems caused by war attend the productions of Greek tragedies as a form of abreaction. These plays were probably useful as a primitive form of psycho-drama in which the troubled soldier identified with the tragic hero as a way of reliving and relieving his own emotions. Aeschylus' play, *Persians*, which portrays the horror of the naval battle of Salamis where Persian sailors, helpless in the water, were 'spit [stabbed] like tuna', is but one example. While the Greeks can be credited with inventing psychiatric diagnosis and treatment for soldiers, Greek physicians did not apply these techniques in any systematic way.

The Romans had the first army to regularly care for psychiatric casualties, where soldiers suffering battle-induced mental problems were treated in the psychiatric wards of legion hospitals.[28] It was not until the Russo–Japanese War of 1905 that any Western army again attempted to deal with the problem of psychiatric casualties in a systematic manner. The Russian Army is credited with reinventing the practice of military psychiatry in the modern age.[29]

Many soldiers suffered from less extreme symptoms brought on by trauma, fear and fatigue. Fear and trauma led many soldiers to suffer from 'nostalgia', a severe form of depression that resulted in coma-like symptoms or even death, first diagnosed by Swiss military physicians in 1678. Union soldiers in the American Civil War suffered from 'soldier's heart', a condition mimicking atrial fibrillation brought on by anxiety. Other conditions called 'disorders of loneliness' such as drug use, alcoholism, fatigue, depression, rage and hysteria are recorded in all armies throughout history. These disorders include high rates of self-inflicted injuries to escape combat. In 1922, the British Army found that most of its gas casualties had collected the residue of mustard gas and rubbed it on their necks and arms before reporting to medical facilities to get out of the line. Other 'accidents' like the famous 'M-1 thumb' that afflicted GIs in the Second World War, venereal disease, frostbite, feigned fatigue, etc. are forms of 'silent' psychiatric conditions. Psychiatric symptoms in response to stress can manifest themselves suddenly or long after the trauma has passed.

Greek society contributed the ideal of military heroism to Western thought, and it comes as no surprise that the Greeks were acutely aware of the failure of nerve that often afflicted soldiers in combat. The culture of heroism in which manliness was demonstrated by bravery in war permitted the Greeks to believe that psychiatric reactions did not happen as a matter of course, but as a result of poor character and lack of bravery. The fault lay with the individual soldier, and condemning the psychiatric casualty as a coward reinforced the traditional heroic culture in the face of much evidence to the contrary. The ideal of individual heroism was transmitted into the mainstream of Western culture, passed down generation after generation until modern times. From the American Civil War to the Vietnam War, the problem of psychiatric collapse in war was still viewed as idiosyncratic human behaviour, the consequence of psychological or sociological 'weaknesses' in the soldier's character.[30] It is only since the Iraq and Afghan wars, with their high rates of Post-Traumatic Stress Disorder, that Western culture is becoming aware that this is not the case.[31]

What modern studies of psychiatric collapse tell us is that it is not so much the fear of being killed as the fear of having to kill another human being that prompts the mind to rebel with such ferocity that it will do almost anything, including injuring itself or the body, to keep from killing.[32] Like other mammals, humans have an innate revulsion to killing their own kind.[33] The critical variable seems to be distance. The closer the engagement in which a soldier must kill, the greater the revulsion to the killing, and the greater the likelihood that the soldier will suffer psychiatric effects.[34] This seems true of all but some 2 per cent of soldiers exposed to close combat: these remain unaffected by the slaughter. Most of these 'two-percenters', however, already showed clinical symptoms of mental illness before engaging in battle.[35] The armies of the ancient world must have been full of psychically damaged soldiers, for to be a soldier then required killing human beings at very close range indeed.

There is no good reason to believe that soldiers in ancient times were any less fearful of dying or being maimed than are today's soldiers. Modern studies of psychiatric collapse in war suggest that the already mentally aberrant appear most able to adjust to the horror of combat, while it is mostly the sane that collapse under its strain.[36] Whether in ancient or modern times, however, exposure to the stress of war is likely to seriously affect one's sanity and ability to function normally in civil society

In describing the life of the soldier in the ancient world, we ought never to lose sight of the fact that his stock in trade was killing, and that killing often had terrible effects on the soldier's psyche. Given the personal nature of combat in the ancient world, to look another human being closely in the eye, making a decision to kill him where he stands, and then striking him with a weapon while watching him suffer and die before your eyes, is perhaps the single most basic, primal and traumatic experience of human existence. To understand this is to understand the most central fact of the life of the ancient soldier. All else is commentary.

Chapter 11

Writing Military History from Ancient Texts

Some were found lying alive with their thighs and hams cut, laying bare their necks and throats, bid them drain the blood that remained in them. Some were found with their heads plunged into the earth ... having suffocated themselves by overwhelming their faces with the earth which they threw over them. A living Numidian, with lacerated nose and ears, stretched beneath a lifeless Roman who lay upon him ... for when the Roman's hands were powerless to grasp his weapon, turning from rage to madness, he had died in the act of tearing his antagonist with his teeth.

This dramatic description of the Battle of Cannae (218 BC) was written by a Roman historian about events that occurred more than 200 years earlier, for which no eyewitness accounts existed. The historian, Titus Livius, had no military experience at all. What often passes as history in ancient 'original source' texts turns out to be dramatic representations of what the writers thought may have occurred. And yet one cannot examine the wars and battles of antiquity without reference to these accounts. The modern historian studying military history in antiquity is a prisoner of these accounts, upon which so much of that study depends.

The most formidable obstacle to our understanding of ancient military history is simply the lack of reliable evidence. The Greeks' invention of history as a search for a rational explanation and understanding of events expressed in written prose or oral recitation created a means by which historians could record events in a manner still comprehensible in the modern age. Three centuries later, the Greeks passed their invention to the Romans. The consequence was an archive of written texts upon which the modern study of Greek and Roman military history is based. Unfortunately, much of the information contained in the texts is unreliable, biased, incomplete and, in many cases, even false.

The accounts of many ancient historians have serious limitations, and the modern reader is right to suspect that there is something different about history written by ancient historians. Greek and Roman historians were often less concerned with a factual accounting of events than with writing accounts that taught moral lessons, or guided the behaviour of powerful political classes or individuals.

Thus the Assyrian bas reliefs or the Egyptian wall inscriptions describing the achievements of their respective kings are grandiose portrayals of the greatness of their respective monarchs more than accurate accounts of actual events. The same may be said of the tales of the Israelite heroes in the Old Testament. This didactic approach to history focused on the achievements of great men, treating biography as the history of individuals. Ancient historians expected their work to be recited more than read, and due care has to be taken to remember that the historian was also a rhetorician. This concern for rhetoric led to the incorporation in the texts of fictitious speeches attributed to famous generals and kings.

At the very least, ancient historical accounts are often unreliable as sources because details and factual accuracy were subordinated to the larger purpose of teaching important lessons to the historian's readers, including of course powerful civic personages. As regards rhetoric first of all, if the bare facts were insufficient for an effective presentation, then the known facts could be adorned, modified or variously combined in the interest of a more dramatic presentation. Secondly, names, numbers, exact dates, chronology and geographical details of battles and important events were frequently inaccurate, invented or sometimes omitted altogether. It is difficult to think of a Greek or Roman ancient text as it relates to military history that does not suffer to some extent from one or both of these shortcomings.

In addition, ancient texts were often written long after the events recorded in them occurred, so that only a few of these source materials address events even remotely contemporary with their authors. Ancient historians usually did not check the validity of the sources upon whom they excessively relied. This was mostly impossible in any case since few useable archives existed, and would probably have required lengthy and dangerous journeys to obtain access to them. Some ancient historians are simply repeating accounts of earlier sources, telling them in a different, often more dramatic fashion. Thus, Livy relies primarily on Polybius' account of the Second Punic War for his military narrative, and Dio Cassius, writing a century later, relies upon Livy's account for the same war. Sources often cannot be evaluated because while they may have been available to the writer, they have since been lost. The accounts of two of Polybius' most valuable sources, Sosylus and Silenus – Greek 'war correspondents' who travelled with Hannibal – are lost to us. Herodotus' sources for the Persian War, on the other hand, are little more than a collection of oral tales and some monument inscriptions. There are, however, a few exceptions. Arrian's *Anabasis*, dealing with the life of Alexander the Great, is the most trustworthy account of Alexander's life precisely because it is based upon earlier eyewitness accounts by Nearchus, Ptolemy and Aristobulus, all soldiers who participated in Alexander's campaigns.

Military historians are thus prisoners of the surviving texts, almost all of which suffer from errors that corrupted the texts when they were translated from Greek to Latin or copied by medieval monks, who often lacked the necessary language skills and knowledge of the military subjects involved. The most common errors involved numbers. The monks often had limited knowledge of ancient numerical systems, and regularly mistranslated or transposed numerical values, sometimes substituting completely new numbers of their own. The tendency of ancient historians to exaggerate the number of enemy combatants and casualties in any case was thus compounded by the monks' errors, further distorting the texts. Speed of tactical movement, rates of march, distances, weights, numbers of animals, the widths of rivers and streams, terrain heights, etc. are often expressed numerically in these texts, so that distortion occurs frequently in information most important to today's military historian. The original historical emphasis on the past as informing the present meant, too, that there was no necessary virtue in having experience of the events one wrote about. Thucydides' invention of contemporary history as the study of events of one's own time changed this, and the Western study of contemporary history as a form of historical analysis is owed to this great soldier-scholar.

The ancient texts dealing with military history can be divided into three categories: (1) those written years after the events by historians who had no military experience upon which to draw for their understanding of military material; (2) those who had some military experience upon which to base their analysis, but not contemporary with the subjects they were addressing; (3) those who had military experience and participated in the events about which they wrote.

Herodotus (480-425 BC), Appian (AD 95–165), Livy (59 BC–AD 17) and Dio Cassius (AD 164–234), all of whom wrote major treatments of military history but had never seen military service, fall into the first category. Appian's *Roman History* covered all the wars fought by the Romans from their early history until Trajan's campaigns. Livy's *The War with Hannibal*, along with Polybius' work, are the basic source materials for the Punic Wars. Cassius Dio's work is extensive, but flawed in its reliance upon uncriticized sources and its dependence upon Livy as a major source. Herodotus' account of the Persian Wars is more a dramatic novel than military history, its technical details of things military often suspect. These sources are more valuable for the general themes that can be extracted from them than for exact details, and must be treated with great caution.

Polybius (200–118 BC), Tacitus (AD 56–117) and Arrian (AD 87–145) fall into the category of military historians who had some military experience and wrote about events that had occurred long before their own times. Polybius' *History* is the best account of military events, details and tactics as they pertain to the Second Punic War and Scipio Africanus' role in it. Polybius was a Greek officer who was the cavalry commander of the Achaean League that fought in the Achaean War, and he commanded troops in battle before being taken prisoner and sent to Rome as a hostage, where he was befriended by the Scipio family. He had access to all of Scipio's papers, interviewed a number of the major commanders of the Second Punic War and visited some of the battlefields of that war about which he wrote. His account of Roman warfare proceeds from an accomplished military eye, and is generally accurate.

Arrian had military experience as a Roman cavalry officer, and saw action in Dacia. Later, as governor of Cappadocia, he was given command of two legions and may have taken part in Trajan's campaign against the Parthians. His treatment of Alexander's campaigns in the *Anabasis* is based on eyewitness source accounts, and is the most reliable source for the campaigns, Macedonian tactics and military organization. Tacitus had been a Roman legion commander, but does not seem to have seen combat. His greatest work is the *Annals*, which provides us with the only extant descriptions of Roman legionary warfare and equipment of the first century AD.

Military experience, of course, is no guarantee of historical accuracy, and even experienced soldier-historians cannot always be trusted to forego the usual biases of both modern retired generals and ancient historians. Sallust, for example, was an experienced soldier who saw combat in the civil wars in Illyricum and Campania, and later in North Africa. Yet *The Jurgurthine War*, his account of the Roman war against Jurgurtha the Numidian, is generally untrustworthy as to numbers, dates, distances, size of forces, etc., all the material of most interest to the military historian. Josephus, another combat veteran who commanded troops both for and against Rome, is a good source for the details of Roman equipment, arms and artillery, but is otherwise untrustworthy. His primary work, *The Jewish War*, may even have been commissioned by the Roman emperor.

The last category comprises the soldier-historians who wrote contemporary history, accounts of the battles in which they themselves fought. This group includes Thucydides, Caesar, Xenophon and Aeneas Tacticus. Thucydides'(455–399 BC) account of the Peloponnesian Wars remains the definitive history of that conflict. He fought in that war on land and at sea, and is one of our few eyewitnesses to fifth-century Greek phalanx warfare and trireme naval tactics. He probably witnessed or participated in every major engagement of the war from 424 BC to the end. His command of tactical and strategic realities of that period is unrivalled among the ancient texts. In the *Commentaries* and *The Gallic Wars*, Caesar (100–44 BC) offers us first-hand narratives of dozens of legion battles and sieges, making him the best source for Roman military capabilities in the first century BC.

Xenophon (430–350 BC) was a mercenary captain who spent most of his life in military service. He served all over the eastern Mediterranean and in the pay of several Greek states, and even fought in the Persian army. He was an eyewitness to and participant in dozens of Greek vs Greek and Greek vs Persian battles, and is the best source for fourth-century Greek land warfare. His best work is the *Anabasis: The March Into the Interior*, the story of his service to one of the Persian kings, the defeat at Cunaxa and his command of the Greek troops in retreat for more than 1,000 miles before returning to Greece. A cavalryman, he wrote a short work on commanding cavalry appended to a treatise on horsemanship, the earliest complete work of its kind still in existence. Aeneas Tacticus (fourth century BC) was one of the earliest Greek writers on the art of war. He wrote several didactic works on warfare, of which the only survivor is *How To Survive Under Siege*, a detailed military manual on how to defend a fortified city. A Greek mercenary captain of the Peloponnese, he saw combat in the Aegean and Asia Minor, and took part in several battles, among them Mantinea (362 BC). His work is also valuable for containing a large number of historical illustrations that allow us to press our knowledge of Greek warfare further back in time.

Although the shortcomings of the ancient texts were well-known, for many years there was little else upon which historians could draw. As a result, the study of ancient military history was left largely to classicists who could read the texts in the original Latin and Greek. The forte of classicists is language, however, including text analysis and translation, and not military affairs. Few had been trained as military historians. Classicists saw military history as a minor field of academic interest, so that accounts of ancient wars and battles were regarded as only one more part of the overall linguistic translation, with little attention paid to military history per se. Fortunately, a European university education of the nineteenth century consisted largely of a classical education in which the original texts were read. Many of the university graduates of the aristocratic classes became high-ranking military officers who had studied the accounts of ancient warfare for modern lessons. A number of these soldier-historians – Liddell-Hart, Fuller, Delbruch, Veith and others – wrote revised accounts of the ancient battles based upon their own experiences with nineteenth century military training and war.

In the late nineteenth century, a movement began among classicists and historians to bring a more empirical eye to the study of ancient accounts of military history. Two developments made this possible. First, the nineteenth century was an age of invention and discovery in which the scientific impulse required carefully measured confirmation of all propositions before they could be accepted as fact. New knowledge from psychiatry, medicine, nutrition, human endurance studies, map making, metallurgy, engineering, etc. – items all relevant to military history – became available to military historians, who could now apply them to the study of ancient warfare.

Second, the nineteenth century saw the emergence of modern war on an unprecedented scale. Large standing and reserve armies required the management of men and material in precise detail. This brought into being tables of organization and implementation. There emerged statistical tables to tell one how much food and water each soldier required to remain in fighting condition; how quickly a brigade could march under different conditions; how many mules and wagons were needed to transport men and supplies over a given distance; how long they could be sustained in the field; what kinds of wounds could be expected from different types of attacks; and how many of the wounded would die from hostile fire, accidents and disease, etc. What had once been the 'art of war' was replaced by 'military science'. The military historian now had at his disposal new information and methods that could be applied to the analysis of the ancient texts.

The new approach was further encouraged by the military reserve mobilization system used by the European armies of the day. European standing armies were relatively small, but their system of reserve units available for mobilization was enormous. Almost every male between the ages of 18 and 45 was assigned to a reserve unit. In the period between the Crimean War and the First World War, many reservists went to war, or at least underwent military training. Many of them were professors, graduate students and university students who became acquainted with the new science of war and its attendant tables, schedules and measurement. They took these methods with them back to the universities, creating an impetus for more empirical analysis of the text accounts of ancient warfare.

By the beginning of the twentieth century, the new approach was gaining credibility, and professors who were not classicists but military historians began securing positions at European universities, only to have the disruption and carnage of the First World War decimate the ranks of the new scholarship and bring it to a halt. After the war, the survivors who still had academic posts to go to and students to teach tried to re-establish the new discipline, and a number of ground-breaking empirical works like Kromayer and Veith's *The Battle Atlas of Ancient Military History* and Delbruch's *History of the Art of War* (4 vols) were produced. The political turmoil following the war and the catastrophe of the Second World War again completely eclipsed the study of ancient military history in Europe. The subject had never been popular in the United States, and the study of ancient military history remains today a minor disciplinary emphasis still firmly in the hands of classicists.

The destruction wrought by the Second World War made a resurgence of the study of ancient military history impossible in Europe until very recently. In the United States, the influence of the Cold War on university curricula retarded any emphasis on the subject for thirty years. Long stays in graduate school were often the method of choice for future academics to avoid the military draft of the Vietnam War, with the consequence that few American historians of ancient military history have any military experience at all. There are few academic positions open to military historians of any type in the US, and fewer still in ancient military history.

It is only in the last two decades that one can detect an emergence of the empirical approach to ancient military history in the United States and Europe, prompted by the electronic revolution in information transfer that has brought the content of the world's libraries and the work of distant scholars to the historian's desktop computer. This same revolution has increased personal communication among scholars sharing similar interests and research results. There are also the beginnings of financial support for research. Oxford University, for example, sponsored the recreation of a fourth-century *trireme* to test its operational characteristics, and the Canadian Defence Academy republished Kromayer and Veith's magnificent atlas of terrain maps of ancient battlefields.

New research has added to the tools that the ancient historian can apply to the texts. Lazenby and J.K Anderson's work on Greek warfare, Hanson's study of the Battle of Cannae, Sabin's research on the battles of the Punic War and Christopher Matthew's empirical groundbreaking recent works on the Greek and later Macedonian phalanx have added to our understanding of the battle mechanics of close combat, the role played by fear and exhaustion, and the role of 'battle pulses' in combat. My own studies of psychiatric collapse in battle are somewhat helpful here. Junkelmann's experiments measuring the speed, loads carried and endurance of marching soldiers have raised new questions about these factors in ancient warfare. Karen Metz's and my efforts at 'experimental archaeology' in our *From Sumer to Rome: The Military Capabilities of Ancient Armies* have provided insights into the killing and wounding power of ancient weapons, as has Aldrete's *Reconstructing Ancient Linen Body Armor*. Engels' excellent study on the logistics of Macedonian armies has been supplemented by Jonathan Roth's analysis of the logistics of Roman armies from 264 BC to AD 235. The result is that modern ancient historians have at their disposal a new set of tools with which to analyze the ancient accounts of warfare. This promises to result in a strongly revised understanding of what war was like in ancient times.

One of the most important factors in our understanding of ancient warfare, the terrain upon which the battles were fought, has remained mostly beyond our ken. Urbanization, industrialization and two world wars have altered the landscape of the ancient battlefields beyond recognition. At this writing, the battlefield of Chaeronea is under development as a shopping mall. But this was not the case before and just after the First World War. Then Johannes Kromayer, Chair of the Department of Ancient Military History at Leipzig University, and Georges Veith, Director of the Military Archive in Vienna, undertook a systematic effort to locate and map the major battlefields of antiquity. Employing military cartographic teams from the Archive, they spent a decade visiting these battlefields and overseeing the production of colour topographic contour maps for each battlefield. After consulting the most famous military historians of the day in England, Austria,

Germany and France, Kromayer and Veith superimposed illustrations of the troop dispositions and manoeuvres of the antagonists in each battle upon the maps. Their *Schlachten-atlas zur Antiken Kriegsgeschichte* (*Battle Atlas of Ancient Military History*) comprises 168 colour terrain contour maps of all the major Greek and Roman battles, beginning with the Greek and Persian Wars (499–448 BC) and ending with Octavian's campaign in Illyria in 35–34 BC.

The *Atlas* was published as several individual folios beginning in 1922 and ending in 1928. Due to the expense and time required to publish the complete atlas, only a small number of complete sets of maps found their way into the hands of scholars or libraries. The devastation of the Second World War destroyed many of these copies. In 2008, only twenty-eight complete copies were in libraries world-wide, most kept safely kept in rare book rooms and not permitted to circulate. In 2005, I gained access to one of the last complete atlases remaining in private hands. In 2008, the Canadian Defence Academy in Kingston, Ontario, published the atlas in English, and made it available to scholarly and military libraries in Canada and Europe. Each library was encouraged to list the atlas on relevant electronic indexes, and make it available to scholars and students of ancient military history through the world-wide inter-library loan programme. With the publication of Kromayer and Veith's unique work, military historians will be able to travel back in time and walk the blood-soaked ground of antiquity. It promises to be a remarkable journey.

Chapter 12

Thutmose III of Egypt and the First Battle in Military History

Thutmose III (1504–1450 BC) was one of the great captains of the ancient world, and the greatest of all generals in Egyptian history. His record of military activity is remarkable. He fought more battles over a longer period and won more victories than any other general in the ancient world. In the sixty years prior to Thutmose's reign, the great warrior kings of Egypt from Ahmose to Thutmose II fought one foreign campaign every 4.6 years. In the seventy years following Thutmose III, from Amenhotep II to Amenhotep III, there was one foreign campaign every 10.5 years. In the nineteen years between regnal years 23 and 42 of Thutmose's thirty-two-year reign, he fought seventeen campaigns in Canaan and Syria, or an average of one military campaign every 1.2 years.[1] In the six years between assuming command of the army and ascending the throne in his own right, Thutmose fought a major campaign in Nubia and, perhaps, another for which there is only tentative evidence. He then led the army that liberated Gaza from rebels.[2]

By the time Thutmose ruled Egypt in his own right, sometime in his twenty-second year, he was already an experienced combat commander. In his first major campaign against the combined Canaanite-Syrian armies at Megiddo in his twenty-third year, Thutmose revealed himself to be a first-rate strategist, tactician and logistician. Thutmose transformed Egypt into a military state, and with Egypt's great resources at his command, he set events in motion that shaped Egypt and the Levant for the next 500 years.[3]

Paradoxically, Thutmose's magnificent military record remained unknown for most of Western history. The Greek and Roman occupation of Egypt produced no histories of the great man, and the Arab invasion and occupation of Egypt from the sixth century to the present completely obliterated any knowledge of Egyptian history in the West. It was not until Napoleon's occupation of the country and the discovery of the Rosetta Stone that Western historians were able to read the surviving ancient hieroglyphic script and papyrus records revealing Thutmose's achievements. For much of history, then, Western military historians were simply unaware of Egypt's greatest warrior king.

Thutmose's intellectual interests ranged beyond military matters and affairs of state, to include history, religion, architecture, pottery and even jewellery design.

His reign witnessed a period of prodigious art production of all forms, and he was one of history's greatest patrons of the arts.[4] He had an abiding interest in botany, and took special scribes with him on campaign to find and record any strange flowers and plants they might encounter. Thutmose was one of Egypt's great builders, and constructed more temples, shrines, votive buildings, pylons and fortresses than any of his predecessors, and all of his successors, with the possible exception of Ramses II, who enjoyed the longest reign (sixty-seven years) in Egyptian history.[5] It was Thutmose who introduced the basilica as an architectural form to Egypt.[6]

As head of the Egyptian state, Thutmose's administrative responsibilities were different and considerably more difficult than those of his predecessors. While the trend toward centralization was already evident under earlier kings, Thutmose's large-scale and almost constant wars accelerated and increased the trend toward governmental centralization, turning Egypt into a military state. Unlike any of his predecessors, Thutmose had to govern an imperial realm.

Thutmose III was probably born in 1504 BC, the son of Pharaoh Thutmose II by a concubine named Isis. Pharaoh's Great Wife and half-sister, Hatshepsut, produced only a daughter, Neferure.[7] It is likely that Thutmose was married to his half-sister, Nefurure, while he was still very young. Marriage to sisters and half-sisters was common among the royalty of Egypt because the bloodline of succession followed the female line. Thutmose II died while his son was still an infant, 'only a nursling' as the texts say, and although his son was recognized as pharaoh from this early time, real power passed to Queen Hatshepsut, Thutmose III's stepmother/aunt, who governed as regent. The two kings, one male child and one mature female, ruled side by side for some fifteen years, but with Hatshepsut wielding the real authority of office until Thutmose removed her from the throne when he was 22.[8] We do not know the circumstances under which Thutmose assumed his rightful position as sole king of Egypt sometime in 1482/1481 BC, or what happened to Hatshepsut. Thutmose III's great achievements on the battlefield inevitably lead one to think of him mostly in military terms, as a great general who excelled in the art of war. But there is more to military greatness than winning battles. It is more often an appreciation for the political dimension of war that give victories on the battlefield any substantial and lasting strategic meaning.

Perhaps the most important and far-reaching of Thutmose's achievements was to change the psychology of Egyptian national character, to set forth a new paradigm altering the way Egyptians thought about themselves and their world. For more than two millennia before Thutmose' reign, Egypt had been an isolated society, almost hermetically sealed by her vast desert borderlands from the great cultural changes that were occurring in the rest of the Levant. The Hyksos invasion of Egypt (circa 1650 BC) and 108 years of occupation provided a shocking awakening. Thutmose was the first to realize that to return to the past would achieve nothing but to eventually place Egypt at risk of invasion once more. It was Thutmose who led a closed Egyptian society into a new era of awareness and international interaction with other cultures. Thutmose gave Egypt a new vision of itself and its place in the world, and that strategic vision remained unchanged in its essentials for the next 500 years.

The new Egyptian security strategy was partially dictated by a change in the nature of the threat that Egypt faced. First, the 'sand dwellers' or city-states of the Canaan land bridge had matured to the point where they now possessed powerful military establishments and fortifications. These circumstances meant that the armies of the small states of the area, especially in coalition with the larger and more powerful Hittite and Mitanni states, had become dangerous antagonists that had to be dealt with if Egypt was to be secure. At the same time, new and more powerful kingdoms were emerging further east. The most proximate threat came from the Mitanni, who occupied the land beyond the Great Bend of the Euphrates in north-east Syria, and whose client states extended south and west to the Litani River into southern Syria, modern Lebanon. To the north-west, the powerful and dangerous Hittites were beginning to appear as major players on the international scene. Both states eventually became competitors with Egypt for hegemony in Syria. The key to the dominance of Canaan, and thus to protecting the Nile, was the ability of Egypt to control political events in Syria. It is testimony to the sophistication of Egyptian strategic thinking that they realized that the defence of the Nile began so far away in the mountains of Syria.

Egypt required a new national security strategy to guide its foreign and military policy in the new and hostile environment in which it was now forced to live. Thutmose's strategic vision of Egyptian security guided Egyptian diplomatic, commercial and military policy for a half-millennium after his death. In this view, Egypt had no safe borders. The security of the nation lay in Egypt's ability to control political and military developments in the Canaan-Lebanon-Syrian theatre of operations. The goal of Egyptian defence policy was to prevent any major power or coalition of Asiatic city-states from assembling an alliance powerful enough to threaten Egypt. This required for the first time the full involvement of Egypt in the politics, economics and military affairs of the states on the Palestinian land bridge and in Syria.

New empires and great powers rose and fell over the five centuries following Thutmose, and during this time they all challenged Egyptian hegemony over the Canaanite land bridge at one time or another. Under Thutmose, Egyptian defence policy became dynamic and proactive, requiring preventive military interventions in support of political objectives, as well as economic policies that guaranteed Egypt access to vitally important strategic materials such as hard wood for ships, chariots and buildings, and tin for manufacturing bronze weapons. After his first foray into Canaan at Megiddo, where he destroyed a coalition of Canaanite and Mitanni princes planning to invade Egypt, Thutmose intervened with military force in the area no fewer than sixteen times.[9] His son, Amenophis II, was kept busy with one campaign after another in similar fashion, as were most of the pharaohs who followed for the next 500 years.

To successfully implement this new strategic perspective, Egypt required a new military establishment. The new army would have to be larger, better equipped and better logistically organized to carry out expeditionary campaigns hundreds of miles from Egypt for months on end. New garrisons had to be constructed and manned, the professional military cadre expanded to organize and train large numbers of conscripts, and new administrative positions created and staffed. Transport of Egyptian forces by sea required the expansion and modernization of the navy, which required new shipyards and a large shipbuilding programne. Sources of important strategic materials also had to be secured, and thousands of new workshops established and manned with skilled craftsmen to produce the new weapons and war machines in substantial numbers. While the restructuring of the new army probably began under Hatshepsut and incorporated previous improvements in supplying new weapons, most of the credit is due to 'the military genius of Thutmose III'.[10]

The new Egyptian national army was raised by conscription, with the levy being one man in ten instead of the traditional one man in 100.[11] It was centrally trained by professional officers and non-commissioned officers, and Pharaoh himself stood as commander-in-chief and personally led his troops in battle. The Vizier served as Minister of War, and there was an Army Council that served as a general staff. The field army was organized into divisions, each of which was a complete combined-arms corps, including infantry, archers and chariots. These divisions contained approximately 6,000 men each, including logistics and support personnel, and each was named after one of the principal gods of Egypt. The two major combat arms of the Egyptian army were infantry and chariotry. Figure 10 portrays a typical Egyptian combined arms combat division of 5,500 men and 1,000 horses. A full field army usually comprised four divisions, or more than 20,000 men and 2,000 chariots.

Thutmose III's strategic vision brought into being another important development, the Egyptian imperial navy. Egypt could not bring Canaan and Syria under its control if it had to move its army overland each time that control was threatened by revolt. The overland march from Egypt to Syria was 350 miles long, took a high toll on the army's men and machines, was difficult and expensive to support logistically, conceded the tactical initiative to the enemy and took too much time, sacrificing any possibility of surprise. In addition, the transit time through Canaan reduced the effective campaign season to such a degree that the

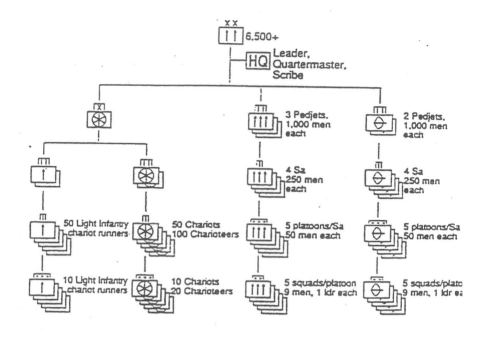

Figure 10: Organization of an Egyptian Division in the Eighteenth Dynasty

Egyptian army would be incapable of conducting sustained operations against the Mitanni across the Euphrates. Maintaining permanent troop garrisons of sufficient strength in Syria was expensive, and probably not possible in terms of manpower. To achieve Egypt's goals in Canaan and Syria, Thutmose had to find a way to move his army quickly into the zone of operations, and to do so at low cost.

The solution was to transport Egypt's army by ship along the Canaan-Lebanon coast, landing it in secure harbours logistically prepared in advance, and then strike inland against the adversary. The Egyptians had been sailors and ship builders from time immemorial, but only on the Nile, and never upon the open sea. Thutmose ordered the expansion of the army and naval presence at the new town of Perunefer (literally, 'good sailing' or 'bon voyage') located on the Pelusiac branch of the Nile leading to the open sea.[12] A large dockyard for building ships was established, where the Egyptians began to construct new and larger ships, including horse and troop transports to sail upon the open Mediterranean.[13] Six years after Thutmose's attack on Megiddo, he transported his army by sea, landed on the Lebanon coast and attacked Kadesh, conducting the 'first great amphibious operation in history'.[14] The Egyptian amphibious force numbered 12,000 troops, 500 chariots, 1,250 horses and 2,000 pack animals, transported by sea 340 miles to Byblos in eighty ships.[15] Over the next three years, Thutmose gained control of a number of the Lebanon port cities, converting them into safe harbours and logistics bases for future expeditionary operations. From this time forward, Egypt had no rival for control of the coastal Mediterranean.[16]

Thutmose's success on the battlefield offers a case study in those personality traits that make a general great. First and foremost is a penchant for clear thinking unclouded by ideological or religious precepts. Thutmose was also an innovative commander in things large and small. The willingness to accept innovation is the mark of a stable, self-confident personality, one who trusts his own experiences and intellect to make sense of his world. The strength of Thutmose's personality is revealed, too, in his willingness to challenge the unknown. He moved armies 800 miles from Egypt into Mitanni territory, about which Egyptians knew little. Time and again, he forged ahead into unknown land, trusting in his ability to learn and adapt to its very strangeness. To challenge the unknown requires a personality of strong will and confidence, and Thutmose's strength of will was prodigious.

Thutmose's will was clearly revealed when he overruled the objections of his senior officers to his plan of advance at Megiddo, and imposed his own tactical vision upon the plan of battle. It is a maxim of military leadership that an army is an instrument of a commander's will. If so, then it is a good idea to begin with a commander who possesses a will of iron, as Thutmose did. Thutmose also possessed the qualities of a good combat commander, including the all important willingness to share the risks of his soldiers. At Megiddo, he personally led the army down the dangerous narrow track he had selected over the objections of his senior officers. The lesson was clear: if he made a mistake and the enemy ambushed the column, he would have been the first into the fight ... and the first to die. In every one of his campaigns for which we have records, Thutmose is portrayed as always participating fully in the battle.

Thutmose III set in motion a series of events that shaped and influenced the Levant and Egypt that can be regarded as a watershed in the military and imperial history of the entire eastern Mediterranean. Thutmose inherited only a rudimentary military establishment that was gravely inadequate to the task of fostering his imperial ambitions. He forged the new model army of the New Kingdom, introducing major reforms in logistics, conscription, weapons, chariotry and a new naval arm capable of supporting ground operations far from Egypt itself. The army that Thutmose brought into being lasted almost four centuries without major changes, remaining a reliable instrument of force projection in the hands of his immediate successors, the rest of the Eighteenth Dynasty and most of the Nineteenth. Had he not done so, Egypt's conquest and administration of the eastern Levant would have been impossible.

Megiddo: Military History's First Battle

Thutmose's military and political genius is clearly revealed in his first campaign to implement his new strategic vision in Canaan and Syria. The first, and most famous, is his campaign against the city of Megiddo, where thirty-four Canaanite and Mitanni princes were gathering with their armies as a prelude to attacking Egypt. The Battle of Megiddo is the first battle for which we have a name and a sufficient account of events from which to reconstruct a portrait of the strategy and tactics employed by the antagonists. In this sense, it can be said that the Battle of Megiddo marks the starting point for the study of military history. In April 1481 BC, an Egyptian army comprised of two combined arms corps, each having 5,000 infantry, and a brigade of 500 chariots marched out of Egypt along the coastal road toward Gaza.[17] The army's advance to Megiddo was divided into four operational phases, each influenced by time, terrain and enemy reaction. In the first phase, Thutmose moved his army from Egypt to Gaza. The army covered the 125 miles from Sile to Gaza in ten days, a rate of march of about 12 miles a day.[18]

The second phase required traversing the terrain from Gaza to Yehem (modern Yemma), a distance of 80 miles, much of it across the open Sharon coastal plain, perfect for an Asiatic chariot attack. Yehem was a key road junction controlling the entrance to the Aruna road that led over the Carmel mountains to the Esdraelon Plain, the Classical Greek name for the Jezreel Valley, and the city of Megiddo itself.[19] The danger in the movement from Gaza to Yehem lay in the possibility of discovery by Asiatic reconnaissance units, or even a collision with advance units of the Asiatic main force already making its way across the Sharon plain en route to attack Egypt. Under these circumstances, security of the Egyptian force was paramount, and Thutmose covered the 80 miles in nine days in a forced march. When the Egyptian army arrived at Yehem, it had been on the march for nineteen days.[20]

Phase three required the army to move over the Carmel mountains and gain the open plain next to the ridge upon which Megiddo sat without being attacked, worn down by enemy harassment along the way or being ambushed as it exited the mountains on to the plain. Phase four required that the Egyptian army force the exits from the mountains, gain the Esdraelon Plain and bring the enemy to battle.

Thutmose spent three days at Yehem, during which time his reconnaissance units explored the routes leading to Megiddo, and discovered the disposition of the enemy force on the Esdraelon Plain. Three roads led from Yehem to the valley. One led to Ta'anach at the southern end of the valley and was heavily guarded by an enemy chariot force. The second led through Aruna, and debouched less than a mile in front of Megiddo itself. It, too, was heavily guarded. A third road led to Djefty, some 5 miles from the city. On 18 May, the Egyptian army left Yehem,

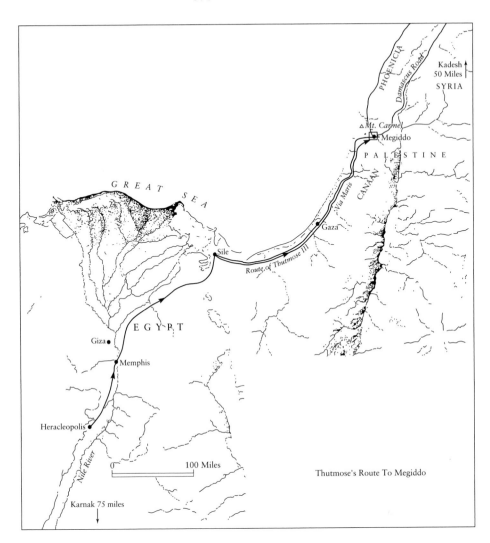

Figure 11: Thutmoses' Route to Megiddo

entered the Wadi Ara through the Carmel Mountains connecting to the Aruna road, and marched 13 miles to the village of Aruna and encamped. Below in the valley, some 300 enemy chariots blocked the exit at Aruna, and another 600 guarded the exit from Ta'anach. The two forces were only 4 miles apart, and could easily reinforce one another.[21] It was only when the Egyptian army arrived at Aruna that the enemy finally learned of its presence. Thutmose had successfully achieved strategic surprise.

The tactical problem of how to get the army from Aruna on to the Esdraelon Plain without being attacked as it exited the ridge remained, however. Egyptian reconnaissance units had discovered a narrow path running left off the Aruna road that debouched on the plain behind the Kina brook that ran across the valley. The brook was about a mile from Megiddo itself. The path down the mountain was narrow, steep and ran 6 miles from Aruna to its exit on the valley floor. Thutmose

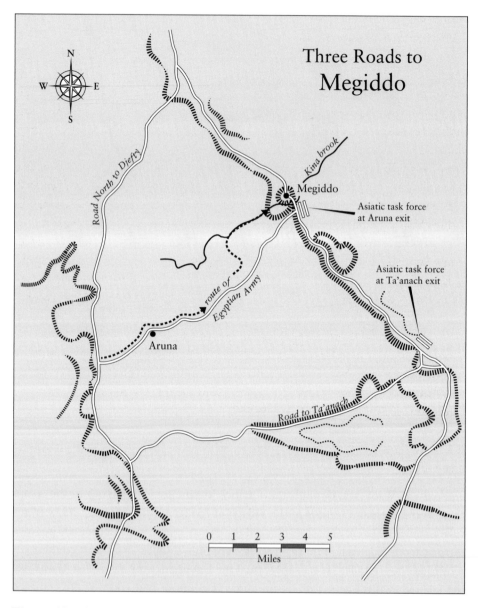

Figure 12: Three Routes to Megiddo

proposed to his officers that the army take the path, and arrive outside the city and behind both enemy forces blocking the other exits. To a man, his senior generals strongly opposed the plan as too dangerous. The 22-year-old Thutmose, now commanding his first major field operation, overruled them, and ordered his army down the path on the morning of 19 May. With himself in the lead, the van of the army reached the plain in three hours, around noon, and began to deploy for battle on the plain along the Kina brook, using it as a defensive obstacle to enemy attack. Outmanoeuvred and surprised, the enemy chariot detachments at the Aruna and Ta'anach exits deployed rearward to defend the city.[22]

The Battle of Megiddo took place the next day. Greatly outnumbered and forced into a narrow tactical box by Thutmose's deployment of his infantry on the wings, the enemy chariots clashed with the Egyptians in the centre, as the Egyptian infantry pressed inward from the flanks. Squeezed between the two combat elements, the enemy broke and fled, some taking refuge inside the city, others fleeing behind the city on the road to Hazor, 20 miles distant. Thutmose placed Megiddo under siege, and on 27 June, sixty-six days after the Egyptians had left Egypt, the city surrendered.[23] The capture of Megiddo placed control of the key communication routes from Egypt to Canaan, Syria and Mesopotamia firmly in Egyptian hands, where they remained for the next five centuries.

Thutmose was 42 years old and in the third decade of his reign when he mounted his last campaign in Syria-Lebanon to put down another revolt. After this, he spent his last years building temples and indulging his intellectual interests. And then one day, the greatest of the warrior pharaohs was gone, dead from natural causes:

> Lo, the king completed his lifetime of many years, splendid in valour, in might, and in triumph; from year 1 to year 54, third month of the second season, the last day of the month under the majesty of King Menkheperre, triumphant. He mounted to heaven, he joined the sun; the divine limbs mingling with him who begat him.

He had lived fifty-three years, ten months and twenty-six days, and in his time had changed Egypt and the world forever.

Chapter 13

Egyptian Shipbuilding and the Invention of Amphibious Warfare

T he use of ships in warfare was a relatively late invention of the middle Bronze Age (1400 BC), and the use of warships to fight other ships upon the open sea came even later, perhaps not before the Greek Archaic Age. One reason for this situation was that most of the great imperial states of the Bronze Age arose on the major rivers of the region – i.e., Egypt on the Nile, Sumer on the Tigris, the Mitanni on the Euphrates and the Harappa and Aryans on the Indus – but only a few had coastlines open to the sea or ocean. These states learned the skill of ship construction relatively early in their history, but all of them used ships only for transportation upon their respective rivers, never really venturing upon the open sea to any extent. When employed in war, these early ships were used only as troop and logistics transports. There is no evidence of ships being used in sea-going combat until much later.

As a coastal and river state, Egypt was among the earliest, if not the earliest, to find a use for sea-going ships in war. To carry out his campaign against the Lebanon coast circa 1467 BC, Thutmose III introduced one of the most remarkable innovations in warfare. He was the first commander in history to conduct large-scale amphibious operations upon the open sea.[1] Egypt was a river state, and the only practical way of transporting troops and supplies was by boat on the Nile. By the Third Dynasty, Egyptians were building boats that were 100 cubits long (1 cubit = almost 1¾ft; thus 170ft long) and 30 cubits wide,[2] capable of carrying 80–100 tons of cargo.[3] The first use of the Egyptian navy in support of ground operations occurred in the Fifth Dynasty (2480 BC) when Pharaoh Sahure transported troops to the Syrian coast. His example was followed in the Sixth Dynasty (2340 BC) by a troop commander named Weni who conveyed Egyptian troops in 'travel ships' to the Antelope's Nose (the end of the Carmel Mountain ridge) near Haifa to deal with a revolt of the 'sand peoples' (Canaanites).[4] These early naval operations on the open sea were small expeditions in support of raids, and not sustained campaigns. They were not repeated until Thutmose III conducted the 'first great amphibious operations in history'.[5]

Egyptian naval operations had been traditionally confined to the Nile, where they played an important role in the wars of liberation against the Hyksos. Kamose's victory stela tells us how he transported his army aboard ship to battle with the occupiers. The king sailed up and down the river, using his fleet as a mobile base from which to deploy his troops. Ahmose I, his successor, used ships to bring the Hyksos capital of Avaris under siege. The reconquest of Nubia begun by Ahmose I could not have been accomplished without the river navy to transport troops and push the southern frontier to Buhen. His successor, Amenophis I, used the navy to extend Egyptian control further south beyond the Second Cataract to Semneh. Thutmose I carried his troops in ships past the Second and Third Cataracts of the Nile, crushing Nubian resistance as far south as Kerma. With Nubia once more under control, the Egyptians dug canals to bypass the cataracts, and heavy naval and commercial traffic over long distances was now carried out on a regular basis.

The Egyptian navy was an integral branch of the army at this time, and not a separate military service. Its importance, however, was evident in the fact that many naval officers were drawn from the Egyptian nobility.[6] Under Thutmose I, when the focus of Egyptian military operations shifted away from Nubia toward Asia, and where the need for a land warfare capability became paramount, the navy became an independent branch of service, and was relegated to a minor role whose mission was to keep the Nile's river traffic open to Nubia. Neither Thutmose II nor Hatsehpsut showed any interest in the Egyptian naval arm, and the construction of naval ships declined considerably. The once important Egyptian navy fell into decay.

Thutmose III rebuilt the Egyptian navy, and ordered the construction of a large dockyard and military base on the site of the old Hyksos capital at Avaris, turning it into a major port city on the Pelusiac branch of the Nile.[7] Just when Thutmose completed the construction of the Perunefer base is unclear, but it may have been near the end of his campaigns in Canaan. It is not impossible, however, that the old dockyards at Memphis remained the main supplier of ships and the major port of military debarkation for Thutmose's earlier campaigns in Syria. It may not have been until his later campaign against the Mitanni that the new facility became fully operational. A Lord of the Egyptian Admiralty, one Nebamun, was appointed fairly early in Thutmose's reign, and some high-ranking army officers were transferred to naval commands, perhaps indicating that the higher ranks of the old navy had fallen into poor condition.[8] The importance that Thutmose attached to the new naval facility can be judged by his appointment of his son, Amenophis II, to command the dockyard and troops stationed at Perunefer.[9]

With the Memphis dockyard working overtime to supply the expanded needs of the new navy, Thutmose had to acquire additional skilled sailors and craftsmen from outside Egypt. Syria and the ports of Canaan were full of experienced shipwrights, rope-makers and sailors who could be hired away with the promise of steady work and Egyptian gold. Most Egyptian boat captains only had experience sailing on the Nile, however, and Thutmose's new navy intended to sail upon the open sea. Attracting captains with sea-going experience must have been a priority. Compared to Canaan, life in Egypt was good. The country was peaceful and food plentiful, and the recruitment of people with the necessary skills was probably not much of a problem.

Thutmose's intention to use the navy in support of his overseas campaigns in Syria explains why he moved so rapidly in his fifth campaign (regnal year 29) to stop Tunip's encroachment on Whalia and Ullaza, and the threat it presented to Byblos and the coast of Lebanon. Control of the Eleutheros Valley was vital to Byblos' ability to access the cedars of the Lebanon Mountains. The straight, long-running lengths of cedar timber were vital to the construction of large Egyptian transport ships. These timbers formed the long central strakes that took the place of keels of the carvel-built Egyptian ships. Cedar timbers were also needed for supporting deck beams, masts and steering oars.[10] Any threat to Egypt's ability to obtain the vital supplies of cedar timber threatened Egyptian naval power at its root. Having already decided to use the navy to transport his armies to Syria, Thutmose moved quickly to reverse Tunip's encroachment and restore access to the vital timber supplies that flowed through Byblos.

Thutmose's revival of Egyptian naval power in the eastern Mediterranean reveals the broad sweep of his strategic thinking. Commercial trade between Egypt, Canaan and Lebanon required ships to make frequent stops along the route. Ships could make between 50–70 miles in daylight in ten hours with favourable winds. Sailing on the open sea was not usually undertaken at night, requiring ships to put in to the beach every evening. Whoever controlled the stopping points along the coast could also control commercial shipping. Thutmose must have realized the vulnerability of the coastal Lebanon ports to an Egyptian assault from the sea. One of the primary reasons for rebuilding the Egyptian navy was to carry out these assaults. Once the Lebanon ports were under his control, there were no other port cities in Lebanon or Canaan powerful enough to mount a serious threat to Egyptian shipping. Thutmose was then able to move his troops and supplies by sea without fear of coastal interdiction.

While a brisk commercial sea trade existed between Egypt and Syria, it is unclear how much of it was actually carried on Egyptian ships. Much of the trade seems to have been carried in Syrian hulls. These ships were small coastal entrepots constructed around keels. The Egyptians called these boats 'Syrian ships'. If Egypt could control the Lebanon ports, then a great deal of commercial shipping would have to be carried in Egyptian ships. As soon as Thutmose gained control of the Lebanon ports, he ordered that all shipping of cedar timber be carried on Egyptian ships.[11] Thus, the new Egyptian navy provided commercial as well as security benefits to the Egyptian state. The major strategic consequence of Thutmose's revival of Egyptian naval power was to establish effective Egyptian control of the eastern Mediterranean coast, one that Egypt did not relinquish for more than two centuries.

The ancient Egyptians were among the oldest civilized peoples on the planet, and were perhaps the first people to construct genuine ships. King Snefru of the Third Dynasty built ships of 40, 60, and 100 cubits long (58ft, 102ft and 170ft respectively) for use on the Nile. The first example of a sea-going ship (*menesh* ships) in Egypt dates from the reign of King Sahure of the Fifth Dynasty circa 2480 BC.[12] By Thutmose I's reign, ships of 100 cubits were commonplace.[13] Queen Hatshepsut had an enormous ship constructed to carry her obelisks from the quarry to Karnak. Francis Elgar, the Director of Naval Construction to the British Government in Victorian times, calculated that 'the two great obelisks of Karnak, each 97 feet 6 inches long, could be carried on a boat about 220 feet long and 69 feet of beam, upon a draft of water of 4 feet 6 inches, or not exceeding 5 feet.'[14] Egyptian ship design, size, speed and carrying capacity reached their peak during Hatshepsut's reign, a development that Thutmose was able to exploit in his programme to expand Egypt's navy.[15]

Most ships in antiquity were built on the foundation of a keel to provide the vessel with its longitudinal strength and stability. Ribs or frames sprang up and outward from the keel at close intervals to support the sides of the hull. The sides of the hull were further strengthened by deck beams that interlocked with the ribs. Sometimes deck beams ran through the hull and were attached to the outside. Modern ships are constructed in much the same manner.

Egyptian ship construction was, however, radically different. The lack of long timbers for keels, ribs and deck beams forced Egyptian shipwrights to invent a unique method of shipbuilding. Herodotus recorded that Egyptian ships were made of 'thorn tree wood' (acacia) and were built 'brick fashion', in the same way that one would build a wall.[16]

Egyptian ships had no keels, and were carvel-built as a shell of planking attached to ribs at comparatively wide intervals. Deck beams did not interlock with the rib frames in the modern manner, but were secured to the planking of the hull.[17] The deck was laid over the beams. The Egyptians had no nails or screws, and invented an ingenious method for joining the planks of the ship's hull together with dowels driven in along the edges where one plank joined another. The ends were similarly held together with dowels. On the inside of the hull, flat double-tongued mortices overlapped the plank edges, pulling them tightly together and giving them vertical strength. The planks of the hulls were staggered and stepped, much like a mason would build a brick wall, so that there were no continuous seams. The staggered lateral seams of the hull planks were caulked with papyrus to make them watertight.[18]

A ship constructed without a keel in the manner described lacked sufficient longitudinal rigidity to sail upon the open sea. In a rough sea, the waves would pitch the boat up and down from bow to stern, breaking the vessel's back. To prevent this, the Egyptians invented the girt rope and hogg-truss. The girt rope was a papyrus cable wrapped around the ship's bow and stern, tightly holding the ends of the hull in place and strengthening the hull's lateral stability. These cables also served as anchors for the hogg-truss. The hogg-truss was a strong cable running longitudinally across the entire length of the hull, and anchored at each end of the ship. The truss passed over two 'crutches' near each end of the ship, raising the cable off the deck. A stout pole wrapped around the cable located between the crutches was tightened to maintain tension on the truss cable itself. The hogg-truss provided sufficient longitudinal stability to allow the ship to sail in heavy seas without risk of breaking in two.[19]

By Thutmose's day, Egyptian sea-going ships had evolved streamlined hulls, and were longer, wider and deeper than the old Nile ships.[20] They were 'comparable to a modern racing craft' in efficiency.[21] Propulsion was by huge rectangular sails wider than they were tall which caught the wind atop masts ranging in height from 6–17 metres, depending upon the size of the ship.[22] The mast was located amidship and was stepped, that is, could be lowered, and was held in place by side supports and ropes. Sails were made of thick linen, and controlled by ropes and yards at their base to allow the ship to reach and tack into the wind.[23] Steering was accomplished by two aft steering oars connected to a steering post attached to the loom of the oar.[24] When entering or departing harbours, propulsion was managed by oarsmen. Rowing also augmented the ship's movement in light wind. A 100ft-long ship might have as many as forty oarsmen.[25] Unlike the Nile boats, sea-going ships did not have deck houses.

The Egyptians developed a standard design and scale for constructing their sea-going vessels that called for a ship to be three times as long as its beam. Crew strengths were calculated at one crew member per cubit of length.[26] Egyptian ships were transports of various types, and were not built as naval combatants to fight other ships on the open sea, a concept that did not dawn upon the military minds of antiquity until late in the New Kingdom. The first use of naval combatants to fight other ships occurred during the reign of Ramses III (1186–1154 BC), who in the eighth year of his reign fought what appears to have been the world's first saltwater naval battle against the marauding Sea Peoples at the mouth of the Nile.[27]

In the eastern Mediterranean, the best time for sailing is between 27 May and 14 September, when the seas are undisturbed by storms and the winds are generally favourable from the north and west at not more than 25 knots.[28] Under these conditions, a ship could make between 4–6 knots, or 5–7 miles an hour.[29] Under unfavourable conditions, the speed dropped to between 2–3 miles an hour.[30]

In antiquity, ships put into shore each night for the crews to rest, eat and sleep. 'Ports' were little more than stretches of open sloping beach protected to some degree by the natural contour of the shoreline.[31] Where an overland march would have taken Thutmose's army almost six weeks to travel the 340 miles from the Nile Delta to Byblos, the journey by boat required slightly more than a week to complete. A sea voyage also avoided wear and tear on the army, so that the Egyptian army arrived reasonably rested and ready to fight.

Chapter 14

The Exodus as Military History

While the Bible is primarily a religious text, it can also be read as an after-action report detailing the military history of the early Israelites. Examined as military history, Exodus tells the tale of a great general who sacked an Egyptian supply depot, outmanoeuvred the Egyptians in a desert campaign, fought the Amelekites to a draw, created and trained the first Israelite national army, won a great victory on the plain of Jahaz, destroyed fortified cities in the Jordan Valley and bequeathed his successor a large, well-equipped, combat-hardened and professionally led military force with which to attack Canaan. This great Israelite general's name was Moses.

Contrary to popular belief, the Israelites in Egypt were neither slaves nor a rag-tag band of wandering Bedouins, but a tribal coalition of *habiru. Habiru* is not a designation for an ethnic or racial group, but a class of wandering peoples in Palestine and Syria who came into contact with the Egyptians during the New Kingdom. They were a people without a country, with no national identity, united now and again in common journeys for pasture and plunder.[1]

The *habiru* sometimes settled in an area for very long periods, and became clients of the host kingdom, where their military arm performed military service as mercenaries. They 'operated as armed groups, semi-independent in the feudal structure, available for hire, as auxiliary troops or resourceful in carrying out freebooting, either on their own or at the instigation of one city-state against another'.[2] The military arm of the *habiru* typically comprised military professionals experienced in war. Their units were formidable military assets, proficient in combat in rough terrain and experts at hit-and-run raids, ambush and surprise attack. The settlement of the Israelites in Egypt at Goshen in exchange for military service, as told in the Bible, is a typical pattern of *habiru* military employment found in Canaan and elsewhere in the region.

The tale of the Exodus in the original Hebrew is explicitly told in military terms. Exodus 13:19 says that the Israelites were armed when they left Egypt: 'Now the Israelites went up armed out of Egypt.' The Hebrew term *hamushim* is used to denote their possession of weapons.[3] Exodus 12:37 describes the Israelites as having 'six thousand footmen – the males besides the dependents'. The term employed for 'footmen' is *ragli*, literally 'he of the leg', meaning infantry.[4] Exodus 12:41 describes these infantry units as being formed into brigades: 'All Yahweh's brigades went out from the land of Egypt.' The biblical account tells us that the Israelites departed Egypt with their weapons in hand and their military units formed up in march formations. Against this background, the adventures of Moses and the Israelites described in Exodus take on new meaning as military history.

Because Exodus has been presented to the world mostly by theologians and religious historians and not military historians, the account of the Exodus has been largely overlooked as an account of military history. Yet even a cursory examination of the texts reveals more than a few examples of the military art competently practiced. Properly seen from a military perspective, the Exodus is the saga of a people equipped and familiar with weapons, led by experienced and tactically proficient commanders, who were not Egyptian slaves, and whose military proficiency and operational capability improved greatly during the desert trek until, with remarkable clarity of strategic aim, they were able to achieve the ultimate strategic objective of conquering Canaan. What follows is an analysis of events described in Exodus from the perspective of a military historian trying to make sense of the Moses tale in military terms.

The Exodus military saga begins with Moses in command as the Israelites prepared to leave Egypt. Evidence of a first-rate military mind is seen quickly in the choice of which routes to take. Exodus 13:17–18 tells us:

> Now when Pharaoh let the people go, Moses did not lead them by way of the land of the Philistines, although it was nearer; for Moses said, 'The people may have a change of heart when they see war, and return to Egypt.' So Moses led the people roundabout, by way of the wilderness at the Sea of Reeds.

Moses avoided the coastal road, the most direct route to Canaan, because it was well-guarded by Egyptian forts and troop garrisons. The Canaanite/Philistine towns along the coastal road were also protected by their own military forces, some including other *habiru* serving as mercenaries to their Canaanite kings. Moses feared his people might be attacked and 'have a change of heart when they see war, and return to Egypt'. His decision to avoid the coastal road made sound military sense.

But having received permission to leave Egypt, why would Moses be concerned about the Egyptians? Exodus 14:5–6 tells us only that Pharaoh changed his mind, but not why. A clue may lie in Exodus 14:8, which says that the Israelites were 'departing defiantly, boldly'. It is important to recall that the *habiru* were not only mercenaries, but brigands and freebooters who could quickly turn from allies to brigands if circumstances required. Exodus 12:39 tells us that 'because they had been expelled from Egypt and could not tarry ... they had made no provisions for themselves'.

Moses must have known that to take the Israelites into the desert without sufficient provisions was to court disaster, especially since the Israelites in Goshen were surrounded by the very provisions they required. Goshen was filled with 'store cities', logistics depots for the Egyptian army in the Delta, and royal estates and farms. It is a reasonable guess that the Israelites sacked one of the towns on the way out of the country to provision themselves for the desert trek. Exodus 12:35–36 tells us that 'thus they stripped the Egyptians'. The Hebrew word used to describe what happened to the Egyptians is *nitzeyl*, usually used to mean 'despoiled', so that the Israelites 'despoiled Egypt'. It is likely that Israelite brigands took what provisions they needed at the point of the sword. If the news of the Israelite sack of an Egyptian town reached Pharaoh, it may have provoked him to punish the Israelites.

The Pillar of Fire and Smoke

The Israelites began their march along the well-travelled road leading from Raamses to the edge of the desert. All along the way the Israelites were accompanied by a strange phenomenon, a pillar of cloud and a pillar of fire. Exodus 13:20–22 describes it this way:

> The Lord went before them in a pillar of cloud by day, to guide them along the way, and in a pillar of fire by night, to give them light, that they might travel day and night. The pillar of cloud by day and the pillar of fire by night did not depart from before the people.

Miraculous explanations aside, Exodus 40:36–37 tells us the pillars have two functions: to guide the Israelites as they move over unfamiliar terrain, and to signal the Israelites when to camp and when to break camp. The pillar of cloud and fire appears to be not so much a divine totem as a practical device to improve Moses' command and control over his followers. This same signalling device is found in the writings of Quintus Curtius, a Roman historian. In his *History of Alexander*, Curtius describes how after conquering Egypt and returning to Babylon, Alexander adopted a number of changes in his regular methods of command and control that he encountered in Egypt. As Curtius tells it, 'also in the military discipline handed down by his predecessors Alexander made many changes of the greatest advantage'.[5] Curtius goes on to describe one of these changes:

> When he [Alexander] wished to move his camp, he used to give the signal with the trumpet, the sound of which was often not readily enough heard amid the noise made by the bustling soldiers; therefore he set up a pole

[*perticam*] on top of the general's tent, which could be clearly seen from all sides, and from this lofty signal, visible to all alike, was watched for, [*ignis noctu fumus interdieu*] fire by night, smoke by day.[6]

Until very modern times, Arab caravans making their way to the *hajj* were commonly preceded by a signal brazier of this sort.[7]

The Crossing of the Reed Sea

Perhaps no event in Exodus has captured the imagination more than the crossing of the Reed Sea. When examined from the perspective of military technique, however, it is clear that what happened at the Reed Sea was a tactical manoeuvre, the night crossing of a water obstacle, and not a miraculous occurrence. Moses and the Israelites had lived in Goshen for a long time, perhaps as long as four generations, and were thoroughly familiar with the area, including the marshy tract (the Reed Sea) where the fertile land met the desert. For years they had taken their herds down the same road they were travelling now to pasture them in the Sinai steppe during the rainy season.[8] As mercenaries serving in Goshen, Israelite commanders were also aware of the locations and strength of Egyptian troop garrisons in the area.

The terrain where Goshen met the desert was marshy and wet, deep in places and shallow in others, neither sea nor lake for the most part, yet subject to strong tidal flows, all elements attested to by other writers in antiquity.[9] That the marshy terrain was dangerous to infantry is clear from the description offered by Diodorus Siculus, a first-century AD Greek historian, who records that during Xerxes' invasion of Egypt in 340 BC, a troop unit of his army drowned in the place.[10]

Moses was aware that the Israelite column would have to pass directly beneath the Egyptian fortress that guarded the road junction leading to Beersheba. He depended upon a peaceful passage. If he had to fight his way through, the results would be a catastrophe, for his people were no match for the Egyptian professionals. Perhaps this was when a message reached Moses that Pharaoh's troops had already left Raamses, and were fast closing in on the road behind him, trapping him between them and the Egyptian fortress to his front. If he remained where he was, Moses would find himself caught between the classic 'hammer and anvil'.

Moses told his assembled commanders (Exodus 14:2–2): 'Tell the Israelites to turn back and encamp before Pi-hahiroth, between Migdol and the sea, before Baal-Zephon; you shall encamp facing it, by the sea.' The order must have struck some of the Israelite troop commanders as insane, for Moses had just instructed the Israelite column to leave the road and head directly into the desert. Unwilling to risk forcing his way through the Egyptian fort to his front, Moses maneouvred to neutralize its tactical significance by moving his people south and west, away from the Egyptian garrison. But why did Moses move further into the desert? Exodus 14:3 tells us what was in his mind when it explains: 'Pharaoh will say of the Israelites, "They are astray in the land; the wilderness has closed in on them."' It is an axiom of war to deceive the enemy as to your intentions, to mislead him into thinking one thing while you prepare to do another. Here Exodus provides us with an example of tactical deception at its best. Moses intends to convince the Egyptians that the Israelites are lost when, in fact, having lived in Goshen for many years, Moses knows exactly where he is.

The Israelites marched into the desert. When they reached a place where the firm ground to their front met the watery marsh to their rear, they encamped and waited for the Egyptian chariots to arrive. Now Moses manoeuvred to deceive the Egyptians further. *Exodus* 14:19 tells us that Moses moved his command tent and its characteristic signal, the pillar of smoke atop a pole, around behind the column to strengthen the impression that the Israelites were facing in a direction of march leading further into the desert. In fact, the Israelites were facing in the opposite direction. The goal was to convince the Egyptians that the Israelites were 'astray in the land'.

It must have been near dusk when the Egyptian chariot units arrived, for they went immediately into camp. From the Egyptian camp it looked like the Israelites were facing in a direction of march that would take them deeper into the desert. Behind the Israelites lay the tidal salt marsh. As dusk gave way to darkness, the pillar of smoke atop the Israelite signal standard burst into flame, and 'the pillar lit up the night, so that the one camp could not come near the other all through the night' (Exodus, 14:20). The bright flame atop the pillar drew the attention of the Egyptian sentries, causing night blindness and completely blocking their ability to see behind it.

Now the *ruah qadim*, or 'forward wind', began to blow. It was springtime, the time when sirocco winds blew out of the eastern desert with terrific force and great noise. As the wind grew stronger, the noise increased and the shallow water covering the sandbar just below the surface began to move, as the tide flowed out to sea. With the desert wind pushing from the south-east and the tide pulling it northward, the water was gone in a short time, and the ground dry enough to hold the weight of man and animals. Moses called his troop commanders together and ordered them to withdraw across the marsh to the desert beyond.

Exodus 14:24 tells us that the Egyptian pursuit began 'at the morning watch', or shortly after daybreak, clearly indicating that the Israelites had crossed during the night. The Egyptians attempted to follow the Israelites, but the wheels of their chariots became 'locked' so 'that they moved forward with difficulty' (Exodus 14:21–23). This seems to be nothing more mysterious than chariot wheels stuck in the mud. While struggling to free their machines, 'the waters turned back and

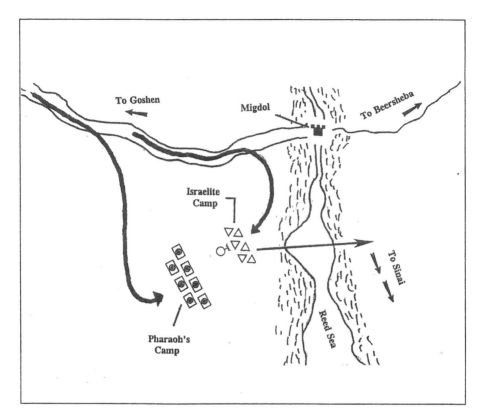

Figure 13: Night Crossing of the Red Sea

covered the chariots and the horsemen'. The tide came in, and perhaps some of the Egyptian troops and horses drowned. The incoming tide filled the marsh, preventing any further pursuit for at least eight hours until the tide receded again.[11]

The Israelites had crossed the marsh, evaded the Egyptians and gained the desert. To return to their original route to Canaan, however, would have required them to turn north to reach the Beersheba road, and taken them close to the Egyptian fort at the junction of the Beersheba-Goshen road. Once more Moses did the unexpected. He turned not toward the land of Canaan, but away from it. Exodus 15: 22 says: 'Then Moses caused Israel to set out from the Sea of Reeds. They went into the wilderness of Shur.' And so began the great desert trek of the Israelites in their attempt to return to Canaan.

The Battle with the Amalekites

Little more than a month after crossing the Reed Sea, and somewhere in the Sinai near Rephidim, the Israelites were attacked by the Amalekites, and forced to fight their first battle. The centre of the Amalekite territory was north of Kadesh-barnea in the Negev desert in the southern part of Canaan.[12] The biblical text suggests an engagement that occurred in two phases. The first (Deuteronomy 25:17–19) was an ambush in which the Amalekites caught the Israelites in column of march at Rephidim, and inflicted serious casualties. The Amalekites then attacked again in the morning. Moses placed command of the Israelite fighting men in the hands of a young troop commander named Joshua of Nun (an Egyptian name), and then 'stationed myself on the top of the hill, with the rod of God in my hand'. The text tells us that for the entire day Moses stood in plain view on the hill overlooking the battle 'until the sun set', while on the battlefield below 'Joshua overwhelmed the Amalek with the edge of the sword' (Exodus, 17: 9–13).

The Amalekites were tribal nomads whose military capability was confined to camel-riding infantry armed with the simple bow. Camel infantry was well-suited to ambush and hit-and-run raids of the type described as having occurred at Rephidim. In uneven or narrow terrain, however, it was at a severe disadvantage, and could not effect a tactical decision without having its riders dismount and fight as infantry.[13] Joshua's tactical problem was how to neutralize the enemy camel infantry.

Joshua took up positions with the Israelite main body behind his soldiers, who deployed in a narrow defile protected by hills on either side. The hills prevented any flanking attack or envelopment by the Amalekite camels. To his front, Joshua's spear and shield infantry offered an impenetrable wall of spear points and shields. Behind the spear infantry were Joshua's archers. Scattered upon both sides of the hills were slingers capable of throwing stone shot the size of a tennis ball about 100 yards.

The Amalekites rushed the wall of spears, firing their bows again and again, only to have their camels pull up short as long as the Israelite spear infantry held fast. Each Amalekite attack was subject to long-range slinger and arrow fire before it reached the wall of spears, inflicting casualties upon the attackers. Exodus 17:12–13 tells us that the battle lasted until sunset, and that when it was over, 'Joshua overwhelmed the people of Amalek with the edge of the sword.'

The word used in the Hebrew text is *chalash*, which means 'overcome', but only in the sense of being overcome by weariness, not by force of arms. The more common meaning of *chalash* is 'exhausted'. Exhaustion is exactly what we might expect from a cavalry force that threw itself again and again against a wall of disciplined spear infantry, only to expose itself to archer and slinger fire as it did so. Sooner or later, the enemy commander would have concluded that he could not carry the day, and would have broken off the battle. This is what probably happened at Rephidim.

Moses' New Army

The Israelite *habiru* who left Egypt possessed a military arm which they employed in self-defence and as mercenaries in the service of Egyptian and Cannanite kings. This army was transformed after the Israelites arrived at Mount Sinai, where they spent much of the next two years creating a new national army. At Sinai, Moses reformed the Israelite military, introducing for the first time a militia levy from which conscripts were to be drawn. The new system integrated the old professionals within it by selecting the best as troop commanders. It was at Sinai that the Israeli Defense Force finds the first evidence of its existence as a citizen army in which all eligible males of the community are required to serve.

Mendenhall's study of the Israelite census permits an estimate as to the size of the overall Israelite community at Sinai.[14] Israelite men became eligible for military service at age 20.[15] We do not know until what age soldiers remained in military service, but with the average age of death around 40 years, it was unlikely that the military could get more than ten years, perhaps fifteen at the extreme, out of a soldier. If the 5,000–5,500 soldiers calculated by the census in Numbers are taken to represent 20–25 per cent of the population of the entire community as Yadin suggests for a community during this period, then the size of the Israelite community during the Exodus was 20,000–25,000 people.[16]

The Israelite army that marched out of Sinai 'on the twentieth day of the second month of the second year' since leaving Egypt was a far cry from the original *habiru* military force. Nowhere is this more clearly revealed than in the Israelite order of march employed in the departure from Sinai. Numbers 10:11–28 gives us the combat organization of the new Israelite national army.

The march column is divided into four divisions, each led by a tribal levy and containing two additional tribal levies within it. Behind the Judah division are the clans of Gershon and Merari transporting the dismantled command tent, while the clan of Kohath carries the sacred objects for the dwelling, presumably the Ark of the Covenant, behind the division of Reuben. One is immediately struck by the fact that the division of the column into four sections, each divided into three sub-divisions, is the same general order of march found in the Egyptian army of the period.[17] The Israelites were most familiar with the army of Egypt, and it is not beyond reason that they might have adopted the Egyptian column of march to their new army.

The order of combat arms units within the column can also be reconstructed from the military specialties attributed to each tribe in various places in the Old Testament.[18] The column that marched out of Sinai had the Judah Division at its head. Far to the front were the men of Issachar, whose special ability was 'to know how to interpret the signs of the times, to determine how Israel should act'.[19] These

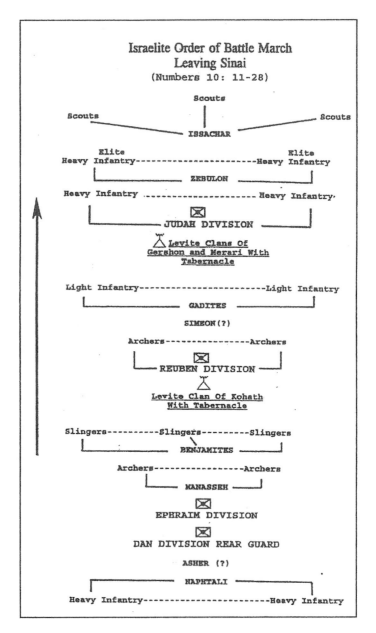

Figure 14: The New Israelite Army at Sinai

were the scouts who excelled at intelligence gathering.[20] Behind them, at the head of the column's main body, were the men of Zebulon, elite heavy spear infantry who fought in phalanx, who 'were expert with all instruments of war … who could keep rank'.[21] Next in the column's van were the troops of Judah 'equipped with shield and spear' as regular heavy infantry protecting the disassembled tabernacle.[22]

Comprising the second division were the tribes of Reuben, Gad and Simeon, an entire division of light troops capable of quick response in all directions. The Gadites were light infantry 'armed with spear and buckler … and were as swift as the gazelles upon the mountains'.[23] The troops of Simeon are mentioned only as 'valiant men', and were probably light infantry, as were the Reubenites 'skilled with the bow'.[24] The Emphraim Division was third in line, comprised mostly of missile troops, archers (Manasseh) and archer/slingers, the Benjamites 'who gave support in battle; they were armed with the bow and could use both right and left hand to sling stones and shoot arrows with the bow'.[25] There is no description of the combat capability of the Ephraimites.

The Dan Division made up the column's rearguard. Aside from knowing that the men of Asher were 'ready to man the battle line' (light or heavy infantry), there is no military capability given for Asher and Dan. The last place in the column was occupied by the men of Naphtali armed 'with shield and lance', that is, heavy infantry.[26] It will not escape students of ancient armies that the distribution of combat arms units throughout the column is very similar to the combat order of march employed by the Egyptian army.

The encampment at Sinai was a momentous event in the history of the Israelites, for it was there that the Israelites created a national people's army to replace the mercenary corps of the old *habiru* society. Israel was becoming a nation, and it instituted a conscript levy to raise sufficient manpower for war, producing an army of 5,000–5,500 men from a society of 20,000–25,000 persons. It was at Sinai that Moses instituted the first formal military command structure staffed by experienced and competent officers, and brought into being the powerful combat force with which Joshua later attempted the conquest of Canaan.

The March to Canaan

Having spent much of their time at Sinai reorganizing, replenishing and training their new national army, the Israelites set out 'in the second year, on the 20th day of the second month' prepared to fight their way into Canaan. After a few days' march, they camped in the desert of Paran. In sound military fashion, Moses prepared for the invasion of Canaan by ordering a thorough reconnaissance of the objective. He assembled a reconnaissance task force of twelve men, one from each tribe, and placed the reliable Joshua in command. Moses instructed his reconnaissance task force to return within forty days. In the meantime, he moved the main body of the Israelite army closer to his objective at Kadesh-Barnea, and there rendezvoused with the returning scouts.

The news was not good. The scouts reported a land of difficult terrain, inhabited by fierce and strong Canaanite peoples with adequate armies and large fortified cities. Worse, the three main avenues of advance were blocked by hostile armies and fortifications (Numbers 13:25–31). There would be no attack. The Israelites remained at Kadesh-Barnea for a long time, though certainly not forty years, but perhaps long enough for a new generation to reach military age and increase the size of the army.

Deuteronomy 2:14 tells us it was thirty-eight years later that the Israelite army departed Kadesh-Barnea, crossed the Wadi Zered and entered the Transjordan, taking the eastern route toward Canaan. This route took the Israelites through hostile territory. In attempting passage through Edom and Arad, the Israelite route was blocked by hostile armies. Except for what appear to have been minor skirmishes, Moses refused to offer battle, choosing instead to march around the two lands. In Moab, too, he adjusted his route of march to avoid a fight.

The Battle of Jahaz

But once Moses and his army crossed the Arnon River, the boundary between Moab and the land of the Ammonites, there was no avoiding battle. With Moab to their rear, the harsh desert to their right and the Dead Sea blocking their progress to the left, there was no choice but to fight if the Israelites were confronted. Moreover, the land of Ammon was the strategic platform from which Moses intended to launch the Israelite invasion of Canaan itself. The Ammonite and Israelite armies met on the edge of the desert at Jahaz. The new Israelite national army gained its first major triumph of arms by destroying the Ammonites. The defeat of the enemy left the rest of the country open to conquest and occupation. The victory at Jahaz allowed the Israelites to occupy the entire country from the Arnon River in the south to the Jabbok River in the north, and east as far as the border of Canaan itself.

It was in the Ammonite campaign that the Israelite army demonstrated a new military capability, the capacity to take fortified towns by storm. After their victory and settlement of Ammon, the Israelites attacked the kingdom of Gilead to the north. Here again we find the Israelite army subduing fortified towns. Deuteronomy 3:3–5 tells us that 'all the cities were fortified with high walls and gates and bars'. Lacking any evidence of a siege capability, the Israelites must have taken these towns by storm. What evidence there is concerning the military capabilities of the armies of Moab, Edom, Ammon and Gilead suggests that the Israelite account of the battles is fundamentally accurate.[27]

The textual evidence suggests that the Israelite army that conquered the Transjordan had become a formidable fighting force. It fought well-organized and disciplined armies and defeated them all. Given that we know the size of other armies of this period to have been between 6,000–10,000 men, the earlier estimate

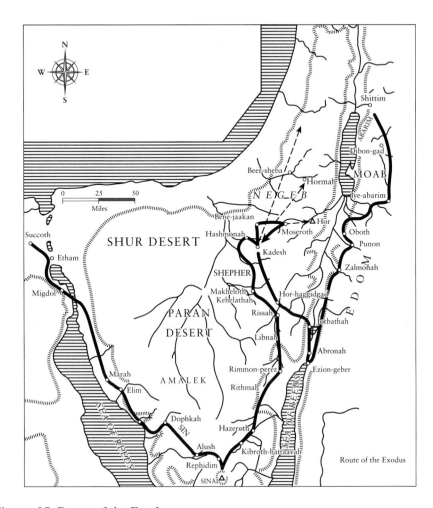

Figure 15: Route of the Exodus

of the Israelite army as having been 5,000–5,500 strong (before any increase at Kadesh-Barnea) might be generally correct.[28]

By force of arms, the Israelites had captured the territory from the Arnon River to the foothills of Mount Hermon, comprising all the cities of the plateau and all of Gilead. While some Israelite tribes remained in the north, the main body settled in the plains of Moab, the lowlands north-east of the Dead Sea, between Jordan and the foothills below Mount Nebo. Here they remained until Joshua led them across the Jordan River in the campaign that conquered Canaan.

What is clear from the preceding analysis is that the Exodus texts reveal the beginning of an Israelite tradition of arms and, thus, a military history, evident before Joshua's campaign against Canaan began. And all of it is owed to Moses, the first great general of the Israelites.

Chapter 15

Joshua At Jericho: A Study in Special Ops

A s shown earlier, the Israelite army that assembled in Jordan under Joshua's command in preparation for the invasion of Canaan was not a rag-tag rabble of poorly armed fugitive ex-slaves without military experience. Joshua's army was a large force led by experienced commanders, and equipped with the same weapons found in Egyptian and Canaanite armies of the day. It was highly trained, and capable of executing a broad array of tactical manoeuvres, including special operations and the ability to take fortified cities by storm. Its commander was a charismatic general, a veteran of many battles who had been a soldier all his life. As he assembled his army at Shittim, Joshua prepared his war of conquest with the single-minded determination that he was doing Yahweh's (God's) will.

Joshua's Army

Mendenhall estimated the size of the Israelite army at Sinai as recorded in the census ordered by Moses (Numbers 1:2–4*)* at 5,000–5,500 fighting men, a number which implies a total Israelite population of 20,000–25,000 people.[1] After two generations at Kadesh-Barnea, and making some reasonable assumptions about fertility rates, the Israelite population that crossed into the Transjordan can be conservatively estimated at 35,000.[2] That the population was of significant size is confirmed by Numbers 22:3–4, which tells us: 'Moab was alarmed because that people [the Israelites] was so numerous. Moab dreaded the Israelites, and Moab said to the rulers of Midian, "Now this horde will lick clean all that is about us as an ox licks up the grass of the field".' Under the militia system established by Moses (Numbers 1:2–4) in which all males over age 20 were conscripted for military service, a population of 35,000 could raise between 8,000 and 9,000 fighting men.[3]

Yigal Yadin notes that in the Biblical period, urban areas were inhabited by approximately 240 people per acre, and that the population of most cities contained from 1,000–3,000. Yadin also says that a city could muster about 25 per cent of its population in its defence.[4] Thus, we arrive at a startling conclusion: in almost every battle between Joshua's Israelite army and the Canaanites, the Israelites held the numerical advantage.

As described in the Biblical text, Joshua's army was armed with the sickle-sword, long and short spear, simple bow, sling and shield, the same infantry weapons used by the Egyptian and Canaanite armies. Moses' reform of the Israelite army instituted at Sinai and its organization is described in Numbers 10:11–12. The text describes the Israelite column of march as it departed Sinai. The division of the column into four sections, each divided into three sub-sections, is the same general organization for an Egyptian army. The order of combat arms units within the column is also specified in the text and includes reconnaissance units (1 Chronicles 12:33), heavy spear infantry (1 Chronicles 12:34), light infantry (1 Chronicles, 12:37), archers (1 Chronicles 12:37) and slingers (1 Chronicles 12:1–2). The arrangement of combat arms throughout the column is identical to the order of march of the Egyptian army.

Moses conquered the cities and lands of the kings in the Transjordan with this army. (Deuteronomy 2:26, Numbers 33:41 and Deuteronomy 3:3–5). The Israelite army's ability to attack and subdue fortified cities in the Transjordan campaign speaks to its sophistication as a military force.[5] The usual method of attack was to use scaling ladders to climb over the walls. The defenders could not usually muster sufficient manpower to check simultaneous assaults at widely spaced points. As noted earlier, the proportion of soldiers and dragooned civilians available to defend a city was about 25 per cent of its population. Under these conditions, the advantage lay with the attacker. Jericho is a case in point. The city enclosed 8½ square acres, with a population of approximately 2,000, forcing its defenders to protect 1,400 metres of perimeter wall with only 500 or so troops, or one man every 2.74 metres. The Israelite army attacking Jericho was 8,000–9,000 men strong, and could encircle the city's entire perimeter wall with one man every metre, six men deep.[6]

Joshua's army was comprised of *melumedey milchamah*, or soldiers 'trained for war' (i.e., veterans). The range of tactical manoeuvres and operational capabilities of Joshua's army as described in the Biblical texts is impressive, and includes tactical reconnaissance, forced night marches over rugged terrain, ambush, tactical surprise, concentration of forces at the *Schwerpunkt* (economy of force), enticement, decoys, deception, coordination of divided forces, tactical communication, indirect approaches, feints, diversionary movements, lethal pursuit and storming of fortified cities. In the literature of the ancient Near East, the books of Joshua and Judges are unique in the number and variety of battle tactics, manoeuvres and military capabilities of the Israelite army that the text portrays.[7] Little wonder, then, that the modern Israeli army still uses the Biblical texts in exercises to train its soldiers.

The Invasion of Canaan

Having been ordered by Yahweh to begin the invasion of Canaan, Joshua sent two spies to conduct a reconnaissance of the objective before committing the army to

cross the Jordan River. He instructed his spies to 'Go, have a look at the land –
and Jericho' (Joshua 2:1). Joshua's broad mission brief implies that the spies were
to do more than scout the defences of the city itself, no doubt reconnoitring the
proposed route of march, location of the river fords and avenues of approach to be
used in the attack on the city. Joshua planned to feed the Israelites and the army off
the land of Canaan, a scheme that required an assessment of the size of the spring
harvest of the farms around Jericho.

Once inside Jericho, the scouts 'rested' at the house of a prostitute named Rahab.
The choice of a whorehouse was sound tradecraft. Not only were these places
sources of loose talk, but they were one of the few locations in a small city where
strangers could appear without raising questions. The Israelite spies, however,
were not so fortunate, and the Canaanite king's counterintelligence agents detected
the spies' presence the night they arrived (*Joshua* 3:3): 'So the king of Jericho sent
word to Rahab. "Bring out the men who came to you, who entered your house this
very night. For they came to explore the whole land!"' The text suggests that the
king was aware of the Israelite army camped at Shittim less than 30 km away, and
also, presumably, their intentions. The king's decision not to engage the Israelites
at the Jordan and use the river as a tactical obstacle was a grave tactical error.

Rahab lied to the king's agents, telling them that the Israelites had left the city
around dusk when, in fact, she had hidden them on her roof. She told the Israelites
that the tales of the Israelite victories over Sihon and Og (on the Golan Heights)
across the Jordan and the slaughter of their populations had reached Jericho (Joshua
2:11): 'When we heard about it, we lost heart, and no man had any more spirit left
because of you.' In return for her cooperation and helping the scouts escape, the
Israelites agreed to spare Rahab and her family when Jericho was attacked.

Jericho's walls were casement walls, in which the inner and outer walls were
divided by cross-chambers that could be filled with rubble for strength or left
unfilled and used for apartments, storage rooms and stables.[8] Rahab's house was
beqir ha-homah e shevah, or 'in the wall of the wall'. The Israelites instructed Rahab
'to tie the length of crimson cord to the window through which you let us down'
(*Joshua* 2:18) so that the Israelites attacking the town would know that Rahab's
house and its occupants were to be spared the slaughter. Then Rahab 'let them
down by a rope through the window – for her dwelling was at the outer side of
the city wall and she lived in the actual wall' (Joshua 2:15). The Israelite scouts
returned to Shittim and informed Joshua of the low state of morale in Jericho,
telling him that 'all the land's rulers grow faint because of us' (Joshua 2:24).
Convinced that he held the psychological advantage, Joshua ordered the army to
prepare to cross the Jordan.

Three days later, Joshua gave the order to attempt the crossing (Joshua 3:1–3)
He ordered the Ark of the Covenant and the priests to lead the people to the

riverbank. Once at the riverbank, the priests touched the water with their feet and (Joshua 3:16), 'the water coming down from above stood still. It arose in one heap a great distance from Adam, the city which is beside Zarethan. And the stream going down toward the Arabah Sea was entirely cut off. The people crossed opposite Jericho.' More miraculous was (Joshua 3:17), 'The priests carrying Yahweh's Covenant-Ark stood firmly on dry ground in the middle of the Jordan; and all the Bene Israel crossed on dry ground until finally the entire nation had crossed over.'

What is the historian to make of this tale? The Jordan typically overflows its banks with the late winter and early spring rains. Even at full flood, the river is little more than a wide stream, never more than 90–100ft across, its channel usually no more than 10ft meandering in zig-zag fashion from bank to bank, which sometimes leaves the midstream the shallowest.[9] When in flood, however, the Jordan can possess a current strong enough to sweep a man off his feet. The current was likely to have been more of a problem than the river's depth. Even a strong but shallow current can be reduced relatively easily by breaking its strength a few yards upstream from the crossing point. So simple a device as placing a line of large stones upstream will work. The Israelites constructed a platform of rocks along the river's bottom under the water's surface by piling one stone atop another in several layers until the bridge was wide and long enough to cross the ford.[10]

The text notes that Joshua was concerned about the stones left behind in the river. After the crossing, he instructed one man from each of the twelve tribes to go to where the priests stood on dry land in the middle of the Jordan and carry twelve of the stones to Gilgal, the next place of encampment, where he placed them in a sacred circle. Other men were sent back to the river to gather more stones, from which a platform was constructed within the circle upon which the Ark was placed (*Joshua* 4:4–9). Joshua's order to remove the stones seems to have been intended to destroy the crossing point into Canaan. If Joshua wished to convey the message that there was no turning back, the destruction of the bridge would certainly have accomplished that.

With the army assembled at Gilgal, Joshua ordered all adult males of military age to be circumcised. The males of military age who had come out of Egypt had been circumcised, but all but Joshua and Caleb had died by this time.[11] None of those born on the trek and now of military age had been circumcised (*Joshua* 5:4–6). Circumcision was a well-established Egyptian practice, and the evidence points to the Israelites having acquired its use in Egypt. Egyptian circumcision was performed on males to mark their passage into adulthood, but does not seem to have been practised by all classes. However, Egyptian military conscripts were circumcised, and circumcision may have been a military ritual marking the 'covenant' between the Egyptian soldier and his Warrior God, Pharaoh.

Joshua probably had opportunity to witness the circumcision of military conscripts while in Egypt, and may have adopted the Egyptian ceremony for the Israelite army, for only males of *military age* were circumcised at Gilgal.[12] When the text reads, 'and it was these that Joshua circumcised' it may mean that Joshua officiated at the circumcision of the troops, endowing the ceremony with a distinctly military character. Joshua may have used circumcision as a way of separating the warriors from the rest of the people by bestowing a special status upon them. In Egypt and Israel, the ceremony was associated with military service, and with the covenant between the soldier and his warrior god.

The Capture of Jericho

On the eve of the attack against Jericho, the text tells us that Joshua encountered an angel who was *sar tseba Adonai*, or a 'commander of Yahweh's army', a story designed to emphasize that Yahweh was present at the battle. The encounter 'happened while Joshua was near Jericho' (Joshua 5:1). What was Joshua doing near Jericho the night before the battle? It had been more than two weeks since the last reconnaissance of the objective (a day's march from Shittim, three days' encampment to build the crossing bridge and ten days for the troops to recover from circumcision), and like any good commander, Joshua was making his own reconnaissance before the battle.[13]

Yahweh himself supposedly revealed the battle plan to Joshua. The army was to form a column with an armed guard marching before and behind the priests carrying the Ark, and to 'march around the city, all the fighting men going around the city once' (*Joshua* 6:3), doing so in complete silence. The silent march was to be repeated for six consecutive days. At daybreak on the seventh day, the column was to assemble again and begin its familiar march. This time, however, it was to march around the city seven times. On the seventh circuit (Joshua 6:20–21):

> The priests blew the trumpets. When the people heard the sound of the trumpets, the people gave a tremendous shout. The wall collapsed on the spot. The people went up into the city, every man straight ahead, and took the city.

The fall of Jericho is yet another Biblical story told in deuteronomic terms. If the tale is analyzed from a military perspective, however, it reveals Joshua's brilliant tactical mind. The text uses the Hebrew term *sabbotem* to describe the movement of the column at Jericho. Taken in context, the term does not mean 'to march around', but more precisely 'to encircle'.[14] It is unclear if the column marched around the city or if the city was simply encircled by the Israelite army. Jericho was fortified by 1,400 metres of perimeter wall. If the Israelite army of 8,000 men encircled Jericho, it did so in a formation where each man occupied a metre of ground in a phalanx six men deep.

But why did Joshua order the army to appear each day and encircle the city, presumably standing silently in place for hours, only to withdraw to its camp each night without attacking? The answer may be that Joshua was attempting to weaken the will of the enemy by playing upon the fear and uncertainty that Rahab the prostitute and the Israelite scouts had reported earlier. Joshua knew that Jericho's army did not engage him at the Jordan when they would have had the tactical advantage. Nor did it attack when he was encamped at Gilgal. And when Joshua moved into position to attack the city, he found that 'Jericho was shut up tight because of the Bene Israel' (Joshua 6:1). Whoever the enemy commander was, he had already shown himself to be timid and unaggressive. Joshua's repeated encirclement at Jericho was designed to increase the enemy commander's uncertainty and heighten fear within the garrison.

In the end, of course, the city still had to be taken by force. If we do not take the text literally that 'the walls collapsed on the spot', and understand it to mean that resistance suddenly collapsed, then we can enquire as to what Joshua did to make the resistance collapse so suddenly. The large Israelite army assaulting a small city of only 500 defenders could easily have overcome the walls with scaling ladders at any time during the six days. Why, then, did Joshua wait until the seventh day? Part of the answer was to weaken the resolve of the defenders. But another reason had to do with Rahab the prostitute. Rahab's 'dwelling was at the outer side of the city wall and she lived in the actual wall' (Joshua 2:15). When the Israelite scouts left Rahab, they had instructed her to 'tie this length of crimson cord to the window through which you let us down' (Joshua 2:19). Tied to the window, the crimson cord would only be visible from outside the city wall, making it useless as an indicator of the location of Rahab's house to Israelite soldiers ravaging the city from inside the walls. That is why the Israelite scouts told Rahab to keep herself and her family inside the house during the attack, warning that 'if anyone ventures outside the doors of your house, his blood will be on his head' (Joshua 2:19). What, then, was the purpose of the crimson cord?

The crimson cord marked the window through which Israelite elite troops could enter the city undetected. The dust and confusion caused by the Israelite army as it assembled and marched around the city or stood silently in place was a distraction to permit small numbers of Israelite commandos to enter the city through Rahab's window. Rahab already had a rope to assist them, the same one she had previously used to let the Israelite scouts down from her window. A few men at a time could have climbed up into Rahab's house, using the army's demonstration outside the wall as a distraction. At only seven or eight men a day, the Israelites could have placed between thirty-five and fifty men inside the house, where they awaited the signal to strike.

When the great roar from the army accompanied by the blast of the trumpets signalled the start of the Israelite attack, the commandos went into action. They could have been used in two ways to bring about the sudden collapse of resistance. The text does not tell us the location of Rahab's house relative to the city's main gate, but hints that it might have been fairly close by. When Rahab was questioned by the king's intelligence agents about the Israelite scouts, she told them that 'when at dusk the gate was about to close, the men [the Israelite scouts] went out' (Joshua 2:5), implying that she was able to see them leave from her window. If this was the case, then the main gate was nearby. When the infiltrators emerged from their hiding place, they attacked the main gate from the inside, overpowered the guard and threw it open to the sudden rush of the attacking Israelite army.

If Rahab's house was some distance from the gate, the infiltrators may have rushed from their hiding place, overpowering the nearest defenders on the wall. They then cleared a section of the wall in short order, making it easy for the troops below to scale the wall with their ladders. With similar attacks occurring all along the perimeter wall, a considerable number of troops could have successfully scaled the cleared wall in a matter of minutes. In either scenario, the defence would have collapsed quickly, perhaps tempting the Biblical text's author to employ the metaphor that 'the walls collapsed on the spot'.

Jericho was the first Israelite objective in Canaan, and Joshua put the city to the sword, commanding his troops to slay *kol han-nesama*, literally 'everything that breathed' (Joshua 6:21, 24): 'They put everything in the city under ban – man and woman, young and old, ox and sheep and ass – at the mouth of the sword ... The city they burned, with everything in it.' But was there any valid military reason to destroy Jericho? The answer is concealed in the more fundamental question: why attack Jericho at all?

Perhaps it was because Jericho commanded the approaches to the central Judean highlands, capture of which was Joshua's ultimate objective. But it is not accurate to say that Jericho 'commanded' the approaches to the central Judean ridge. There are several approaches north and south of the city that Joshua could have used. With its modest size and small garrison, Jericho presented no significant threat to the Israelite rear, even if it had been bypassed. Why go through the trouble of attacking a city that was not going to be used for Israelite resettlement? This was, after all, a war of conquest and resettlement, a fact which might explain why, except for Hazor and the northern royal towns, Joshua did not burn the other cities captured in his campaign.

In ancient times, Jericho already had a reputation for being an unhealthy place.[15] Its water supply depended on a single well, Elisha's Well, located below the city.

Archaeological investigations have uncovered evidence of *bulinus truncatus* in its water, the tiny snail that carries the parasite for *schistosomiasis*, or 'snail fever', which is still endemic to Egypt and Iraq. The disease also produces genito-urinary discharge (which Rahab might have been aware of, given her profession!), weakness, low fertility and high rates of miscarriage.[16] Perhaps it was these conditions that prompted Joshua to place a curse on the city and whoever attempted to rebuild it.

But if Joshua knew that Jericho was a pesthole and did not intend to settle Israelites there, why attack it at all? The reason was psychological. Joshua's war was one of extermination, and Jericho was destroyed with utter ruthlessness to strike fear in the minds of the rulers and inhabitants of other cities that Joshua planned to attack. By any military calculation, Jericho was a 'soft' target. It was attacked and destroyed as part of Joshua's campaign of psychological warfare to terrify his enemies. Jericho was the first battle to be fought on Canaan's soil, and Joshua wanted to make certain that the first combat in the Promised Land was a success. Nothing so excites an army as a successful bloodletting, and nothing rattles the nerve of one's enemies like a bloody example of the fate that awaits them. In these respects, Joshua demonstrated his understanding of the psychology of war. He also provided a textbook example of how to use special operations forces successfully.

Chapter 16

The Catastrophe:
The Violent End of the Bronze Age

The Bronze Age (3200–1100 BC) was among the most creative periods in human history. It would have been difficult to believe that it would become so at its outset. Then, humans lived in small villages in huts made of mud and wattle, subsisted on a marginal form of agriculture supplemented by hunting and generally lived a harsh and primitive existence. Some peoples lived in pit-houses, holes in the ground and even caves. Over the next 2,000 years, however, humans proved themselves the most inventive of the planet's creatures. In that relatively short time, humans invented large-scale agriculture, irrigation, great palaces, fortified cities, ships, writing, music, art, religions, administrative bureaucracies, metals manufacture, a number of new weapons and other killing technologies, armies and, of course, war, all important accompaniments of the human condition ever since.

By the Middle Bronze Age (2100–1500 BC), the original villages had grown into towns, that grew into large fortified cities surrounded by extensive agricultural areas to support ever larger populations. The population of Thebes during this period was 80,000, of Pi-Ramses 160,000 and of Memphis 50,000, all of which were in Egypt. These large populations made it possible for the emerging political entities to raise very large armies. The development of metals manufacture, wealthy economies and the international trade in tin made possible their equipment with a range of bronze weapons and armour.

The result was a period of frequent war between rival states of increasing imperial dimensions that provoked a period of increased and more sophisticated defensive fortifications around cities. The cities and towns of the various civilizations of the Levant began to coalesce into large political-military realms or empires, centred in powerful capitals and encompassing scores of vassal states. Thus it was that the Middle Bronze Age witnessed the rise of the powerful empires of the ancient world: the Egyptian empire, the Mycenaean kingdoms of Greece, the Hittites and Mitanni in Anatolia, Babylon on the Euphrates and Azawa in western Antolia.

By the middle of the period, the great imperial states had settled down into fairly stable and regular relations with one another. There were certainly important conflicts among them, but for the most part the imperial states had come to a general *modus vivendi* with one another, and mostly accepted each other's geographical limits. All the empires maintained relatively large infantry and chariot armies, but they were careful to maintain stable political and diplomatic relations with each other, a political and economic regularity that served as a mechanism for resolving conflicts short of large-scale violence. Also contributing to stability was the gradual interdependence of the economies of the various states. It was the first truly international system based around trading economies, in which states became greatly interdependent for imported materials such as tin for weapons. Most importantly, there was a great interdependence based on the movement of food, a practice that helped mitigate the effects of droughts, fires, insect invasions, plagues and earthquakes on the state populations. The period is exceptional in the treaties, laws, diplomacy and exchange that created the first great international era in world history.

The Catastrophe

But then, in less than a century (1225–1179 BC), the whole international system of cross-cultural contact collapsed, followed quickly by the economic and political collapse of the great empires. All, with the exception of Egypt, disappeared or were greatly weakened. Within a period of fifty to seventy-five years, beginning at the end of the thirteenth century BC, extending through to the beginning of the twelfth century BC, almost every major city in the eastern Mediterranean was destroyed. Figure 16 shows the forty-seven sites that archaeologists have suggested were destroyed during this time, with most showing evidence of having been destroyed by fire and sword. Historians have called this period of violence that marked the end of the Bronze Age 'The Catastrophe'.

The Catastrophe seems to have begun in the last quarter of the thirteenth century, about 1215 BC, with sporadic attacks. In 1207 BC, the king of Libya formed a coalition of mercenary contingents from southern Italy and Greece, and attacked Egypt, only to be defeated by an Egyptian army under Pharaoh Merneptah. It is generally thought that these mercenary contingents of disparate ethnic peoples later became part of the famous Sea Peoples that some archaeologists believe were the main forces implicated in the wider destruction of cities in the Levant that followed. By 1190 BC, the attacks increased, gathering momentum and finally raging to full fury in the 1180s.

In 1177 BC, another major invasion was launched against Egypt by the Sea Peoples. Pharaoh Ramses III defeated the invaders in a battle in southern Canaan, and then again in a land-sea battle with their invasion fleet in the mouth of the Nile.[1] The invaders retreated back into Canaan, where they settled with Pharaoh's permission on the southern coast in an area that had previously been the location of five Egyptian military garrisons. In a relatively short time, these five garrisons

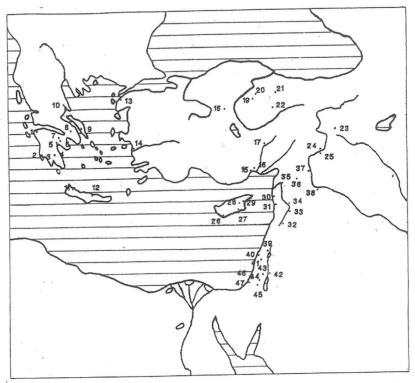

The Eastern Mediterranean: Major sites destroyed in the Catastrophe

GREECE

1. Teichos Dymaion
2. Pylos
3. Nichoria
4. The Menelaion
5. Tiryns
6. Midea
7. Mycenae
8. Thebes
9. Lefkandi
10. Iolkos

CRETE

11. Kydonia
12. *Knossos*

ANATOLIA

13. Troy
14. *Miletus*
15. Mersin

16. Tarsus
17. Fraktin
18. Karaoglan
19. Hattusas
20. Alaca Höyük
21. Maşat
22. Alishar Höyük
23. Norşuntepe
24. Tille Höyük
25. Lidar Höyük

CYPRUS

26. Palaeokastro
27. Kition
28. Sinda
29. Enkomi

SYRIA

30. Ugarit
31. Tell Sukas

32. Kadesh
33. Qatna
34. Hamath
35. Alalakh
36. Aleppo
37. *Carchemish*
38. Emar

SOUTHERN LEVANT

39. Hazor
40. Akko
41. Megiddo
42. Deir 'Alla
43. Bethel
44. Beth Shemesh
45. Lachish
46. Ashdod
47. Ashkelon

Figure 16: Major Sites Destroyed in the Eastern Mediterranean during the Catastrophe

became the five cities of the Philistine Pentapolis – Ashkelon, Ashdod, Ekron, Gath and Gaza – recorded in the Hebrew Bible. The Egyptians knew these settlers as the *Peleset*;[2] they are known to history as the Philistines.

By 1175 BC, the worst of the destruction in the Levant was over, and the results were truly catastrophic. The mighty kingdoms of the Late Bronze Age were mostly destroyed, or so greatly weakened that they could no longer sustain themselves as imperial realms. The system of international trade and diplomacy collapsed. Robert Drews described the effects of these events: 'Altogether the end of the Bronze Age was arguably the worst disaster in ancient history, even more calamitous than the collapse of the Western Roman Empire.'[3] The great cities of the eastern Mediterranean either remained unoccupied for centuries, or were gradually replaced by much smaller city-states and towns that came to characterize the early Iron Age that followed. Many, if not most, of the cultural and technical advances of the Bronze Age were lost to human memory, not to be reinvented for centuries or, in some cases, millennia.

The question that has concerned historians and archaeologists for more than eighty years is, who was responsible for the calamity? It is important to note that there is currently no scholarly consensus as to the cause or causes of the Catastrophe. Culprits blamed by scholars include attacks by foreign enemies, i.e., the Sea Peoples, societal unrest and revolts, natural catastrophes, the collapse of the international trading system and changes in warfare.[4]

The most commonly accepted explanation, however, is that the cities were destroyed by invaders who came from the sea. These Sea Peoples may have originated in Mycenaean Greece, and may have been forced to flee when invasions from the Balkans drove them out of their homeland. The evidence for this proposition is that the palace civilization of Greece was also destroyed by fire and sword at about this same time, setting their populations in motion.[5] Alternative explanations suggest that the Mycenaean civilization collapsed around 1205 BC when a massive earthquake destroyed many of their palaces and towns. It is generally agreed that some of the Sea Peoples came from Greece.

If it was the Mycenaeans who formed the core of the Sea Peoples, it is clear that over time the invaders came to comprise a coalition of diverse ethnic groups, perhaps mercenaries or professional raiders (pirates?), or even survivors from the destroyed cities who joined them. It is clear, however, that the sea raiders came to include various peoples who came from different areas of the Mediterranean. Thus, in the Libyan invasion of Egypt in 1207 BC, the Libyan king's army had contingents of five different groups with it: Shardana and Shekelesh (probably from Sardina and Sicily), and the Eqwesh, Lukka and Teresh – 'northerners coming from all lands'. Scholars have suggested that the Eqwesh may have been Mycenaeans, the Lukka a people of south-western Turkey and the Teresh might be linked to the Etruscans.[6]

Later invasions, as in 1177 BC when a large army of Sea Peoples launched a massive combined land and sea invasion against Egypt during the reign of Ramses III, were accompanied by other groups, like the Peleset, who originally came from Crete, the Khatte from Anatolia, the Qode from south-western Turkey (maybe Arzawa), Carchemish and Alashiya (Cyprus).[7] Whoever they were and from wherever they came, these raiders from the sea are generally regarded as comprising the invading armies that destroyed many of the cities of the Late Bronze Age. In short, the Catastrophe may have a military explanation.

The Military Explanation

A good place to start in assessing the military explanation is with the targets of the attacks, that is, with the cities that were attacked. These cities were not 'soft targets', and would present considerable difficulties for an attacking force to deal with. Most of the cities were of considerable size and held substantial populations. The chart below gives the size of the urban acreage enclosed by the defensive walls of five major cities that were destroyed in the Catastrophe. Using Yigael Yadin's accepted formula that in the Late Bronze Age a walled town or city could, on average, house and support approximately 240 inhabitants per acre allows us to compute the size of the resident populations in our group of cities.[8]

Table 5: Size, Populations, Walls and Defenders of Late Bronze Age Cities

City	Area Enclosed	Population	Defenders	Length of Wall	Defenders per Metre
Jericho:	8.5 acres	2,000	500	1400 m	.1
Hazor:	250 acres	60,000	15,000	3,600 m	3.3
Qatna:	75 acres	46,000	11,500	2400 m	4.7
Dan:	200 acres	48,000	12,000	2,000 m	6
Megiddo:	13 acres	3,100	775	2400 m	.4
Kadesh:	25 acres	14,600	3,650	1300 m	3.5
Ugarit:	240 acres	60,000	15,000	4100 m	3.6

Note: Calculations based on Yigael Yadin's formula that at this time, the cities in Israel and Syria were capable of supporting some 240 people per acre; family size, including possibility of more than one generation living in the same house, was about 5.2 people per dwelling unit.

Note: Yigael Yadin says at maximum effort, 25 per cent of the population could be mobilized for defence: this does not include any manpower that might be deployed as normal garrisons in each city. Also, does not include any population that lived outside the city walls or in the vicinity for farming, trade, etc.

Note: The length of the walls needed to surround the enclosed area of a settlement can be calculated by multiplying 800 metres by the square root of the acreage enclosed.

According to Yadin, approximately 25 per cent of a city's population, mostly able-bodied males, could be turned to the defence of a city's walls. Table 5 calculates the number of defenders that each city under attack could muster relative to its total population. Note that these numbers include only defenders drawn from the resident populations, and do not account for others living outside the walls in proximity to the city who would have rushed to the metropolis in the event of any attack. Nor does it account for the strength of any military garrisons that almost certainly would have been stationed in the larger cities. Table 5 also calculates the number of defenders that could be put atop the city walls in their defence, given both the length of the walls that encircled the city and the population density. These figures are also important in estimating the relative sizes of the attacking and defending forces.

For an attacker to successfully overcome a walled city requires a considerable numerical advantage in manpower that permits the attacker to assault multiple points of the wall simultaneously, thus making it difficult or impossible for the defending force to cover all points of attack at the same time.[9] Some idea of the relative size of forces required to achieve this result can be seen in Joshua's attack on Jericho, probably sometime around 1210 BC. Jericho's walls were 1400 metres long, creating a defensive perimeter around 8½ acres of interior land that housed a population of approximately 2,000 people living in about 385 dwelling units, calculated at 5.2 persons per dwelling unit.[10] Under these conditions, the people of Jericho could field about 500 citizens to defend their walls, while Joshua's army could attack with an army of 8,000–9,000 men.[11] As outlined in the previous chapter, while the defenders could put one man on every 3 metres of wall, Joshua could actually surround the entire perimeter of the city with soldiers deployed six-men deep. Under these conditions, there was no need for a miracle to capture Jericho. The relative size of attacking and defending forces becomes a critical element in the chances of success.[12]

We can calculate the number of men that could be assembled to defend each city's walls. Thus Hazor, with 3,600 metres of wall, could place 3.3 defenders per metre on its walls: Dan, with 2,000 metres of wall, could field six men per metre; Megiddo and Qatna, both with 2,400 metres of walls, could deploy only one man every 4 metres; Kadesh, with 1,300 metres of wall, could deploy 3.5 men per metre; and Ugarit, with 4,100 metres of wall, could deploy 3.6 men per metre in defence of its own walls.[13] Assuming that the populations of the cities were not drastically reduced by famine, earthquake, drought or social unrest before they were attacked, the populations of the cities would have been sufficiently large to mount a significant defence against an invader. Or, said in another way, the attacking force of Sea Peoples would have had to be very large to have any real prospect of success in taking a city by storm.

If a ratio of six attackers for each defender is assumed (considerably less than the advantage Joshua enjoyed at Jericho), it is possible to calculate the size of an attacking force needed to overcome the defenders in each city. Thus, Jericho required 3,000, Hazor 90,000, Qatna 69,000, Dan 72,000, Megiddo 4,650, Kadesh 21,900 and Ugarit 90,000. Armies of the Late Iron Age could field forces of such size. In the Late Bronze Age, however, armies were much smaller. Many, if not most of these cities, were vassals of the larger imperial realms. It has been argued that the large chariot and infantry armies characteristic of the Middle Bronze Age had grown smaller during the Late Bronze Age as a consequence of the cost of maintaining such large military establishments, and the generally stable political conditions that prevailed as a consequence of the established international order.[14] In addition to reduced size, especially of the chariot units, the imperial armies were dispersed in smaller garrisons throughout the empire to protect and control the various vassal cities. Much of the control over food production and trade in the vassal cities fell to the imperial armies to oversee and administer, thus further dispersing and reducing the size of the garrisons. It is possible that when the cities were attacked, these smaller dispersed garrisons were unable to mount an effective defence by deploying in force outside the walls, engaging the enemy with chariots and infantry, and thus could not disrupt a sustained attack against the city walls. These forces would have been available to defend the walls, but could not prevent the cities from being attacked by a determined invader.

Defensive Fortifications

An attempt to storm these cities had to deal with their considerable fortifications. The period of greatest fortification of urban areas occurred during the Middle Bronze Age (2100–1550 BC) when the Mediterranean civilizations were developing into large imperial realms. These imperial civilizations were comprised of a native heartland combined with a number of vassal towns and cities that had to be protected from the predations of rivals. The result was a great period of constructing defensive fortifications throughout the region.

In the Late Bronze Age (1550–1200 BC), the imperial civilizations had largely established their territories, and developed the international trading system and diplomatic practices that reduced conflicts between the great powers. Thus, the period saw only little activity in creating new fortifications, although there is no reason to believe that they permitted the existing ones to fall into decay.[15] We may safely conclude with support from archaeology that the cities of the period still had significant defensive fortifications, i.e., walls, fortified gates, ramparts, towers, etc. that could be of some use in mounting a defence if the city was attacked.[16] It is worth noting that in Israel and Egypt these fortifications were commonly constructed of mud brick in the manner of casement walls. Fortifications in Syria northward, however, were mostly of natural or shaped stone forming solid walls that were much more difficult to breach than casement walls.[17]

Fire

If we assume that a large coalition of Sea Peoples attacked and successfully captured the major cities of the Levant, what happened next? The evidence of soot and ash layers found in the rubble at various dig levels within the city walls seems to suggest that the cities were destroyed by fire. It is important, then, to see how difficult it was for an invading army to destroy a city by setting it ablaze.

First, the number of dwellings that would have to be set ablaze would have been considerable. Consider the following data: Hazor had 11,538 dwelling units within its walls; Qatna 8,846; Dan 9,230; Kadesh 596; and Ugarit 11,538.[18] Second, most of these dwellings were simple structures made of mud brick walls (mostly south of Syria) or fired brick or stone (from southern Syria north), materials that do not ignite easily if at all. Third, the typical arrangement of houses packed so closely to one another and often sharing one or more walls made it difficult for flames to jump from one unit to another. The lack of space between units deprived the fire of sufficient oxygen and draught. Fourth, most of the dwellings had roofs of 3in wooden poles carried by two large beams covered by a thick layer of brushwood to fill in the spaces between the wooden framing. Covering the brushwood were 2–3in of packed, dried and sun-hardened mud that served as a roof.[19] What little wood was used in the construction of these dwellings was found in casings for the single door or for one or two window frames. Sometimes the second floor of a larger house might be constructed around a wood frame, but this would commonly be covered in mud or faced with mud or fired brick. Nothing in the external construction of a typical urban dwelling in the Late Bronze Age cities burned easily.

The British Army operating in the Indo-Afghan borderlands in Waziristan during the 1919–1920 rebellion encountered the same type of dwelling construction found in Bronze Age cities.[20] A British officer, D.H. Gordon, who went on to become a noted archaeologist, suggests that firing these units was no easy task, based on his personal experience as a troop commander in Waziristan whose unit often attempted to burn villages.[21] He notes that a good deal of time and labour was required to prepare a dwelling for firing. Fire needs a draught, and the first step was to send soldiers up to the roof with shovels to dig a good deal of mud off the roof and expose the thick layer of brushwood. Using a pick, a number of draught holes had to be hacked through the brushwood layer, itself thick with packed, sun-baked, hardened mud. Gordon notes that 'this was a most laborious method and one likely to be attended by fatalities if the enraged householders were being fussy over the damage being done to their property'.[22]

The internal furnishings of these dwellings rarely provided sufficient materials (furniture, bedding, clothing, etc.) to start and maintain a serious fire. Objects mostly of seasoned wood and ceramic were very difficult to set to flame. Gordon notes in this regard: 'I have learned by experience that the casual application of a torch will not necessarily set fire to anything.'[23] To fire the inside of the dwelling, it was first necessary to 'prepare' it by stacking brushwood from floor to ceiling on at least two interior walls of the dwelling, and on both sides of the door. This, too, required considerable manpower and effort, assuming there was a source of wood to be harvested nearby, an unlikely circumstance in an urban area or even in the immediately surrounding lands that had been turned to agriculture. Gordon explains: 'The stacked brushwood on each side of the door was sprinkled with kerosene and this was fired with a torch made of kerosene-soaked sandbag wired to a stick.'[24]

Ancient raiders, of course, possessed no such accelerants to help start fires. In an ancient urban neighbourhood, it is unlikely that a sufficient supply of brushwood or straw was available to be used in this manner. Gordon notes that when the Waziris saw that the British were using the brushwood kept for their animals to burn their houses, they burned the wood themselves: 'This effectively made house burning impossible.'[25] Without the means to set fire to the dwellings, they were destroyed by explosives. But, 'even where houses were thoroughly burned they could be, and in fact were, made habitable after a few months'.[26]

Turning to the question of whether the Bronze Age cities could have been burned, as was commonly assumed in Gordon's day (he wrote his account in 1953), he concludes that if the houses made of mud with flat mud roofs were of the type used in the Middle East during the Late Bronze Age, then it is clear that these houses 'could not have been fired at all' if extra fuel was not available.[27] He goes on to conclude 'that there are two possibilities, either the tentative reconstruction of houses with flat mud roofs that are often [attributed to the Bronze Age] are in many cases incorrect or equally in many cases, the so-called destruction level is nothing of the kind'.[28]

How, then, are we to account for the layers of soot and ash found in the ancient dwellings from which scholars have deduced that the dwellings were destroyed by fire? Gordon suggests the interiors of the Bronze Age dwellings, like those in Waziristan, contained open hearths with no chimney and little ventilation, where cooking and heating fires burned for many years. This produces a 'floor thickly coated with a fine grey dust hopping with fleas and a brushwood ceiling kippered black with smoke'.[29] In Waziristan, when a house wall or roof collapsed, usually from heavy monsoon rain,[30] the site was levelled for a new one 'where the debris contain a thick layer of ashy earth floor and blackened brushwood which would in

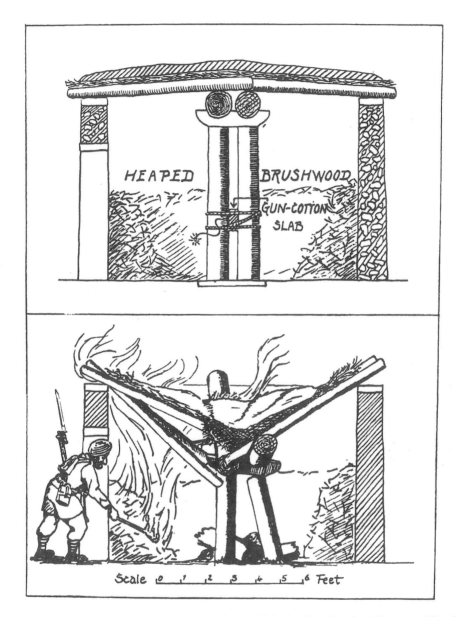

Figure 17: Sketch by D.H. Gordon of a British Soldier Setting Fire to a Hut in Waziristan

due course present an archaeologist with conclusive evidence of an invasion and destruction by fire and sword'.[31] Thus, the discovery of layers of ash and soot at different levels among the ruins of ancient cities is more likely evidence of how many times, over the millennia, the dwelling had collapsed and been rebuilt over its own debris, and not evidence of destruction by fire at the hands of raiders.

Sword

If and when the invaders gained entrance into the city, there was still the problem of prolonged street fighting. There is no reason to believe that the defenders would have simply ceased fighting once the walls were breached. More likely, they would have continued to resist, withdrawing to the citadel to make a final stand.[32] Civilians caught in the midst of the melee would have also been killed or injured. The point is that the invaders are likely to have suffered significant casualties in the street fighting. The battle to put an end to all resistance would certainly have taken at least several days, and perhaps longer, with the death and injury toll rising on all sides.

The narrative of cities attacked and destroyed by invading armies assumes, in more than a few cases, that the population was massacred. This raises the question of what was done with the corpses. One could imagine that they were simply left in the street, the raiders sailed away and the returning survivors buried them. Or, if the raiders decided to stay a while, they may have forced the remaining civilian populations to gather up the corpses and bury them someplace nearby. In either case, one might expect that evidence of mass graves holding the victims' bones would have come to light. An analysis of bone injuries might also reveal how they died. Alas, nothing of this nature has yet been found.

When the Catastrophe is examined as a military operation, it is clear that the accepted explanation that the Levantine cities were destroyed by attacking forces leaves much unanswered. The number of soldiers required to carry out these operations would need to have been much larger than is usually supposed. Small numbers of raiders from the sea simply did not possess the manpower to attack, overcome and destroy so many cities of such size and population typical of Bronze Age settlements.[33] If the cities of the Levant were indeed destroyed by fire and sword, then it could only have been done with much larger forces. One possibility is that a whole people was on the move in all its thousands, equipped with a considerable military arm, or able to recruit more manpower and mercenaries along the way. The attack on Egypt in 1179 BC may have occurred in just this way.

It is also difficult to see what an invading army might achieve by killing a city's population and burning its dwellings.[34] If the destruction was wrought by raiders or mercenaries seeking loot, then once the city was looted, the attackers would have likely departed, perhaps seeking their next target. If attacked by a large army as part of a bigger migration of peoples, then why destroy the city? Why not move into the available housing and use the existing populations as slaves and tillers of the surrounding farms? If the migrants remained and made the city their new home (as the Philistines did in southern Canaan), surely there would be substantial evidence over time of their presence.[35] In either case, the destruction of the cities would have required a substantial source of manpower and taken considerable time to complete. The evidence for most cities was that they remained deserted for long periods, in some cases centuries, before they were inhabited again.

We are left with D.H. Gordon's observations that the cities of the Levant may not have been destroyed by fire and sword after all. Perhaps drought, famine, earthquakes, disease and other natural disasters so greatly reduced the populations that it was possible that smaller forces of raiders and/or migrants could have overrun the great cities of the Levant. Even so, there was no reasonable need to destroy the city by fire and sword. In truth, we do not yet know what caused the great Catastrophe that brought an end to the magnificent Bronze Age.

Chapter 17

The Dawn of the Iron Age:
The Iron Army of Assyria

T he collapse of the Bronze Age (1100 BC) produced radical changes in the social and economic structures of the Mediterranean world. The great urban cities with large populations were replaced by small towns and smaller cities with much reduced populations. The large and efficient governmental administrative structures that gave coherence and direction to the urban civilizations mostly disappeared, as did the robust international trading system in food and metals upon which the cities were highly dependent. The tin trade collapsed, effectively making it impossible to manufacture bronze implements and weapons at a reasonable cost, if at all. Over the next three centuries, new social and economic institutions arose. The great Bronze Age kingdoms and empires were gradually replaced by smaller city-states during the Early Iron Age that followed.[1] A major characteristic of this transition was the replacement of bronze with iron as the most common material in metal manufacture. This new age that began in earnest in the tenth century BC, and ended in the third century, is known as the Iron Age.[2]

Wrought iron is inferior to bronze in almost every respect. It is softer, far more subject to corrosion and its high melting temperature (1,540 degrees Fahrenheit) made it impossible to pour into moulds to make castings, as was done with bronze. Heating iron ore produced a hot, spongy bloom of iron mixed with slag. By hammering, the blacksmith could produce a usable lump of iron that could be reheated and hammered into the desired shape, a very labour-intensive process, but one that was much simpler to master than with bronze. The main advantage of iron is that, unlike the tin and copper needed to make bronze, iron ore was available almost everywhere. Indeed, it is 100 times more plentiful than copper and 4,000 times more so than tin.[3] Its wide availability made implements made of iron much cheaper than bronze. The armies of the new period could now supply iron weapons more cheaply than bronze weapons. The result was that the armies of the Iron Age were much larger than those of the Bronze Age.

From 1200–1000 BC, iron metallurgy developed at about the same time across a broad area ranging from the Levant to Iran, and in the Indus Valley in India. It is noteworthy that once iron working got underway, all the necessary technology for producing effective tools, implements, weapons, etc. of quenched iron developed and spread quickly. Interestingly, the use of iron for weapons seems to have lagged behind its other more common uses. Of all the weapons and armour found in twelfth-century BC contexts in the eastern Mediterranean, only a little more than 3 per cent are iron, while over 96 per cent are bronze. For the eleventh-century BC contexts, the proportions are 20 per cent iron and 80 per cent bronze. It is not until the tenth century BC that iron weapons appear more frequently (54 per cent) than bronze (46 per cent).[4] It was in Assyria that we encounter the first huge, well-administered and highly centralized iron empire in history, far exceeding in its extent the great powers of the earlier era.[5] It was also the first army in history armed primarily with weapons and military equipment made of iron.

The Iron Army of Assyria

The Assyrian army of the ninth century BC was the most sophisticated of its time in terms of size, weaponry, tactics, siegecraft, innovation, mobility, logistical support and overall military efficiency. No army equalled its overall organizational sophistication until that of Rome. The Assyrian army was thoroughly integrated into the larger social, political and economic institutions of the Assyrian state, and much of its success was due to its ability to take maximum advantage of this integration.

Like the other settlements of the Tigris-Euphrates valley between 1500–1200 BC, Assyria was a city-state that sat astride important trade routes that the major powers of the day – Egyptians, Hittites and Mitanni – sought to control. In the twelfth century BC, Hittite power collapsed and Assyria began a 300-year rise to power under the direction of successive powerful kings that resulted in the establishment of the Assyrian Empire in the ninth century BC.

Assyria emerged as the most powerful and successful military empire the world had seen to that time. Warfare, conquest and exploitation of neighbouring states became the primary preoccupation of the Assyrian kings. Between 890–640 BC, the height of Assyrian power, they fought 108 major and minor wars, punitive expeditions and other significant military operations against neighbouring states.[6] During the reign of Sargon II (721–705 BC), the Assyrians carried out no fewer than ten major wars of conquest or suppression in sixteen years.[7] The result was the establishment of an empire that ran from the Persian Gulf to the Mediterranean Sea, from Armenia and northern Persia to the Arabian desert, and west to include parts of the Egyptian Delta. This large empire was sustained by the largest, best-equipped and best-trained military organization that the world had ever witnessed.

The economic base of the Assyrian Empire centred on the three major cities of Nimrud, Nineveh and Ashur, all located on the Tigris River in what is now

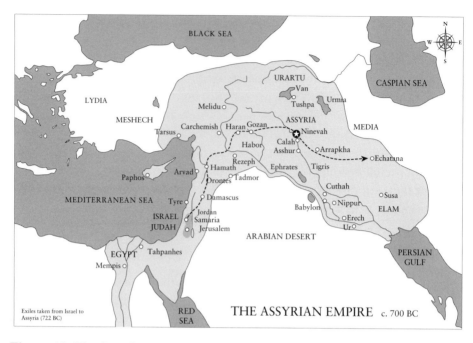

Figure 18: The Assyrian Empire

north-western Iraq. Like Egypt, Assyria was an alluvial state that depended on agriculture, and its agriculture depended upon the fortunes of a major river. The Tigris is not a friendly or gentle river, however, and its ever-present threat of violent floods required that major irrigation projects be constructed and maintained. These massive irrigation networks required a large supply of manpower that Assyria lacked. Military conquest as a source of slave manpower, and the wholesale resettlement of foreign peoples, provided the Assyrian solution. As long as the irrigation system could be maintained, the Assyrian fields could feed its people.

In most other respects, however, Assyria's economic base was sorely deficient. Assyria's geography afforded few of the vital strategic materials from which to forge its military strength. In an age of iron, Assyria possessed few easily available iron deposits for manufacturing modern weapons. It also lacked stone for its building projects, most pointedly for defensive walls and irrigation projects. Except for the weak and thin wood of the palm tree, Assyria had no wood at all. Long, straight wooden beams were required to construct fortifications, public buildings and temples, and it was wood from that Assyrian chariots, forty high siege towers and battering rams were made. In an age of chariot warfare, Assyria had no grasslands upon which to breed horses. The solution to these strategic shortages was to conquer and occupy its neighbouring states, all of which could provide the raw materials Assyria required.

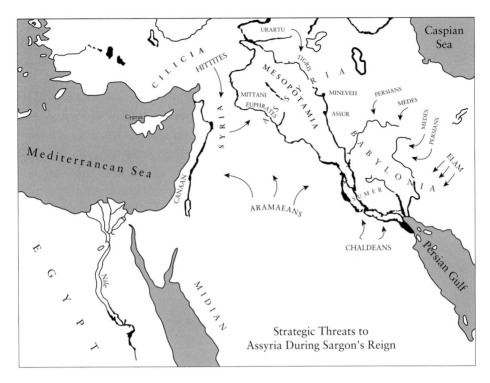

Figure 19: Strategic Threats to Assyria

Assyria's geographical position left it vulnerable to hostile neighbouring states whose aggressive designs placed Assyria under constant threats. Map 2 portrays the geo-strategic position of Assyria relative to her hostile neighbours. In the early days (1500–1200 BC), Assyria was the target of Mitannian, Hittite and Babylonian expansion and vassalage, and even at the height of Assyrian power, Babylon always had to be watched closely. South-west of Babylon were the Chaldeans, who posed a constant threat to Assyria's southern borders. To the north-west, in the area of modern Armenia, the Urartu posed an even greater threat, as did the Medes in the Zagros Mountains further to the east. Assyria was surrounded by hostile powers which frequently raided its trade routes, disrupted its economic supply lines and attacked it outright whenever Assyria was weak. In the Assyrian view, the world was a dangerous place, and there could be no real security unless these hostile states were brought to heel. The instrument of this policy was the new iron army.

The Assyrian army was forged in the crucible of 200 years of near constant warfare. The rulers of Assyria during this period proved to be strong and talented men who provided the direction needed to sustain a constant reign of conquest and suppression of revolts. Moreover, it was Assyria that gave the world what was to become the imperial system of provincial management of conquered peoples, a system that reached its height under the Romans.[8] The need to respond to a number of new technologies and strategic needs required that the Assyrian army undergo periods of significant reform, reorganization and re-equipment. All these challenges were accomplished by the great warrior kings of the period.

The imperial period witnessed the reigns of six important monarchs, beginning with Assurnasirpal II (883–859 BC), who was followed by his son Shalmaneser III (858–824 BC). There then was a period of eighty years in which the archaeological records reveal little about monarchical rule until Tiglath-Pileser III (745–727 BC) came to power. Six years after his death, the greatest Assyrian ruler and military conqueror, Sargon II (721–705 BC), came to the throne. History has accorded this greatest of the Assyrian kings the title of Sargon the Great. He was succeeded by his son Sennacherib (704–681 BC) and, thirty years later, by his grandson Ashurbanipal (668–630 BC). Under three of these monarchs – Assurnasirpal II, Tiglath-Pileser III and Sargon II – significant reforms of the Assyrian army were carried out that allowed the development of a powerful and modern military machine.

The Assyrian Empire was not an easy one to govern. In an age of primitive communications, the empire was widely scattered, and in some places was geographically isolated by mountain ranges and deserts. It was, moreover, comprised of conquered peoples that harboured strong nationalist feelings, often tied to local religious, tribal and blood loyalties. The Assyrians mastered the administration of this state through the use of a modern bureaucracy comprising over 100,000 civil service functionaries, the establishment of a provincial system of authority later copied by the Romans, the use of auxiliary armies, deportation of whole peoples and ruthless use of police and military terror supported by an efficient intelligence system.[9] The creation of an excellent system of national roads under control of the army permitted the rapid movement of troops for use against internal and external enemies.[10]

Behind the civil service stood a police and intelligence apparatus centred in the personal bodyguard of the king. These praetorians, about 1,000 in number, had the task of ensuring the loyalty of the civil service and anyone else in a provincial area who might in any way represent a threat to the royal will.[11] The intelligence service employed spies and other agents to accomplish their task, and it was they who enforced the order for recall, interrogation or termination of provincial officials who had fallen from the favour of the king. The control of an empire containing so many disparate peoples required a heavy reliance upon native auxiliary troops. While Tiglath-Pileser III seems to have been the first to use these auxiliaries, by the time of Sargon II the practice had been institutionalized. Native auxiliaries were used mostly to garrison the provinces, but after a while they became an integral part of the Assyrian field fighting force.[12]

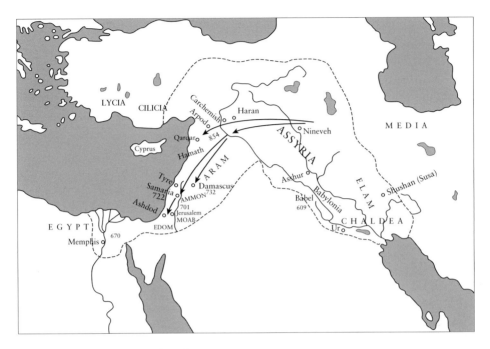

Figure 20: Map of Assyrian Conquests

Behind the imperial system rested the sure knowledge among potential revolutionaries that punishment would be swift and extremely cruel. The Assyrians were the first to practise psychological warfare on a grand scale as a matter of state policy. What made the Assyrians different from other conquerors is that they boasted about their cruelty and raised monuments to it as a form of propaganda to convince actual and potential adversaries that resistance was futile and carried terrible penalties. In almost every instance of Assyrian victory, the vanquished were dealt severe and public punishment. Defeated monarchs, generals and high government officials often met horrible and painful deaths in full view of the newly subjugated population.

To maintain an empire the size of Assyria's required a military establishment of great size. No accurate figures exist as to the total size of the army, but at the very least the Assyrian army would have to comprise between 150,000–200,000 men.[13] A large part of this force, probably as much as one third, was composed of auxiliary troops used to garrison the provinces. They were called to actual combat service as the need arose. Probably as much as 20 per cent of the total army was comprised of reserve troops that functioned in peacetime as local militia, but could be called to national service when needed. An Assyrian combat field army numbered 50,000 men, with various mixes of infantry, chariots and cavalry.[14]

In the early days of the empire, the army was recruited from the general population by forced conscription. Local provincial vassals sustained feudal militias that the vassals were required to provide to the king in time of war.[15] Tiglath-Pileser III (745–727 BC) broke the power of the feudal aristocracy and formed the nucleus of a standing professional army centred around an elite royal guard of 1,000 men.[16] Records reveal the use of auxiliary troops under Assurnasirpal II (883–859 BC), and the practice seems to have been expanded by Tiglath-Pileser. It was formally institutionalized by Sargon II, who also expanded the professional army.

Under Sargon II, the professional praetorian corps of the army was expanded to several thousand, and an inner elite known as 'the companions', or 'troops of the feet', formed the spine of the army.[17] Provincial governors were required to raise and support local forces for use in time of war, but the governors were no longer powerful enough to use these forces to resist the king. Yet local forces were substantial, in at least one instance being comprised of 1,500 cavalry and 20,000 archers.[18] Auxiliary units were thoroughly integrated into the field fighting force, but still retained the major function of garrison duty to ensure control of captured populations.

A number of other important reforms increased the fighting power of the army. Assurnasirpal II introduced the first use of cavalry to the Assyrian army.[19] Indeed, the Assyrians invented cavalry as a new military combat arm. Assurnasirpal's armies were the first to employ heavy, mobile siege towers and the mobile battering ram. Under his reign, there appears the first use of units of 'wall-breakers' who specialized in climbing scaling ladders and weakening defensive walls with axes and levers.[20] Cavalry units were integrated into the force structure, and eventually replaced the chariot corps as the elite striking arm.[21] In 854 BC, at the Battle of Karkar, Shalmaneser III fielded a force of 35,000 men comprised of 20,000 infantry, 1,200 chariots and 12,000 cavalry.[22] Even allowing for exaggeration, what is important are the force ratios: at Karkar, there were ten times as many cavalry as chariots.

By Sargon's time, the army had been reorganized into a thoroughly integrated fighting force of infantry, chariots, cavalry, siege machinery and specialized units of scouts, engineers, intelligence officers and sappers. Sargon also equipped the army entirely with weapons of iron, thereby producing the first iron army of the period.[23] The Assyrian army was also equipped with iron armour and helmets. The production and storage of iron weapons and other metal materials of war became a central feature of the army's logistical base. The weapons depot in Sargon's palace at Dur-Sharrukin (Fort Sargon) contained 200 tons of iron weapons, helmets and body armour.[24]

The combat forces of the field army were organized in units of ten formed around national and regional formations, each of which specialized in the weapons and tactics at which it excelled. The ten-man squad under the command of a non-commissioned officer was the smallest fighting unit. The normal tactical unit was the company, which could be tailored into units of 50–200 men.[25] In battle, infantry units of spearmen deployed in phalanxes with a ten-man front and files twenty men deep, each commanded by a captain. These units were highly trained and disciplined in manoeuvre. Their gradual but persistent movement toward and through enemy ranks, killing as they went, represented the main shock force of the Assyrian army.[26]

Assyrian infantry was divided into spearmen, archers and slingmen. The spearmen deployed in phalanxes to anchor the main line in the centre of the battlefield. Assyrian spearmen were heavy infantry armed with a long, double-bladed spear and a straight sword for hand-to-hand combat. The sword was secured to a thick belt that ran around a knee-length coat of iron mail armour. The spearman carried a small iron shield and wore a conical iron helmet.[27] An important Assyrian innovation was the introduction of knee-high leather boots reinforced with iron plates to protect the shins.[28]

Archer units comprised the second type of Assyrian infantry. The Assyrian composite bow seems to have been of a more advanced type than that usually found in the Near East at the time.[29] This bow was very powerful and fired iron-tipped arrows that had great penetrating power. For protection, the archer wore a long coat of mail armour, the weight of which considerably reduced his mobility. A shield bearer carrying a large man-sized shield of braided reeds protected the archer from missiles fired from defensive walls. The Assyrian archer also carried a sword for close combat. The Assyrians increased the rate of fire of their archers by introducing an innovation in the arrow quiver. Carried on the back and secured by a shoulder strap, the Assyrian quiver had a short rod protruding from the bottom front opening slightly above the shoulder. This allowed the archer to reach back and pull down on the rod, tipping the quiver forward and bringing the arrows within easy reach. This innovation increased the rate of fire by as much as 40 per cent.[30]

The final type of Assyrian infantry were the slingmen. The sling was probably introduced to the Assyrians by mercenaries or conquered peoples, and the Assyrians were slow to adopt it. While some bas-reliefs show slingmen deployed alongside archers in battle on open terrain, the slingmen saw their primary use in siege warfare. Slingers could direct high-angled parabolic fire against the defenders on the wall.

The chariot corps originally constituted the primary striking arm of the Assyrian army, but gradually underwent major design changes over the imperial period. The Assyrian chariot was previously used in much the same way as the Egyptian and Mitannian chariot, as a mobile platform for archers. But the Assyrian chariot was always a heavier machine, with a stiff and heavy front end, a characteristic that made it less manoeuvrable at high speed.[31] Originally the crew had consisted of a driver and an archer. The mission of the chariot was to attack massed infantry formations, deliver shock, and then, as the Assyrian infantry clashed at close range, aid in the pursuit.

Over time, the Assyrians developed an even heavier chariot carrying a crew of three, with the third man acting as a shield bearer to protect the archer and driver. By the time of Ashurbanipal, however, the Assyrian chariot had evolved into a four-man vehicle with a driver, archer and two shield bearers. The weight of the machine required three and then four horses to pull it, and the wheels became thicker, requiring eight spokes for strength.[32] All crewmen now carried a spear, sword, shield and axe, a development that turned the chariot corps into mounted infantry. After administering the initial shock to the enemy by mounted charge, the chariot crew dismounted and fought as heavy infantry. As the Assyrian Empire grew, the army was required more and more to traverse difficult terrain, and to conduct operations in areas where the ground was not favourable to the chariot. The need to fight in other than open terrain required another combat arm that could manoeuvre and deliver firepower. The solution was cavalry.

It was the steppe peoples who lived in the northern areas above the Tigris Valley to whom armies of the Near East owed the development of the horse as a fighting vehicle.[33] At first the horse was too short, light and weak to carry a mounted rider for any distance, and found its primary military use in pulling the light chariot. The presence of Assyrians in Armenia and in the Zagros Mountains most likely brought them into contact with the horse-riding steppe peoples from whom they obtained the stronger breeds of horses.

The introduction of horses to the Assyrian army required that they be obtained in adequate supply. Since Assyria itself lacked grasslands and offered few of the conditions necessary to breed these animals in sufficient numbers, the Assyrians developed a remarkable logistical and supply organization to ensure an adequate supply of horses for the army. The horse recruitment officers, called *musarkisus*, were high-level government officials appointed directly by the king. The fact that they reported directly to the king and not the provincial governors under whom they served testifies to the importance of their function as horse quartermasters. Usually two horse-recruitment officers were assigned to each province. Assisted by a staff of scribes and other officers, they ensured that adequate numbers of horses were purchased, imported, assembled and trained for military use.[34]

The *musarkisus* obtained horses on a year-round basis, and were responsible for sustaining them in a national system of corrals and stables. Surviving documents indicate that in the city of Nineveh alone these officers were able to secure 3,000 horses a month arriving on schedules of 100 animals a day. These reports also note that the horses were received from every province of the empire. One report notes that of the 2,911 horses received for a single month, 1,840 were used as yoke horses in the chariot corps, twenty-seven were put to stud and 787 were riding horses assigned for cavalry use.[35] Horse-recruitment officers were also responsible for securing adequate supplies of mules and camels for use in the logistics train. This efficient logistical apparatus was unknown in any other army of the world at this time.

Originally the Assyrian cavalryman was an ordinary foot soldier equipped with armour, lance, sword, shield and heavy boots. This great weight severely limited his mobility. Over time, the armoured coat was reduced to waist-length, and the shield made smaller. The Assyrians used a blanket, saddle girth, crupper and breast straps to stabilize the rider.[36] Later, Assyrian cavalrymen learned to control their mounts with their legs and the heel pressure of their boots (the spur had not yet been invented). This made it possible to place archers on horseback and gave birth to the first use of mounted archers in the Near East. Writers of the Old Testament called these cavalry archers 'hurricanes on horseback'.[37]

The Assyrian army was the first of the Near East to develop an all-weather capability for ground combat. They fought in winter as well as in summer, and even conducted siege operations during the winter months.[38] The fact that the army was almost continually at war somewhere in the empire for more than 200 years provided adequate opportunity for developing field technique by trial and error. The Assyrians also experimented with mixed units, combining infantry, archers and slingers in a single unit.[39] So adaptable were the Assyrian ground forces that they also fought well in marshlands: placed aboard light reed boats, they became water-borne marines using fire arrows and torches to burn out the enemy hiding among the bushes and reeds of the swamp.[40]

In open terrain, Assyrian tactics were straightforward, relying upon shock, firepower and discipline to carry the day. Once the army had been formed for battle, archer and slinger units began firing their missiles from a distance to inflict casualties upon the enemy infantry. Other archer units were specialists at killing chariot horses, directing their fire at these units.[41] Then Assyrian chariots attacked from as many different directions as the terrain would permit, their archers firing as the machines closed with the enemy infantry. The purpose of the attack was to deliver shock at a number of different points in an effort to shatter the enemy infantry. As the chariots drove into the mass of infantry, their crews dismounted and fought in close combat. As the enemy mass began to waver, the phalanxes of Assyrian spearmen, supported by direct fire from archer units, began in a disciplined and slow march to close with the enemy. The cavalry, which to this point had been used to pin the enemy flanks, now took up positions to prevent the retreat of the broken enemy, sometimes acting as an anvil against which the infantry and chariot units could drive the fleeing remnants. Once the enemy army broke ranks, the charioteers and cavalry singled out individual targets, rode them down and killed them.

An army of such size and complexity as Assyria's required a sophisticated logistics apparatus to support and supply it in the field. With few exceptions, such as the recruitment of horses mentioned earlier, we know very little about the organization of the logistics system. This being said, however, it is obvious that being forced to fight in so many different climates and types of terrain must have required a high degree of logistical flexibility and planning. The provincial system allowed the positioning of supplies near the borders in advance of a campaign, but once in enemy territory, the Assyrian army lived off the land and on captured enemy stores. This need for supplies explains the penchant of early armies to attack cities even when it made little tactical sense for them to do so. Like the armies that came after them, the Assyrians timed campaigns to take maximum advantage of the seasons to assure an adequate supply of food in captured areas.

Even when food and water were adequate, there remained the problem of transport. The spine of the supply transport system was the mule and the camel. So valuable were these animals that they took high priority as captured loot.[42] In the campaign against Egypt, the Assyrians used camels to cross the Saudi Desert to attack Palestine. The camel served another function as the main transport of the commercial caravan system. As caravan traders themselves, the Assyrians no doubt had maps of every trail, water hole and oasis of possible military use.

Military power is always slave to political events, and this fact brought about the end of the Assyrian Empire. In 668 BC, Ashurbanipal, the last great Assyrian king, ascended the throne upon the death of his father. He inherited an empire that had been weakened and overextended by constant border wars and suppressions of domestic revolts. The numerous captive peoples grew increasingly restless under the harsh rule of their Assyrian masters. Political control from the centre was weakened as auxiliary forces became more and more unreliable, even as they became more necessary to control frequent revolts.

In 664 BC, the Elamites sacked Babylon, only to do it again in 653. In 656 BC, Shamash-shum-ukin, the brother of Ashurbanipal, struck at the Assyrian throne by forming an alliance with Babylon, the Elamites, Arameans, Arabs and Egyptians against his brother. The result was a costly civil war that tore apart the army, pitting national and regional forces against one another. The period between 648 BC and the death of Ashurbanipal in 630 was marked by another civil war provoked by Ashurbanipal's sons fighting over the mantle of power.[43] The weakness at the political centre encouraged local governors and generals to pursue their own interests through revolts and corruption. The situation was compounded by a number of large-scale popular uprisings that occurred at the same time.

The end came in 612 BC when a coalition of Medean and Babylonian armies sacked Nineveh and destroyed what was left of the most powerful empire and army the world had ever seen. The destruction of Nineveh was complete, and a terrible vengeance was wrought upon the Assyrians. A biblical commentary captured the sense of terrible vengeance for all history:

> Cursed be the city of blood, full of lies, full of violence..The sound of the whip is heard, the gallop of horses, the rolling of chariots. An infinity of dead, the dead are everywhere! My anger is on thee, Nineveh, saith Jehovah … I will show thy nakedness to the nations and thy shame to the kingdoms. And then it will be said: Nineveh is destroyed! Who will mourn her?[44]

So complete was the destruction of the Assyrian capital that two centuries later, Xenophon and his Greek mercenary army of 10,000 men passed the ruins of Nineveh completely unaware that they were passing one of the great cities of the ancient world.[45] Not a single vestige of the city remained; it had disappeared from the face of the earth.

Chapter 18

Animals In War

The size of armies increased enormously during the Iron Age, along with the scope of the battles and length of campaigns they fought. Ancient armies had to master the task of supporting these larger armies in the field over greater distances and for longer periods. The most important supplies were, of course, food and water for the soldiers and the pack animals. The main means of moving supplies in antiquity was the animal pack train comprised of donkeys, mules, horses, oxen, camels and elephants in some appropriate mix. These animals were used either as draught animals (load-pullers) or pack animals (load bearers). Iron Age armies were as heavily dependent upon their pack animals as they were upon their fighting animals. No army of antiquity went to war without its war animals.

The number of pack and draught animals in the baggage trains of Iron Age armies was substantial. A Roman legion of 4,800 men had 1,400 mules,[1] or one animal for 3.4 men. This number of mules equalled the carrying capacity of 350 wagons.[2] By comparison, an American army of 10,000 men during the Mexican War (1844–1846) required 3,000 mules and 800 wagons.[3] General Sherman's American Civil War army (1864) of 100,000 men had 32,600 pack-mules and 5,180 wagons.[4] In ancient armies, the number of pack animals to be fed and watered included cavalry and chariot horses that also had to be cared for. The number of these animals was also substantial. An Indian field army during the Mahabharata period (400 BC) had 6,561 chariot horses and 19,683 cavalry horses.[5] At Arbela (331 BC, also known as Gaugamela), Darius III put 40,000 cavalry in the field, and at the Battle of the Hydaspes (326 BC) Alexander deployed 13,000 Macedonian cavalry and 18,500 mercenary cavalrymen recruited from Central Asia.[6]

Fodder for the animals was the largest logistical requirement of any army of the ancient period, often amounting to three times the amount of foodstuffs needed to feed the troops.[7] Ten thousand animals required 247 acres of acreage per day to obtain sufficient fodder,[8] and an army would quickly consume its supply of fodder in a few days if it didn't move. Livy tells us that armies often waited 'until there was an abundance of pasture in the fields' before undertaking a campaign.[9] At the Battle of Marathon, for example, Miltiades, the Greek commander, delayed giving battle for eight days. As each day passed, the Persian cavalry was forced to find another location to forage its horses, forcing it further and further from the battlefield. When Miltiades attacked eight days later, the Persian cavalry was so far from the battlefield that it could not take part in the battle.[10] No army could carry sufficient grain to feed its troops and fodder to feed its animals, so that finding sufficient fodder was an important concern in planning the route of march.

The Donkey

The donkey derives from the Nubian and Somalian subspecies of the African wild ass that was first domesticated around 3000 BC in Egypt.[11] The animal may have been first domesticated by pastoral people in Nubia. Donkeys quickly replaced the ox in ancient cultures, and the animal was vital to the development of long-distance trade across Egypt as a consequence of its ability to be ridden and carry goods. By 2675 BC, Egyptians employed large numbers of donkeys in agriculture, as dairy producers, meat animals, and transport and pack animals. The tomb of Pharaoh Hor-Aha, one of Egypt's earliest kings, contained the skeletons of ten donkeys buried in a manner usually reserved for high-ranking humans, indicating the high regard with which Egyptians held the animal.[12] By 1800 BC, the main breeding centre for donkeys had shifted to Mesopotamia. Damascus became famous for its breed of large white riding asses. It seems to have been the Greeks who introduced the animal to Europe sometime in the second millennium BC.[13]

The animal varies considerably in size from 30–63in in height and 180–1,060lb in weight. Donkeys have a life expectancy of twelve to fifty years, depending upon nutrition and how they are worked. The animal is commonly interbred with a horse to produce the mule. The donkey's reputation for stubbornness is attributed to its much stronger sense of self-preservation than exhibited in horses.[14] This stronger prey instinct makes it considerably more difficult to force or frighten a donkey into something it perceives as dangerous. The donkey was the most common transporter of goods in the civilian economies and military establishments of the ancient period. Properly equipped with pack saddles, panniers or wooden frames, a donkey can carry a 220lb load.[15]

The donkey has a number of characteristics to recommend it for military use. Compared to other pack animals, the donkey was cheap to purchase and raise, commonly available even on the march and an excellent source of high-calorie milk to supplement march rations. Old or injured animals could be butchered for meat. The animal's digestive system easily breaks down roughage and scrub plants that the horse cannot eat, so that the donkey can often feed itself by foraging. A donkey requires only half as much food per body weight as a horse, and its system is more efficient at converting food into energy.[16] The animal's hooves are more elastic than those of horses, and do not wear down as fast, giving them greater range on the march. Donkeys are herd animals, and will bond with other animals if no other donkeys can be found. Curiously, this makes the donkey an excellent watchdog, and it was often used to guard the herds of sheep and cattle that went along with armies on the march. Donkeys have the ability to calm horses, a trait that made them useful to the grooms that attended the cavalry and horse-drawn chariot brigades of antiquity. No army of the ancient period could move very far without its large horde of donkeys.

The Mule

The mule is the offspring of a male donkey (jack) and a female horse (mare). The Kashka peoples of Anatolia in the area of Phaphlagonia on the coast of the Black Sea and in Nicea on the south-western coast of Anatolia along the Sea of Marmara may have been the first to breed mules as a regular economy sometime around 1400 BC.[17] The *Iliad* mentions mules arriving from Henetia in Asia Minor, and hieroglyphic records reveal that the Egyptians preferred the mule to horses and camels as pack animals. The horse made its appearance in Egypt around 1680 BC when the Hyksos invaded the country with horse-drawn chariots. Mule breeding in Egypt probably did not begin until the Hyksos were driven out more than a century later. In the Old Testament, the mule replaced the donkey as the 'royal beast', and both King David and King Solomon rode them at their coronations. Muhammad commanded his army from atop a white mule.[18]

As a hybrid, the mule inherits and exhibits traits of each of its parents. From its sire, the mule inherits intelligence, sure-footedness, toughness, endurance and a natural cautiousness. From its dam, the mule acquires speed, size, ground-covering ability, conformation and agility. The mule is more intelligent than either of its parents, lives longer than the horse and is less obstinate than the donkey.[19] Depending upon the breed of its female parent, the mule can be bred to be larger than a horse, and to weigh over 1,000lb, and makes an excellent mount for cavalry.

As regards military use, the mule shows more patience, persistence and composure under stress and heavy weight. Their skin is tougher and less sensitive than that of horses, rendering them more capable of resisting sun and rain. Their hooves are harder than horses', they have stronger muscles and are less likely to come up lame, and they show a greater resistance to disease and insects than both the horse and donkey. The mule, like the horse, can be packed with dead weight at about 20 per cent of its body weight.[20] But the mule can live on coarser forage than the horse, and can forage en route on small shrubs, lichens and branch-laden tree foliage. Horses have to be fed on grass and grains, two feeds not usually found in abundance in harsh terrain when the army is on the move. The mule can obtain sufficient nutrition from foraging alone, and unlike the horse does not require the pack train to carry large amounts of high energy grains (oats, barley) and forage (hay, straw) to feed the horses. Freed of this burden, a mule pack train can carry considerably more cargo than a horse train.

Mules are relatively slow travellers, making only about 4–5 miles per hour, or slightly faster than a marching soldier. But the animal possesses incredible endurance, and can march continuously for ten to twelve hours.[21] A mule can easily travel 40 miles a day. In the nineteenth century, US Army mule trains could make 80–100 miles a day under forced march conditions.[22] The Romans were particularly fond of mules, and found that a mule-drawn wagon could make 19 miles a day.[23] During the Soviet war in Afghanistan, the Central Intelligence Agency transported weapons and supplies to the *mujahadeen* fighters on mule pack trains.[24] Mule trains are still being used by US forces in the current (2017) Afghan war.

The Camel

The camel was first domesticated in Arabia as early as the third millennium BC, where it had been used primarily as a source of food.[25] By 1000 BC, the animal had become a common load-bearing animal in the armies of the ancient Near East. Camels are more difficult to control than mules and horses, and have softer feet that make them unsuitable for mountainous or rocky terrain, but ideal for desert use and transport. The ability of the animal to endure long periods without water also makes them ideal for desert campaigns. The animal can consume up to 40 gallons of water at a time, which it stores in its stomach and not, as is commonly thought, its hump, which is comprised of fat upon which the animal draws for nutrition when forage is not available. The camel can go for very long periods, more than three weeks, between watering because of its unique metabolism. Most mammals, including humans, become dehydrated once they lose 15 per cent of their body's water. The camel can lose up to 25 per cent of its body water before becoming dehydrated.[26] The animal's mouth helps reduce water loss. The camel's thick coat reflects the sun, keeping it cool in hot climates. The camel's ability to retain water results in faeces so dry that they can be used as fuel for campfires for cooking and warmth in desert areas where wood is scarce. The campfire is an important source of warmth for soldiers in the cold desert night. The camels' nostrils are designed to retain water vapour that can be returned to the body of the animal. In windy conditions with blowing sand, the camel can close its nostrils completely. The nostrils close in between breaths, preventing sand from entering their lungs. Camels' eyes have three eyelids and two rows of eyelashes to keep out blowing sand.[27]

Other features make camels good military beasts. They can eat almost any vegetable or fauna they encounter. Their tough mouths are such that they can eat thorny twigs and other sharp plants that might cause injury to a horse or mule. With no need to transport forage or grains to feed them, camel pack trains can carry heavy loads for long distances without interruption. Outfitted with panniers, a camel can carry between 400–600lb.[28] When used as cavalry, the camel easily outperforms the horse, at least in desert or hot climates. A camel can run at speeds of 40 miles an hour, faster than a horse. As regards endurance, a camel can easily last longer than a horse or mule, and move up to 25 miles an hour almost all day long.[29] The armies of the Muslim Conquest used these characteristics of their mounts to move their armies much more quickly than the Roman armies, often allowing the Muslims to established ambushes into which the enemy fell by surprise. Camel milk has more iron and vitamin C than cows' milk, and is a good supplement for military rations. A camel that is severely injured on the march or dies from exhaustion can be butchered and eaten. One camel can provide food for ninety men.[30]

By 1200 BC, the camel had become the primary means of human and goods transport for the Arabian desert tribes that invented the use of the camel in war. The first recorded instance of Bedouin camel cavalry in war is recorded in the book of Exodus, when Amalekite camel cavalry archers attacked the Israelite column of march at Rephadim, and were driven off by Joshua and his men.[31] At the Battle of Karkar (853 BC), the Assyrian King Shalmaneser III fought a battle against a coalition of forces led by Hadadezer of Damascus in which Hadadezer's Arab Bedouin allies, led by Gindibu the Arab, fielded 1,000 archer-cavalrymen on camels.[32] This was the first recorded instance of camel cavalry in a regular army of the Near East. Xenophon tells us that Cyrus the Great of Persia at the Battle of Thymbra (547 BC) against Croesus of Lydia used his baggage camels as cavalry to frighten the Lydian horses.[33] Herodotus notes that sixty years later, Xerxes invaded Greece during the Second Persian Expedition with a huge army that contained Arab mercenary archers mounted on camels. The Romans did not use camels in any numbers until the Imperial period when, under Emperor Hadrian, they equipped some of their North African units (*Dromedarii*) in the desert provinces of Africa with the animal. Although never used extensively as an implement of war in either the ancient Near or Far East, camels were often used by the Persians and other armies as pack animals.[34]

All of the desert economies of the ancient period were heavily dependent upon the camel, including the long-distance trade to China. The military tradition of the camel lived on in Arabia, however, and re-emerged in the fifth century AD when camels were used to transport the infantry in the campaigns of Muhammad and his followers.[35] Subsequently, camels were used extensively by armies of the Muslim Conquest to transport troops in battles with the horse-mounted Sassanid and Byzantine armies.

The Elephant

Both types of elephants, the larger Asian elephant and smaller African forest elephant, have been used in war from early antiquity. The first elephants to be tamed for use in agriculture were the Asian elephants used by the Indus Valley Civilization in India, but the animals were not used in war until the Aryan period much later (950 BC). There is evidence of the elephant in China dating from early in the first millennium, and they were used in battle in the later part of the sixth century BC.[36] The animal never found an important place in Chinese warfare because they were rapidly becoming extinct in China. By the close of the fourth century BC, the elephant had disappeared in China.

The elephant roamed wild in Syria and Mesopotamia from early times. Egyptian records note that Pharaoh Thutmose III (1450 BC) hunted these animals at Niy in northern Syria on his way back from his Euphrates campaign.[37] Assyrian records tell us that King Tiglath Pileser I (1100 BC) killed ten elephants and captured four alive in a forest near the middle Euphrates region.[38] By 850 BC, human population growth, hunting and deforestation had driven the Syrian elephant to extinction.

The use of war elephants remained alive and well in India, and the animal was quickly adopted into the armies of the Persian invaders of the Punjab under Cyrus the Great. The first European military contact with the animal occurred at the Battle of Gaugamela (331 BC) between the Persians and Alexander the Great. It was the first time Western troops had encountered the animal, and it struck fear in the hearts of Alexander's soldiers. Fortunately, the elephants had been driven to fatigue on the march, so when the battle began, they left their place in the centre of the line and retreated to the baggage train, expecting to be fed. Alexander's victory opened his way to Persia and India, and he incorporated a significant number of elephants in his army.

Alexander faced war elephants again at the Battle of the Hydaspes River (326 BC). It is possible that the Macedonian troops' terrifying experience with the elephant in that battle provoked the mutiny that forced Alexander to abandon his plans to invade India. Greek spies had reported that Porus was only a minor king, and that one of the kings that awaited Alexander across the river, Xandrames, had mobilized 4,000 elephants to oppose the Macedonians.[39] Worse, the Nanda king could deploy another 6,000 animals against him. Alexander abandoned his plans to invade India and turned back.

Alexander's successors, the Diadochi, used large numbers of elephants in their wars against each other in Asia during their struggle over Alexander's empire. The first use of elephants in Europe was in 318 BC, when Polyperchon, one of Alexander's generals, used the animals in the siege of Megalopolis. The siege failed, and Cassander captured the animals which he transported by sea, and were used in other battles in Greece.[40] The wars in Greece prompted the Ptolemies of Egypt and the Carthaginians to incorporate large elephant corps into their armies, where they replaced the chariot. At the crucial Battle of Raphia (217 BC), Ptolemy's elephants played a key role in his victory. The elephants used in the West were mostly the smaller North African forest elephants.

The introduction of the animal to wars in the western Mediterranean is owed to the Epirot king, Pyrrhus. He brought twenty elephants to the battle at Heracles (280 BC), driving the Romans from the field with his animals. A year later, Pyrrhus attacked the Romans at the Battle of Asculum. The Romans came prepared with flame weapons, ox-drawn wagons with long spikes, pots of fire and light infantry troops to attack the animals with javelins. The day was finally carried when Pyrrhus' elephants broke the Roman line in a final charge. Pyrrhus suffered very high casualties, however: a Pyrrhic victory.

Elephants played a significant role in the First Punic War (264–241 BC) when the Carthaginians used them at the Battle of Abyss (255 BC), at Panormus (251 BC) and the Battle of Tunis (255 BC), where a charge of Carthaginian elephants disrupted the Roman legions, allowing the Carthaginians to carry the day. During the Second Punic War (218–201 BC), Hannibal crossed the Alps and invaded Italy with a contingent of thirty-seven elephants in his army. Only a handful survived the winter crossing, but they played an important role in the Battle of the Trebia River, where Hannibal first defeated the Romans. In the southern Italian campaign, Carthage managed to smuggle ten elephants through the Roman naval blockade to strengthen Hannibal's army. It was to no avail, and Hannibal was forced to withdraw to Africa. At the Battle of Zama (202 BC), Hannibal deployed eighty elephants against Scipio Africanus' Roman infantry. When the beasts charged, the Roman ranks opened, allowing the elephants to pass harmlessly through their infantry lines. The Roman infantry charged, broke the Carthaginian reserve and killed more than 20,000 Carthaginians.[41] Only eleven elephants died at Zama. Scipio took the rest back to Rome, where they were integrated into the Roman army as special combat units.

Although not well-known, the Romans used elephants extensively in their wars following the Punic Wars. The conquest of Greece saw the use of the animal in many battles, including the invasion of Macedonia (199 BC), Battle of Cynoscephalae (197 BC), Battle of Thermopylae (191 BC) and Battle of Magnesia (190 BC). In 168 BC, the Romans deployed twenty-two elephants at the Battle of Pydna, and in a bit of historical irony, the Romans used elephants to destroy the Carthaginian army at the Battle of Carthage in 146 BC. The Romans captured Carthage, massacred the population and set the great city on fire. The blaze lasted for seventeen days. The last significant use of the elephant by the Romans was by Metellus Scipio at the Battle of Thapsus (46 BC) against Julius Caesar, who armed his Fifth legion with axes and ordered them to strike at the elephants' legs.[42] The legion withstood the elephant charge, and the elephant became the legion's symbol. Thapsus was the last significant use of the war elephant in the West.[43]

Elephants live for about seventy years, but cannot be trained for war until they are 20 years old, by which time they have reached full body size and strength, and have become accustomed to being around humans. At full growth, an Asian elephant stands 13ft at the shoulders, and can weigh 15,000lb. The animal is very strong and sure-footed, and can negotiate steep and rough ground that would cripple a horse or a mule. On the march, elephants walk at 3–4 miles per hour, and cover 20 miles a day carrying a heavy load. Without a load, the animal can cover 40 miles a day.[44] At the charge, elephants can run at 20 miles an hour. Elephants have terrible eyesight, and cannot see a man more than 50 yards away.

Elephants were used in four ways in ancient battles. They can act as a screen against enemy cavalry by being deployed on the flanks or to the rear of the infantry to prevent envelopment or cavalry attack from the rear. Most often, elephants have been used to attack and disrupt enemy infantry formations by rushing headlong into the enemy line. Unlike horses, which will not crash into an infantry line, elephants have no such hesitation. Elephants can also be used to break through fortified positions and destroy obstacles to the infantry's advance. The main difficulty in their use in war is getting them to the battlefield in shape to fight. On the march, an elephant consumes 300–400lb of fodder, fruits and grain a day, or about 10 per cent of its body weight. The animal also requires enormous quantities of water, some 18–26 gallons a day under normal use, but under heat and stress, 40–50 gallons a day are needed.[45] To supply twenty elephants on the march requires hundreds of soldiers, pack animals and carts to transport feed and water for the animals. Failure to provide sufficient water to the animal can be disastrous.

The elephant has great difficulty releasing body heat, and is extremely susceptible to heat stroke. If the animal is not provided for adequately, it becomes irritated and difficult to control, and its use in battle becomes unpredictable. At Gaugamela, Darius had fifteen elephants deployed in the centre of the line. Fatigued from the long march and not sufficiently fed or watered, the elephants abandoned their positions when the battle began and walked to the rear. Alexander found them gathered around the baggage train waiting to be fed. Once ancient armies learned how to deal with the tactical application of the elephant by simply opening ranks and allowing the animals to pass harmlessly through the infantry, or equipping special teams with axes or long spears to cut their leg tendons or stab their eyes, or simply waving flags or blowing trumpets to frighten the animal, the elephant's value as a battle asset declined. As armies incorporated their elephant units into their own armies, and soldiers and horses became familiar with the elephant, the psychological impact of the animal's presence on the battlefield disappeared.

As noted above, the last use of the elephant in war in the West was at the Battle of Thapsus. The animal's use in war continued undiminished in Asia, however, where even the effects of the modern rifle did not curtail its use. It took the modern cannon to finally drive the elephant from the battlefield. Viet Cong units used elephants as logistics animals in the heavily jungled areas of

Vietnam. This led to the elephants being declared legitimate military targets by the US Air Force, and hundreds of the poor beasts were killed by air strikes.

The Horse

The earliest domestication of the horse occurred in the fourth millennium BC on the Pontic steppe, the large area of grasslands in far Eastern Europe, located north of the Black Sea, Caucasus Mountains and Caspian Sea, and including parts of modern Ukraine, southern Russia and north-west Kazakhstan. The Indo-European peoples of this region practised a form of pastoralism that required their cattle herds to be moved frequently to feed them sufficiently. Capturing wild horses, learning to ride them and then to hitch them to carts made this mobile form of pastoralism possible. The Indo-Europeans gradually became a warrior culture centred around the early horse-drawn chariot.

Sometime around 2000 BC, the Indo-Europeans began a great movement of peoples out of the Pontic steppe, first south-west into Europe and then south-east into the Middle East and due east into India. The Hittites were the first to arrive in Anatolia, followed by the Mitanni, sometime around 2000–1800 BC. These Indo-European horse and chariot-borne warriors imposed themselves upon the local inhabitants, becoming the dominant culture in Anatolia. Thus was the horse and chariot introduced to the Near East, from where it spread throughout Europe. Improvements in technologies to control the horse and in chariot design and weapons turned the chariot into a major mechanism of war that dominated the battlefield for the next 1,000 years.

The horse had been known in Asia and the Near East for more than a millennium before anyone thought to use it as an instrument of war in a manner separate from the chariot. The animal had been domesticated and ridden in India during the era of the Indus Valley civilizations (third–fourth millennium BC). The Hittites imported Mitanni horse trainers and used the horse to carry messengers in war.[46] There are also references in Assyrian records to Urartu and Ethiopian soldiers riding horses.[47] The *Rig Veda* refers to Vedic horsemen fighting on horseback, but not as cavalry units.[48] Training horses for chariot teams required grooms who were riding other horses. Thus, military men had been riding around on horses for a very long time before anyone thought of using soldiers on horses as implements of war.

The chariot dominated the ancient battlefield from 1800 BC until the ninth century BC, when it began to be replaced by horse cavalry. Several reasons account for the decline of the chariot as a battlefield weapon. First, chariots were very expensive to maintain. The cost of the chariot itself and the horses was not unreasonable, but that was only a small part of the overall expense.[49] Horses had to be fed, and in most countries of the Near East there were no grasslands so horses had to be fed on grain. It required the grain output of approximately 9 acres of land to feed a single horse for a year. Other costs included stables, grooms, armour and equipment. Second, training charioteers for war was a full-time occupation maintained at government expense. Since charioteers had no other function, maintaining large numbers of them was a significant burden on the military budget. Armour for a charioteer was also very expensive. Third, chariots were fragile machines requiring large numbers of craftsmen to keep the vehicles in fighting trim. Fourth, the chariot was unable to traverse uneven terrain, greatly reducing its scope of tactical application. The chariot's dominance of the battlefields of India for almost 1,000 years came to an end once the Aryans began to push out beyond the Ganga plains, encountering thick forests and jungles where the chariot was useless. It was then that the elephant began to replace the chariot as the primary battlefield 'vehicle' in India.[50]

It was the Assyrians who invented the new combat arm of horse cavalry. The new 'cavalrymen' still fought in the manner of the old chariot system of driver and archer, operating in pairs with one 'charioteer' riding his horse while holding the reins of another, upon which sat the chariot archer with his composite bow. The 'charioteer' managed both horses, leaving the archer free to concentrate on shooting, just as if he were in a chariot.[51] The 'charioteer' was armed with a spear, and both he and the archer wore the standard armour, helmet and other equipment of the Assyrian chariot team. The cavalry team used the same horse harness and bit used for chariot horses. The Assyrians used these cavalry teams for almost fifty years before the individual horseman armed with either spear or bow made his appearance during the reign of Tiglath-Pileser III (745–727 BC), giving rise to the true horse cavalryman.

The value of cavalry to ancient armies was that they could do everything a chariot could do and more. Cavalry could act as reconnaissance scouts and range further afield and over rougher terrain than could the chariot. On the march, cavalry units could move further and faster in a day than chariots, and provide flank security through forested terrain where chariots could not go. Without the horseshoe, horses in antiquity often went lame, but far less so than when they operated in chariot teams. Cavalry horses were put out of action far less often than chariot horses, which were useless when the chariot broke down. A single cavalryman armed with the lance and bow provided more firepower than a chariot crew, which often needed a shield bearer and driver along with the archer or spearman. Cavalry could manoeuvre much more quickly than chariots on the battlefield, and their ability to assemble and reassemble for attack after attack made cavalry a far more flexible combat instrument than chariots.

Still, the chariot remained a part of most ancient armies to the end of antiquity. The original identification of the chariot as the vehicle of kings and nobles, along with the high status the charioteer had acquired over centuries, enticed armies to keep the chariot around in small numbers for centuries after it had lost any real value as a weapon of war.

In no army of antiquity, with the exception of that of Philip II of Macedon and, later, Alexander, was cavalry used as the combat arm of decision.[52] In Assyria, Persia, Carthage, Classical Greece, India, China and Republican Rome, the infantry remained the combat arm of decision for centuries after the cavalry made their appearance. In India, cavalry never acquired important status, first being subordinate to the chariot and then to the elephant corps of Indian armies. Mounted warriors did not make their appearance in China until at least the fifth century BC,[53] and it was another two centuries before cavalry was used routinely by Chinese armies.[54] It was not until the reign of Diocletian (AD 284–305) that the Romans finally adopted large cavalry forces, the heavily armoured *cataphracti*, to meet the mobile threat of invasion from barbarian horsemen. By Constantine's time (AD 306–337), one in every three soldiers in the Roman army was a cavalryman, and cavalry became the Roman army's most important and powerful combat arm.

But why did horse cavalry not play a more important role in the tactics of the armies of antiquity? Several reasons, some cultural and others technical, suggest themselves. The lack of a firm saddle and stirrups made it almost impossible for a cavalryman to wield his lance or spear effectively without being knocked from his horse by the force of impact. Mounted on saddle-cloths and without stirrups, encumbered with lance, sword and shield, most horsemen were unable to remain mounted, and tumbled to the ground, where they continued to fight on foot.[55] To become an effective combat arm, cavalry had to await the invention of the saddle and stirrup, something which did not occur in the Near East or West until around the sixth century AD, when both were introduced by the Hun invaders.[56] Nor, for the same reasons, could cavalry engage at the gallop. The instability of the horseman on the animal's back made it difficult for him to wield his bow with any accuracy. The shock power and lethality of later Medieval cavalry made possible by the introduction of the high-backed saddle and the stirrup were absent in the cavalry units of antiquity. The appearance of cavalry on the ancient battlefield forced infantry formations to find ways of dealing with them, all of which resulted in the infantry being better able to defend themselves. The Persian, Macedonian, Assyrian and Classical Greek armies deployed very dense infantry formations that were invulnerable to cavalry as long as they retained their integrity.

It is one of the interesting questions of military history why it was that the horse persisted as the dominant war animal in the armies of antiquity, when it is clear that they are less hardy biologically, have weaker legs, have a greater tendency to panic, are much more difficult to sustain nutritionally on the march (and in garrison for that matter), are less intelligent, more susceptible to disease and injury, have softer hooves that wear out faster, suffer greater injuries from more frequent falls, are less sure footed and have less endurance than the mule. This fragility was clearly on display during the First World War, when the armies employed thousands of horses and mules. In that conflict, for every mule that became debilitated, five horses were lost to the same causes. For every mule that suffered from or died from intestinal disorders, no fewer than eight horses were afflicted in the same way. Most mules that died during the First World War were killed by enemy fire rather than from exhaustion or sickness that killed most horses.[57] Except for the ability to gallop instead of ramble, and the ability to jump over fences or ditches, there appear to have been no real advantages to having horse instead of mule cavalry.

Why, then, did the horse persist as the dominant war animal in ancient armies? Perhaps it was that the horse became strongly identified with the conquerors who introduced the animal and the chariot to the Near East and Europe. Additionally, the horse became identified with the ruling nobility. The *maryannu* system of chariot warfare that dominated the period involved only nobles as horsemen. The horse was also a symbol of virility, a fact that led the animal to often be portrayed in statues and bas relief with intact, but anatomically forwardly misplaced, genitalia so as to be visible to the viewer, when most chariot horses were in fact geldings. Whatever the reason, the horse remained the dominant war animal throughout most of Western history.

Chapter 19

Buddha's Military Experience and PTSD

It is one of the more interesting curiosities of military history that three of the four founders of the world's major religions – Moses, Muhammad and Buddha – were soldiers. It will probably come as a surprise to many to learn that the founder of Buddhism was also a soldier. The ancient accounts of Buddha's early life tell the story of a child born to a powerful Indian king named Suddhodana. It was prophesied that the boy, named Siddhartha Gautama, would become either a great king or a great teacher. To prevent Gautama from giving up the pleasures of this world and becoming a teacher, Suddhodana raised his son in great luxury, preventing him from witnessing the evils of the world. One day, the tale continues, Siddhartha ventured beyond the palace grounds with his charioteer, where he came upon an old man, a sick man and a dying man. He was shocked by the realization that he, too, might suffer their fate, and resolved to become an ascetic and discover how he might escape the cycle of perpetual rebirth that Indians believed to be the central affliction of humanity. At 29, Siddhartha left his wife and child, slipped past the palace guards and began a life of wandering and contemplation that lasted until his death at age 80. His teachings were written down centuries later, and became the scriptures of the Buddhist religion.[1]

This tale was first encountered by Marco Polo, but written texts of the account did not reach the West until late in the eighteenth century.[2] The story remains the generally accepted account of Buddha's early life. It is, however, largely inaccurate, and fails to account for the historical and sociological circumstances of the age in which Buddha lived. The images of Buddha are often misleading as well. By the time the first images of Buddha reached the West in the eighteenth century, Buddhism had spread through Asia, where these images had taken on the racial and ethnic characteristics of the different peoples of the region. Indian portrayals often show Buddha as dark-skinned, while those of other countries show him as oriental. In fact, Buddha was an Indo-Aryan, a Caucasian whose people had invaded and subjugated India for two millennia. Familiar Western portrayals of Buddha as doughy and overweight, an image intended to portray his passive character, are also misleading. The oldest texts describe him as at least 6ft tall and of muscular build. One obtains a more ethnically accurate picture of Buddha by looking at a modern Afghan: tall, muscular, white-skinned, with dark hair and eyes, physical characteristics typical of the Indo-Aryan warriors from whom Siddhartha

Gautama was descended. The Macedonian Greeks described these same physical characteristics as typical of the Indo-Aryans they fought during Alexander's Indian campaign.[3]

The original home of the Aryans was southern Russia, in what is now the far eastern and northern Ukraine. Probably provoked by overpopulation, a great migration of these peoples began sometime around 1800 BC, first south to Europe, then south-east into Anatolia and northern Iraq, and then further east into the mountains of Iran and the valleys of Afghanistan and Pakistan. A fierce warlike people, the Aryans introduced the horse and chariot to warfare. Wherever they conquered, their superior military technology and fighting ability allowed them to impose themselves as a warrior aristocracy upon native, less advanced peoples. From north-west India, the Aryans moved south along the Indus River, destroying the native Indus Valley civilization. Over the next 1,000 years, the Aryans conquered most of India, bringing the Ganges River plain and north-east Bengal under their control only a century or so before Buddha was born.[4]

The Aryans regarded war as the most noble calling, and all able-bodied males were trained in war from childhood. By the seventh century BC, the Aryans had settled throughout India, imposing themselves upon a large population of indigenous peoples that tilled the land. To maintain their superior position, the Aryans forbade intermarriage with the dark-skinned aboriginal peoples, and restricted their place and roles in society. Over time, Indo-Aryan society became organized into four castes: *brahmans* (priests), *kshatriya* (warriors), *vaisya* (merchants and farmers) and *sudra* (serfs), the latter comprised mostly of the conquered indigenous population.

By the sixth century BC, the Aryan tribes had coalesced into organized states with large standing armies and governmental administrative systems. This was the age of the *mahajanapadas*, sixteen major states organized as monarchies, oligarchies and republics that frequently fought one another to establish regional empires.[5] Two of these states, Kosala and Maghada, were the main rivals in Bengal during Buddha's lifetime. They fought frequent wars until Kosala was destroyed and absorbed into the Maghada Empire. The major states also fought wars with the smaller republics. These republics often formed alliances to prevent their absorption by the larger states.

Siddhartha Gautama (563–483 BC), known to history as the Buddha, or 'the enlightened one', was born in the Indo-Aryan Sakya republic in the foothills of the Himalayas north of the Ganges River, in the province of north-east India known today as Bengal. The Aryan republics (*samghas*) of Buddha's day were tribal kingdoms (*rashtra*) governed by an oligarchy of nobles (*sabha*) led by a warrior chief. The *rashtra* was comprised of tribes (*jana*), sub-tribes (*vish*) and villages (*grama*). The nucleus of the tribe was the family (*kula*), with the oldest male as its head

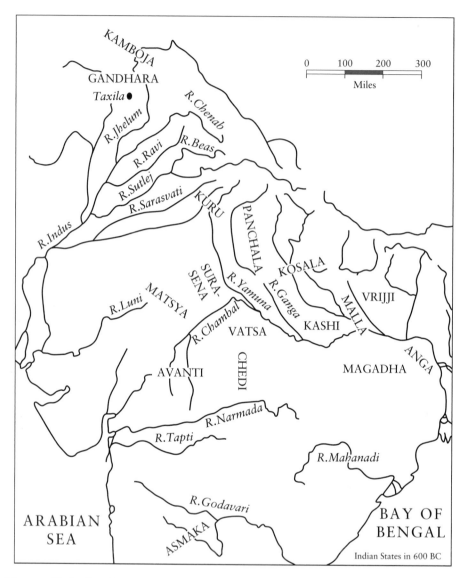

Figure 21: Indian States circa 600 BC

(*kulapa*).[6] The Sakya social organization was closer to the traditional organization of the earlier Aryan tribes than to the more complex social organization of the newly emerged *mahajanapanda* states. Although Buddha's father is portrayed in the scriptures as a mighty king living in great luxury, he was in fact a warrior chief, or *raja*, a term equivalent to the Latin *rex*. Although the office had originally depended upon consent of the nobles, by Buddha's day the position of chief had become hereditary.[7] All able-bodied men were trained for war, and were led in battle by a professional warrior caste called *kshatriyas*. The warrior chief personally commanded the army in battle.

Although the republics were smaller than the new states, they were not insignificant military powers.[8] The texts record that the Sakyas comprised 160,000 families, and that their capital at Kapila-vastu on the banks of the Rhoni River (modern Kohana) was surrounded by seven defensive walls. Other towns were also fortified. Kapila-vastu was the location of a famous school of archery for training troops. The country was about the size of modern Belgium. Besides having to contend with the predations of Kosala and Magadha, both of which sought to control the Ganges River plain, the Sakyas were surrounded by other republics that were often hostile. As with the larger states of India at this time, war was an almost constant occurrence for the Sakyas.

Buddha was the son of the *raja* of the Sakyas, a people 'of great heroes', as Buddha himself describes them. According to the Aryan rule of primogeniture, as the oldest son of the chief, Buddha was expected to succeed his father.[9] The ancient texts tell us that like all *kshatriya* men, Buddha was trained from a very young age to be a soldier. The term *kshatriya* means 'noble warrior'. He was taught the alphabet and numbers at age 3. By the age of 6 he entered the formal educational and military training programme that lasted until he was 16.[10] The curriculum included courses in logic, politics and economics. *Kshatriyas* also studied the ancient Vedic religious texts, but were only required to memorize the first line of the Vedas. For over a decade, the young warrior was subjected to a rigorous curriculum of studies and military training that required proficiency in all the Aryan weapons of war, including handling the chariot, warhorse and elephant.[11]

The weapons curriculum was called the *Dhanur Veda*. Buddha's instructors were professional tutors, and military subjects were taught by experienced warriors. Instruction was personalized, students living in the homes of their instructors for the duration of the course of study. Special tutors called *sutas* recited the *Itihasa*s to the student at fixed times during each day. The *Itihasas* were the historical accounts of the exploits of great warriors and battles of the past. Great stress was placed upon accustoming the student to discipline, hardship and endurance.[12]

At age 11, the young warrior underwent the important rite of *upanayana*, or 'second birth', whereby the boy was recognized as a full member of his class. This rite was very ancient, having its origins in a time before the Aryans invaded India. The youth was dressed in the clothing of an ascetic, and carried a staff in his hand. It was then that the *yajnopavita*, or 'sacred thread', was hung over his right shoulder and under his left arm. He was expected to wear the thread continuously for the rest of his life.[13]

The Aryans believed that luxury weakened the spirit required of a warrior. Before being consecrated as a knight at age 16, the young soldier was required to demonstrate his competence with weapons. If he passed the test, he was also given the special dress of the *kshatriya* warrior fashioned of dyed flax cloth, and a girdle of *munja* grass adorned with pieces of iron.[14] The consecrated warrior was now allowed to take part in war, and enjoy the privilege of rendering and receiving the military salute. He was also allowed to marry, although only within his caste, a requirement enforced by the Aryans to keep themselves separate and racially distinct from the darker-skinned conquered peoples.

Ravana in Full Battle Array. (1) Dagger axe, (2) club, (3) mace, (4) lasso, (5) metal trident spear, (6) crescent axe, (7) cane arrow, (8) incendiary arrow, (9) unknown, (10) bronze leaf-point javelin, (11) iron-tipped spear, (12) sickle-sword, (13) sword, (14) battle-axe, (15) trident dagger, (16) club, (17) stimulum (?), (18) composite bow.

Figure 22: Ravanna and the Full Array of Aryan Weapons

The texts are clear that Buddha went through the *kshatriya* ceremony of becoming a warrior. When Buddha was 16, his father announced that his son would become his heir apparent. The accounts tell us that Buddha was required to demonstrate his martial prowess by a display of weapons drill. He had to demonstrate competence in the 'twelve tests', including proficiency with the bow, sword, spear, lasso, iron-dart, club, battle-axe, thrown iron discus and trident. Also included were fencing, swimming, wrestling, hand-to-hand combat, horsemanship and shooting the bow from a moving chariot. The texts say that Buddha passed with flying colours, was named heir apparent, and that the nobles were satisfied that he was capable of leading them in war. A short time later, he married his cousin. Buddha was now a *kshatriya* warrior.[15]

The ancient Aryan law texts are clear that a warrior was forbidden to give up the military life and take up a life of asceticism, as Buddha later did after leaving his father's court at the age of 29. The texts note that even then he left on his war horse, Kanthaka, and carrying his broadsword, his hair still worn in the warrior's top-knot. As a member of the *kshatriya* caste, Buddha was also forbidden to pursue any other profession except that of the solider.[16] Military life was an all-consuming profession for the Indo-Aryans. The *Samyutta* scripture tells us that, 'For the *kshatriya* there is no other rule but to fight', and the *Adi Parva* that, 'among men, the highest duties are those performed by the *kshatriya*'. The Aryan gods were warrior gods, like *Indra* who helped the warrior in battle, and *Agni*, the fire-god, loved for the blessing of fire with which to destroy enemy strongholds. The entire weight of Indo-Aryan religious sanction and social conditioning required warriors to fight. Being born warriors and prohibited from taking up other professions, the *kshatriya* were impatient of peace. It was this 'psychological barrenness of peace' that led to many wars in India's long history.[17] War was a fundamental function of the Aryan state, and waging it was the primary responsibility of the *kshatriya* caste.

The code of the *kshatriya* required that the soldier die gloriously in battle, for only then could he attain salvation (*moksha*) and enter paradise (*swarg*), freeing him from the cycle of rebirth and suffering. Cowardice was punished by death. Offenders were stoned or beaten to death, or wrapped in grass and set on fire. Senior officers who showed a lack of resolve were required to dress in women's clothes until the public disgrace drove them to suicide. To live long enough to die in bed was a sin. Many warriors, of course, did die in bed. Under these circumstances, the dying warrior was laid upon a bed of *kusa* grass, and his body cut with a sword as special prayers were said over him. In this manner, the hero was permitted to achieve heaven.[18] After a battle, the dead were gathered and cremated in a huge funeral pyre. The wives of the dead climbed upon the pyre, and were burnt with the corpses of their men (*suttee*). This custom was still being practised in India when the British put an end to it in the colonial era.[19]

Against this background, some key elements of the story of Buddha's early life can be questioned. First, it is clear that the story of Buddha being raised in luxury by his warrior chief father cannot be true. The *kshatriyas* regarded luxury as a sin. If Buddha had been raised in this manner, he would never have been able to become a warrior, which would have made it impossible for him to succeed his father. Second, it is also clear that as the oldest son of a *kshatriya* aristocratic family and the son of an Aryan chief, Buddha must have been trained from childhood as a soldier, as all Aryan males of his caste were. He would have had no choice in the matter. Had he failed to meet the warrior standard, he would have been relegated to a life of obscurity and never anointed as his father's heir. Third, during Buddha's life north-east India was wracked by frequent wars. While Buddha was still alive, the Sakya republic was attacked and its entire population massacred, and we hear no more of the people which produced the greatest of the Indians. While we have no accounts of Buddha's activities from age 16 when he became a warrior knight until he left home at 29, it is all but certain that he experienced the horrors of war as a soldier in the Sakya army. There is no reason to believe that Buddha did not behave in the manner expected of a *kshatriya* warrior, including going to war, before he left his father's house. It is inconceivable that the son of the warrior chief and heir apparent would not have accompanied his father into battle.

We have only fragmentary information regarding the Sakya wars that occurred during Buddha's lifetime in which he would have participated. There seems to have been some sort of revolt of the smaller tribal republics in which the Sakyas, Koloyas, Moriyas and Mallas attempted to break free of the influence of the larger Kosalan state.[20] These event caused an almost continuous state of simmering conflict between the Sakas and the Kosalans that persisted off and on until the Kosalans finally exterminated the Sakyas during Buddha's lifetime. When Buddha was 24 years old and a member of the tribal council, a conflict broke out between the Sakyas and the neighbouring Colias over irrigation rights to the Rohini River that formed the boundary between the two states. A series of serious battles and skirmishes took place over the next four years in which both sides suffered significant casualties.[21] It is likely that Buddha participated in some of these skirmishes.

We are left to explain why Buddha abandoned his wife and child, and left his father's court to embrace the life of a wandering ascetic. Whatever caused Buddha to do this must have been some sort of traumatic event. The story that he was shocked by his first encounter with a sick man, an old man and a dying man is hardly credible, though it may contain a kernel of truth. One possibility is that Buddha's war experiences may have rendered him a psychological casualty.

The accounts of Buddha's wanderings for the six years after he left home reveal a soldier suffering from symptoms that a modern psychiatrist would associate with post-traumatic stress disorder (PTSD).[22] He abandoned his wife, child and extended family (disruption of traditional social ties), and cut off the top-knot of his hair, the distinguishing mark of his warrior caste (alienation). He took off his uniform and donned the saffron robe worn by condemned criminals on their way to execution (identification with the guilty and damned). He found his way into a forest, where he wandered, sometimes with others, other times alone (aimlessness). During this time, he inflicted what the texts call 'tortures' upon himself (self-destructive behaviour), going without food until he looked like a skeleton. He rarely ate (lack of appetite), and one text says he was so thin that his stomach touched his spine (anorexia). He remained silent for long periods, often falling into deep trances (fugue states/disorientation), and suffered from disturbing dreams about battles with demons (night terrors). Buddha was homeless during this time, and slept outdoors.[23]

After six years of this penitent existence, Buddha encountered a young girl who brought him a bowl of milk and rice. He came to the realization that his life of self-inflicted suffering was not the way to achieve nirvana and relief from the birth-death-rebirth cycle. He renounced asceticism for what he called 'the middle path', left the forest and began a new life as a wandering teacher. Buddha went on to live a long life, travelling through the Gangetic Plain and southern Nepal, attracting converts and establishing schools and monasteries to support the new faith. This activity speaks to his likely recovery from post-traumatic stress disorder. It is worth noting that Buddha's founding of a new religious practice, complete with initiation rites, theology, monastic rules and institutions, is not without its modern equivalent. Soldiers recovering from severe psychological trauma often turn to some form of religiosity as part of their redemption from suffering and return to normality.[24]

It may have been Buddha's war experiences that also led him to renounce the warrior caste into which he had been born. The central ethical claim of the *kshatriya* was that the warrior protected the society, and his selfless service and glorious death in battle gained him salvation and paradise. Buddha rejected this claim in the *Samyutta* when he admonished a soldier that death in battle did not bring the soldier salvation at all. Instead, Buddha asserted that the soldier would be reborn as an animal or suffer the purgatory of yet another life, directly challenging the moral legitimacy of the warrior class. Buddha also forbade soldiers to join the monastery (*sangha*). Others forbidden to join were criminals, slaves and lepers. Placing *kshatriya* warriors in the company of the outcasts of Aryan society demonstrates Buddha's strong rejection of the warrior caste and its ethos. Monastic rules also forbade monks from visiting an army that had marched out of its camp preparing to fight. A monk could visit a military camp if he had good reason, but could stay no longer than three days. Monks were also forbidden to attend mock combats or military reviews. Along with the well-known Buddhist pacifism and rejection of war per se, Buddha rejected the very notion of the warrior class as possessing any moral legitimacy. Simply by virtue of being a soldier, the soldier violated many of the basic ethical principles of Buddhism.

It may have been Buddha's public rejection of the moral legitimacy of the *kshatriya* that led to the attempts on his life. As Buddhism gained popularity, it was said that many soldiers joined the movement, although not as monks. Buddha's teaching may have been seen as a threat to the fighting elan of the warrior class, as well as to the caste system itself, which he also rejected. Sometime after 491 BC, several attempts were made to kill Buddha. The texts imply that it was Buddha's cousin and second-in-command, Devadatta, who conspired with King Ajatashatru of Maghada to carry out the plot.[25] If the popularity of Buddhism was indeed eroding the moral status and martial spirit of the warrior caste, then Ajatashatru, a paracide who came to the throne by murdering his father and was engaged in a protracted war at the time, may have had reason to neutralize Buddha.

As it was, Buddha died in 483 BC. The circumstances of his death remain somewhat suspicious, however, and murder cannot be entirely ruled out. Buddha visited the town of Kushingara and took to sleeping in a grove. A person named Chunda came to him and offered to feed him. This in itself was not unusual, since monks routinely received food from people who offered it to gain merit. The texts tell us that Buddha ate the meal at Chunda's house and immediately became violently ill and died.[26] The suddenness with which he was stricken and succumbed suggests the possibility of poisoning. The most likely suspect again was Ajatashatru, who was still at war and had committed genocide against the Sakyas, Buddha's people, only a few years before. It is interesting that the destruction of the Sakyas (about 490 BC) seems to have occurred about the same time that the first failed attempts to assassinate Buddha took place.

Modern medical analysis, however, suggests that Buddha may have died from mesenteric infarction, a condition accompanied by acute abdominal pain and the passage of blood, symptoms attributed to Buddha in the Pali Canon and commonly found among the elderly. Mesenteric infarction is caused by an obstruction of the blood vessels of the mesentery, that part of the intestinal wall that binds the intestinal tract to the abdominal cavity, and results in a laceration of the intestinal wall.[27] The condition causes massive blood loss, and is usually lethal. If the modern medical analysis is correct, Buddha died a natural death from old age.

We are forced to glimpse the life of Buddha through the dark and clouded glass of time, where reliable material sources are only partially extant or lacking completely. The task of discovery is not made easier by the tendency of Buddha's followers to express the relevant information about the subject in mythic and even supernatural terms. It is still possible, if somewhat speculative, to examine the ancient accounts of Buddha's life, while interpreting them within the context of the known history and sociology of the times, and reach reasonable conclusions about what the facts may be. On this basis, it seems likely that the usually accepted story of Buddha's life is questionable on a number of key points that are at least worthy of reconsideration, if we are ever to understand the man who created one of the world's great religions.

Chapter 20

Philip II of Macedon: Greater Than Alexander

Philip II of Macedonia (382–336 BC), father of Alexander the Great, dynastic heir to the Agead kings who traced their lineage to Herakles (Hercules in Latin), son of the Temenid family from Argos that had ruled Macedonia since the eighth century BC, unifier of Greece, author of Greece's first federal constitution, creator of the first national state in Europe, the first general of the Greek imperial age, founder of Europe's first great land empire and Greece's greatest general, was one of the pre-eminent statesmen of the ancient world. It was Philip who saved Macedonia from disintegration, military occupation and eventual destruction by defeating and securing it against external enemies, bringing into existence an entirely new form of political organization in the West, Europe's first national territorial state.[1] Having made Macedonia safe, Philip developed mining, agriculture, urbanization, trade, commerce and Greek culture to transform a semi-feudal, tribal pastoral society into a centralized national state governed by a powerful monarchy and protected by a modern army.

Philip achieved all this over a twenty-three-year reign marked by a programme of territorial expansion and military conquest, in the process creating a Macedonian army that revolutionized warfare in Greece and became the most effective fighting force the Western world had yet seen. A brave combat officer, Philip was wounded no less than five times, wounds that left him blind in one eye, paralyzed in one leg and with only limited use of his left hand. Through shrewd statecraft and military force, Philip doubled the size of Macedonia and incorporated most of the Balkans into the Macedonian state. This done, he overpowered the Greek city states, uniting them for the first time in history in a federal constitutional order under his political leadership, and directing them toward the greater strategic vision of conquering Persia. Philip used every means at his disposal in his efforts to achieve his goals – diplomacy, bribery, intimidation, deceit, subversion, sabotage, assassination, marriage, betrayal, war and, on occasion, even scrupulously keeping his promises.[2] In short, Philip used all the same means commonly used by his enemies, the political leaders of the Greek city states.[3]

Philip was the first great general of the Greek imperial age, one of those rare military men who saw that the political and cultural world around him was changing, and that by mastering that change one could shape the future. His military and political brilliance shaped both his own age and the future. Had there been no

Philip to bring the Macedonian national state into existence, to assemble the economic and military resources to unite Greece, to create the bold strategic vision of conquering Persia and to invent the first modern, tactically sophisticated and strategically capable military force in Western military history as the instrument for accomplishing that vision, the exploits of Philip's son, Alexander, in Asia would not have been possible. It was Philip who provided the means, methods and motives that lay behind Alexander's achievements. History remembers Alexander as a romantic international hero. But it was Philip who was the greater general and national king.[4]

The claim that Philip of Macedon was Greece's greatest general invites the question of whether or not Philip was 'greater' than Alexander. Alexander's exploits were recorded early on by ancient historians, so that even in ancient times he had already become the great romantic warrior hero for kings and generals to emulate.[5] The theme of Alexander's greatness survived the ages almost unchallenged, arriving in modern times largely intact. One consequence was to neglect Philip's contributions to Alexander's accomplishments, and Philip's own accomplishments as they compare with Alexander's. It has been commonplace for Alexander's supporters to assert, usually in passing, that Alexander's 'inheritance' from Philip was important without, however, examining that inheritance in detail. In fact, Philip's legacy was so important that without it, there would have been no Alexander the Great.

Alexander's opportunity for greatness began with the single truth that Philip was a great national king who created the first national territorial state in Europe, uniting disparate peoples under Macedonian leadership into a powerful national political entity. Philip enlarged, urbanized and developed Macedonia's natural and human resources to a degree never seen before in Greece or the West. In doing so, Philip made Macedonia the wealthiest and most resource-rich state in Greece. With Macedonia as his national power base, Philip expanded his sphere of political and military dominance into the first great European land empire in history, uniting all of Greece into a single political entity with common political institutions and a single constitution. It was this imperial state that provided the material resources – ships, food, troops, reserve manpower, military equipment and animals – that made Alexander's successful assault on the western half of the Persian Empire possible.

The composition of the expeditionary force that Alexander took with him to Persia amply illustrates the extent of the resources provided by Philip's new imperial state. Alexander's army included 12,000 Macedonian infantry (phalanx and Guards Brigades), 7,000 Greek hoplites drawn from the League of Corinth's troops, 7,000 troops from the subject tribes, including light cavalry, *peltasts* and javelin men, 1,000 archers and Agrianian mounted javelineers, and 5,000 mercenaries (heavy infantry). These are in addition to the 11,000 or so troops already in Ionia as the advance expeditionary force sent under the joint command of Attalus and Parmenio. Alexander also took with him 1,800 Macedonian cavalry, including the elite Companion cavalry, 1,800 Thessalian heavy cavalry, 900 Thracian and Paeonian scouts and 600 League cavalry, in addition to the 1,000 cavalry already in-country with the advance expedition.[6] Alexander's force amounted to 49,100 men. Usually not mentioned but surely present were Philip's siege engineers and sappers. It was Philip's creation of the Macedonian empire that made raising such large numbers of troops and equipment possible.

Raising and deploying this force was itself an achievement. Sustaining its manpower levels in the field was quite another. Alexander's campaigns lasted for a decade and covered 10,000 miles of marching and fighting. His army would have been worn to helplessness without some system of manpower replacement. While it is true that Alexander made some use of Persian and tribal troops, he did so only minimally. Most of Alexander's replacements over a decade of war came from Macedonia, sent by Antipater who had been left behind as regent. Often these troop replacements exceeded 10,000 men at a time and, in one instance, 19,000. It was Philip who introduced a system of nation-wide recruitment and training of Macedonian militia troops, a system that made it possible to provide large numbers of trained and disciplined soldiers to Alexander on a regular basis. Other than Macedonia, no Greek state had such a large and comprehensive system of military recruitment and training, and none could have sustained Alexander's army in the field for very long.

It is often overlooked that wars and campaigns take place within a political context, and that they are made possible by more than armies, troops and equipment. Alexander's campaign against Persia would not have been possible had Philip not first established a civic peace among the warring Greek states. More than anything, it was Philip's peace and its accompanying guarantee that the Greek states would observe their obligations to the League of Corinth that made Alexander's attack on Persia possible. Without the guarantee of peace among the Greek states, no commander would have dared risk invading Persia, exposing himself to revolt or attack in his rear. Without Athenian assurance to use its navy to oppose any Persian attempt to attack Greece by sea while Alexander was in the field, Alexander's expedition risked being cut off and destroyed piecemeal. Even the crossing into Asia itself depended upon Philip's previous successes. Alexander crossed at the Hellespont. The crossing was possible only because Philip had previously secured Thrace and the Chersonese in a year-long military campaign, creating the strategic platform from which Alexander could launch his invasion.

The strategic vision of taking a Greek army into Asia and conquering the Great King of Persia was far more Philip's than Alexander's. The idea had been around for at least a decade, espoused by men like Isocrates as a way of stopping Greek civil strife by bringing the warring states together in a common effort against Persia. The idea was less than fully formed at best, and the political conditions necessary to make an invasion possible were completely absent until Philip brought them into being. It was only after he had done so that a war against Persia became possible with some expectation of success. It was Philip who gave the idea strategic possibility, and who planned the invasion in detail. Alexander carried out the invasion, but it was Philip who transformed thought into action, and first gave practical expression to the strategic vision itself.

It is not too strong a statement to say that Philip was a military genius who invented the military instrument that allowed Alexander to carry out his conquest of Asia. Philip's innovations revolutionized the Greek way of war, bringing into existence new and more powerful combat capabilities without which Philip's own conquests and Alexander's in Asia would not have been possible. Philip's invention of a new form of infantry warfare constructed around a new combat formation, the pike-phalanx, armed with a new weapon, the *sarissa*, and capable of greater flexibility, stability and manoeuvre than the hoplite phalanx, bequeathed Alexander his main combat arm for controlling the infantry battlefield. Philip's new phalanx could be employed in a number of new ways: in defence to offset the numerical superiority of the Persian infantry, in offence to strike at the Persian line with sufficient force to penetrate it, and as a platform of manoeuvre to anchor the battle line and freeze enemy dispositions while the Macedonian cavalry sought a weak spot through which to penetrate and turn inside the Persian lines. Philip's introduction of the long pike (*sarissa*) also afforded his infantry a great advantage in close combat over Persian infantry armed mostly with short spear, shield, bow and little armour, and which was far less formidable than Greek heavy infantry.[7]

Philip also revolutionized the killing capability of Greek cavalry. Until Philip, cavalry in Greece had been only a minor combat element with little killing power, incapable of offensive action, limited in the pursuit and unable to break infantry formations. Philip changed all this by replacing the short cavalry javelin with the longer *xyston* lance, designed for close combat, and introducing the cavalry wedge to drive through infantry formations. Philip taught the Macedonian cavalry to fight as units instead of individual combatants, and trained them in close combat and horsemanship to a level heretofore unseen in Greece. Unlike traditional Greek cavalry, Philip's cavalry was designed to close with the enemy, shatter its formations and kill it where it stood. If the enemy took flight, Macedonian cavalry was expert in the lethal pursuit, hunting the enemy in small groups and striking it down with the lance and sabre.

Philip's cavalry innovations transformed Greek cavalry from an impotent combat arm into the Macedonian army's combat arm of decision. It was the killing power of the Macedonian cavalry in close combat that made Alexander's cavalry so effective against both Persian infantry and cavalry. Persian cavalry was employed mostly in the traditional manner, to ride close to the enemy and throw javelins, and lacked an ability for effective close combat. Again and again, Alexander used his cavalry to close the distance with the enemy and bring the killing power of his cavalry to bear upon his adversaries in close quarters. If Alexander had been equipped with traditional Greek cavalry, his main combat arm against the Persians would have been practically useless.

It was Philip's military genius in devising and introducing new infantry and cavalry formations, expanding their tactical roles and increasing exponentially their combat killing power that created the military instrument that gave Alexander the advantage in battle that made his victories possible. Robert Gaebel sums up this advantage in the following terms:

> Except for numbers, Alexander always had superior fighting ability at his disposal, so that a significant military asymmetry existed between his forces and those of his enemies. Most of this superiority resulted from the inherent qualities of the Macedonian army and was based on discipline, training, arms skill, professionalism, and cultural outlook, all of which had been enhanced by experience.[8]

Had there been no Philip to invent a new army, the odds are very good that there would have been no Alexander the Great.

Another innovation that made Alexander's success possible was Philip's creation of an engineering and siege capability for the first time as an integral part of a Greek field army. Philip's siege engineers had almost two decades of field experience before Alexander took them to Asia, and were equipped with the new Macedonian torsion catapult that gave Alexander's army the capability to batter down the walls of cities. Alexander's chief engineer, Diades, had been trained by Polyiedos, Philip's chief engineer. The siege corps itself had been trained to a fine edge by Philip, who employed them in at least eleven sieges in his previous campaigns. The importance of a siege capability to Alexander's success cannot be overestimated. Before Alexander could invade the interior to meet the Persian army, he had first to secure his hold on the Persian coast. To achieve this, and not to leave hostile garrisons across his line of communications, he had to reduce the major coastal cities, and do so quickly to avoid being caught from behind by the Persian army, as almost happened at Issus. It was Philip's besiegers that reduced Miletus, Hallicarnasus, Tyre and Gaza in relatively short order. Had they not done so, and had Alexander been forced to rely upon the usual Greek siege practice of isolation and starvation, it is likely that he would never have got much beyond the Ionian coast, giving the Persian army plenty of time to come up and attack him, with results that may have been far different from what history records.

The fourth of Philip's major innovations upon which Alexander depended was the commissariat corps. Philip introduced the science of logistics to Greek armies, allowing his armies to march long distances and sustain themselves in the field for months on end. By Alexander's time, Philip's logisticians had been at their work for two decades. Alexander's march up country lasted a decade and covered 10,000 miles, much of it through hostile territory. It was Philip's logistics officers who made this projection of force possible by finding the means to supply the army over some of the most hostile terrain on the planet. To be sure, the Persians were excellent logisticians themselves, and had an excellent system of interior roads that aided Alexander. But once Alexander moved east over deserts, mountains and through jungles, he depended heavily upon those Macedonian logistics officers who had been trained by Philip to supply his army.

While there is no doubt that Alexander was a brilliant tactician in his own right, and like Napoleon was gifted with a *coup d'oeuil* that permitted him to quickly assess the terrain and weakness of the enemy's disposition and to fashion a tactical plan on the spot, his tactics were not radically different from those he had learned from Philip.[9] In Alexander's early battles, the Persian advantage in numbers presented the risk of single or double envelopment to his formations. Alexander countered this threat with a swift penetration of the enemy line, turning inward toward the enemy commander's position, while assaulting the interior ranks as he advanced. The key to a successful penetration of the Persian line was the ability of Alexander's cavalry to close with the enemy at the *Schwerpunkt*, engaging in violent close combat until it drove through the line and exploded behind it. The infantry, always deployed in the centre-left of the line across from the location of the enemy commander, was used primarily as a platform of manoeuvre, that is, to hold the enemy infantry in check while the Companion cavalry, almost always deployed on the right under Alexander's personal command, manoeuvred until it found the weak spot in the enemy line through which to attack. To weaken the ability of the enemy cavalry across from him to resist his cavalry assault, Alexander employed mounted skirmishers in front of his cavalry to engage the enemy and force it to throw its javelins and expend its energy in the defence. Alexander then attacked with his fresh Macedonian cavalry.

It was Philip who first used his infantry as a platform of manoeuvre while unleashing his cavalry to achieve penetration of the enemy line. Philip first used this tactic in his battle with Bardylis, and then again at Chaeronea. There would have been no point to training the Macedonian cavalry as he did if Philip did not use them to penetrate the enemy line. Philip was also adept at reading the terrain and adjusting his forces accordingly, as he did at Lavahdi, Illyria, the Crocus Field and Chaeronea. It is by no means clear that Philip was inferior in this talent to Alexander.

The tale of Alexander's pursuit of Darius was one of the most widely told battle stories of antiquity to demonstrate Alexander's use of strategic pursuit in his campaigns. But here again, we witness Alexander doing what Philip often did first. It was Philip who made strategic pursuit possible by introducing a logistics system that made sustaining his forces in the field over long-distance forced marches a practical possibility. Philip not only used pursuit to destroy fleeing enemy armies, but for strategic political ends as well. Philip often conducted lethal pursuits with the political objective of destroying as many of the enemy's leadership corps and aristocracy as possible, to make it easier for the survivors to come to terms with him. Alexander used it for the same purposes in hunting down Darius; he later used pursuit to utterly destroy the leadership of opposing tribal armies, almost to the point of genocide. The invention and effective use of the strategic pursuit within the context of Greek warfare must be credited to Philip, and by Alexander's day it was a stock element in the Macedonian commander's tactical repertoire.

Alexander is often given great credit for his innovations in assembling units of mixed arms for use on specific missions. Arrian identifies twenty-seven examples of Alexander combining forces of different arms for specific tactical missions.[10] Later, Alexander redesigned the Macedonian phalanx, mixing Persians with Macedonian pike-men to make it heavier, although these mixed units were never used in battle. Alexander's 'tailoring' of tactical units, as today, depended upon the terrain over which they had to operate, the mission they were to accomplish and the nature of the force to be engaged. It was a light force of mounted infantry, for example, that Alexander used to close the gap in the pursuit of Darius.

While Alexander certainly utilized mixed arms units more often and on a greater scale than Philip, this was probably a consequence of the varied nature of both Persian and tribal armies that Alexander confronted. Many of Arrian's examples apply to the counter-insurgency operations that Alexander mounted in Afghanistan and the Indus Valley, where his opponents were highly mobile units armed with bow and javelin. While specialty units (archers, slingers, *peltasts*, javeliners, etc.) had been used by traditional Greek armies for decades, albeit in minor roles, it was not until Philip that these units were regularly incorporated into a standing military force, the Macedonian army. Moreover, Philip's wars in the mountains of western Macedonia and the Balkans forced him to deal with highly mobile tribal forces operating in difficult terrain. It was during the Thracian campaign, however, that Philip seems to have used mixed forces with some regularity and size, so much so that as the campaign went on he found himself short of regular infantry and had to request replacements from Macedonia.

Great generals are not the only causes of their greatness. War is a cooperative enterprise by its nature, heavily dependent upon the talents and abilities of others orchestrated by the commander into a coherent tapestry of activity. The quality of leadership and experience is vitally important at all levels of command to the overall success of any army. Perhaps it is in the qualities of leadership, training and experience of the Macedonian officer and non-commissioned officer corps that Alexander owes his greatest debt to Philip.

Most of the important officers in Alexander's army had served with Philip at various levels of command over the years. They included Parmenio, the old war horse, who was Philip's best field commander; his sons, Philotas and Nicanor, commanding the horse and foot guards respectively; Hephaestion, Alexander's lover, closest friend, and the commander of half the Companion cavalry; Craterus, commander of the left half of the phalanx; Seleucus, commander of the foot guards; Antigonus the One-Eyed; and Ptolemy, a fellow-student with Alexander under Aristotle's tutelage.[11] Even some of Alexander's peers had seen their first combat under Philip, and had risen in rank under Philip's tutelage. Equally important were the unnamed and unremembered battalion commanders, squadron commanders, file commanders and section leaders, the small-unit officer and non-commissioned officer corps upon which the effectiveness of any army depends most, who had served under Philip as well. Perhaps no general in history had ever received a better-trained, experienced and well-led army than Alexander's legacy from Philip.

Both Philip and Alexander were heads of state as well as field generals, a fact that radically changes the meaning of military greatness. In modern times, and even in times later in antiquity, generals were most often not simultaneously heads of government. Accordingly, they are properly judged only by their achievements on the field of battle, and not usually held responsible for larger political concerns. In these circumstances, military performance may be regarded as an end in itself. But Alexander and Philip must be judged by a different standard, that is by the degree to which their military achievements worked to support their objectives not only as military men, but as heads of governments. In these circumstances, military competence becomes not an end, but a means to other ends for which the general is also responsible. The concerns of the general *qua* general are the tactical and operational elements of war. The concerns of the general *qua* statesman are the strategic objectives of the national state.

For the general as strategist, war is but one means to achieve national objectives within the political and cultural context within which wars are fought for specified goals. Philip always properly saw war as a means to strategic goals, and much preferred to achieve his objectives by other 'less kinetic' means such as diplomacy. Even to as Homeric a warrior as Philip, the search for glory and heroism had but little place in his strategic thinking. Alexander, by contrast, was the prototypical Homeric warrior, fighting only for personal glory and reputation, a military adventurer almost entirely lacking in strategic vision. One is hard pressed to discern in accounts of Alexander's adventures any strategic vision that might have reasonably been achieved by his many campaigns. When the Indian philosopher, Dandamis, met Alexander, he seems to have grasped Alexander's strategic mettle correctly when he asked, 'For what reason did Alexander make such a long journey hither?'[12]

Some of Alexander's campaigns, such as crossing the Gedrosian Desert, were undertaken simply to surpass the achievements of other generals:

> Alexander chose it, we are told, because with the exception of Semiramis, returning from her conquests of India, no one had ever brought an army successfully through it ... the Persian king, Cyrus the Great, supposedly had lost all but 7 of his men when he crossed it. Alexander knew about these stories, and they had inspired him to emulate and hopefully surpass Cyrus and Semiramis.[13]

With only personal glory and reputation to concern him, Alexander became a fierce and recklessly brave warrior who was wounded seven times.[14] He apparently had little regard for his personal safety, and even less for the consequences of his death for either Macedonia or the Aegead dynastic line. He 'seems to have been possessed of some sort of restless, almost irrational desire for glory unchecked by a larger political sense', that is, by any strategic calculation or vision.[15] For Alexander, war was the crucible of fame, an end in itself, its exploits the stuff of history and legend.

Philip, by contrast, was the ultimate strategist, fighting wars only when forced to because other means had failed to achieve his objectives that were rooted in Macedonian national interests more than personal reputation. When at war, Philip showed himself to be an innovative and brave field commander who was wounded no fewer than five times, three of which were life-threatening. But Philip was also the first Western general to abandon the Homeric practice of fighting in the front ranks of the battle line. He had designed his army to manoeuvre and strike at his command. But to control the flow and tempo of battle, Philip had to command from outside the battle space. He would probably have agreed with Scipio Africanus, who, when criticized for moving around the battlefield surrounded by guards with shields to protect him, responded: 'My mother bore me a general, not a warrior.'[16]

Generals were becoming too valuable to be risked in foolish heroics. Philip had already moved beyond the general as warrior-hero to the general as battle manager. Alexander, in doing the opposite, was already an anachronism in Greece, and would soon be everywhere else as well. Alexander was a magnificent throw-back to a simpler age of warfare. The future, however, belonged to the Philips, for the Alexanders were already obsolete even in their own day.

Chapter 21

Stolen Valour: An Analysis of Alexander the Great's Wounds

Alexander the Great is the most heroic figure in Greek and Roman literature, and we hear of no other person's wounds as much as we hear of Alexander's. But the Alexander we read about is more a literary creation of Greek and Roman authors than he is an historical personality. Ancient historians did not attempt to provide accurate accounts of events as much as to produce history that served as inspiration for the young and instruction and example to the powerful. Accordingly, their accounts of events need to be regarded with great caution, and their claims empirically verified wherever possible.

The accounts of Alexander's life portray him as a warrior hero driven by the search for fame and glory. But Alexander did not die a warrior's death: he died in bed of disease aggravated by his abuse of alcohol. Without a glorious death to celebrate, ancient historians exaggerated his wounds as evidence of his 'reckless bravery'. In fact, most of his wounds were neither serious nor suffered during heroic actions. If Alexander's seven wounds are examined from a modern medical perspective, it appears that there is significant exaggeration, if not outright fabrication, in their descriptions. Alexander's war record may be somewhat less imposing than it is often assumed to be.

In the first place, it was somewhat difficult to wound Alexander. Whether fighting on horseback or on foot, Alexander was well protected and never fought alone. On foot, he was always accompanied by a seven-man bodyguard (*somatophylakes*) chosen for their loyalty, bravery and combat experience. Standing in front of him at all times was his shield bearer, who wielded Athena's shield to deflect arrows and javelins fired in the direction of the king. When mounted, Alexander fought with the Royal Cavalry Squadron protecting him. It is significant that six of Alexander's wounds were from missiles (arrows and rocks), and only one from a sword, an indication of how difficult it was for an enemy to get close enough to do him harm.

Second, Alexander wore linothorax body armour comprised of three layers of overlapping linen plates glued together to a thickness of ½in. Modern tests reveal linen armour to be very effective by remaining sufficiently pliable to flex inward to absorb much of the impact energy of missiles and thrusting weapons. Linen armour easily prevented penetration sufficient to reach the body, so that

Alexander's chest, neck and back were almost impervious to wounding by arrows, swords, spears, slingshot or javelins. Modern tests show that an arrow fired at a distance of 4 metres from a 60lb bow will not penetrate linen armour.[1] In addition, Alexander always wore an iron or bronze helmet, usually of the Corinthian design. No weapon of the day could be wielded with sufficient force to penetrate it.[2]

An examination of Alexander's wounds as provided in the accounts of the ancient historians suggest a fair degree of exaggeration as to their seriousness.

The Granicus River (May–June 334 BC)

Facing a Greek-Persian force, Alexander opened the battle with a battalion of infantry and a squadron of cavalry moving across the enemy front searching for a gap in their line. With Parmenio engaging on the left wing, Alexander led the Companion cavalry into the gap on the right.[3] During the melee, Alexander was attacked by a Persian cavalryman who 'brought his sword down on Alexander's head with such a fearsome blow that it split his helmet and inflicted a slight scalp wound'.[4] Arrian adds that the blow knocked off a piece of the helmet, but does not record a wound at all.[5] Curtius says the split helmet fell from Alexander's head,[6] while Diodorus tells us that Alexander 'withstood two blows to his breast plate and one to his helmet'. Three other blows were absorbed 'by the shield which he had taken from Athena's temple', that is, by his shield bearer.[7]

It is unlikely that a sword blow could split open Alexander's helmet, as 151 foot pounds of energy are required to split a bronze helmet, and 251 foot pounds to do so to an iron helmet. A sword swung by muscle power can produce no more than 101 foot pounds of energy.[8] The blow may have shifted the helmet and caused a 'rub-wound' on the scalp, but it was not the blow of a sword blade that caused the wound. The claim that Alexander took three blows to his shield is also suspicious. Macedonian cavalry did not carry shields. At the Granicus River, Alexander passed his first test as a field commander, but did not receive a battle wound.

The Battle of Issus (November 333 BC)

Curtius says that as Alexander led the Royal Squadron in a cavalry attack, he suffered 'a sword-graze to his right thigh'.[9] Arrian says Alexander was 'hurt by a sword thrust in the thigh', and Didorus says Alexander 'was wounded in the thigh'. Thigh wounds were the most common suffered by Macedonian cavalrymen, and were rarely serious.[10] Macedonian cavalrymen wore high leather boots, metal greaves and thick leather coverings up to the tops of their thighs, so any wound was likely to be minor. That Alexander's wound was not serious is evident from Arrian's comment that it did not prevent Alexander from visiting the wounded or holding a funeral for the dead.[11] It is curious that all our sources mention it, however. This may be because it was the only wound Alexander suffered by a sword, implying that it was received in close combat.

The Siege of Gaza (September–November 332 BC)

At Gaza, the Persians sallied forth from the gate and engaged the Macedonians in an infantry skirmish in which Alexander 'fought courageously in the front rank'.[12] Curtius tells us Alexander was hit by an arrow 'which passed through his cuirass and stuck in his shoulder, from which it was extracted by Philip, his doctor'.[13] Alexander ordered the bleeding to be staunched, the wound bandaged, and returned to the front where he remained 'for a long time' until the wound began to bleed again. Then, 'he began to faint, his knees buckled, and the men next to him caught him and took him back to camp'.[14] Arrian's version has Alexander struck by 'a missile from a catapult that pierced his shield and corselet and penetrated his shoulder ... the wound was serious and did not easily yield to treatment'.[15] Tellingly, Diodorus does not claim that Alexander was wounded at all at Gaza.

If the wound was as serious as described, the claim that Alexander returned to the fighting immediately after being wounded and remained there 'for a long time' is difficult to believe. Alexander's linen corselet was relatively impervious to arrow fire. Most likely the arrow that hit Alexander's corselet penetrated to only a short depth, surely less than the 2in required to produce a serious wound. That Alexander's physician extracted the missile without removing Alexander's armour also suggests a wound of shallow depth that could not have been as serious as the texts suggests.

There is no mention of cautery or tourniquet to stop the bleeding, another indication of a shallow flesh wound, and the claim that Alexander passed out from blood loss is unlikely to be true. Bleeding sufficient to cause physiological collapse, as the sources claim, would not have been so easily stopped only with a pressure bandage, and would not have stopped on its own. Moreover, the sources tells us that after the arrow had been extracted and the bleeding resumed, Alexander 'did not even lose colour', i.e., become pale, suggesting that the blood loss was not serious.[16] The account of Alexander's bleeding may have been exaggerated to convey a sense that Alexander was more seriously wounded than he was.

Alexander was back on the battlefield within a few days. Such a short recovery would have been unlikely had Alexander been seriously wounded. When the attack was resumed, 'Alexander himself led the advance troops, and, as he approached somewhat recklessly, he was struck on the leg with a rock. He supported himself with his spear, and though the scab had still not formed on his first wound, kept fighting in the front line.'[17] Note that the only evidence of his previous wound is a scab, and not the much prized battle scar, suggesting that the wound was merely a flesh wound and not serious.

Skirmish on the Jaxartes River (June 329 BC)

On the march to Maracanda (modern Samarkand), Alexander's foragers came under attack. After inflicting heavy casualties, the attackers withdrew to a redoubt atop a steep hill. Alexander led his troops in an attack, and Arrian says 'many were wounded, including Alexander himself, who was shot through the leg with an arrow and had the fibula broken'.[18] Plutarch adds that Alexander 'was shot in the shin, right through, and a piece of his fibula was broken off by the arrow'.[19] Curtius' version has Alexander 'hit by an arrow, the head of which was left firmly lodged in his leg'.[20]

Macedonians wore heavy knee-high leather boots covered by metal shin greaves, making an arrow wound to the shin very unlikely. The claim that Alexander's fibula was broken or had a piece of the bone shot off is also suspicious. A bone fragment would have left an external wound or, perhaps, produced a compound fracture, neither of which is mentioned. A break in the fibula in which both pieces of the bone are disarticulated, that is, left beside each other, can leave a person permanently crippled. If the fibula is not disarticulated, it might be possible to walk with the injury, although painfully. That Alexander was hindered by his injury seems evident from the fact that he was carried from the battlefield and transported on a litter when the army continued its march. Three days later, however, Alexander was back in action, burning villages as his army approached the city, a very rapid recovery that suggests either a stress-cracked fibula or, at worst, a broken bone that was not disarticulated.[21]

Curtius' claim that the arrow head 'was left firmly lodged in his leg' seems unlikely, in that it would certainly have caused the wound to become infected.[22] Alexander was probably wounded in the leg by an arrow whose impact was greatly reduced by first having to penetrate his thick leather boot. The arrow may have penetrated the skin and, perhaps, some surface viscera, but not very deeply, and its extraction was easily accomplished. The wound was probably painful, but not terribly so. The fact that Alexander was able to move around quite readily after a few days suggests that there was no fracture of the fibula.

The Siege of Cyropolis (Summer 328 BC)

While besieging Cyropolis in Afghanistan, Curtius tells us that 'Alexander was struck so severely on the neck by a stone that everything went dark and he collapsed unconscious. The army wept for him as if he were dead.'[23] Arrian says the injury was to the back of the head and neck, while Plutarch says it was to the back and the side of the neck, that is, the occipital and parietal area of the skull.[24] Alexander lost his sight, and Plutarch says 'for many days he was in fear of becoming blind', before recovering.[25] Curtius tells us that Alexander had still not fully recovered from his wound a month later, 'and in particular had difficulty speaking'. Alexander was so weak that 'he could not stand in the ranks, ride a horse, or give his men instructions or encouragement. Alexander's words were spoken in a quivering voice that became increasingly feeble, so that it was difficult even for those next to him to hear.'[26] It was several weeks before Alexander's symptoms disappeared and he was able to put on his corslet and 'walk to the men, the first time he had done so since receiving the most recent wound'.[27] Altogether, Alexander was incapacitated for more than two months.[28]

The blow to Alexander's head likely caused a severe concussion that resulted in transient cortical blindness.[29] His difficulties with balance, walking and speaking, however, suggest further damage to the brain. The damage caused by the blow to the back and side of Alexander's head, the loss of his sight, was not confined to that area. A blow to this area drives the fluid surrounding the brain forward, propelling the frontal lobe of the brain into the bony structure of the skull, causing damage to the frontal lobe. In this 'contra-coup' injury, the functions of the frontal lobe can be greatly affected. Long-term emotional effects of frontal lobe concussion include depression, anger, irritability, shortened temper, paranoia, memory loss and inappropriate displays of emotion, all dysfunctions of the frontal lobe. Severe concussions can, over time, also result in chronic traumatic encephalopathy, producing severe emotional outbursts and paranoid states. This type of concussion can also create disinhibition, a state of reduced control over one's behaviours, impulses, attention and emotions.[30] Hypersexuality, hyperphagia, mania, aggressive outbursts and paranoid states are also common effects. Alexander's heavy drinking increased markedly at this time (hyperphagia), as did his open displays of homosexual affection with his lover, Hephaestion (hypersexuality).

Alexander was 27 years old when he was injured at Cyropolis. He had been at war for seven years, and had already begun to show symptoms of post-traumatic stress disorder: explosive anger, cruelty, paranoia, depression, heavy drinking and suicidal impulses. These symptoms became more frequent after this injury at Cyropolis, as he increasingly lost his ability to control his impulses, emotions and behaviour.

Alexander's behaviour after the injury reveals this to have been the case. At Maracanda, he killed Cleitus in a fit of drunken anger. His paranoia became more acute, and he had Callisthenes and the Pages executed when he believed they were involved in a conspiracy to kill him. Four senior generals were executed on suspicion of disloyalty. Upon his return from India, Alexander ordered scores of

Macedonian and Persian officials liquidated in a mass purge. His depression and paranoia grew worse, and on at least two occasions he was suicidal; Alexander became more convinced that he was divine, and paid excessive attention to even the smallest event as signs of his divinity.

He became more brutal than ever. At Cyropolis, he ordered the death of 7,000 enemy soldiers who had surrendered. At Maracanda (328 BC), he ordered the destruction of every village and town, killing every male of military age. When he captured the city, he ordered the entire population butchered. In 327 BC, Alexander returned to Sogdiana and destroyed every village, town and tribe encountered en route of the line of march. Estimates of the losses begin at 120,000 people. Forty thousand were killed in a single engagement. After taking the town of Massaga in the Kabul Valley, he granted the Indian mercenaries safe passage, then surrounded them and their families, slaughtering every man, woman and child, some 7,000 people in all.

In India, Alexander slaughtered the entire town of Sangala in 326 BC. Seventeen thousand people were killed, and 70,000 taken prisoner. When Alexander came upon the sick and wounded they had left behind, he had them all killed too. In 325, Alexander attacked the Malians, destroying their town and slaughtering the inhabitants. Some 50,000 souls were slain in this single engagement. A few months later, he encountered the Brahmins at Sambus. Again he ordered a terrible massacre in which 80,000 people were slaughtered. In 324 BC, Alexander and his army spent forty days in a campaign against the Cossaeans in which the entire nation was put to the sword to soothe Alexander's grief over the death of his lover.

Even allowing for exaggeration by our sources, it is clear that Alexander's brutality was much worse after his injury at Cyropolis than it had previously been. J.M. O'Brien summed up the changes that had taken place in Alexander since his injury:

> This change, which deepened during the last seven years of his life, was marked by a progressive deterioration of character. He became increasingly suspicious of friends as well as enemies, unpredictable, and megalomaniacal. Towards the end, he was almost totally isolated, dreaded by all, a violent man capable of anything.[31]

Fight with the Aspasians (Winter 327 BC)

Moving through the Swat Valley (Afghanistan) toward the Indus River, Alexander attacked the first Aspasian town he encountered. Arrian tells us that 'during the operation, Alexander was wounded in the shoulder by a missile which pierced his corselet. The wound was not serious, and the corselet prevented the missile from going right through his shoulder.'[32] There is no evidence that the wound was treated in any way, or that it pierced Alexander's flesh. It must have been a minor wound, since Curtius tells us Alexander proceeded to take the town and butcher its inhabitants to a man.

Massaga (early Spring 327 BC)

Alexander took the town of Massaga under siege. While leading his infantry too close to the walls, Alexander was struck by an arrow that 'wounded him slightly in the ankle'.[33] Curtius tells us that 'someone on the walls hit him with an arrow which happened to lodge in his leg. Alexander pulled out the barb, had his horse brought up and without even bandaging the wound, rode around fulfilling his objectives no less energetically.'[34] Alexander's ankles were protected by thick leather boots, and it is likely that the arrow lodged in the leather without piercing his flesh.

Sudrace (January 325 BC)

Continuing his march along the Hydraotes River, Alexander attempted to take the Mallian capital at Sudrace by storm. Angry that the assault was not going well, Alexander climbed a scaling ladder, gained the top of the parapet and jumped inside the wall to engage the enemy in what Curtius and Diodorus say was an attempt to die gloriously in battle (one of two suicide attempts by Alexander). He was struck in the chest by an arrow.

Arrian says that 'the arrow penetrated his corselet, and entered his body above the breast'. Curtius adds that Alexander was wounded 'above his right side' by an arrow, and 'when he received his wound, a thick jet of blood shot forth'. Alexander 'dropped his weapons and appeared to be dying'. Arrian says:

> [T]he blood from the wound was mixed with air breathed out from the pierced lung. Despite the pain, Alexander continued to defend himself so long as the blood remained warm; but there was soon a violent hemorrhage, as was to be expected with a pierced lung, and overcome by giddiness and faintness, he fell forward over his shield … Alexander was almost unconscious from loss of blood.[35]

Rescued by his bodyguard, Alexander was taken to his tent for medical treatment. The arrow had pierced Alexander's corselet, nailing his armour to his chest. The doctors 'cut off the shaft of the arrow embedded in his body without removing the arrow head'. Alexander refused to be held down while the wound was enlarged, and 'submitted to the knife without flinching'. When the arrow head was extracted, 'a stream of blood now began to gush forth. Alexander started to lose consciousness … In vain they tried to check the bleeding with medications … finally the bleeding stopped; Alexander gradually regained consciousness.'[36] Alexander did not make a full recovery until sometime in late August, some seven months after he was wounded.

Although the wound was serious, it is difficult to believe that Alexander was hit by an arrow that penetrated both his corslet and his body so deeply as to puncture his lung 'above the breast', as Arrian says. The musculature in that area is considerably thicker than at or below the breast line, and would have required much greater force to penetrate the corselet and the body deep enough to puncture the lung.[37] Curtius may be closer to the truth when he says Alexander was struck 'above his right side'. The musculature on the side of the chest is considerably less thick than in the front, and the arrow may have struck the seam where the two halves of Alexander's body armour were laced. The area of the wound puts the puncture at the top of the lung, a location of less lung tissue area, blood circulation and aeration function than lower areas of the lung. If punctured at the apex, the lung will collapse, but have less effect on breathing capacity, which shifts to the other lung. Unless infection sets in, the lung will heal naturally. A puncture wound to a major area of the lung, however, would have been fatal.

It is unlikely that Alexander's lung was punctured, however. Arrian's statement that air mixed with blood rushed out of the wound cannot be correct. The lungs function in a vacuum created by the pleural space of the chest cavity. When the pleural space is pierced, air rushes into the vacuum. Modern military physicians refer to this type of wound as a 'sucking chest wound' for just this reason. It is also possible to pierce the pleural space without piercing the lung, especially at the top of the lung where Alexander was likely hit. The bleeding came from simple tissue injury, not a pierced lung. It is instructive that the heavy bleeding occurred only after the wound had been enlarged by the physician to extract the arrow head which, apparently, the physician had little difficulty locating. Perhaps the surgeon punctured a vein when enlarging the entrance wound, or there was profuse capillary bleeding.

Curtius's statement that Alexander's wound had not closed after seven days is misleading in that he means the outer entrance wound. The wound would have naturally begun to heal from inside very quickly. However, it would have taken more than a week for the inside wound to reseal the pleural space. Once this occurred, the body would begin to re-establish the vacuum in the pleural space, and gradually reinflate the collapsed lung. The lung would gradually heal and recover its function. This is consistent with the claim that thirteen days after being wounded, Alexander was able to lift himself off the litter and meet his troops, even though his condition was 'still very fragile'. Alexander required five more months to recover fully, a length of time consistent with what modern physicians would estimate.

The descriptions of Alexander's wounds provided by the historical sources merit the suspicion that some accounts may have been enhanced to convey the impression of greater severity than can be explained medically. Moreover, except for the wound at Sudrace, none of Alexander's wounds were received in direct combat or under heroic circumstances. Most wounds were minor, while others are clearly unbelievable from a medical perspective. The wound that probably did the most damage to Alexander, the blow to the head at Cyropolis, went mostly unnoticed in its importance by our sources, probably because it left no obvious physical injuries. It is possible, then, that Alexander's reputation for heroic bravery resulting in serious battle wounds may very well have been exaggerated by ancient historians seeking to create an heroic exemplar with which to instruct their audiences, the very purpose of history in the eyes of the ancient historians.

Chapter 22

Rome against Carthage: Why Hannibal Lost

'Hannibal was never more than a great solider, a brilliant innovator in the art of war, who applied his powerful mind and personality to one end – that of winning battles.'[1] The difficulty is, of course, that wars are not won only by winning battles. Battles are means to strategic ends, not ends in themselves. For Hannibal, however, the war in Italy was the only war. Hannibal never regarded his operations in Italy as one campaign in a larger war, but as the only campaign in the only war. This narrow perspective on the war between Rome and Carthage caused Hannibal to commit a number of operational mistakes that led eventually to his defeat in Italy. Paradoxically, Hannibal's defeat in Italy had little to do with Carthage's defeat in the larger strategic arena.

At the root of Hannibal's view of war was his Hellenistic education and the influence of Hellenistic culture on his thinking. In the Hellenistic view, the object of war was not the destruction of the enemy's state or political regime. Instead, armies fought to win battles until it became clear to the political leadership of one of the combatants that there was nothing to be gained by continuing the fighting and, perhaps, much to lose. At this point, the antagonists entered into negotiations, and a settlement of a commercial or geographic sort was reached. Thus, Hannibal believed his victories would force Rome to the negotiating table. He would then have won the war, and other outstanding issues could be addressed. It was Hannibal's Hellenistic thinking that caused him to fail to attack Rome itself when he had two opportunities to do so.[2]

One of Hannibal's most significant failures was to not understand the conservative culture and moralistic values that underlay Roman society and that ultimately shaped the Roman view of war. For Romans, war was a predatory exercise, employed precisely to bring down and destroy the enemy's regime. Battles were means to the larger political ends of conquest, occupation and economic exploitation of the enemy. From this cultural perspective, to accept defeat risked these conditions being imposed upon the Romans themselves, something they would pay any price in blood and treasure to prevent. In the Roman view, then, wars were fought until they were won and the enemy defeated. Only then did negotiations follow.

Wars, especially successful ones, are always fought within the cultural contexts that the adversaries bring to the conflict. Hannibal brought to the battlefield a Hellenistic cultural context that caused him to make assumptions as to what ends

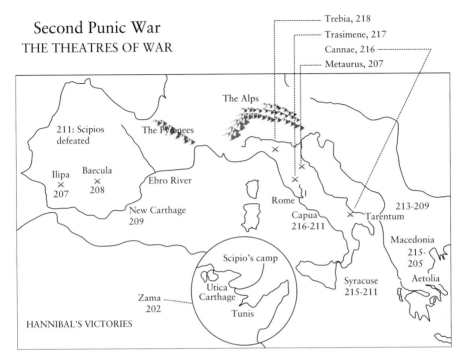

Figure 23: Hannibal's Victories in the Punic War

and means might be successfully employed against the Romans. The result was that he completely misjudged Roman motives and resolve. In the same way that American commanders never understood the cultural context of the Vietnam War, and Russian commanders the war in Afghanistan, so too Hannibal failed to understand the cultural context of the Romans. The many victories of the Americans, Russians and Hannibal on the battlefield all failed to achieve a single strategic end.[3]

When the Romans refused to discuss peace even after the disaster at Cannae, Hannibal's original strategic plan, such as it was, began to unravel. It was one thing to expect the Gauls to join him against Rome, but the assumption that the Latin allies or Roman colonies would join him in any significant numbers was completely unfounded, and based upon a lack of understanding of Roman culture and history.[4] If this had not been clear to Hannibal before, it must surely have been after Cannae. As an alternative strategy, Hannibal hit upon the idea of creating a league of Italian and Greek states in southern Italy that would become a de facto protectorate of Carthage once the war was over. For this idea to have any chance of success, however, required sufficient manpower to accomplish two things. First, Hannibal required enough troops to maintain an army of occupation to hold the towns and cities with sufficient strength to protect their surrounding agricultural lands to provide food for his army and to ward off Roman attacks. Second, he needed sufficient troops to sustain a large field army to meet and blunt any Roman military operations undertaken against him or the towns. The problem was that Hannibal's strategy required far more manpower to succeed than he possessed, or could possibly raise and supply in Italy alone.

Hannibal's manpower and supply requirements, therefore, depended heavily upon Carthage to provide them from outside Italy, something which it refused to do for sound strategic reasons. Moreover, Hannibal's plan gave no consideration to the ability of the Roman navy to blockade the southern Italian peninsula and disrupt supply convoys that might be sent from Carthage. Most important, Hannibal's southern Italian league was essentially a defensive strategy, and it left the Roman manpower and resource base to the north of the Volturnus River intact and unchallenged until Rome could rebuild her armies and go over to the offensive against Hannibal in the south. Even within the Hellenistic concept of war, Hannibal's creation of a league of rebel states in southern Italy could hardly serve to damage the Roman war effort sufficiently to provide Rome with an incentive to seek peace.

By his own admission, Hannibal's failure to attack Rome was his greatest failure, and perhaps so. But if it was, it was only so within Hannibal's compounded failure to understand the larger strategic plan with which Carthage, not Hannibal, was conducting the war. Livy tells us that when Hannibal was recalled to Carthage in 203 BC, 'he called down on his own head for not having led his armies straight to Rome when they were still bloody from the victorious field of Cannae'.[5] Here again we encounter Hannibal's limited strategic view that the war was primarily about his operations in Italy, and little more.

Both Carthage and Rome, in contrast, saw the war in a much larger strategic context: Rome to preserve her gains obtained after the First Punic War and, perhaps, seize Spain; and Carthage to retain Spain and recover those territories and ports that it had lost in the previous war. Rome immediately understood Carthage's strategic intent. Of the eleven legions deployed after Hannibal arrived in Italy, two were sent to Spain, two to Sardinia, two to Sicily and one to the key port of Tarentum to block any invasion of southern Italy by Philip V of Macedon, even though at this point Philip was not allied with Hannibal. These deployments were intended to defend the expected Carthaginian attacks on its former possessions now in Roman hands.

Had Hannibal understood this broader strategic perspective, he would have seen that an attack on Rome would have made sound strategic as well as tactical sense. Had he attacked Rome after his victory at Trasimene, Hannibal would have forced the Romans to come to the city's aid, drawing off its forces from outside Italy. At the time, there was only one intact legion in Italy, at Tarentum. The nearest two

Roman legions were on Sardinia, but there were seventy Carthaginian warships deployed between the island and Italy that could attack the Roman troop transports. Rome could have recalled the two legions from either Sicily or Spain, but never in time to meet the attack on the capital. Had Hannibal brought Rome under attack after Trasimene, either as a genuine effort or a feint, Rome would have had to recall at least *some* of its legions from abroad, exposing Sicily, Spain or Sardinia to a Carthaginian attack and invasion. Goldsworthy observes that Hannibal did not attack Rome because 'he did not think it was necessary' and believed that Rome would eventually seek peace.[6] Hannibal's Hellenistic conception of war and his failure to appreciate the larger strategic situation of which he was only a part led him to fail to take advantage of an opportunity that even he, in hindsight, realized might have turned the tide of the war.

After Cannae, Carthage's strategic view of the war was no longer, if it had ever been, the same as Hannibal's. When Carthage gave Hannibal a free hand to deal with the problem that arose in Spain over Sarguntum, it is by no means clear that they anticipated or wished a general war with Rome. But once war was declared, Carthage had little choice but to support Hannibal in his Italo-centric strategy. But after Cannae, Carthage's strategic view of the war changed. Hannibal was a field general focused on defeating the Roman armies in Italy. Once it became clear that this was not going to succeed in driving the Romans to negotiations, the government of Carthage changed strategy in favour of a more direct approach to regaining its lost possessions.

What Carthage wanted foremost out of the war was to retain possession of Spain, its silver mines, its commercial bases and its monopoly on the inland trade. It probably would have been satisfied with allowing the Romans to remain north of the Ebro River, as was the case before Hannibal's attack on Sarguntum. If possible, Carthage wanted to regain its bases in Corsica, Sardinia, Sicily and some of the offshore islands. When Hannibal could not bring the Romans to terms after Cannae, Carthage moved quickly to strengthen its grasp on these possessions by reinforcing them, as in Spain, or attempting to seize them outright, as in Sardinia, Sicily and Corsica, by military means. If Carthage could create a significant military presence in these former possessions, it would be in a much stronger position to retain them once the war ended. In this strategic view, Hannibal's operations in Italy were little more than a localized campaign designed to tie down as many Roman armies as possible while Carthage sought to bring military pressure to bear at strategic points elsewhere. This shift in strategy had little to do with factional rivalry or familial jealously, as both Polybius and Livy imply. Rather, Carthage had its own strategic view as to the conduct and purpose of the war which originally had been forced upon them by Hannibal's actions at Saguntum. The new strategy was the consequence of the failure of Hannibal's original strategy to succeed in Italy.

We have Hannibal's own words that he felt betrayed by Carthage after Cannae. When Carthaginan envoys arrived in 203 BC to order Hannibal to abandon his campaign in Italy and return to Africa, Livy says: 'Hannibal groaned and gnashed his teeth and could hardly refrain from tears.' Hannibal blamed Carthage for its failure to support his Italian campaign with sufficient troops, supplies and money. 'For years past they have been trying to force me back by refusing me reinforcements and money.' He went on to say that he was not defeated by the Romans 'but by the envy and disparagement of the Carthaginian Senate'.[7] Hannibal accused the Senate of not sending him critical supplies and troops when he needed them most, and, indeed, he is correct that they didn't. In all the long years of the war, Hannibal received only one resupply expedition, and that in 215 BC, comprised of marginal forces of 4,000 troops, forty elephants and some money. He received nothing after that.

Hannibal's charge that he was being ignored is curious in light of Polybius' claim that Hannibal alone was in charge of Carthaginian military affairs, including the decisions to send reinforcements to various theatres of the war.[8] Polybius is unlikely to be correct here. Communications in antiquity were primitive, and the Roman navy had a strong presence in and around southern Italy. The texts record only two examples of communications between Carthage and Hannibal during the war. The first was when Hannibal sent his brother, Mago, to Carthage after Cannae to ask for supplies and troops, and the second when Carthaginian envoys came to Hannibal in Croton to recall him to Africa. If Polybius is correct that Hannibal directed the war in all theatres – Sicily, Sardinia, Spain, Italy and Illyria – then we would have expected there to be more evidence of that direction in various communications between Hannibal and Carthage. In any case, if Hannibal was directing the war from Italy, then it is hardly credible that he should complain that Carthage was depriving him of troops and supplies. Carthage was using its resources to pursue a strategy different from Hannibal's, in which victory in Italy no longer occupied a central place or was important at all.

The facts are that Hannibal's shortages of supplies and troops cannot be blamed on the lack of resources available to Carthage to prosecute the war. The manpower and resource base of the Carthaginian Empire was greater than Rome's.[9] The troop and resupply expeditions sent out by Carthage in support of its military operations outside Italy were quite substantial, in some cases larger than Hannibal's army in Italy. In 215 BC, 12,000 infantry, 1,500 cavalry, twenty elephants and twenty talents of silver were sent to Spain. Later that year, an even larger force of 22,000 infantry, 1,200 cavalry and some warships were sent to Sardinia. In 213 BC, Carthage sent an army of 25,000 infantry, 3,000 cavalry and twelve elephants to Sicily to attempt to rescue Syracuse. A year later, Bomilcar attempted to relieve the siege of Syracuse by sea with a fleet of 130 warships and 700 transports. When the Carthaginian army in Sicily was almost wiped out by an epidemic, Carthage sent reinforcements of 8,000 infantry and 3,000 cavalry. In 207 BC, 10,000 troops were sent to Spain to reinforce the forces there that had been lost at the Battle of Baecula. Finally, in 205 BC, Mago and a force of 12,000 infantry, 2,000 cavalry and thirty ships were sent to invade Liguria in northern Italy. A year later, he was reinforced with 6,000 infantry, 800 cavalry, seven elephants and twenty-five warships. With the money sent to him, Mago was able to raise another 10,000 Ligurian mercenaries, for a total force of 30,000 men.[10] Right to the end, Carthage had enough troops and cavalry to support Hannibal in Italy. It simply chose not to do so.

It is sometimes thought that the failure to resupply Hannibal was due to the Carthaginian lack of ships and the preponderance of Roman naval power to intercept supply convoys. The Romans were certainly always apprehensive about the Punic navy, mostly based on the fear that they would attack the Italian coast. While the Roman fleet surely outnumbered the Carthaginian fleet in warships, by the end of the war the disparity could not have been more than about three-to-two.[11] In any given escort operation, however, this disparity might easily disappear or shift to the Carthaginian advantage. Carthage never seems to have had any difficulty in escorting its troop and supply convoys to Spain, Liguria, Corsica, Sicily and Sardinia. Carthaginian naval assets even operated in Greek waters to support Philip V's campaigns, although to no great military effect.[12] When Scipio ordered the Carthaginian fleet burned in the harbour at Utica at the end of the war, Livy says that 500 ships of all kinds were destroyed.[13]

When considering the ability of Carthage to resupply and reinforce her armies in the various theatres of operations, the number of naval combatants to act as escorts was really of little importance. Of more importance were the number of transports available, and Carthage never seems to have had any difficulty in acquiring sufficient transports. This is not surprising for a commercial and shipbuilding nation like Carthage that could construct or hire whatever transports it needed from its commercial traders. Using naval combatants to escort transports only reduced the range and speed of the transports, which could sail day and night over longer distances, without having to regularly stop and rest the crews of the warships.

The Roman naval presence around southern Italy was never sufficient to cover all bases at once, and there was no good reason why supply transports could not have got through to Hannibal in southern Italy, either through Locri or the other Greek coastal city ports in Bruttium. Carthaginian ships reached Hannibal there in 215 BC, and again in 203 BC when the envoys ordered him home. Mago was able to sail to Carthage in 215 BC to inform the Senate of Hannibal's victories, and Hannibal was able to evacuate his army from Croton in 203 BC without incident. In 207–206 BC, the Roman fleet in Sicily was reduced from 100 ships to a mere thirty, clearly opening up an opportunity to reinforce Hannibal in Italy. Hannibal was on the defensive by then, his forces dwindling and his army suffering from lack of supplies and malnutrition. Carthage finally made an attempt to support Hannibal the next year. In 205 BC, a fleet of transports set sail for Italy, only to be blown off course and captured by the Romans.[14] For most of the war, however, supplies and reinforcements did not get to Hannibal in southern Italy because Carthage did not send them. And it did not send them because Carthage no longer considered Italy to be at the centre of its strategic war effort.

Carthaginian strategy shifted away from Italy after Cannae, precisely when Hannibal's achievements were at their greatest. Ironically, it was Hannibal's successes in the field that led Carthage to reconsider Hannibal's strategy. When Mago returned to Carthage in 216 BC to request troops and supplies for Hannibal, he addressed the Carthaginian Senate. At that meeting, Hanno, the leader of the faction that had opposed the war from the beginning, asked Mago the following: 'First, in spite of the fact that Roman power was utterly destroyed at Cannae, has any single member of the Latin Confederacy come over to us? Secondly, has any man belonging to the 5 and 30 tribes of Rome deserted to Hannibal?' Mago had to answer in the negative. Hanno continued: 'Have the Romans sent Hannibal any envoys to treat for peace? Indeed, so far as your information goes, has the word "peace" ever been breathed in Rome at all?' No, said Mago. 'Very well then,' replied Hanno. 'In the conduct of the war we have not advanced one inch: the situation is precisely the same as when Hannibal first crossed into Italy.'[15] Hanno's point was that Hannibal's strategy to bring Rome to the peace table by defeating its armies in the field in Italy had already failed. If none of the Latin Confederacy or the Roman tribes had deserted by now, it was very unlikely that any defections in the south of Italy or additional victories that Hannibal might win there were likely to cause Rome to seek peace.

If one accepts Hanno's view that Rome could not be coerced by Hannibal's victories in Italy, as seems likely that the Carthaginian elites eventually did, then what was the war about? In true Hellenistic fashion, it was not about destroying Rome, but about maintaining Carthage's control of Spain and regaining Sardinia, Corsica and some ports in Sicily that it had lost in the previous war. If that was the strategic objective of the war, then how did Hannibal's continued presence in Italy contribute to that objective? The answer was to tie down as many legions in Italy as possible so they could not be used elsewhere, while Carthage concentrated its military efforts in the other theatres of operations. Thus, Carthage left Hannibal to his own resources and his own fate while it applied its resources in Spain, Sardinia, Corsica and Sicily in the hopes of establishing strong military positions there so that when the war ended, Carthage would be in a position to hold on to what it had won.

At base, Hannibal failed to understand the conservative culture and moralistic values that underlay Roman society and shaped the Roman view of war. The Romans were not Hellenes, a culture they considered soft and corrupt. The Roman response to Hannibal's victories was to raise more legions and keep on fighting. It was this prodigious effort that permitted the Republic to raise and maintain its armies in the field at whatever the cost. It is estimated that nearly all fit male Roman citizens served in the army at some time or other during the war with Hannibal. For some periods, as many as half the eligible men were under arms. Of a military manpower pool of 240,000 male citizens, fully 120,000 died in the war, and it is possible that some 80,000 of them died as the result of combat, the rest from disease, shipwreck or accidents.[16]

In the same way that American commanders in Vietnam and Russian commanders in Afghanistan failed to understand the cultural context of their respective enemies, so too did Hannibal fail to understand the cultural context of his war with the Romans. As a result, despite their many battlefield victories, the Americans, Russians and Hannibal all failed to achieve their strategic objectives and lost the war.

Chapter 23

Marcus Agrippa: The Forgotten Genius behind the Roman Empire

istory has treated Marcus Agrippa (63–12 BC) cruelly, a great Roman soldier whose life exerted an enormous influence upon the foundation of the Roman Empire, perhaps even more so than Augustus himself. The Roman historian, Cassius Dio, gives us the most substantial account of Agrippa's life, with Pliny the Elder and Nicholaus of Damascus making lesser efforts.[1] Agrippa is mentioned by only a handful of other Roman historians, mostly in passing in their wont to exaggerate the contributions of Augustus. As a result, many of Agrippa's achievements have been attributed to Augustus, and Augustus's very name (the Augustan Age) dominates the history of the period in which Agrippa exerted a powerful force on events. It is no exaggeration to say that Agrippa's military and administrative talents in the service of his boyhood friend at critical junctures made Augustus' success possible.

It was Agrippa who reorganized the Roman navy with new ships, tactics and weapons, and Agrippa who crushed Sextus Pompey at the battles of Mylae and Naulochus, giving Augustus control of Italy and Sicily. Agrippa was present at every major battle that Augustus fought, and in some it was Agrippa who actually commanded the troops, while Augustus remained in his tent, sick and incapacitated. Agrippa won a great victory against the Acquitani in Gaul, and suppressed disturbances in Germany, being the first Roman since Caesar to invade Germany. Later (20 BC), he laid out the four major trunk roads in Gaul that are still in use, conquered the Cantabri of Spain, finally bringing the 100-year war there to a conclusion, and put down a revolt of the Dalmatians. As *aedile* of Rome, Agrippa used his personal fortune to modernize the city's water supply and sewer system, naming many of the new structures after Augustus. Agrippa's brilliant victory at Actium won for Augustus undisputed mastery over the entire Roman world. Without Agrippa's aid in these critical situations, Augustus' ambitions might never have been realized.

With the Civil War against Antony won, Augustus faced the challenge of rebuilding the Roman state. Augustus' talent lay in politics, and he knew little of administration and military affairs. He turned to Agrippa to solve the numerous problems of reconstruction, the reorganization of the state's government and political system, the administration of Rome, Italy and the provinces, all of which were in disarray, the re-establishment of the imperial frontiers and the reform and reorganization of the imperial army and navy. The great challenge was finding a way to disarm hundreds of thousands of mercenary soldiers who represented a threat to the new order, and to transfer their loyalty from their *condottieri* commanders to Rome's new ruler. Agrippa contributed greatly to solving these problems, although Roman historians credit Augustus with his achievements. It was Agrippa's brilliant efforts that largely made possible the establishment of the new Roman imperial order.

Marcus Agrippa was probably born in Arpinum to a poor family. Pliny describes his early life as *miseria* ('misfortunes of his youth'), and poverty might have prompted him to join Caesar's legions during the Civil War when he was only 13.[2] By the time he was 18 and acquainted with Octavian, he was an experienced soldier who had fought under Caesar in Africa and in the Spanish campaign (46–45 BC), including the Battle of Munda. Agrippa had come to Caesar's attention for some reason we do not know, along with another young soldier of plebeian origins, Q. Salvidienus Rufus. Caesar brought these young men into the company of his nephew, Octavian, then 18. The three were sent to Apollonia in Greece, the headquarters of the Macedonian legions, where it was expected that Octavian would acquire some military experience.[3] Four months later (March 44 BC), Caesar was assassinated. The friendship between Octavian and Agrippa lasted until the latter's death in 12 BC. Salvidienus Rufus served Octavian as his field general until after the Perusian War (40–41 BC), when he attempted to betray Octavian to Antony, and was executed.[4] Agrippa then became Octavian's top general and military advisor.

We have very little information about the part the young Agrippa played in the events that immediately followed Caesar's murder – Octavian's decision to claim his inheritance, his journey to Rome, his protracted duel with Mark Antony, his rise to popularity, the Civil War against Antony and conflict at Mutina, the reconciliation with Antony, the formation of the First Triumvirate, the bloody proscriptions that followed, the defeat of Caesar's assassins at Philippi and other events. It is safe to assume, however, that the loyal Agrippa was always at Octavian's side, and one of the few advisors to whom Octavian turned for advice. It is almost certain that Agrippa raised and commanded troops at the Battle of Mutina and at Philippi, and it may well have been one of Agrippa's units that saved Octavian's life at Philippi, when he was caught by surprise in his tent as the Roman camp was overrun. Octavian was forced to hide in a marsh for three days until the danger passed.[5]

The Perusian War (41–40 BC)

The Perusian War marks the first appearance of Agrippa as a military commander in his own right. Mark Antony's brother, Lucius, and Antony's wife, Fulvia, raised armies and invaded Italy. Octavian appointed Agrippa to lead an army against Lucius.[6] Agrippa blocked Lucius' attempt to reach Gaul, and penned him up in the town of Perusia. There, Octavian and Salvidienus laid siege to the place, while Agrippa met and blunted three attempts by enemy armies to relieve the siege. In February 40 BC, Lucius surrendered. Before leaving for Gaul to secure the loyalty of Antony's legions there, Octavian entrusted Agrippa with the defence of Italy against Antony. Agrippa moved quickly to put a temporary end to Pompey's sea-borne raids in Sicily. He then attacked Sipontum, taking it by storm and defeating the last of Antony's allies. When news of Agrippa's victories reached Antony, he agreed to a peace with Octavian. Agrippa was involved in the negotiations, and it was here that Octavian learned of Salvidienus' treachery, and had him executed.

Triumph in Gaul and Germany

In 39 BC, Agrippa was sent to Gaul to pacify the Gallic tribes that had grown restless following the withdrawal of Antony's legions there. Near the end of 38 BC, Agrippa won a major victory over the Acquitani, his first great military success. A year later, he crossed into Germany to put down a local rebellion, leading his men in person to put down the menace. Dio notes that in doing this, Agrippa was only 'the second of the Romans to cross the Rhine for war'.[7] For his efforts, Octavian granted him a triumph. Agrippa graciously declined. Agrippa was later offered triumphs after his victories at Mylae and Actium, and again declined. Military men raised to prominence by public triumphs had been a cause of the Roman Civil War, and Agrippa wanted to put an end to this dangerous practice. Agrippa's refusals led to the abandonment of triumphs for anyone but the *principe* (Augustus himself). Successful generals were awarded medals instead. Agrippa was rewarded by being named consul designate, and took office on New Year's Day 37 BC. The office bestowed the *consular imperium* upon Agrippa, the legal right to lead troops in war.

Father of the Roman Navy

Before being sent to Gaul, Octavius had assigned Agrippa the task of constructing a fleet of ships, and recruiting and training crews for use in war against Sextus Pompey, whose pirate ships had been plundering southern Italy and Sicily for almost a decade. Agrippa set the preparations in motion before being ordered to Gaul, and the work continued in his absence. Agrippa was recalled from Gaul and placed in charge of preparations for the campaign against Pompey. Agrippa was 27, and had no experience in naval warfare.

The new ships were constructed at several locations along the Italian coast that had easy access to pine timber. Agrippa realized, however, that once the ships were built, they needed a single assembly point for final outfitting and training crews and marines. Agrippa found a location at Cumae, between Misenum and Puteoli, where a small bay led to the open sea. Inland were two lakes connected by a narrow isthmus.[8] In what was a massive engineering project, Agrippa cut across the inland shore and widened the inner isthmus between the lakes, creating an outlet to the open sea. He named the new inland harbour *Portus Iulius*, in honor of Octavian. Pliny the Elder called the new harbour one of the most magnificent man-made wonders of Italy.[9]

Agrippa designed a new type of high, heavy warship to fight against Pompey's smaller, lighter and shallower draft vessels. The Roman ships were equipped with three new devices: a type of iron-covered grapnel (*harpax*) that could be fired from a catapult, two collapsible shipboard towers that could be raised when needed to provide a better angle of fire for the ship's archers, and the *corvus* (raven's beak), a moveable bridge that could be swung outboard of the carrying ship and lowered upon the enemy vessels, over which Roman infantry could cross and engage the enemy crew. All three of these devices are found on earlier ships, but it was Agrippa's innovation to employ them all together. Agrippa had no intention of trying to manoeuvre against Pompey's faster vessels. He planned to close, grab the enemy ship with his *harpax,* pull the ship close with windlasses and allow his marines to board. In short, Agrippa intended to transform a naval clash at sea into a fight that more resembled combat on land.[10]

The harbour at Misenum became the main base for what would become the Roman imperial navy. Historically, Rome had not maintained a standing naval arm, relying instead upon creating one whenever the need arose. But the naval battles of the civil wars, especially the decisive Battle of Actium, convinced Agrippa to establish the navy he had constructed and commanded on a permanent basis. The Roman navy became 'the most organized, widely-based naval structure in antiquity'.[11] For the next 500 years, the Roman Empire depended as much upon its fleets as upon its legions and roads for its survival. It was Marcus Agrippa who created the first permanent standing Roman naval force.

Battle of Mylae (August 36 BC)

During the summer 36 BC, Agrippa and Octavian went hunting for Pompey in the waters off Sicily. As the Roman fleet approached Sicily, it was struck by a powerful storm that disabled many ships, forcing the fleet to put in for repairs. Octavian relinquished command, and appointed Agrippa to continue the effort to find and attack Pompey. Pompey's fleet lay at anchor off Messana (modern Messina), preventing

Octavian's legionnaires from crossing to Sicily. In mid-August, the two fleets clashed at Mylae on the northern shore of Sicily. Pompey's 150 ships outnumbered the 100 or so of Agrippa, but the taller and heavier Roman ships equipped with the new towers and grapnels carried the day. After several hours of combat, Pompey withdrew his shallower draft vessels into the shoals and broke contact. Agrippa's heavier ships could not follow, but the battle ended in a Roman victory.

Battle of Naulochus (August 36 BC)

With Pompey engaged elsewhere, Octavian took command of the transports and attempted to cross with his army into Sicily from Tauromenium. The result was disaster. Pompey's fleet was able to reach the strait, and fought two battles during the same day. Some of Octavian's ships were captured, many were burned or sunk, and others fled for the Italian shore. At least sixty Roman ships were lost, and Octavian was forced to abandoned the crossing.[12]

With Pompey's fleet continuing to block the crossing at Messina, Agrippa's fleet engaged it off Naulochus on the north shore on 29–30 August, some 10 miles from the Messana Strait.[13] The *harpax* proved a success once again, and the grapnels reduced the ability of Pompey's superior pilots to manoeuvre. At the end of the day, the Romans had burned, captured or run aground all but seventeen of Pompey's ships, losing only three vessels themselves. Pompey and his remaining ships fled, abandoning Sicily.

The consequence of Agrippa's naval victories was that the seas around the Italian peninsula were now peaceful, trade was restored, and Sicily and its manpower and agricultural resources were now at Octavian's disposal. Octavian created a special one-of-a-kind military decoration, a golden wreath surmounted with a ship's *rostra* called the naval crown (*corona navalis*), and awarded it to Agrippa.

The Illyrian War (35–34 BC)

Revolt broke out among the tribes in Illyria and Pannonia, forcing Octavian to take the field against them, accompanied by Agrippa. The region was a patchwork of independent tribes, all with different cultures, languages and social systems, not unlike the situation in the Balkans today.[14] Octavius wanted to strengthen Roman control over the area to deny its possible use by Antony to attack Italy. Agrippa conducted extensive naval operations all along the Dalmatian coast, and was with Octavian at the siege of Metulum. In the following year, Agrippa was sent against the Dalmatians alone, and Octavian joined him later. While Agrippa and Octavian were leading a charge across a bridge, the bridge collapsed, severely injuring Octavian's leg and leaving him with a limp. Despite difficulties involving poor logistics and a mutiny, Agrippa finally subjugated most of the tribes. The entire region, including new areas that had not been under Roman control, was proclaimed the Roman province of Illyricum, administered by a senatorial *proconsul*.[15] Agrippa had once more acquitted himself well in the service of his old friend.

Commissioner of Public Works

In 33 BC, Agrippa was made *aedile* of Rome, responsible for all the public buildings and roads of the city, which he repaired at his own expense, establishing the expectation that the wealthy would thereafter be expected to adorn the city with public works. Pliny tells us that Agrippa rebuilt the city's two main aqueducts, and constructed a new one that he named the *Aqua Julius* after Octavian. Pliny says Agrippa constructed 700 cisterns, 500 fountains and 130 *casella*, or basins, for distributing water, upon which he placed 300 figures of bronze and marble as adornments.[16] To keep the water system running, Agrippa trained a company of slaves to act as repairmen. Later, the slaves were freed and became public employees, creating the world's first public water department.[17]

Agrippa's constructions provided an opportunity to improve the health and sanitation of the citizenry. Pliny tells us that Agrippa built 170 free public bath houses for use by the general population.[18] Daily bathing quickly became a famous Roman habit. The great amount of water now flowing from the taps, fountains and baths through the city's antiquated pipe system was too much for it to accommodate, bringing it to near collapse. Agrippa had the city's entire drainage system cleaned and repaired so that the main sewer, the Cloaca Maxima constructed in 600 BC, once more flowed into the Tiber. Agrippa's improvements made Rome one of the healthiest and cleanest cities in the ancient world.

After the Battle of Actium, Agrippa commissioned the construction of the Pantheon, completed the foundation for the first Roman public bath in the city and established a number of important monuments on the Campus Martius, all at his own expense.[19] He constructed the *Diribitorium*, the vote counting office, the largest building under a single roof ever constructed up to that time.[20] The wealthy of Rome soon followed Agrippa's example, and public works projects sprang up across the city. All the civic buildings were rebuilt, and the city's streets were improved. When Octavian later boasted that he had found Rome a city of brick and left it a city of marble, the transformation was due largely to Agrippa.

The Battle of Actium (September 33 BC)

Agrippa was now entrusted with the preparations for the war against Antony in the East. To conduct coastal raids and counter Antony's heavier ships, Agrippa had a new type of smaller, faster and shallower draft ship constructed, the *Liburnae*, that later became the vessel used by the new riverine force that patrolled the empire's rivers. Agrippa crossed over to Greece in the spring in what probably was a combination feint and reconnaissance in force to determine Antony's dispositions. Agrippa encountered a small flotilla of Antony's supply ships on the way, which he immediately engaged and captured or sunk. He then attacked the coastal town of Kekyra.[21]

Antony had moved his fleet to the harbour at Actium, deploying his army on the ground to protect the harbour from the south. He had established a series of logistics bases to supply his forces on islands and the Greek coast, reaching all the way back to Egypt. In a brilliant strategic move, Agrippa quickly attacked Antony's long and exposed line of communications, capturing Methone on the Greek coast. He then sailed north, attacking more of Antony's coastal supply depots. Finally, he captured Corcyra before joining Octavian, who had moved his army into position north of Actium.

Agrippa now moved to completely cripple Antony's supply line, and starve his army and fleet. Staging from Corcyra, he captured the island of Leucas south-west of Actium, seizing more of Antony's supply transports. Next he captured Cape Ducato, and then Patrae near the western end of the Gulf of Corinth. In a surprise attack, Agrippa seized Corinth itself, closing off all access to the Peloponnese. With his supply lines now completely cut, Antony's army began to starve and suffer from disease.[22]

The Battle of Actium was anticlimactic in that Antony had already decided not to fight, but to break through Agrippa's naval blocking force and make for Egypt, while his land army marched north through Macedonia and Greece to join him there. Antony manoeuvred against Agrippa's right wing in an effort to thin out his centre, allowing Cleopatra and her sixty ships to break though and run for Egypt. Antony's tactics worked well enough, and he was able to salvage some 100 vessels and 20,000 of his best marines against truly incredible odds. Antony planned to fight again once he reached Egypt, but disaster struck when the commander of his land army, Canidius Crassus, went over to Octavian after negotiating favourable terms for his troops.[23] Although politically decisive, the Battle of Actium was not a major military action. Only in later accounts written to glorify Octavian was the tale magnified to heroic stature. Once Agrippa cut off Antony's supplies, the outcome was inevitable, and the credit for the victory belongs rightly to Agrippa.

The Foundations of Empire

Octavian was a sickly sort, given to bouts of paralyzing anxiety, superstition and physical disability, often at the most critical moments.[24] Twice at Philippi and once at Actium, he fell ill and took to his tent, while command fell to others. He lacked the energy and experience for sustained effort, and had little interest in administrative and military matters, which he often left to Agrippa. Agrippa's genius for organization and administration made him an invaluable asset in meeting the challenges of the new imperial realm, and he spent the next decade of his life occupied with organizing and administering the new empire. Agrippa aided Octavian in the establishment of the *principate*, at the same time preserving the forms, if not the powers, of the old Republican institutions. The Senate was reformed, its numbers reduced, powers limited and new members appointed. In 28 BC, Agrippa was appointed consul for the second time, and was made of equal rank with Octavian whenever the two were in military command. At Octavian's urging, Agrippa married Octavian's niece, becoming a member of the royal family.

Of all the imperial reforms, the most important was the reform of the Roman military system, for it was the army that became the defender of the new order, the foremost instrument in organizing and governing the empire, the instrument of civil order and the means of defending Rome against her enemies. These reforms were to a great extent the work of Agrippa. There were some fifty legions, around 300,000 men still under arms, who could not be discharged without provoking great civil unrest. The number of legions was reduced to twenty-five, and the remaining soldiers paid off in money or land grants. The legions were transformed into a professional army with regular pay, retirement accounts and tax privileges upon retirement. They were posted outside Italy to prevent them from once again becoming a threat to the political order.[25]

The Senate was no longer permitted to appoint military commanders, and reports from field commanders were now passed directly to Octavian, bypassing the Senate. To ensure the loyalty of the soldiery, the practice of swearing loyalty to their commanders was outlawed. Soldiers now swore an oath, the *sacramentum*, to Rome itself upon entering military service. At the beginning of each year, soldiers were required to repeat the oath amid solemn ceremony. With only 150,000 soldiers in service, the new practice of raising auxiliary legions from Rome's allies to serve alongside the regular legions when called to service proved an excellent solution to the military manpower problem.

Agrippa's reforms, always carried out in the name of Octavian, transformed the mercenary armies of the Civil War into an impartial instrument of the new state. Had the reforms failed, sooner or later Rome would have succumbed again to the ambitions of a new generation of *condottieri*, pressing their ambitions by military means. Agrippa's reforms remained the fundamental basis of the Roman army for the next two centuries.

The empire's finances were reformed with the establishment of a national mint, bringing an end to the ruinous inflation caused by the debasement of the currency. The tax system was changed so that all taxes now flowed directly to the national treasury, prohibiting the old practice of having often corrupt provincial governors levy and collect imperial monies.[26] Among the most important reforms was the creation of an administrative structure to govern the provinces. Until now, Rome had attempted to govern the empire with the same machinery with which it had governed the city-state, with the result that the ability to control events from the centre was almost non-existent. Provincial governors were no longer appointed by the Senate, but by the emperor, with strong oversight by a system of *procurators*, who kept close watch on the province's finances. Provincial governors no longer held military command, and could be removed at will and prosecuted. Retired centurions were offered posts in civil government at the local level, the provincial law courts reformed and elements of Roman law and protection extended to all residents of the empire. These practices became the groundwork for the gradual establishment of the imperial civil service that became the spine of imperial government for the next four centuries.[27] Again, it was Agrippa who played an important role in their establishment.

In 23 BC, Agrippa was sent east to reorganize the eastern provinces, and may have conducted negotiations with the Parthians for the return of the legion standards lost by Crassus in 53 BC. At Octavian's initiative, Agrippa divorced his wife and married Octavian's daughter, Julia, in 21 BC. Without male heirs of his own, Octavian planned to make Agrippa his successor. In 19 BC, Agrippa was sent to Spain to put down a revolt by the Cantabri. In more than a year of hard fighting, Agrippa broke the back of the insurgency and resistance that had plagued the Romans in Spain for two centuries. Agrippa's victory allowed the Romans to complete the conquest of the Iberian peninsula and begin its economic exploitation and settlement by Roman veterans. Once more Agrippa was offered a triumph; once more he refused.

In 18 BC, again at Octavian's initiative, the Senate granted Agrippa the power of *tribunicia potestas*, officially making him co-regent with Octavian. In 17 BC, Agrippa left again for the East on an inspection tour where he settled soldiers from two legions in Berytus (modern Beirut), establishing the first Roman colony in Syria. In 15 BC, he put down a minor rebellion in the Bosporus, and spent an extended visit with his old friend, Herod the Great. Herod named a wing of the great Roman fortress in Jerusalem the Agrippinium, after Agrippa. The remains of the Roman fortress form the present Wailing Wall. Agrippa supported the Jews against the resident Greeks in retaining the special privileges granted them by Julius Caesar. Agrippa returned to Italy in late 13 BC, and a year later he was dead at the age of 51. His ashes were entombed in Octavian's mausoleum.

Renowned during his life, Agrippa was ignored by Roman historians after his death. Always a loyal friend to Octavian, Agrippa served the empire without ambitions of his own. In doing so, he laid down many of the institutional foundations of the new Roman imperial realm. Cassius Dio called him 'the noblest man of his time'.

Chapter 24

The Roman Navy: Rome's Other Military Arm

In 31 BC, the last two great generals of the Roman civil wars faced each other at Actium off the coast of Greece in a battle for the future of Rome. For months, Mark Antony and Cleopatra had tried without success to break Octavian's land and naval blockade of their armies. Now Antony's armies were running low on supplies, and were ravaged by disease. His fleet of 200 ships, with 20,000 marines and 2,000 archers, put to sea on 2 September to break Octavian's blockade. The Roman fleet under the command of Agrippa had more than 260 ships carrying 30,000 marines and 2,000 archers.[1] Antony's fleet was comprised of large *quinqueremes* and a number of even larger ships of Levantine design. The large ships rode high off the water, affording Antony's marines and archers a significant advantage in close combat. Agrippa's ships were mostly *liburnae*, biremes of Illyrian design constructed two years earlier in Naples, and were smaller, lighter, lower and faster than Antony's ships. Antony intended to fight a typical Roman sea battle, to close with the enemy ship, hold it fast with grappling hooks, board it with marines and finish off the enemy in close combat. Agrippa was the most daring and imaginative commander Rome had produced since Caesar, the real genius behind Octavian's military successes. And he had a different plan in mind.

The battle opened with Antony's 5,000 yard-long line of ships moving into the attack. For four hours the fleets skirmished and manoeuvred in light winds without result. Just past noon, the breeze freshened and Antony's ships manoeuvred to lengthen their line and prevent an envelopment by Agrippa's longer line (8,000 yards) of ships. This is what Agrippa had been waiting for. At Agrippa's command, the fast *biremes* raced toward the heavier and slower *quinqueremes*, breaking the enemy ships' oars and rudders as the Roman ships passed by. Agrippa brought his numerical advantage to bear by having several *biremes* attack a single *quinquereme*. Whenever a *bireme* successfully rammed a *quinquereme*, it did not engage with its infantry, but backed off the target and manoeuvred away. In a few hours, many of Antony's large ships were dead in the water, helpless victims awaiting the final boarding attack.[2]

The Roman attack never came. Agrippa's *biremes* manoeuvred close to the drifting *quinqueremes* and launched flaming pots of pitch and charcoal with their on-board *ballistae* at the helpless ships. Dio Cassius says the crews tried to quench the fiery projectiles with water, but, as their buckets were small and few and half-filled they were not always successful. Then they smothered the fires with their mantles and even with corpses. They hacked off burning parts of the ships and tried to grapple hostile ships to escape into them. Many were burned alive or jumped overboard or killed each other to avoid the flames.[3]

Thousands of Antony's sailors drowned or were burned alive.

The Battle of Actium was the last naval battle of the great Roman Civil War. Rome was now master of the Mediterranean, and would not relinquish its control for 500 years.[4] The naval battles of the Civil War convinced Octavian that Rome needed a permanent navy. Before then, Rome had not maintained a standing naval arm, but relied upon creating one whenever the need arose. The victory at Actium resulted in the establishment of the Roman imperial navy, 'the most organized, widely-based naval structure in antiquity'.[5] For the next 500 years, the Roman Empire depended as much upon its fleets as its legions and roads for its survival.

The Roman Republican Navy

The First Punic War (264–241 BC) between Rome and Carthage brought the first Roman naval force into being. Carthage was the pre-eminent naval power in the western Mediterranean with a fleet of 300 ships, while Rome had no navy at all. The Senate ordered Cornelius Scipio, the grandfather of Scipio Africanus, to construct the first Roman fleet. Italy had large forests of fir and pine from which to build boats, but had no ship designers or crews or captains to take them to sea. The Romans hit upon the idea of copying a *quinquereme* that had fallen into Roman hands. It was not, as is often thought, a Carthaginian ship, but a Rhodian vessel from the navy of Hannibal of Rhodes.[6] Using the captured boat as a template, the Romans constructed a fleet of 100 *quinqueremes* and twenty *triremes*. Polybius says the task was accomplished in two months, and required 165 woodcutters, carpenters and metal workers on each of the ships working full-time, or a labour force of 20,000 men.[7]

Shortages and the cost of trained crews more than the cost of the ships themselves were usually the most important factors in determining the size of a country's navy in antiquity. Galley crews were not slaves, but skilled freemen who were very expensive to hire. Rome used her army conscripts and trained them in the rudimentary skills of rowing and manoeuvre in wooden ship mock-ups on shore.[8] This was the Roman fleet that put to sea to fight the Carthaginians, the largest and most experienced naval force in the western Mediterranean.

The *quinquereme* had been the basic warship of Mediterranean navies since the late Hellenic period, when it replaced the lighter and smaller *trireme*. The *quinquereme* was 120ft long, 18–20ft wide, 10ft high below deck, with a draft of 5ft displacing close to 50 tons. It had two side rudders, an attached metal ram in the prow, raised ends and a single mast and sail 1,400ft² in area. The boat required twenty-eight vertical banks of oars per side, three oars to a bank, the top two oars each worked by two men, the bottom oar by one man, for a total of 280 oarsmen, plus 75–100 marines and twenty-five sailors and officers, a total ship's complement of around 400.[9] Deck space of some 2,000ft² accommodated the marines when boarding or resisting attack. *Ballistae*, siege engines, artillery and fore and aft castles were added later as the ships became larger. Under sail with fresh winds without much sea (i.e., close to shore), a *quinquereme* could make 9 knots.[10] Powered only by oars, it could make 4–6 knots for about two hours before the crew was exhausted. Only three to four days' food and water could be carried aboard. Unlike transports that could sail across the open sea without stopping, warships had to put into shore every few days to rest and replenish the crews. This made naval power dependent upon a friendly shore from which to operate. The Romans learned this lesson quickly, and during the Second Punic War rendered Carthage's fleet useless by controlling the land around the sea, denying her warships safe harbours.

The naval tactics of the day relied upon the skill of captains and rowers to manoeuvre their vessels to pass by an opponent at speed, breaking his oars and leaving his boat dead in the water. The helpless boat could then be rammed with the heavy metal ram built into the attacker's prow. The victor would then back off and watch the victim sink. Lacking trained crews and skilled captains, the Romans played to their strongest military capability: close infantry combat. Roman captains used grappling irons (*manus ferreae*) fired by catapults to grasp the enemy ship and hold it fast, while their marines boarded and engaged in close combat. To facilitate boarding, the Romans introduced the *corvus*, or raven, to naval warfare. This was a swinging wooden boarding ramp. Polybius says it was 6 *oguira*, or 36ft, long and 4ft wide, with railings on each side.[11] Controlled by ropes, the ramp could be swung over the side. A long metal spike extended from the bottom of the ramp, so when the *corvus* was swung out over the enemy's deck and lowered its weight would drive the spike into the deck, holding both ships together and steadying the ramp as Roman marines poured onto the enemy ship. The new tactics caught the Carthaginians by surprise at the Battle of Mylae in 260 BC, destroying their ships one by one.[12]

In 256 BC, the Romans struck at Carthage using a fleet of 250 warships and eighty transports to move a force of 60,000 men in an amphibious invasion of North Africa.[13] Two hundred Carthaginian warships attacked the Roman fleet off Mount Economus. For the first time in Rome's short naval history, the battle was decided by Roman seamanship and manoeuvre rather than seaborne infantry. Squadron commanders acted upon their own initiative to thwart multiple attacks against the troop transports. The Romans lost twenty-four ships, while the Carthaginians suffered thirty sunk and fifty others captured.[14] The battle was a draw, but the Roman invasion force got through and landed in North Africa, where it was later defeated in a land battle and forced to withdraw.[15]

Roman naval losses during the First Punic War were extremely high, due mostly to their practice of sailing in rough weather. Moreover, the weight of the *corvus* and its position on the bow made Roman ships unstable in rough seas. As many as 600 Roman warships and 1,000 transports were sunk during the war.[16] Polybius called the First Punic War the bloodiest in history; Rome lost over 400,000 men, a number almost equal to the total American dead in the Second World War.[17] Probably no war in naval history has seen such casualties to drowning, losses approximately equal to 15 per cent of the total number of able-bodied men of military age in Italy.[18] Despite these high losses, the Romans pressed on, replacing lost ships and training fresh crews to continue the war.

In 241 BC, the Carthaginians tried to lift the Roman siege of Lilybaeum in Sicily by sending a naval force to attack the Roman blockade. Certain of victory, the Carthaginians sent no marines with their ships, planning to acquire them in Lilybaeum once the siege had been lifted. The weather turned foul, but the Roman captains put to sea anyway to intercept the Carthaginian fleet. In a battle off the Aegates Islands, the Romans sank fifty ships and captured seventy of the 200 Carthaginian combatants that took part.[19] Her last fleet gone, and lacking money and raw materials to build another, Carthage surrendered. Rome was now mistress of the western Mediterranean.

Twenty years later, Rome and Carthage were again at war. Probably for financial reasons, Carthage had not rebuilt her combat fleet. When the Second Punic War (219–202 BC) broke out, it had no more than fifty warships to counter the Roman fleet of 220. Carthage's lack of a navy forced Hannibal to take his army overland through Spain, rather than descending directly on the Italian mainland. Without a navy, Hannibal could not shift his forces from theatre to theatre, as could the Romans, and his long overseas supply lines to Carthage were always under threat. As a result, there were no major sea engagements during the long war. In 204 BC, a Roman invasion force of 400 transports carrying 30,000 troops and 1,200 horses, protected by fifty warships, crossed from Sicily and invaded North Africa.[20] Two years later, Scipio defeated Hannibal at Zama and Carthage surrendered. Now only Antiochus of Syria stood between Rome and complete dominance of the entire Mediterranean Sea.

Rome had learned that the proper role of a navy was to support ground operations, and that naval combatants by themselves could not bring about a strategic decision. Thus it was that Rome placed emphasis upon her transport ships as well as combatants. Although there were larger vessels, the most common transport ship of this period could carry about 80–100 tons. These vessels were about 90ft long by 16ft wide and 14ft deep from keel to deck.[21] They were shallow-draft, open-decked, barge-like boats in which men and animals were exposed to the elements during the voyage. A typical troop transport could accommodate forty-eight benches, arranged back to front like pews. This permitted each soldier 5in of leg room and 2in of shoulder room on either side. Configured in this manner, a troop transport could carry about 380 men. Used as a supply ship, a Roman transport could carry 8,000 *modi*, or 120,000lb, of grain.[22] A horse transport required special configuration of its internal hull to create a flat surface upon which the animals could stand. A typical horse transport had fifty horse tie-stalls, each 9ft long and 3½ft wide. A sling in each stall supported the horse and kept the animal from falling. A rope barrier separated each stall from the one in front of it. Horse transports had flat platforms in their sterns to prevent the animals from falling and breaking their legs when boarding or unloading.[23]

The war with Antiochus broke out in 192 BC. Antiochus maintained a large fleet, which made transporting the Roman army from Greece across the Aegean a risky proposition. Lucius Scipio, the brother of Scipio Africanus, marched his army overland to cross the Hellespont and take the war to the Asian mainland. Navy transports ferried his troops across the strait, while other naval units blockaded the Syrian fleet at Ephesus. Both sides skirmished off the coast for weeks. In December 190 BC, as the Roman army was marching down the coast to bring Antiochus to battle, the Syrian fleet tried to break out of its blockade. In a battle fought off Myonnesus, the Romans carried the day.[24] A few weeks later, Antiochus' army was defeated at Magnesia. Rome now controlled the entire Mediterranean. Only Rhodes, a Roman ally, and Egypt, a broken reed, remained in possession of significant naval assets.

But Rome considered herself a land power, and over the next century 'the Romans carried out the most complete process of naval disarmament that the world has ever seen and let her own naval establishment rot away'.[25] The result was one of the worst waves of piracy in classical times. By 102 BC there were more than 1,000 pirate ships preying on Mediterranean shipping, and over 400 coastal settlements had been sacked, their populations sold into slavery in Roman slave markets. Rome finally reacted when the pirates threatened the grain imports upon which Rome depended to feed her people. In 67 BC, Pompey the Great was given a special command by the Senate to eradicate the pirate scourge. Dividing the sea into twenty-five districts, each with its own ships and admirals, Pompey swept the pirates from the sea. He then proceeded to attack their strongholds on land. Within a year their threat was considerably reduced. The experience convinced Rome to rebuild her naval fleet.[26]

Until now, Roman naval experience had been restricted to the tideless Mediterranean. It fell to Julius Caesar to fight the first Roman naval battle upon the open ocean. In 55 BC, Caesar launched his first invasion of Britain. Never having encountered ocean tides, Caesar found his ships grounded on the British coast in shallow water at low tide.[27] The incident is even more embarrassing in light of his having fought the first Roman ocean battle the year before in his campaign against the Veneti in Gaul. The Veneti were a Gallic people living around the coast of the Bay of Biscay, and were excellent sailors. While Caesar moved his armies overland, Decimus Brutus commanded the fleet that engaged the Veneti navy.

The Gallic ships were superior to the Roman *quinqeremes* in every respect. Constructed of oak, they were almost impervious to ramming. Their bottoms were flat and could sit more easily in shallow water. They were higher at the deck line and had high sterns and prows from which to fight off Roman marines. Large leather sails could withstand the high winds better than canvas, allowing the ship to run faster before the wind and elude the Romans.[28] But the Romans found their weak spot. The Gallic ships had no oars, and relied upon the mainsail for propulsion. The halyards supporting the sail were tethered at the sides of the deck on either side.

The Romans devised a new weapon to cripple the ship. Caesar described it thus:

> [S]harp and pointed hooks secured to the ends of long poles, after the fashion of siege hooks. When these contrivances had caught the halyards supporting the yards, the Roman ship was driven away by the oars and the halyards were cut in consequence, so the yards fell to the deck.[29]

With their mainsail halyards cut by these scythes, the Gallic ships were unable to move. The Romans could now close with their grappling irons, and send their infantry aboard to deal with the crew.

The naval engagements that took place during the Roman Civil War saw no changes in Roman tactics or ship design until the Battle of Actium. Two years earlier, Agrippa had constructed a new fleet with a different kind of ship, the Roman *bireme*. At 109ft long, 16ft wide, with a draft of only 3ft, the new ship was smaller and faster than the traditional *quinquereme*, and was probably a larger warship version of the Illyrian pirate vessel, the *liburna*.[30] Two rows of oarsmen pulling eighteen oars per side required 108 rowers. The ship could make 14 knots under sail and more than 7 knots under oars.[31] The boat had two raised platforms, one forward and one aft, from which javelin men and archers could deploy their weapons. The boat carried a complement of eighty marines.[32] A peculiarity of the design was the placement of a gangway above the outrigger frames on either side that was lower than the deck, so marines standing on the deck could hurl their spears over the marines standing below on the gangway. Though built for speed and manoeuvre, Agrippa used them at Actium mostly as platforms for artillery and *ballistae* to attack Antony's larger and slower ships.

The Roman Imperial Navy

The history of the Roman imperial navy began after the Battle of Actium when Octavian sent Antony's 300 captured ships to Forum Iulii (modern Frejus) on the south coast of France, establishing a permanent naval base controlling the northern Mediterranean. From then on, the Roman Empire maintained standing naval forces until the end of its existence.[33] Octavian created two new major naval commands to support large fleets, one (*Classis Praetoria Misenensis*) at Misenum on the Bay of Naples to protect Italy itself and its imported grain supply in the south, and another (*Classis Praetoria Ravennatis*) at Ravenna at the head of the Adriatic to deal with trouble in Dalmatia and Illyria. To protect Egypt, the source of Rome's grain supply, Octavian created the Alexandrian Fleet (*Classis Augusta Alexandrina*). [34]

The Roman campaigns in Germany (AD 5–16) along the Rhine forced the creation of the *Classis Germanica*, with its heavier sea-going ships based near the mouth of the river and lighter river squadrons at Altenburg near Cologne. The invasion and eventual conquest of Britain (AD 43–60) required strong naval logistical support to carry out. The main Roman naval base was at Gesoraicum (modern Boulogne), which became the headquarters for the *Classis Britannica*. One of the significant achievements of the Roman navy during the conquest was the circumnavigation of Scotland, proving that Britain was an island.[35]

The Danube was the other great river border protecting the Empire. The river is naturally divided at the Kazan Gorge, leading the Romans to create two river fleets, the *Classis Pannonica* in the west and the *Classis Moesica* in the east. It was the *Classis Moesica* that provided naval and logistical support to Trajan's conquest of Dacia (AD 101–106). After the Armenian wars, Nero (AD 54–68) created the *Classis Pontica* to control the Black Sea. Under Hadrian (AD 117–138), control of this area was shared with the *Classis Moesica*, which had responsibility for controlling the mouth of the Danube and the area to the north, while the *Pontica* had responsibility for the south and the Hellespont. Later, other smaller fleets such as the *Classis Nova Libyca* and *Classis Aegeptae Alexandrinae* were created to patrol the western littoral, while a larger fleet, the *Classis Syrica*, was created to support Roman forces on the border with Parthia.[36]

Naval bases were usually co-located with legion camps (*castra*), and their major missions were logistical support of the army, transport of troops and patrolling the rivers and coasts with complements of marines aboard. The navy remained

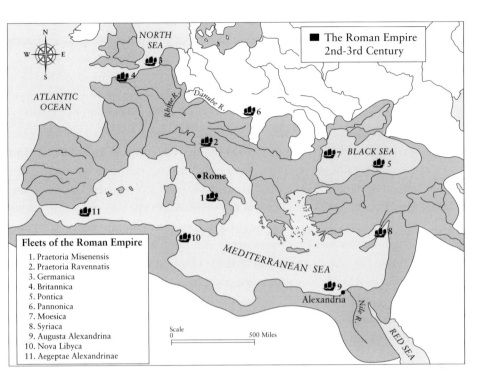

Figure 24: Fleets of the Roman Empire, second third Century AD

subordinate to the army throughout the imperial period. Naval personnel did not think of themselves as sailors (*natuae*) but as soldiers (*milites*), and often had themselves portrayed on their tombstones as legionnaires. Naval crews were organized along military lines into centuries just like the army, and each ship had a centurion aboard assisted by an *optio*, who seems to have served as a first sergeant. The centurion was responsible for training the crew to fight as infantry, repel boarders or act as an assault party under his command.

The fleets were organized into squadrons of probably ten ships, each commanded by a *navarch*, or squadron commander. A ship was commanded by a *trierach* (captain) assisted by a small administrative staff under a *beneficarius*. Commanding officers were drawn from the equestrian class of Roman nobles, and fleet commanders carried the rank of *praefecti*. The sailors were freemen drawn from the lower ranks of society. Few were Romans, however, most being drawn from among the sea-faring peoples of the eastern Mediterranean or the provinces. Service was for twenty-six years, and citizenship was awarded upon discharge.

The function of the navy during the imperial period changed considerably. A navy originally intended for combat at sea under the Republic evolved into one largely comprised of multi-purpose military vessels, and then into river fleets comprised of smaller vessels intended mostly for transport and patrolling. The ships of the Republic had been designed for combat, with full decks upon which to muster marines for battle, a formidable ram and a removable mast to provide for a high degree of manoeuvre. By the first century BC, the undecked ship, less useful for combat but more suitable for transport of supplies and troops, became common. With no rival navies with which to contend at sea, emphasis shifted to the river fleets (Rhine, Danube and the Nile) that supported ground operations in securing the imperial borders. By the third century AD, ships of Byzantine design came into wide use. These vessels had fore and aft posts, fixed masts making them less agile in combat, and were rowed from deck level. Some even lacked a ram. Other ships associated with the peoples of northern Europe also came into use as transport vessels, some resembling the flat, long, narrow Viking longboats.

The change in mission from combat on the open sea to logistics and troop transport along the coasts and upon inland waterways forced changes in ship design. As early as AD 15, Tacitus records that Germanicus' campaign in Germany required a new type of ship to sail on the inland waterways and canals. These ships had wide hulls, narrow sterns and bows and flat keels to navigate the shallow rivers. They could be sailed or rowed, and had covers to protect the men and cargo from wind and weather.

The defence of the river borders also required combat ships that were faster, lighter and of shallower draft than the sea-going combatants still in service in the ocean-going fleets. The most prominent of these combat ships was the *liburna*, a design copied from the Illyrian pirates of Liburnia (modern Balkans). The *liburna* had been used by the Romans even before Actium, but now became the basic ship of the river and coastal fleets. About 80ft long and of shallow draft, the boat had only two rows of oars and a crew of sixty rowers. It had a forward-raking mast and a single sail, and could be built decked or undecked. Under sail it could make close to 14 knots, and carried thirty to fifty marines depending upon the mission.[37] It was fast and highly manoeuvrable, and its low hull made it easy to put into riverbanks for loading and unloading. While the word *liburna* was first used to describe a specific type of warship, in the course of time it became synonymous with warships in general, and the crews of warships came to be called *liburnarii*.

The Roman fleets and naval squadrons were vitally important to the defence and survival of the Empire by patrolling the larger rivers that were the Empire's borders and safeguarding the regional river traffic routes to protect trade. In times of crisis, the navy served primarily as a transporter of troops and supplies. Even then its light combatants could be brought into play in direct support of ground operations.

Rome ruled the seas for more than four centuries. But weakened by repeated invasions of barbarians from the East, internal political discord, civil wars and even a great plague, Rome found itself unable to sustain its naval establishment. By the time Diocletian became emperor AD (284), the imperial navy in the West had shrunk to little more than a handful of local flotillas. However, in the eastern Empire at Constantinople, the imperial navy remained vigorous and strong. It played a crucial part in resisting the Arab invaders two centuries later. By AD 450 in the West, the Vandals had established a kingdom in North Africa and constructed a powerful navy that their king, Gaiseric, used to raid the coasts and shipping of the Mediterranean, and to attack Rome itself. By the time of Gaiseric's death in AD 477, Roman naval power had been completely eliminated in the western Mediterranean, and the Vandals were masters of the once Roman sea.

Chapter 25

Rome: The Death of a Superpower

The Roman Empire was the largest and most powerful empire of antiquity. It reached its greatest expanse under Trajan (reigned AD 98–117), encompassing an area of 3 million square miles, and containing a population of over 60 million. The Empire was tied together by more than 53,000 miles of paved roads, and another 200,000 miles of secondary roads. Roman engineers founded or improved more than 1,000 cities and towns, transforming the rural European landscape into a marvel of urbanization. At one time, a quarter of all humanity lived under Roman rule. In the fourth century AD, the Roman army could put 435,000 infantry and cavalry and 45,000 sailors and marines in the field. By the time of its death with the fall of Constantinople in 1453 at the hands of the Ottoman Turks, the Roman army had existed for more than 2,200 years, the oldest continually existing social institution in the West.[1]

The city of Rome itself was a magnificent example of Roman cultural, technological and social superiority over other extant civilizations. In AD 356, Rome had twenty-eight libraries, ten basilicas, eleven public baths, two amphitheatres, three theatres, two circuses (the *Circus Maximus* could seat 200,000 people; the *Colosseum* 55,000), nineteen aqueducts, eleven public squares, 1,352 fountains and 46,602 *insulae,* triple-storey apartment houses, each forming a city block. Yet, in little more than a century, barbarian invaders stood astride the Empire's corpse, the capital in ruins.

The reasons for the Empire's demise remain among the great unsettled questions that occupy historians. Nonetheless, it is possible to identify some of the major forces that rendered the imperial government incapable of dealing with the lethal challenges that beset it. Of all the factors draining the Empire of its ability to survive, four seem most important: (1) the changing nature of the external threat to the Empire's western borders; (2) the frequent civil wars among various claimants to the imperial throne; (3) the migration and settlement of large, armed and culturally hostile barbarian populations within the imperial borders; (4) the gradual erosion and eventual demise of the Empire's manpower and taxpayer base required to sustain the defence and administrative capability of the Roman state.

The Changing Barbarian Threat

The Romans called the area beyond the western imperial border that followed the Rhine and Danube rivers the *barbaricum*, or land of the barbarians. The Roman historian Publius Cornelius Tacitus in his *De origine et situ Germanorum* provides us with a description of the peoples that inhabited the border area in the first century AD. These mostly Germanic-speaking peoples were relatively few in number and lived in small villages, their populations limited by their primitive agricultural technology. Employing only the wooden scratch plough, German farmers could not turn the earth sufficiently to sustain its fertility. With no knowledge of irrigation or the value of manure, the soil's ability to sustain adequate agricultural production quickly declined after only a few seasons of production, forcing the population to move every generation or so in search of fertile land.

The small populations and nomadism of the German tribes retarded development of their political structures. Government was only local, and comprised clan chiefs (whom the Romans often called kings) whose ability to enforce governance was limited by councils of advisors drawn from among other important persons in the clan. The 'king' did not have the wealth or manpower to form a warrior group loyal to him alone. Instead, military forces, such as they were, were comprised of an assembly of clan warriors that came together as circumstances required. These warrior groups were usually small and capable of only conducting plunder raids in very limited fashion. Roman diplomacy employed subsidies, trade, military honours and punitive expeditions against the recalcitrant to guarantee the loyalty of the tribes, often playing off one against another. Under these conditions, the Germanic tribes on the western border presented no real threat to Roman garrisons. The limited size of the tribal populations presented no threat of mass migration and, occasionally, small groups were resettled as farmers on the Roman side of the border to keep the peace. In a few instances, the tribes provided warriors to serve in limited military capacities in the Roman army.

By the third century AD, all this had changed. The presence of Roman garrisons and merchants on the border lands led to the economic and further socio-political development of the border tribes. The Roman garrisons provided a lucrative market for agricultural products, manpower for slaves, military recruits and metals for weapons. Increased Roman demand transformed the old German subsistence economy. The introduction of Roman agricultural techniques – the iron deep plough, manure fertilization and irrigation – led to larger farms, more available food, an explosion in population and the establishment of towns, all of which stabilized the tribal populations and put an end to the traditional agricultural nomadism.

These larger tribes required more complex political and organizational structures. Among the most important developments was the ability of now wealthy tribal kings to support a significant warrior class. By the end of the second century AD, the populations of the Germanic tribes on the imperial borders had grown considerably. When the kings of the tribes arranged themselves in confederation under the temporary authority of elected leaders, these confederations could easily field armies in excess of 10,000 men.

The discovery of large metal ore deposits beyond the imperial border created a local armaments industry. Just two deposits in Poland produced 16,000,000lb of raw iron during the Roman period. Before this, metal weapons were individually produced, very expensive and strictly controlled by Roman authorities. By the third century, local factories in the border areas were producing thousands of weapons and many of the Roman garrisons were now equipped with weapons produced locally. The tribal warrior classes could now be equipped with the same weapons at low cost.

The political unity necessitated by the confederations enhanced the tribal populations' sense of common identity. The civilian populations of these confederations ranged between 50,000 and 100,000 in some cases. As long as their warrior classes were content to remain under Roman control and limit their military activities to periodic raiding, the tribes presented no real difficulty for the Romans. However, under pressure from other, more inland tribes on the move for better land or plunder, the large border tribes now presented the threat of mass migration across the imperial borders.

The tribal kings borrowed the Roman practice of compulsory, full-time military service. Instead of calling upon warriors only when needed, as had been the traditional practice, kings were now able to support and equip armies of considerable size. The result was the emergence of a semi-professional, large and well-armed warrior class. These armies often came to be well-led and well-trained in Roman military methods, acquired from service in the Roman army as allied units. Arminius, the German chieftain who massacred three Roman legions at the Battle of the Teutoburg Forest in AD 9, had served in the Roman army. His brother was still an officer in Roman service when the battle occurred.

By the end of the second century, the nature of the threat faced by the Romans along the western imperial borders had changed drastically. Instead of the small, quasi-nomadic clans described by Tacitus in the first century, there were now large, politically organized confederations led by warrior kings that had large military forces under their command living in the border zone. For the most part, these tribes were still content to carry out raids aimed at plundering the Roman settlements on the other side of the border. These raids sometimes brought harsh Roman retaliation. But just as often they brought higher subsidies and more economic opportunities, including the chance for warriors to obtain service in the Roman army itself. But if pushed from behind by the development of tribes further inside the *barbaricum*, or pulled by the lure of a better economic life, the German tribes would be a problem.

In the winter of AD 166, this new reality burst forth when the Langobardi and Ubii began raiding the Roman province of Pannonia (modern Hungary south of the Danube). A year later, two long-time Roman clients, the Marcommani and Victuali, demanded to cross the Danube and settle in the Empire. The cause of these demands was pressure from tribes beyond the frontier zone moving in force to conquer the area for their own use. Emperor Marcus Aurelius (reigned AD 161–180) was at war with the Parthians in modern Armenia, and had weakened the German frontier by diverting troops to the Parthian war. The Romans were eventually able to contain the pressure, but not before some Germans had raided Aquileia in Italy itself, and the war had gone on for ten years.

The Macromanni war is noteworthy for its scale. This was no border raid. Damage was serious, with a number of cities sacked. The raids were accompanied by an attempt at large-scale migration by some of the German tribes. Between AD 233–275, major barbarian raids occurred all along the Roman western frontier, some resulting in the settlement of significant barbarian populations inside the imperial borders. Scholars have called this period the Third Century Crisis. The military strength of the tribes was now a reality, and would remain so for the next two centuries until Roman defences on the Rhine and Danube frontier collapsed completely.

Frequent Civil Wars

A major cause of Rome's inability to deal with the growing barbarian threat was the frequent civil wars fought between emperors and usurpers. The challengers to the emperors were usually army generals or those who supported some rival claimant to the purple. These civil wars set Roman units against one another in open battle, often causing high casualties and disrupting training and the manpower supply needed to defend the Empire against its external enemies. Often, units along the Rhine and Danube frontier were transferred to other areas of the Empire to participate in civil wars, weakening Rome's ability to defend its borders. In just two of these conflicts, Magnus Maximus (AD 383–387) and Eugenius (AD 392–394) so depleted the Roman garrisons on the western frontiers to fight against the emperor of the eastern Empire, Theodosius, that the defence of the Rhine was dependent almost entirely upon the loyalty and good will of local barbarian client kings.

Before the reign of Marcus Aurelius, there had been only a few serious civil wars. But between his death in AD 180 and the deposition of the last western Roman emperor, Romulus Augustus, in AD 476, there were more than 100 instances of armed violence in the western Empire alone, as rival claimants challenged sitting emperors. Some of these conflicts were local rebellions that lasted only a few months, and were quickly put down. Others, however, lasted years, sometimes for more than a decade, destroying Roman military manpower and stripping the frontiers of much needed troops. There is no way of knowing exactly how many Roman soldiers were killed by other Roman soldiers during these wars, but the number must have been considerable. Ironically, most of the emperors and usurpers died at the hands of their own subordinates. After AD 217, there were only a few decades without some sort of violent struggle for power within the Empire. Tiberius was correct when he observed that 'to govern Rome was like holding a wolf by the ears'.

The frequent civil wars did more than weaken the army through combat losses. The fear of usurpers had now become the most pressing concern for the emperors, more important than even the threats to the Empire's borders. Since no usurper could hope to succeed without the support of substantial military units, the old and larger Roman provinces were broken up into smaller ones so that the military forces under command of any given provincial official were kept small enough to prevent a threat. The break-up of the provinces began under Septimus Severus (reigned AD 193–211), and Diocletian (reigned AD 284–305) continued the process until some of the provinces and their military garrisons were so small that they were unable to deal with even local raiders.

Early in the fourth century, the Roman army's organizational structure was drastically changed by Constantine (reigned AD 306–337). The reason for these reforms, begun under Diocletian, had little to do with national defence or military efficiency. Constantine, himself a usurper who gained power through civil war, was most concerned with protecting himself from other would-be usurpers. The emperor created new mobile field armies called *comitatenses*, the name derived from *comitatus*, the imperial household. These were large armies commanded by the emperor himself, designed to protect his person and deter attempts against the throne. As part of these new security arrangements, the emperors abandoned the city of Rome as a national capital, moving frequently from city to city to avoid threats to their persons. This crippled the central administration of the Empire, since slow communications and uncertainty at the court made it difficult for the bureaucracy to operate efficiently. This was important because the army did not control its own logistics, but relied on state bureaucrats to provide the materials, manpower and finances for war. Paradoxically, the size of the bureaucracy increased greatly during this time, mostly to reward friends with official positions. Rome ceased to be an effective national administrative and military capital. Now the capital was wherever the emperor was in residence.

Milan and Ravenna were frequent residences for Roman emperors because of their excellent natural defences.

The *comitatenses* had no permanent barracks or fortresses, and were billeted with the civilian population, dispersed in towns and villages wherever the emperor held court. The army's logistical support remained with the distant bureaucracy in Rome which, when coupled with the dispersion of the army units, made it very difficult to supply and direct the army in field operations. The old frontier legions of 5,000 men were reduced in size, as were all garrison commands on the frontiers, again to prevent large military units from supporting usurpers. These smaller units were called *limitanei*. Many of the forts and strongpoints on the frontier were also made smaller, and others simply abandoned. This forced the army to rely on drafts of barbarian recruits from local kings to defend the frontier. Even the *comitatenses* armies were mostly pieced together from the remnants of the various civil war armies. The quality of Roman military forces declined considerably. By the middle of the fourth century AD, the Roman emperors possessed a very much weakened and badly positioned military to deal with the threat on the frontiers and the internal rebellions and raids launched by the barbarian tribes that had already been settled within the Empire.

Invasion and Migration

Despite the civil wars and the Empire's weakened military capability, Roman emperors were able to contain the border threats fairly well. The dynamic beyond the border of new tribes pressing the more settled tribes nearer the border continued to operate, with the result that Roman power was used in support of client kings to resist the invaders. In some cases, tribes of moderate size were settled within the Empire's borders, their populations dispersed to work vacant farm land.

Far to the east, however, a large coalition of nomadic tribes led by the Huns began moving toward the Danube frontier in a campaign of raiding and plunder. Recruiting warriors from the conquered tribes along the way, the Hunic army swept over the middle Hungarian plain, setting the local populations fleeing toward the Roman border in search of protection. In the summer of AD 376, two groups of Goths numbering together some 10,000–15,000 warriors and 60,000 women, children and elderly suddenly appeared on the banks of the Danube requesting asylum within the imperial borders, and permission to settle in Thrace. The Danubian frontier had been stripped of its forces to fight Emperor Valen's war against Persia. Unable to resist, Valens agreed to their settlement.

Things went horribly wrong. There was an acute shortage of food, and a corrupt Roman commander (Lupicinus by name) gathered up all the dogs in the area and sold them to the starving Goths. The going rate was one child for one dog. This set the Goths on a rampage, and they ravaged the area in northern Thrace, cutting several Roman units to pieces. Valens made peace with the Persians in AD 377, and set out to deal with the Goths. In the summer of AD 378, the Goths and Romans met in battle at Adrianople. Two-thirds of the Roman army was killed, along with the emperor. For the next four years, the Goths continued to ravage Thrace until concluding a peace in AD 382 that allowed some of them to settle in Italy and the rest in Thrace.

The dam had burst. Weakened Roman frontier defences, the success of the Goths in obtaining resettlement, the desire for a better life and Hunic pressure from behind spurred more tribes to cross the weakly defended border. The defeat at Adrianople had destroyed 60 per cent of the Roman army of the East, many of whom had been withdrawn from the western border. The Romans tried hard to stop what had now become a mass migration, attacking the migrating columns as they attempted to cross the rivers, and hunting them down after they had made the crossing and moved inland. Between AD 405–408, other large-scale barbarian invasions attacked the Empire, a time historians refer to as the Fourth Century Crisis. Roman losses during the campaigns between AD 395–410 were horrific. A.H.M. Jones estimates that some eighty regiments – close to 50 per cent of the Roman field army in the West – were ground to dust fighting the various invaders. Roman commanders were so short of manpower that they resorted to hiring the warriors of the tribes already settled in the Empire. Barbarians were now fighting for Rome to prevent the entry of other barbarians.

Once the barbarians were inside the border defences, Rome lacked the military strength to expel them, although great and bloody efforts were made to do so. The invaders were settled in various provinces of the Empire, often with the requirement of providing troops to the Roman army. Settling the migrations did not end the problem, however. The barbarian settlements had their own kings and armies sufficient to resist Roman efforts to control them. Within a few years, the barbarian kings took to fighting one another and raiding and occupying neighbouring Roman settlements. Most of the interior cities and towns lacked defensive walls, the product of the long Roman peace, and the barbarian raids and Roman counterattacks devastated several of the provinces. These barbarian settlements became the prototypes of the feudal kingdoms that emerged later.

Taxes and Military Manpower

Sustaining the Roman army was always the Empire's greatest expense. Now with the barbarian settlements and outright occupation of some of the provinces, the flow of tax money to the imperial capital dried up. Instead, the money went directly to the barbarian chiefs who provided warriors for the Roman army. With

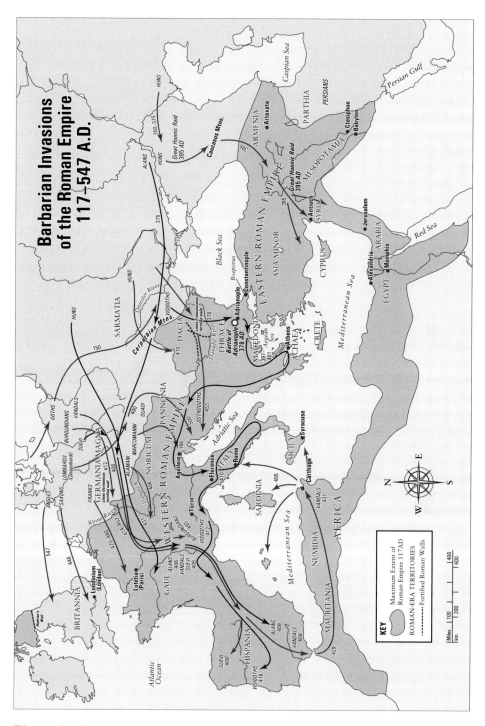

Figure 25: Barbarian Invasions of the Roman Empire, AD 117–547

the transfer or seizure of large landed estates to the barbarian occupiers, much of the tax revenue simply stopped flowing to Rome. By the end of the third century, it is estimated that two-thirds of the Empire's tax revenue no longer reached the imperial administration. With the loss of the silver mines in Spain to the Vandals in AD 411 and the Vandal conquest of the North African provinces in AD 435, Rome's richest provinces in terms of grain supply and tax revenue, imperial finances were crippled beyond repair.

Without sufficient funds, the imperial administration, or what remained of it, could no longer raise sufficient manpower or train them adequately to meet the Empire's manpower and logistics requirements. In short order, the Roman army became a coterie of barbarian war bands serving under their own chiefs, not the imperial eagle. Some of these warrior chiefs had come to think of themselves as Romans and remained loyal, and sometimes the barbarian armies were commanded by an imperial officer. But there was no denying the truth that the once magnificent army and Empire of Rome were now in their death throes.

Why the Eastern Empire Survived

The collapse of the Empire in the West throws into sharp relief the success of the Eastern Empire's ability to function as an important state for another 1,000 years. For the most part, the circumstances that brought down the Western Empire did not confront the Empire of the East.

Geography: The only natural obstacles to invasion in the West were the Danube and Rhine rivers. In the East, the main geographic barrier was the Bosporus. To cross this barrier in any force required ships, sailing ability and the power to confront the formidable Roman navy, resources the barbarian tribes lacked. The imperial capital was protected in the north-east by mountains and easy-to-defend narrow passes. Roman diplomacy maintained good relations with the mountain tribes that provided manpower and early warning against any invasion threat. Even so, in AD 395 a large force of Huns broke through and raided Antioch, before being driven back. To the south and east, the Parthians and later the Sassanid Persian Empire acted as a blocking force to Arab invasions from that direction. Although the Romans had outstanding security issues with the Persians, dealing with an organized state was much easier than with a number of tribes attacking across a long and vulnerable border. The zone of vulnerability to invasion and the nature of the frontier threat were very different in the East.

Few Civil Wars: The Eastern Empire was not entirely free of threats to the throne posed by usurpers that resulted in civil wars, but there were far fewer such attempts than in the West. What few civil conflicts that occured were short-lived, and mostly resulted in victories for the legitimate imperial rulers. The Eastern court was a snake pit, but its politics and conflicts were not as violent nor as destructive as in the West. The Eastern emperors were rarely murdered as they so commonly were in the West. The habit of Western emperors in moving the imperial capital out of fear of assassination did not occur in the East. Constantinople remained the administrative, political and military capital, effectively controlling the army, bureaucracy, finances and logistics required of the imperial state. The stability of the capital also contributed to a persistent sense of national identity with the old Empire, an identity that had been lost in the West. To the very end, the inhabitants of the Eastern realm thought of themselves as Romans.

No Barbarian Settlement: The geography that made invasion of the Eastern Empire difficult had the effect of diverting the invaders to the West, where the geography was more accommodating to assaults on the imperial frontiers. Both the Huns and Goths moved west after their movement to the east had been blocked. The combination of geography and a still effective Roman army was such that the migrating tribes were never able to break through the Eastern defences in large numbers. In the few instances where they did, as with the Goths in Thrace, they were hunted down by the army and forced to surrender. The remnants were dispersed throughout the imperial lands in small groups, and their warriors disarmed. The Eastern emperors were never forced to settle large barbarian populations possessed of independent armies capable of threatening the Empire from within. The Roman army of the East deliberately pursued a policy of reducing the number of barbarian soldiers allowed in its ranks, and never became dependent upon large barbarian contingents as it did in the West.

Financial Stability: Without major invasions, the disruptions of civil war, no large barbarian settlements and possessing adequate military manpower resources, the provinces of the Eastern Empire remained mostly peaceful, wealthy and agriculturally productive. The widespread destruction caused by the wars amongst the barbarians settled within the Western imperial borders did not occur in the East, and the economic infrastructure of the Eastern state remained intact and functional. Even the rich North African provinces were recaptured from the Vandals. These circumstances sustained the financial and manpower resources that the imperial capital required to operate the state bureaucracy and support the army.

After the collapse of the Empire in the West, the Eastern Empire withstood the efforts of various attackers for another 1,000 years. In 1453, Constantinople came under lethal assault from the Ottoman Turks. The Roman army faced certain death. But perhaps mindful of its noble heritage, it put up one hell of a fight.

Chapter 26

Muhammad: Islam's First Great General

To think of Muhammad (AD 570–632) as a military man will come as something of a new experience to many. And yet Muhammad was truly a great general. In the space of a single decade, he fought eight major battles, led eighteen raids and planned thirty-eight other military operations where others were in command, but operating under his orders and strategic direction. He was wounded twice, suffered defeats and twice had his positions overrun by superior forces before rallying his troops to victory. Muhammad was more than a great field general and tactician, however. He was also a military theorist, organizational reformer, strategic thinker, operational-level combat commander, political-military leader, heroic soldier, revolutionary, the inventor of the theory of insurgency and history's first successful practitioner of the art.

Muhammad proved to be a master of intelligence in war, and his intelligence service eventually came to rival that of Byzantium and Persia, especially in the area of political intelligence. He often spent hours devising tactical and political stratagems, and once remarked that 'all war is cunning', reminding us of Sun Tzu's dictum that 'all war is deception'. In his thinking and application of force, Muhammad was a combination of Clausewitz and Machiavelli, for he always employed force in the service of political goals. He was an astute grand strategist whose use of non-military methods (alliance building, political assassination, bribery, religious appeals, mercy and calculated butchery) always resulted in strengthening his long-term strategic position, sometimes even at the expense of short-term military considerations.

Muhammad's unshakable belief in Islam and his role as the Messenger of God revolutionized warfare in Arabia, and created the first army in the ancient world motivated by a coherent system of ideological belief. The ideology of holy war (*jihad*) and martyrdom (*shahada*) for the faith was transmitted to the West during the wars between Muslims and Christians in Spain and France, where it changed traditional Christian pacifistic thinking on war, brought into being a coterie of Christian warrior saints and provided the Catholic Church with its ideological justification for the Crusades.[1] Ideology of the religious or secular variety has remained a primary element of military adventure ever since.

It was Muhammad who forged the military instrument of the Arab conquests that began within two years of his death by bringing into being a completely new

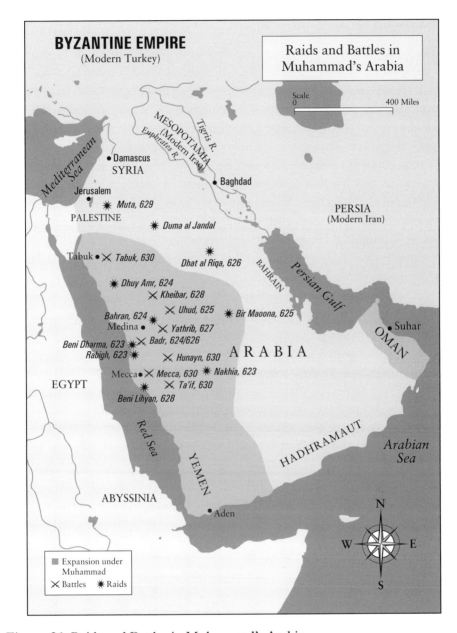

Figure 26: Raids and Battles in Muhammad's Arabia

kind of army not seen before in Arabia. Muhammad introduced no fewer than eight major military reforms that transformed the armies and conduct of war in Arabia that his successors used to defeat the armies of Persia and Byzantium and establish the heartland of the Empire of Islam. Had Muhammad not transformed the armies, the Arab conquests would likely have remained a military impossibility.

Muhammad the Revolutionary

Although his reforms and military achievements afford him much in common with the greatest generals in antiquity, Muhammad was not a conventional field general. He was, instead, a new type of warrior, one never before seen in antiquity. Muhammad was first and foremost a revolutionary, a fiery religious guerrilla leader who created and led the first genuine national insurgency in antiquity that is comprehensible in modern terms. Unlike conventional generals, Muhammad's goal was not the defeat of a foreign enemy or invader, but the replacement of the existing Arabian social order with a new one based upon a radically different ideological view of the world. To achieve his revolutionary goals, Muhammad utilized all the means recognized by modern analysts as characteristic of a successful insurgency. Although Muhammad began his struggle for a new order with a small guerrilla cadre capable of undertaking only limited hit-and-run raids, by the time he was ready to attack Mecca a decade later that small guerrilla force had grown into a large conventional armed force with integrated cavalry and infantry units capable of conducting large-scale combat operations. It was the first truly national military force in Arab history.

Muhammad's rise to power was a textbook example of a successful insurgency, indeed the first such example in antiquity. If the means and methods used by modern military analysts to define insurgency warfare are employed as categories of analysis, it is clear that Muhammad's campaign to spread Islam throughout Arabia fulfilled all of the criteria. One requirement for an insurgency is a determined leader whose followers regard him as special in some way, and worthy of their following him. In Muhammad's case, his own charismatic personality was enhanced by his deeply held belief that he was God's Messenger, and that to follow Muhammad was to obey the dictates of God himself.

Insurgencies also require a messianic ideology that espouses a coherent creed or plan to replace the existing social, political and economic order with a new order that is better, more just or ordained by history or even God himself. Muhammad used the new religious creed of Islam to challenge basic traditional Arab social institutions and values as oppressive, unholy and in need of replacement. To this end, he created the *ummah*, or community of believers, God's community on earth, to serve as a messianic replacement for the clans and tribes that were the basis of traditional Arab society. One of Muhammad's most important achievements was the establishment of new social institutions that greatly altered and, in some cases, completely replaced those of the old Arab social order.

Successful insurgencies also require a disciplined cadre of true believers to do the work of organizing and recruiting new members. Muhammad's revolutionary cadre consisted of the small group of original converts he attracted in Mecca, and took with him to Medina. These were the *muhajirun*, or Emigrants. The first converts among the clans of Medina – the *ansar*, or Helpers – also filled the ranks of the cadre. Within this revolutionary cadre was an inner circle of talented men, some of them later converts. Some, like Abdullah Ibn Ubay and Khalid al-Walid, were experienced field commanders and provided a much-needed source of military expertise. Muhammad's inner circle advised him, and saw to it that his directives were carried out. These advisors held key positions during the Prophet's lifetime, and fought among themselves for power after his death.

Once Muhammad had created his cadre of revolutionaries, he established a base from which to conduct military operations against his adversaries. These operations initially took the form of ambushes and raids aimed at isolating Mecca, the enemy's main city, and other trading towns that opposed him. Only one-in-six Arabs lived in a city or town at this time; the others resided in the 'countryside' or desert, living as pastoral nomads.[2] Muhammad chose Medina as his base of operations. Medina was strategically located in that it was close to the main caravan route from Mecca to Syria that constituted the economic lifeline of Mecca and other oases and towns that depended upon the caravan trade for their economic survival. Medina was also sufficiently distant from Mecca to permit Muhammad a relatively free hand in his efforts to convert the Bedouin clans living along the caravan route. Muhammad understood that conversions and political alliances with the Bedouins, not military engagements with the Meccans, were the keys to success.

Insurgencies require an armed force and the manpower to sustain it. It was from the original small cadre of guerrillas that the larger conventional army could be grown that ultimately permitted the insurgency to engage its enemies in set-piece battles. Muhammad may have been the first commander in history to understand and implement the doctrine later espoused by General Vo Nguyen Giap of North Vietnam as 'people's war, people's army'.[3] Muhammad established the belief among his followers that God had commandeered all Muslims' purposes and property for His efforts, and that all Muslims had a responsibility to fight for the faith. Everyone – men, women and even children – had an obligation for military service in defence of the faith and the *ummah*, the community of God's chosen people on earth. It is essential to understand that the attraction of the ideology of Islam more than anything else produced the manpower that permitted Muhammad's small revolutionary cadre to grow into a conventional armed force capable of large-scale engagements.

The rapid growth of Muhammad's insurgent army is evident from the following figures. At the Battle of Badr (AD 624) Muhammad could only put 314 men in the field. Two years later, at Second Badr (AD 626), 1,500 Muslims took the field. Two years after that (AD 628) at Kheibar, the Muslim army had grown to 2,000 combatants. When Muhammad mounted his assault on Mecca (AD 630), he did so with 10,000 men, and at the Battle of Hunayn a few months later, the army numbered 12,000 men. Some sources record that Muhammad's expedition to Tabuk later that same year was comprised of 30,000 men and 10,000 cavalry, but this is probably an exaggeration.[4]

Like all insurgent armies, Muhammad's forces initially acquired weapons by stripping them from prisoners and the enemy dead. Weapons, helmets and armour were expensive items in impoverished Arabia, and the early Muslim converts, drawn mostly from among the poor, orphaned, widowed and otherwise socially marginal, could ill afford them. At the Battle of Badr, the first major engagement with an enemy army, the dead were stripped of their swords and other military equipment, establishing a practice that became common. Muhammad also established the practice of requiring prisoners to provide weapons and equipment instead of money to purchase their freedom.[5] Muhammad was eventually able to supply weapons, helmets, shields and armour for an army of 10,000 for his march on Mecca.

Muhammad's ability to obtain sufficient weapons and equipment had an important political advantage. Muhammad often supplied converts with expensive captured military equipment, immediately raising their status within the clan and guaranteeing their loyalty to him, if not always to the creed of Islam. Horses and camels were equally important military assets, and Muhammad obtained his animals in much the same manner as he did his weapons. At the Battle of Badr, the insurgents had only two horses. Six years later at the Battle of Hunayn, Muhammad's cavalry squadrons numbered 800 horse and cavalrymen.[6]

An insurgency must be able to sustain the popular base that supports the fighting elements. To accomplish this, Muhammad changed the ancient customs regarding the sharing of booty taken in raids. The chief of an Arab clan or tribe traditionally took a quarter of the booty for himself. Muhammad decreed that he receive only one-fifth, and even this he took not for himself, but in the name of the *ummah*. Under the old ways, individuals kept whatever booty they had captured for themselves. Muhammad required that all booty be turned in to the common pool, where it was shared equally among all combatants who had participated in the raid. Most importantly, Muhammad established that the first claimants on the booty that had been taken in the name of the *ummah* were the poor and the widows and orphans of the soldiers killed in battle. He also used the promise of a larger share of booty to strike alliances with Bedouin clans, some of whom remained both loyal and pagan to the end, fighting with Muhammad for loot rather than for Islam.

The leader of an insurgency must take great care to guard his authority from challenges, including those that come from within the movement itself. Muhammad had many enemies, and he was always on guard against an attempt upon his life. Like other insurgent leaders, Muhammad surrounded himself with a loyal group of followers who acted as his bodyguard, and who carried out his orders without question. For this purpose he created the *suffah*, a small loyal cadre of followers who lived in the mosque next to Muhammad's house. Recruited from among the most pious, enthusiastic and fanatical followers, they were from impoverished backgrounds with no other way to make a living. The members of the *suffah* spent their time studying Islam and leading a life of spiritual avocation. They were devoted to Muhammad, and served not only as his life guard, but as a secret police that could be called upon at a moment's notice to carry out whatever task Muhammad set for them, including assassination and terror.

No insurgency can survive without an effective intelligence apparatus. As early as when Muhammad left Mecca, he left behind a trusted agent, his uncle Abbas, who continued to send him reports on the situation there. Abbas served as an agent-in-place for more than a decade until Mecca itself fell to Muhammad. In the beginning, Muhammad's operations suffered from a lack of tactical intelligence. His followers were mostly townspeople, and had no experience in desert travel. On some of the early operations Muhammad had to hire Bedouin guides. As the insurgency grew, however, Muhammad's intelligence service became more organized and sophisticated, using agents-in-place, commercial spies, interrogation of prisoners, combat patrols and reconnaissance in force as methods of intelligence collection.

Muhammad himself seems to have possessed a detailed knowledge of clan loyalties and politics within the insurgency's area of operations, and used this knowledge to good effect when negotiating alliances with the Bedouins. He often conducted advance reconnaissance of the battlefields upon which he fought, and only once in ten years of military operations was he taken by surprise. In most cases, Muhammad's intelligence service was able to provide him with sufficient information as to the enemy's location and intentions in advance of any military engagement. We have no knowledge of how Muhammad's intelligence service was organized or where it was located. That it was part of the *suffah*, however, seems a reasonable guess.

Insurgencies succeed or fail to the degree that they are able to win the allegiance of the great numbers of the uncommitted to support the insurgency's goals. Muhammad understood the role of propaganda in the struggle for the minds of the uncommitted, and went to great lengths to make his message public and widely known. In an Arab society that was largely illiterate, the poet served as the major conveyor of political propaganda. Muhammad hired the best poets money could buy to sing his praises and denigrate his opponents. He publicly issued proclamations regarding the revelations he received as the Messenger of God, and remained always in public view to keep the vision of the new order and the promise of a heavenly paradise constantly before his followers and those he hoped to convert. He sent missionaries to other clans and tribes to instruct the pagans in the new faith, sometimes teaching the pagans to read and write in the process. Muhammad understood that the conflict was between the existing social order and its manifest injustices and his vision of the future, and he surpassed his adversaries in spreading his vision to win the struggle for the hearts and minds of the Arab population.

The use of terror seems to be an indispensable element of a successful insurgency, and no less so in Muhammad's case. Muhammad used terror in two ways. First, to keep discipline among his followers by making public examples of traitors or backsliders. Muhammad also ordered the assassination of some of his political enemies, including poets and singers who had publicly ridiculed him. Never one to forget a slight, when his armies marched into Mecca, Muhammad's *suffah* set about hunting down a list of old enemies marked for execution. Second, Muhammad used terror to strike fear into the minds of his enemies on a large scale. In the case of the Jewish tribes of Medina, Muhammad ordered the death of the entire Beni Qaynuqa tribe, and the selling of their women and children into slavery, before being talked out of it by the chief of one of his allies. On another occasion, again against a Jewish tribe of Medina, he ordered all the tribe's adult males, some 900, beheaded in the city square, the women and children sold into slavery and their property distributed among his Muslim followers. Shortly after the conquest of Mecca, Muhammad declared 'war to the knife' against all those who remained idolaters, instructing his followers to kill any pagans they encountered on the spot. Such public displays of ruthlessness and brutality strengthened Muhammad's hand when dealing with opponents and allies.

When examined against the criteria used by modern analysts to characterize an insurgency – a charismatic leader, revolutionary creed, disciplined cadre, base of military operations, recruited manpower, weapons, popular base of support, secret police and terror apparatus – Muhammad's campaign to establish Islam in Arabia qualifies in all respects. Over time, the violent origins of all revolutions are forgotten, and only the faith in the new order remains, with the result that the founders of the creeds come to be remembered as untouched by the violence of the historical record. In Muhammad's case, the result has been to de-emphasize the military aspects of his life and his considerable military accomplishments as Islam's first great general, and the inventor of the theory and practice of insurgency.

Muhammad's Military Revolution

Muhammad also brought about a revolution in the manner in which Arabs for generations had fought wars, transforming their armies into instruments of large-scale combat operations capable of achieving strategic objectives instead of only small-scale, clan, tribe or personal objectives. In doing so, he created both the means and historical circumstances that transformed the fragmented Arab clans into a genuine national military entity conscious of its own unique identity. Under these conditions, Arab military brilliance thrived, with the result that the greatest commanders of the early Arab conquests were identified and developed by Muhammad.

Had Muhammad not brought about a military revolution in Arab warfare, it is possible that Islam might not have survived. Within a few months of Muhammad's death, many of the clans that had sworn allegiance to Islam recanted, resulting in the War of the Apostates, or *Riddah*.[7] It was the military brilliance of Muhammad's generals and the superior combat capabilities of his new army that made it possible for Islam to defeat the apostates, and force them back into the religious fold. It was these same generals who commanded the new Arab armies that carried out the Arab conquests of Persia and Byzantium. The old Arab way of war would have had no chance of success against the armies of either of these empires. Muhammad's military revolution was an event that shook the ancient world, and changed its history by creating the means that made the Arab conquests possible.

Muhammad's successful transformation of Arab warfare marks him as one of the great military reformers of the ancient world, along with Thutmose III, Philip of Macedon and Gaius Marius of Rome. Muhammad changed the social composition of Arab armies from a collection of clans, tribes and blood kin loyal only to themselves into a national army loyal to a national social entity called the *ummah*, or community of believers in God. The *ummah* was not a nation or a state in the modern sense, but a body of religious believers under the unified command and governance of Muhammad. It was the new locus of loyalty that transcended Arabia's clans and tribes, and permitted Muhammad to forge a common identity, national in scope, among the Arabs for the first time in their history. Loyalty to the *ummah* permitted the national army to unify the two traditional combat arms of infantry and cavalry into an effective combined-arms force. Historically, Bedouin and town dweller had viewed one another with considerable suspicion, each living a very different way of life and fighting very different types of battles. Arab infantry had traditionally been drawn from people living in the towns, settlements and oases of Arabia. Arab cavalry was traditionally drawn from Bedouin clans whose nomadic warriors excelled at horsemanship, speed, surprise attack and elusive retreat, skills honed to a fine edge over generations of raiding.[8]

Coming from different socio-economic backgrounds, these two types of combatants possessed only limited experience in fighting alongside one another. Bound by clan loyalties and living in settlements, Arab infantry was steadfast and cohesive, and could usually be relied upon to hold its ground, especially in defence. Arab cavalry, on the other hand, was unreliable in a fight against infantry, often breaking off the fight to escape damage to their precious mounts or make off with whatever booty they had seized. Bedouin cavalry was, however, proficient at reconnaissance, surprise attack, protecting the flanks and pursuing ill-disciplined infantry. Each combat arm lacked the strengths of the other. Muhammad was the first commander of an Arab army to successfully join both into a unified national Arab army, and to use them in concert in battle.

This was more than a mere technical reform. The ability to combine both combat arms was the result of Muhammad's creation of a new type of community that made possible the submergence of clan and blood loyalties of traditional Arab society into the larger religious community of believers, the *ummah*, and combine the two primary elements of traditional Arab society, town dwellers and Bedouin tribes, into a single Arab national identity. The change in the social composition of Arab armies under Muhammad rested upon a change in the social composition of Arab society.

Before Muhammad, Arab military contingents fought under the command of their own clan or tribal leaders, sometimes assembled in coalition with other clans or tribes. While the authority of these clan chiefs was recognized by their own clan, every clan chief considered himself the equal of any other, with the result that there was no overall commander whose authority could compel the obedience or tactical direction of the army as a whole. Clan warriors fought for their own interests, often only for loot, and did not feel obligated to pursue the larger objectives of the army as a whole. They often failed to report to the battlefield, arrived late or simply left the fight once they had captured sufficient loot. Warriors and horses were precious, and clan leaders often resisted any higher tactical direction that might place their men and animals in danger. Under these conditions, Arab battles often resembled little more than disorganized brawls lasting but a short time, and producing no decisive outcome.

To correct these deficiencies, Muhammad established a unified command for his armies. Command of the army was centred in the hands of Muhammad himself. Within the *ummah* there was no distinction between the citizen and the soldier. All members of the community had an obligation to defend the clan and participate in its battles. The community of believers was truly a nation-in-arms, and all believers followed the commands of Muhammad, God's Messenger. As commander-in-chief, Muhammad established the principle of unified command by appointing a single commander with overall authority to carry out military operations. Sometimes a second-in-command was appointed as well. Muhammad often commanded his troops in the field himself. All other commanders were appointed by him, and operated under his authority.

As Muslims, all members of the army were equally bound by the same laws, and all clan members and their chiefs were subject to the same discipline and punishments as all Muslims. When operating with clans who were not Muslims, Muhammad always extracted an honour oath from their chiefs to obey his orders during the battle. The establishment of a unified military command gave Muhammad's armies greater reliability in planning and in battle. Unified command also permitted a greater degree of coordination among the various combat elements of the army, and the use of more sophisticated tactical designs that could be implemented with more certainty, thereby greatly increasing the army's combat power.

The moral basis of traditional Arab warfare placed an emphasis on the courageous performance of individual warriors in battle. While every warrior recognized that he was part of a larger kin group, Arab warfare placed no emphasis on the ability of the clan to fight as a unit. The Arab warrior fought for his own honour and social prestige within the kin group, not for the clan per se. One consequence was that Arab armies and the clan units within them did not usually reflect a high degree of combat unit cohesion, the ability of the group to remain intact and fight together under the stress of battle. Muhammad's armies, by contrast, were highly cohesive.

These armies usually held together even when they fought outnumbered, or were overrun. Muhammad did not just strengthen the blood and kin ties of the traditional Arab clan. He went far beyond that in creating the *ummah* as a higher locus of the soldier's loyalty that transcended the clan. Religion turned out to be a greater source of unit cohesion than blood and clan ties, the obligations of faith replacing and overriding the obligations of tradition and even family. Muhammad's soldiers quickly gained a reputation for their discipline and ferocity in battle, soldiers who cared for each other as brothers, which under the precepts of Islam they were.

Muhammad's armies demonstrated a higher degree of military motivation than traditional Arab armies. Being a good warrior had always been at the core of Arab values. Muhammad raised the status of the warrior to an even greater degree. It was a common saying among Muslims that 'the soldier is not only the noblest and most pleasing profession in the sight of Allah, but also the most profitable'.[9] Muhammad's soldiers were always guaranteed a share in the booty, and were often paid better than Persian and Byzantine soldiers.[10]

But better pay was only a small part of the motivation of the soldiers of Islam. The idea of a soldier motivated by religion in the certainty that he was doing God's work on earth was one of Muhammad's most important military innovations. No army before Muhammad placed religion at the centre of military motivation and defined the soldier primarily as an instrument of God's will on earth. The soldiers of Islam were usually extremely religious, and saw themselves as fighting under

God's instructions. The result, often seen in Islamic societies today, was a soldier who enjoyed much higher social status and respect than soldiers in armies of the West.

A central element in the motivation of the Islamic soldier was the teaching of his faith that death was not something to be feared, but to be sought. Muhammad's pronouncement that those killed in battle would be welcomed immediately into a paradise of pleasure and eternal life because they died fulfilling the command of God was a powerful inducement to perform well on the field of battle. To die fighting in defence of the faith (*jihad*) was to become a martyr. Life itself was subordinate to the needs of the faith; to die a martyr was to fulfill God's will. Muslim soldiers killed in battle were accorded the highest respect on the Arab scale of values. While those who died in battle had been traditionally celebrated as examples of courage and selflessness, it was never suggested that death was to be welcomed or even required to be a good soldier. Muhammad's religious pronouncements changed the traditional Arab view of military sacrifice, and produced a far more dedicated soldier than Arab armies had ever witnessed before.[11]

Arab warfare prior to Muhammad's reforms involved clans and tribes fighting for honour or loot. No commander aimed at the enslavement or extermination of the enemy, nor the occupation of its lands. Until Muhammad, Arab warfare was tactical localized warfare, nothing more. There was no sense of strategic war in which long-term, grand-scale strategic objectives were sought, and toward which the tactical application of force was directed. Muhammad was the first to introduce the notion of war for strategic goals to the Arabs.

Muhammad's ultimate goal, the transformation of Arab society through the spread of a new religion, was strategic in concept. His application of force and violence, whether unconventional or conventional, was always directed toward this strategic goal. Although Muhammad began as an insurgent, he was always Clausewitzian in his thinking in that the use of force was seen as a tactical means to the achievement of larger strategic objectives. Muhammad was the first Arab commander to use military force within a strategic context. Had he not introduced this new way of thinking to Arab warfare, the use of later Arab armies to forge a world empire would not only have been impossible, it would have been unthinkable.

Once war was harnessed to strategic objectives, it became possible to expand its application to introduce tactical dimensions that were completely new to Arab warfare. Muhammad used his armies in completely new ways. He attacked tribes, towns and garrisons before they could form hostile coalitions; he isolated his enemy by severing their economic lifelines and disrupting their lines of communication; he was a master at political negotiation, forming alliances with pagan tribes when it served his interests; and he laid siege to cities and towns. Muhammad also introduced the new dimension of psychological warfare, employing terror and massacre as means to weaken the will of his enemies. Where once Arab warfare had been a completely tactical affair, Muhammad's introduction of strategic war permitted the use of tactics in the proper manner, as means to greater strategic ends. War, after all, is never an end in itself. It is, as Clausewitz reminds us, always a method, never a goal.

As an orphan, Muhammad had lacked even the most rudimentary military training provided by an Arab father. Probably to compensate for this deficiency, he surrounded himself with men who were experienced warriors, and constantly sought their advice. He frequently appointed the best warriors of his former enemies to positions of command, once they had converted to Islam. As commander-in-chief, Muhammad sought to identify and develop good officers wherever he found them. Young men were appointed to carry out small-scale raids in order to give them combat experience, and he sometimes selected an officer from a town to command a Bedouin raid to broaden his experience in the use of cavalry.[12] Muhammad always selected his military commanders on the basis of their proven experience and ability, and never for their asceticism or religious devotion.[13] He was the first to institutionalize military excellence in the development of an Arab officer corps of professional quality. It was from this corps of trained and experienced field commanders that the generals who commanded the armies of the Arab conquests were drawn.

Muhammad had been an organizer of caravans for twenty-five years before he began his insurgency, and possessed the caravaneer's concern for logistics and planning, an expertise that permitted him to project force and conduct military operations over long distances across inhospitable terrain. Planning a caravan required extensive attention to detail, and knowledge of routes, rates of march, distances between stops, water and feeding of animals, location of wells, weather, places of ambush etc., knowledge that served him well as a military commander. Muhammad never seems to have had to change or abandon his plans due to logistical difficulties. Muhammad's armies could project force over hundreds of miles. In AD 630, he led an army of 20,000–30,000 men (the sources disagree) over a 250-mile march from Medina to Tabuk lasting eighteen to twenty days across the desert during the hottest season of the year. By traditional Arab standards, Muhammad's ability to project forces of such size over these distances was nothing short of astounding. Without this capability, the Arab conquest that followed Muhammad's death would have been impossible.

The conclusion that emerges from an examination of Muhammad's military life is that he revolutionized the conduct of Arab warfare in ways that made possible the transformation of Arab armies from entities fit only for tactical engagements to ones capable of waging war on a strategic level where they could engage and defeat the major armies of their day. This military transformation was preceded by a revolution in the manner in which Arabs thought about war, what I have called the moral basis of war. The old chivalric code that limited the bloodletting was abandoned by Muhammad, and replaced with an ethos less conducive to restraint, the blood feud. Extending the ethos of the blood feud beyond the ties of kin and blood to include members of the new community of Muslim believers inevitably worked to make Arab warfare more encompassing and bloody than it had ever been.

Underlying all these changes was a change in the psychology of war introduced by Muhammad's teaching that soldiers fighting in defence of Islam were doing no less than God's work on earth, and that to die in carrying out His will earned the soldier eternal life in paradise. The usual sense of risk to life that tempered the violence of the battlefield was abandoned, replaced by the doctrine that 'war to the knife', or fighting until one kills the enemy or is slain oneself, is the ideal to be aimed at in the conduct of war. In every respect, Muhammad's military revolution increased the scale and violence of the military engagements that Arab armies were capable of fighting.

Chapter 27

Riddah: The Great Muslim Civil War

The fragile unity of the Islamic insurgency that Muhammad had managed to hold together during his lifetime began to crumble even before his death. Now it threatened to come apart altogether. At the time of Muhammad's death, no more than perhaps a third of Arabia had been exposed to Islam in any way, and far less than a third of the population, perhaps no more than 20 per cent or so, had actually professed it. Once outside of Mecca, Medina and Ta'if, and the Bedouin tribes in the immediate vicinity of these towns, the attraction of Islam was weak if evident at all.[1] Even within the insurgency, many professed loyalty to Muhammad himself more than to the creed. In the traditional fashion of Arab covenants, upon Muhammad's death many tribal and clan chiefs no longer felt bound by their old agreements with the Prophet.

The crux of the problem was the *zakat*, the annual tax that Muhammad had imposed. The *zakat* had been announced at the Meccan pilgrimage, but Muhammad died before the tax could be collected from all but the tribes nearest Medina and Mecca. Some of the allied tribes sent delegations to Medina to negotiate new agreements with Abu Bakr, who had been elected to succeed Muhammad, promising to remain Muslim and say the daily prayer in exchange for repealing the tax. Abu Bakr refused, saying, 'By Allah, if they withhold a rope of a camel they use to give its due *zakat* to Allah's Messenger, I will fight them for it.' The result was the *Riddah*, or the War of Apostates.

It was Abu Bakr who was responsible for the ultimate success of Islam by using the Muslim armies to suppress all opposition to it, and to enforce conversion on all Arabia by military force. During the two-year period of the wars of the *Riddah* (AD 632–633), we see Muhammad's reformed armies operating on a larger scale over greater distances than ever before, with several campaigns taking place at once, all of them operating under unified command to implement a single strategic goal formulated by Abu Bakr. The same operational characteristics that became typical of the armies of the later Arab conquest were first revealed during the *Riddah*, and it was Abu Bakr who was the political and military genius behind this performance.[2]

Abu Bakr assumed leadership of the insurgency when the movement was on the verge of collapse. He reckoned correctly that to accede to the tribes on the issue of the *zakat* meant the end of centralized control over the movement, opening it to schism, eventual disintegration and perhaps even absorption by other monotheistic religions. To prevent this, Abu Bakr declared war on all those who would not obey. He proclaimed withdrawal from Muhammad's coalition to be a denial of God's will (the concept of *kufr*), and declared secession from the coalition and the *umma* as apostasy (*riddah*) punishable by death. Once the tribes had joined Muhammad, he asserted, they were no longer free not to be Muslims. Nor could they be loyal to God under any leader whose legitimacy did not derive from Muhammad. This fusion of two once separable phenomena, membership in Muhammad's community and faith in Islam, became one of Islam's most distinctive features. To forestall the influence of others who had already arisen in Arabia claiming to be prophets during Muhammad's lifetime, Abu Bakr declared Muhammad to be the last prophet that God would send. Although these tenets were originally devised and introduced as part of Abu Bakr's political strategy to isolate and destroy the enemies of the insurgency, over time they became important religious tenets of Islam.

The term *al-Riddah* has been used by traditional Arab historians who wished to cast the opposition of the tribes in religious terms, as apostasy, a falling away from the faith and thus an attack upon Islam. These traditionalists saw the war as a religious and defensive one to save the true faith.[3] But this view is only partially correct. An apostasy could only apply to those tribes and clans who had already agreed to the tax. Muhammad had died before his agents could collect the *zakat*, and most chiefs had never agreed to pay it at all. Now that it was demanded by Abu Bakr, they saw no reason to pay it to a man in whose election they had played no part. These chiefs could only be deemed apostates under Abu Bakr's new tenets of Islam, and not under the old tenets with which Muhammad had governed.

While certainly a war about religion, the *Riddah* was also a war declared by Abu Bakr, his Meccan allies and the local loyal Bedouin tribes to spread the authority of Medina and the faith of Islam throughout Arabia. The conquest of Arabia served the interests of the Meccan aristocracy to expand their financial and commercial markets; it also served the interests of those, among them certainly Abu Bakr, who wished to spread the true faith and destroy the idolaters; and it served the interests of the loyal Bedouin tribes for battle and booty. Seen in this larger context, the *Riddah* was not so much a war against apostates as a war of outright conquest, driven by a combination of political, economic and religious motives.

The decision to attack the apostates was not a popular one with many of the faithful, including some of Muhammad's field commanders and advisors. Abu Bakr removed these commanders from their positions and appointed Meccan officers who had supported his election over the opposition of the *ansar* and some Emigrants.[4] Once the conquest of Arabia had been accomplished, however, the removed commanders were reinstated, and went on to play important roles in the campaigns against the Persians and Byzantines.[5] Abu Bakr appointed Khalid al-Walid as commanding general of the Muslim forces during the *Riddah*. Abu Bakr assembled a Muslim army from the tribes around Medina, and immediately marched to Dhu al-Qassah (north-east of Medina), where he attacked several of the tribes of Najad and defeated them. Abu Bakr then ordered a general mobilization of all Muslim forces, and ordered his Meccan commanders to join him at Dhu al-Qassah. From there he dispatched eleven armies, supposedly at the same time, to all parts of Arabia with the mission of subjugating the 'apostatizing' tribes.[6]

Tabari provides a list of the Muslim commanders and the tribes against which they fought.[7] Figure 27 depicts the major campaigns of the *Riddah*. Abu Bakr's military operations were carried out simultaneously and in four different directions over eighteen months, with the result that all Arabia fell to the Muslim armies and accepted Islam. The first campaign was carried out to the east and north-east of Medina under the overall command of Khalid al-Walid against the tribes of Tayii, Ghatafan, Asad, Tamin, Bani Hanifah and Rabi'ah. The most famous engagement of this campaign was the Battle of Aqraba which al-Walid fought against the Bani Hanifah under the command of Musaylimah. The Bani Hanifah supposedly put 40,000 men in the field, and had already crushed two Muslim armies sent to bring them to heel.[8] Khalid al Walid attacked with 5,000 men, driving the Bani Hanifah back until they took refuge in a walled orchard known to Arab history as *Hadiqat al-Mawt*, the Garden of Death. In desperate hand-to-hand combat, most of the Hanifah army was slain, including its commander. Muslim losses were 1,200 dead.[9] Among the dead were a number of '*Quran* reciters', men who had memorized the sayings and instructions of Muhammad that would later be collected in the *Quran*.[10] Had all of them been killed, the *Quran* might have been lost to history.

The second campaign was undertaken to the south-east under the leadership of Ikrimah bin Abi Jahl, Hudhayfah bin Mihsah and Arfajah bin Harthamah against the tribes of Uman and Mahrah. In the south-west, the third campaign was led by al-Muhajir bin Abi Umayyah and Ziyad bin Labid, who conquered Yemen and Hadrawawt. In the north and north-west, the fourth campaign was aimed at the Arab tribes along the Syrian border that had once been allies of the Byzantines. Two generals, Amr bin al-As and Khalid bin Sa'id, succeeded in getting some of these tribes to defect to the Muslims before undertaking a series of major operations into Palestine and Syria. By the time the Byzantines' former allies had gone over to the Muslims, some fourteen months after the start of the *Riddah*, most of Arabia had been pacified and Khalid al-Walid was on the border of Iraq. Abu Bakr ordered al-Walid to march to the aid of Amr bin al-As in his campaign on the Syrian border. As the other victorious Muslim commanders began to return to Medina from different parts of Arabia with their armies, Abu Bakr also ordered them to the Syrian front to reinforce the Muslim armies there with troops

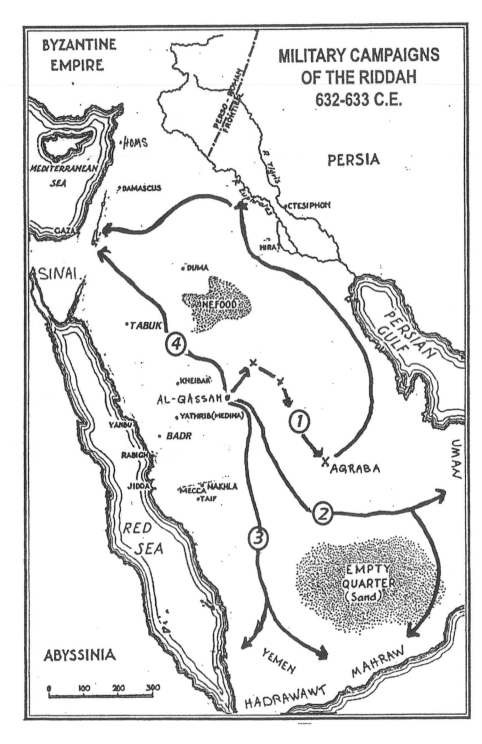

Figure 27: Military Campaigns of the *Riddah*, 632–633 AD

recruited from among the newly converted tribes in Arabia. The result was the collapse of the Byzantine defences on the Syrian frontier, and the beginning of the Arab conquest in the West.

The armies that carried out Abu Bakr's campaigns left Medina as relatively small contingents, each numbering perhaps 4,000–5,000 men or even less, comprised of *ansar*, Emigrants and tribal contingents of local Bedouins under the leadership of experienced field commanders. Only Khalid al-Walid's army seems to have been substantially larger, a circumstance that made sound military sense given that he had the mission of subduing some of the larger and more powerful tribes in Arabia. The size of the Muslim contingents seems to have been only large enough to engage and defeat those small clans and tribes encountered along their routes of march. These contingents were expected to recruit more manpower along the way with promises of religion and loot. If this failed, then military action could be undertaken to inflict a defeat on the recalcitrant clan, which would then make a peace agreement with the victors that required them to accept Islam and join the campaign. Once within the area of operations of the target, Muslim commanders would seek to take advantage of local rivalries to attract additional manpower to their armies.[11] It was a technique Muhammad had used on several occasions, and it worked well for the armies of Abu Bakr.

The armies of the Arabian conquest demonstrated all the operational capabilities that Muhammad had introduced into Arab warfare. The Muslim officer corps was competent and experienced, and in Muhammad's wars had acquired the skills needed to command large armies over long distances. Abu Bakr, while remaining in Medina, was able to coordinate the eleven major campaigns and to shift forces as needed from one front to another.[12] The units within the armies, while mostly organized on tribal or clan lines, nevertheless operated under a unified command in which all subordinate commanders were expected to carry out the missions assigned to them as part of a larger tactical plan.

Abu Bakr's campaigns also demonstrated the primacy of strategic objectives in tactical planning, something which had been absent in Arab warfare until introduced by Muhammad. Even the idea of a single tribe or political group conquering all of Arabia was inconceivable until Muhammad showed the Arabs how to think in strategic terms. Logistics and supply for large armies had improved considerably under Muhammad, and were put to good use in Abu Bakr's campaigns. We have no reports of serious shortages of water, fodder or armaments in any of the campaigns of the *Riddah*. Muslim morale and fighting spirit were superior to those of any tribe the armies engaged, with the possible exception of the Beni Hanifa who fought to the death to retain their freedom. Muslim soldiers had learned to fight as units operating within a larger tactical design, while the warriors of most tribes fought in the old manner as individuals. Finally, the quality of Muslim combat leadership, certainly at the field commander level and probably in the major subordinate units as well, was superior to their adversaries. Muslim field commanders were never selected on the grounds of piety, but always on the basis of demonstrated competence in war.

Muhammad's legacy of new operational capabilities passed intact to the armies of Abu Bakr and produced the conquest and conversion of all Arabia. The Muslim military experience against the border garrisons of Byzantium and Persia had demonstrated that both empires were hollow and ripe for defeat. By spring AD 633, the *Riddah* was over and Arabia was an armed camp full of warrior tribes seeking new adventures and loot. Islamic Arabia lacked sufficient resources of food and wealth to sustain itself under the limitations that the new Islamic laws placed upon the old way of life. If new sources of wealth were not found, the Muslim state that Abu Bakr's military campaigns had brought into being would soon fragment into warring tribal groups. Muhammad's earlier raids attempted against the Byzantine border provinces provided the guiding strategic concept behind Abu Bakr's decision to use the united Arab tribes as a means to an even larger conquest. In AD 633, Abu Bakr ordered three Muslim armies to attack the Byzantines. The great Arab conquests had begun.

Abu Bakr's ideological pronouncements created serious difficulties less than a decade after his death. His pronouncements on apostasy for the first time made it legitimate for Muslims to kill Muslims. Abu Bakr's claim that only elected leaders were legitimate laid the basis for the Shia-Sunni antagonism over who were Muhammad's rightful heirs. And contrary to Muhammad's practice, religion, state and army were now inseparable. This made it inevitable that dynastic and civic conflicts would become religious conflicts, while religious disagreements became civic conflicts. The result was more than 1,000 years of intra-religious civil war among Shia, Sunni and Sufi factions of Islam.

In AD 645, intra-religious *jihad* flared into the open. The appointment of Abu Bakr's successor, Uthman, as caliph precipitated a division between those who believed rulers should be selected by the Prophet's companions (Sunni) and those who believed only God could appoint the ruler (Shia) who should be a blood relative of Muhammad or his family. The Khawarij, or 'seceders', declared a *jihad* against the Sunni caliph on the grounds that his improper election made him a *takfir*, an apostate who must be killed. Uthman was assassinated and his successor, Ali (AD 656–661), declared a *jihad* against the Khawarij. In revenge, he was assassinated in the mosque at Kufa in AD 661. The Sunni-Shia dispute turned increasingly violent, each regarding the other as heretics who could be legitimately slain 'in defence of Islam'. Sufis soon joined the fray with a new mystical theory of '*jihad* of the sword' that threatened everyone. From AD 661–750, Muslims fought three dynastic-religious civil wars that became the stimulus for the emergence of a formal ideology of *jihad* that first appeared in a treatise on the subject in AD 797.

It is only necessary to mention a few of the Sunni-Shia *jihads* to make the point. In AD 680, the beheading of Imam Hussein, the first Shia imam, at the hands of the Sunnis in Iraq is remembered in Shia history as the Shia Martyrdom. *Jihad* against infidels and Shia became the official ideology the Ottoman state used to expand its territory and control Shia and Sufi elements within it. In 1124, Shiites opposed to Ottoman rule in Iran, Iraq and Syria formed a group dedicated to using murder and assassination to overthrow the ruling Sunni order. This group, known in the West as the Assassins, plagued Ottoman officials with violence for three centuries. In 1501, Shah Ismail Safavid, a Shia and the first ruler of the Safavid dynasty, made Shiaism the official religion of the Persian state, and launched a ten-year *jihad* of persecution against Sunnis. Much of the centuries-long conflict between Persia and the Ottomans had its roots in the Shia-Sunni divide.

The rise of Wahhabism (1744) injected an even more violent strain into these religious conflicts. The Wahhabis were a fundamentalist Sunni sect originating in what became Saudi Arabia who believed most Muslims were insufficiently observant in their faith. Along with massacring fellow Sunnis, the Wahhabis declared unrelenting war against the Shia. In 1802, they slaughtered thousands of Shiites in their holy city of Karbala in Iraq. The Wahhabis formed an alliance with the house of Saud in Arabia, and the present Saudi regime is still Wahhabist in its religious orientation. During the Iran-Iraq War (1980–1986), Iran's Ayatollah Khomeini declared the conflict against the Sunnis in Iraq a *jihad*. The current 'civil war' in Syria is an extension of the historical Shia-Sunni conflict, with Saudi Arabia supporting the *jihadist* rebels and Iran propping up Assad's Shia Alawite regime. After more than 1,400 years, it is unlikely that there is a solution to what is surely one of the world's longest-running religious civil wars between adherents of the same religion. One of *jihad*'s great paradoxes is that far more *jihads* have been fought among Islamic co-religionists than between Muslims and non-Muslims.

Without doubt Muhammad's greatest military legacy was the doctrine of *jihad* or holy war. It is indisputable that divinely justified warfare became a force of major importance during the early Islamic period, and remained a powerful motivator for the Islamic conquests that followed Muhammad's death. This is even more amazing when it is recalled that pre-Islamic Arabia knew no notion of ideology of any sort, and certainly not of religiously sanctioned war. Pre-Islamic warfare was directly linked to the economic and social circumstances of pasturage, material wealth and prestige, and there is no evidence of any kind to suggest any religious or ideological motivation for Arab warfare prior to the influence of Muhammad and Islam.[13] Under these circumstances, martyrdom had little meaning, and no transcendent meaning was applied to warfare as a reward for carrying out the instructions of

God.[14] The idea of warfare as a command of God rewarded by martyrdom and paradise was an innovation with no precedents in Arab culture, custom or practice, brought about completely by Muhammad's thinking and influence on events.

The concept of *jihad* came to have many meanings over the years as a consequence of the influence of Muslim legalists, scholars and theologians. The term derives from the root *jahada*, which is defined as 'exerting one's utmost power, efforts, endeavours, or ability in contending with an object of disapprobation'.[15] There are, therefore, many kinds of *jihad*, most of which have nothing to do with warfare. Thus the 'greater *jihad*' (*al-jihad al-akbar*) refers to a struggle within or against one's self, while the 'lesser *jihad*' refers to warring in the path of God. *Jihad*, therefore, may not have always been equated with holy war, although that is the primary meaning that Muhammad seems to have given it. With regard to *jihad* as holy war, most Muslim scholars subscribe to what is called the classic evolutionary theory of holy war: that what Muhammad meant by *jihad* depended upon the historic circumstances and needs at different times during his prophetic mission. Thus:

> At the beginning of his prophetic career in Mecca when he was weak and his followers few, the divine revelations encouraged avoidance of physical conflict. Only after the intense physical persecution that resulted in the Emigration (*Hijra*) of the Muslim community to Medina in 622 were Muhammad and the believers given the divine authority to engage in war and only in defence. As the Muslim community continued to grow in numbers and strength in Medina, further revelations widened the conditions and narrowed the restrictions under which war could be waged, until it was concluded that war against non-Muslims could be waged virtually at any time, without pretext, and in any place.[16]

It is this classical interpretation of Islam as a 'religion of dominion' that provided the ideological justification for the Arab conquests, and that is very much alive in the minds of Islamic *jihadists* of the present day.[17]

Muhammad's military legacy lives on in the memories of *jihadists* in their memory of Muhammad as a great general and passionate revolutionary who created and fought a successful insurgency to achieve his political and religious goals. It is this legacy of Muhammad as successful revolutionary that motivates Muslim insurgents and revolutionary leaders in Iraq, Afghanistan and elsewhere. In their portrayal of their insurgencies as divinely sanctioned acts, these modern revolutionaries are imitating Muhammad. It can scarcely be denied that at least to a certain extent some suicide bombers are motivated by their desire to become martyrs in the same manner that many of Muhammad's soldiers were willing to die for their faith. The Osama bin Ladens of the Muslim world, like Muhammad, speak of creating a more moral world in which to live, a community of believers living according to the instructions given by God himself. Like Muhammad, they are prepared to use violence to bring that new moral order into being.

Chapter 28

Constantinople: The Most Fought Over City in History

The original name of Constantinople was Byzantion (Latin: Byzantium) when it was founded on the European coast of the Bosporus in 657 BC by colonists from Megara in Greece. In AD 330, the Roman emperor, Constantine I, moved his imperial residence there, and the name of the city was changed to Constantinople. It was the capital of the Byzantine Roman Empire until 1453, when the city fell to the Ottoman Turks and became the capital of the Ottoman Empire until 1918, when the empire collapsed. The Turks called the city Istanbul, a Turkish corruption of the Latin 'est in polis', or 'in the city'.

The city occupies perhaps the most valuable piece of strategic terrain in military history, sitting at the centre of the known world from antiquity until modern times. Constantinople controlled the strategic trade and military routes leading from Asia to Europe (east to west and reverse), and access to the Mediterranean to the south and the Black Sea to the north. It controlled overland access to the Danube and Dnieper rivers, and the inland trade routes leading west and north. To the east and southeast, Constantinople dominated the land routes to Turkestan and India, Antioch, Alexandria and the Silk Road. There is no place on the planet more apropos of Napoleon's observation that 'a nation's geography is its destiny' than Constantinople. More battles for control of the city have been fought over Constantinople than in any other place in military history. It is the most fought over place on earth.

Battle History

492 BC: As part of the wars between the Persian Empire and an alliance of Greek city states (499–449 BC), Persia invaded Greece, capturing Thrace and Macedon, during which the Persian general Mardonios attacked and captured Byzantion. Later, the Greeks defeated the Persians at the Battle of Marathon, bringing an end to the Persian invasion.

480 BC: To avenge the previous failure, the Persian King Xerxes (reigned 519–465 BC) personally led an invasion of Greece, defeating them at the Battle of Thermopylae and burning Athens. The Persians recaptured Byzantion, installed a permanent garrison in the city and reoccupied Thrace.

478 BC: The allied Greek states defeated the Persians at the Battle of Plataea (479 BC), driving them out of Thrace. A Greek allied force, led by the Spartan general Pausanias, 'the hero of Platea', attacked and captured Byzantion, expelling the Persian garrison. Shortly thereafter, when Pausanias began to adopt Persian habits and lost the support of his troops, the Persians recaptured the city.

476 BC: Pausanias was now little more than an agent of the Persian king in control of a strategic city on the Greek mainland. The Athenians assembled troops and a fleet of ships, and attacked Byzantion. After a short siege, they captured the city and expelled Pausanias and his supporters. Athens established an Athenian-style government in the city.

411 BC: The Persians and Spartans provoked a revolt in Byzantion, using it as a pretext to send troops and ships to support the pro-Persian rebels. Part of the invasion fleet was wrecked in a storm, but sufficient troops were able to attack by land and capture the city. The Athenians sent a flotilla to reverse the takeover, but a naval battle under the walls of the city proved inconclusive. Byzantion was now back in Persian hands.

407–406 BC: Led by the famous general Alcibiades, Athens sent troops aboard ships in the early spring to capture Chalcedon and Byzantion in order to protect the sea route of the Athenian grain supply leading to the Black Sea. Having taken Chalcedon, Alcibiades turned toward Byzantion and brought it under siege, constructing walls of circumvallation and using sharpshooters and assaults against the city's walls. The Spartan commander had given the city's grain supply to his troops, leaving the citizenry to starve. This provoked a Byzantine citizen to outrage, and he opened the Thracian Gate to the Athenian army, who captured the city after considerable street fighting.

405 BC: The Peloponnesian War (431–404 BC) between Sparta and Athens for control of Greece came to an end after twenty-seven years of bloodshed with the destruction of the Athenian fleet at Aegospotami. This left Sparta the leading power in Greece. As part of the peace treaty, Byzantion was handed over to the Spartans, and a Spartan, Sthenelaus, was appointed governor general of the city. The Byzantines who had supported Athens by betraying the city to Alcibiades were given safe passage to Athens.

399 BC: Xenophon (431–355 BC), one of the most famous generals in Greek history, successfully led his army on the long trek back to Greece after the defeat of the Greek mercenary army at the Battle of Cunaxa (401 BC). He took the army across from Asia to Byzantion under the promise of supplies and ships to take the army home. When denied the promised supplies, the army broke into revolt, attacked the city and captured it from the small Spartan garrison. Xenophon prevented the army from plundering the city, and in short order the supplies and transport were forthcoming.

394 BC: In an effort to shore up their support in the eastern Mediterranean, the Athenians dispatched Thrasybulus and forty ships to the area to secure the friendship of the cities in the region. Xenophon tells us that Thrasybulus was well received in Byzantium, and 'by another stroke he converted the oligarchy of Byzantium into a democracy. The result of this was that the Byzantines were no longer sorry to see as vast a concourse of Athenians in their city as possible.'

340 BC: Philip II of Macedon (383–336 BC), father of Alexander the Great, attacked Byzantium with a force of 15,000 men. Moving 54 miles from his base camp, Philip planned to attack at night, with the movements of his assault teams muffled by a rainstorm. Barking dogs alerted the defenders, who were able to repulse the assault. Philip found himself bogged down in a siege. When the Persians came to the aid of the city, Philip withdrew. It was at this siege that the new torsion catapults developed by Philip's engineers were first used in warfare.

AD 196: Septimius Severus, Roman Emperor (reigned AD 193–211), attacked Byzantium for its support of his rival in another of the interminable Roman civil wars. The city walls were made of thick squared, faced stones fastened together with bronze plates, and was heavily fortified with artillery of all kinds. The Romans besieged the city by land and sea for three years. When the food supply ran out, the inhabitants ate hides before resorting to cannibalism. Eventually, the Byzantines surrendered the city, whereupon the Romans executed all the soldiers and magistrates and demolished the city's walls. Severus later rebuilt the city, transforming it into one of the most beautiful of the Roman Empire.

AD 532: The Nika ('Victory') riots began in Constantinople after contestants from two chariot teams were arrested for murder and sentenced to death. Tens of thousands of fans took to the streets, besieged the emperor's palace and began plundering the city. The great Byzantine general Belisarius took command of a 3,000-man force and put down the riot with great brutality. In the end, 30,000 people were killed and half the city damaged.

AD 559: A Bulgar-Slav invasion of Thrace reached the walls of Constantinople and brought the city under attack. Emperor Justinian (reigned AD 527–565) recalled general Balisarius from retirement to meet the threat. With a force of only 300 veteran cavalry and a few thousand hastily raised infantry levies, Belisarius defeated the invaders at Melanthius, just outside the city's walls, then counter-attacked to drive the invaders back. Beslisarius was credited with saving Constantinople again.

AD 626: The Byzantine army was occupied with yet another war with Persia when a 100,000-strong Avar, Slav, German and Bulgar tribal confederation army attacked Constantinople, first overwhelming its forward defences before attacking the city walls. On 1 August, the invaders mounted a fierce attack in concert with the Persians, who attempted an amphibious landing across the Bosporus behind the city. The engagement lasted ten days, during which the Persian flotilla was intercepted and wrecked by the Byzantine navy, while the army, under the command of Emperor Heraclius's son, Constantine, defeated the enemy ground attack. Having suffered terrible losses, and running short of supplies, the Avar coalition withdrew. This is regarded as one of the greatest victories in the history of Constantinople.

AD 669: In a continuation of the Arab-Byzantine wars, an Arab army invaded Anatolia and reached Chalcedon. The Moslems crossed the Bosporus and attacked Constantinople, but the force was small and easily repulsed. The Byzantines counter-attacked, and destroyed the main Arab army already weakened by famine and disease at the Battle of Armorium. The first attempt by the new Umayyad Caliph to expand his empire against the Byzantines had ended in failure.

AD 672: Assembling a large fleet of warships and transports, the Arabs again attacked Constantinople, with the hope of establishing both a land and sea blockade of the Byzantine capital. The initial naval attack on the city was repulsed, and at a second naval battle at Cyzicus in the Sea of Marmara, the Arab fleet was destroyed. The use of Greek fire played a large role in the Byzantine victory.

AD 673–677: The Arabs attempted again to mount a naval and land blockade, hoping to deprive Constantinople of its food supply from the surrounding farms. A number of land engagements were fought that prevented the invaders from occupying the farms. At sea, the antagonists fought one battle after another, and again the use of Greek fire played a vital role in destroying Arab ships. In AD 677, the Byzantines destroyed the Arab fleet at the Battle of Syllaeum in southern Asia Minor. The disaster led Caliph Mu'awiya to sue for peace, in which he promised to evacuate Cyprus, keep the peace for thirty years and pay an annual tribute to the Byzantines.

AD 705: In AD 695, Byzantine Emperor Justinian II (reigned AD 685–695/705–711) was overthrown and banished to the Crimea, where he made an alliance with the Bulgar king Terbelis (reigned AD 695–715). With the Bulgar army in his service, Jusintian attacked Constantinople in a surprise move, and captured the city. He executed all his opponents in a reign of terror that lasted for six years.

AD 711: Justinian II sent a military expedition to the Crimea to punish his subjects who had mistreated him while he was in exile. The army mutinied under the leadership of Bardanes Philippicus, who led the army back to Constantinople. With the assistance of the Khazars, he defeated and killed Justinian in a battle in north-western Anatolia. Philippicus took the city and seized the throne.

AD 716: Philippicus (reigned AD 711–713) proved to be an incompetent ruler, although he succeeded in turning back a Bulgar attack on Constantinople in AD 712. The Byzantine army mutinied, removed Philippicus and installed Anastasius II (reigned AD 713–715) in his place. His attempt to reform the army led to another mutiny, in which the army installed Theodosius III as emperor. Theodosius III (reigned AD 715–717) captured Constantinople after a six-month siege, and banished Anastasius to a monastery. Theodosius was overthrown by Leo 'the Isaurian', who assumed the throne as Leo III (reigned AD 717–741).

AD 717–718: The Second Arab Siege of Constantinople in AD 717–718 was a combined land and sea offensive that marked the culmination of twenty years of attacks and progressive Arab occupation of the Byzantine borderlands. In July AD 717, an Arab army of 80,000 crossed the Hellespont and laid siege to Constantinople. In August, the Arabs attacked the city and were repulsed. In September, the Arab armies were reinforced with another 80,000 men and a fleet of 1,800 ships. Leo III attacked the Arab fleet, keeping them bottled up in the Sea of Marmara, and won a great victory. This allowed Constantinople to be resupplied by sea, while the Arab army was crippled by famine and disease during the hard winter that followed.

In spring AD 718, two Arab fleets sent as reinforcements were destroyed by the Byzantine navy, and an army sent overland through Asia Minor was ambushed and defeated. Attacked by the Bulgars in their rear, the Arabs were forced to lift the siege of Constantinople on 15 August AD 718. On its return journey, the Arab fleet was almost destroyed by natural disasters, while Byzantine attacks crippled the Arab army as it withdrew. Of the more than 200,000 Arabs committed to the siege of Constantinople, only 30,000 returned home. The successful defence of Constantinople saved Christian Europe from Moslem invasion, and is regarded as one of history's most decisive battles.

AD 813: Between AD 811–817, King Krum of Bulgaria (reigned AD 796–814) continued a series of wars against the Byzantines. Krum won a number of battles, culminating in the Battle of Versinikia (AD 813), which allowed him to capture Adrianople and advance to bring Constantinople under attack. The Byzantine Emperor, Leo V 'The Armenian' (reigned AD 775–820), repulsed the Bulgar attack, but not before Krum had ravaged the area around the city. In AD 817, Leo defeated Krum's son in a major battle that forced the Bulgarians to agree to a thirty-year truce.

AD 822–824: Emperor Michael II (reigned AD 820–829), known as 'The Stammerer', came to the Byzantine throne following the assassination of Leo V. His fellow general, Thomas the Slav, led a revolt against Michael to gain the throne himself. He attacked the city twice in two years, finally investing it by siege. His army was attacked from the rear by the Bulgarians, who came to Michael's aid. A few months later, Michael took the field and defeated Thomas, who was captured and executed. Thomas' rebellion was one of the largest in the Byzantine Empire's history.

AD 860: With the Byzantine army and navy occupied in another of the Arab-Byzantine wars, the defences of Constantinople were seriously exposed. The Rus, a Viking people living north of the Black Sea, attacked Constantinople in June AD 860. Typical of Viking raiding parties, they arrived in a fleet of 200 ships. The Viking invaders raped, stabbed and pillaged their way through the suburbs of the city, then sailed into the Sea of Marmara and attacked Greek settlements there, in one case cutting some monks to pieces with axes. In August, the Rus sailed for home loaded with loot.

AD 907: Oleg of Novgorod (reigned AD 879–912), the leader of the Kievan Rus (Vikings settled in Kiev, the centre of the Viking slave trade in Ukraine), attacked Constantinople, probably in response to the Byzantine attempt to poison him. His fleet of longboats found the Bosporus barred with chains, and were unable to approach the city. Oleg landed on the shore, and for some reason had 2,000 dugout canoes equipped with wheels which he towed to the gates of the city. In typical Byzantine fashion, the defenders negotiated a treaty in which Oleg was paid a fixed sum of money for each Rus boat in the fleet, counting, no doubt, the dugouts as boats. Flush with cash, Oleg and the Rus returned to Kiev.

AD 941: Igor of Kiev (reigned AD 912–945) led the Rus on another attack against Constantinople. Allied with the Pechenegs, he disembarked on the northern coast of Asia Minor with 1,000 ships and 40,000 men. The capital's defences were weakened by the absence of its naval and ground forces engaged in another war with the Arabs, but a small Byzantine flotilla equipped with Greek fire-throwers were able to destroy a large number of Rus ships. This did not prevent the Rus from ravaging Constantinople's suburbs, crucifying and driving nails in the heads of some captives. A combined Byzantine naval and infantry relief force reached the city, and drove the invaders back into Thrace, where the Byzantine navy destroyed their fleet. Only a handful of Rus boats were able to return to the Crimea. The Byzantines beheaded all the captured Rus prisoners.

AD 1185: The Byzantine Emperor Andronicus Comnenus (reigned AD 1183–1185) was overthrown in bloody riots that beset Constantinople in reaction to the emperor's cruelty and defeats by the Normans. He was replaced by Isaac Angelus (reigned AD 1185–1195). Andronicus was paraded in front of the new emperor. Andronicus' beard was torn out, his head shaved and his teeth extracted. His right hand was cut off with an axe, and one of his eyes was gouged out. Then he was seated on a camel and paraded in the marketplace, where his nostrils were stuffed with cow dung. Finally, after 'assaults upon his genitals',[1] the former emperor was killed with a thrust of a sword down his throat. The city's populace had apparently had their fill of Andronicus' tyranny and cruelty.

AD 1186: The great Byzantine admiral-general, Alexios Branas, was an Andronicus partisan who won several key victories against the Normans. He assembled a rebel army and some naval components and attacked Constantinople, with the intention of removing Emperor Angelus. The emperor took the field against him and defeated Branas in a battle near Constantinople. This was but the first attempt to remove Angelus by force. In 1195, he was finally overthrown by his brother, Alexis III, who had Angelus blinded and imprisoned.

AD 1203–1204: The Fourth Crusade (AD 1202–1204) to reconquer Palestine was diverted by church and secular politics into a devastating attack on Constantinople. Twenty-five thousand European troops aboard several hundred transports, financed by the Venetians, sailed for Constantinople as a staging area for the attack on Palestine. The son of the deposed Emperor Isaac II conspired with the Crusader commanders for their support in installing him on the Byzantine throne. In return, Alexius promised to reunite the Eastern Church with Rome, pay the Venetians 200,000 marks and support the Crusaders in Palestine. In June AD 1203, the Crusader army landed near the city, and its navy forced its way into the Golden Horn. The ground army forced their way into the city, where they established Alexius as emperor. The Crusader army and navy returned to their bases to await the payment of the promised 200,000 marks. Resentment at the

Crusaders, however, provoked a revolt that arrested the new emperor. Denied their money, between 11–13 April the Crusaders attacked Constantinople in an orgy of violence, slaughter, loot and rape. The last bulwark of Christendom against Islam in the East was smashed by fellow Christians.

AD 1236: The Crusaders continued to occupy Constantinople, while other regions of the old empire remained in opposition. In AD 1204, Baldwin of Flanders proclaimed himself emperor in Constantinople of the new Latin Empire. For the next three decades, Byzantine nobles fought a running war with the Crusaders to re-establish the old empire. In 1236, John of Nicea, a Byzantine noble, made an alliance with Ivan of Bulgaria to attack Constantinople and break the grip of the Crusaders on the city. Their plan was abandoned when a Venetian fleet and a Latin army arrived to occupy the city.

AD 1261: A small Nicaean army under general Alexius Stragopulos took advantage of the withdrawal of the Venetian fleet. He captured Constantinople in a surprise attack, and established Michael VIII Peleologus on the throne (reigned AD 1261–1282). Michael re-established the old Byzantine Empire, now much reduced, and formed an alliance with Genoa against the hated Venetians. Over the next four years, the Byzantines won campaigns against the Latins in Greece and the Bulgarians in Thrace, Macedonia and Epirus, recapturing some of the old Byzantine provinces.

AD 1347: Between AD 1341–1347, a civil war broke out between two rival claimants for the Byzantine throne, ravaging the provinces of Thrace and Macedonia. Both sides called in Serbs and Turks in a series of shifting alliances. Finally, one of the claimants, John VI Cantacuzene, attacked and captured Constantinople through treachery. The result of the war was that most of the former Byzantine provinces were lost to the Turks and Serbs.

AD 1355: Although John V lost his fight for the throne, he refused to give up. Assembling another army, he captured Constantinople and forced Cantacuzene to abdicate, assuming the throne himself. John V was a weak ruler, and lost Adrianople to the Turks. He was involved in a long dynastic struggle (AD 1376–1392), of which the Turks took advantage and overran most remaining Byzantine territory.

AD 1391–1399: The Ottomans had established their first permanent European settlement in Gallipoli (AD 1345), after which they expanded into Thrace, reducing the Byzantine Empire to an Ottoman fief. They then fought a series of engagements aimed at capturing Constantinople itself. French Marshal Jean Bouciquaut, commander of a small Byzantine force, repulsed repeated Ottoman attacks on land and sea, bringing the Ottoman assault to a halt. Having captured Adrianople earlier, the Ottomans made it their capital.

AD 1422: Murad II (reigned AD 1421–1451), Sultan of the Turks, undertook a full-scale siege of Constantinople in reprisal for the Byzantine emperor's interference in the succession struggle that occurred after the death of Sultan Mehmed I in 1421. The siege marked the first use of cannon by the Turks. Both sides were evenly matched, and the Ottoman assaults failed. The Turks lifted the siege to respond to renewed Venetian naval assaults in the Aegean.

AD 1453: Sultan Mohammed II (reigned AD 1451–1481), called 'The Conqueror', brought Constantinople under siege from February–May with an army of 80,000 men and a siege train of seventy heavy cannon. The Byzantine Emperor Constantine XI (reigned AD 1449–1453) had less than 10,000 troops and a handful of Genoese mercenaries with which to defend the city. A number of Turkish assaults against the walls failed. In May, a heavy Turkish bombardment collapsed a large part of the city wall. As Turkish troops rushed through the breach, they were met with a force commanded by the emperor himself. Rather than flee, Constantine fought on in the breach until he was killed. The Turks captured the city and pillaged it for three days. Constantine was the last Byzantine emperor, and the fall of Constantinople marked the final end of the Byzantine Empire. Constantinople became the capital of the Ottoman Empire.

AD 1807: During the Napoleonic Wars (AD 1800–1815), a British naval squadron under Sir John Duckworth forced a passage through the Dardanelles against a small Turkish flotilla, and approached Constantinople. Duckworth issued an ultimatum to Sultan Selim III (reigned AD 1789–1807) to dismiss the French ambassador. The Sultan responded with a bombardment from 1,000 guns placed on the city's walls. Duckworth's fleet suffered considerable damage before attempting to withdraw back through the Dardanelles, where it was further mauled by Turkish shore artillery as it attempted to gain the passage into the Mediterranean. A similar fate befell the English fleet when it attempted to force a passage of the Dardanelles in 1915.

AD 1909: The Young Turk nationalist movement urged reform of Sultan Hamid II's government, and in April the I Army Corps revolted and seized control of Constantinople. Loyal troops from Macedonia moved into the city and brutally suppressed the uprising. When other disorders broke out in Anatolia, the Turkish army ruthlessly put them down, committing a number of outrageous massacres.

AD 1912: During the First Balkan War (AD 1912–1913), the Bulgarian army drove the Turkish defenders back behind Adrianople and prepared to assault Constantinople. In November, the Bulgars launched an ill-prepared attack on the city against improved Turkish defences, and were driven back with heavy losses. In December, hostilities came to an end with a temporary armistice.

AD 1918: After a disastrous defeat at Megiddo (September 1918) that cost the Turks three armies, 76,000 prisoners and 360 captured guns, they signed an armistice at Mudros in October. In November, British, French and Italian troops entered Constantinople, where they remained until September 1923 as occupying armies. This was the only time the city had changed hands since the Ottomans captured the old Byzantine capital in 1453.

Endnotes

Chapter 1: The Invention of War

1. For an excellent exposition of the view that war has accompanied man's social and even genetic evolution from the beginning, see the groundbreaking work of Lawrence Keeley, *Before Civilization: the Myth of the Peaceful Savage* (Oxford: Oxford University Press, 2001). A contrary and more balanced view can be found in Wayne E. Lee's *Warfare and Culture in World History* (New York: New York University Press, 2011).

2. Wayne E. Lee, 'When Did Warfare Begin?', *Military History Quarterly* (Winter, 2015), pp.66–67.

3. For an analysis of the development of weapons from the Stone Age to the present, see Richard A. Gabriel, 'Armaments', *Italian Encyclopedia of Social Science* (Rome: University of Rome, 1990).

4. The first states for which we have evidence of war as an established social institution are Uruk in Mesopotamia around 3500 BC, pre-dynastic Egypt around 3100 BC, the Harappan culture in India around 2500 BC and the Xia or Erlitou culture in China around 1800 BC.

5. Richard A. Gabriel, *The Culture of War: Invention and Early Development* (Westport, CT: Greenwood Press, 1990), p.20.

6. See Lee, 'When Did Warfare Begin?', pp.68–69, for evidence of human cannibalism.

7. Currently, there are only twenty-seven Neanderthal and nineteen Homo Sapiens skeletons from the Paleolithic that show evidence of violent death. Lee, ibid., p.68

8. Arther Ferrill, *The Origins of War* (London: Thames and Hudson, 1985), pp.23–24.

9. James Mellaart, *The Neolithic of the Near East* (New York: Charles Scribner, 1975), p.198.

10. Of all the evidence compiled on Neanderthal man by archaeologists, the only hint of conflict comes from a single skeleton with a small hole in its pelvis that may have been made by a spear. Among the other twenty-seven Neanderthal skeletons extant, some show evidence of violent death, but not by spears.

11. For a discussion of the Mureybet site and its importance to agriculture, see Mellaart, pp.45–50.

12. Ibid.

13. Ibid., pp.68–71.

14. Ibid., p.54.

15. At least in the early stages of development, the ability of the new warrior caste to influence policy seems to have been strongly controlled by a social structure that left power in the hands of civilian 'peace chiefs'. Only later do warriors seem to have acquired the ability to dominate policy. See Christian Feest, *The Art of War* (London: Thames and Hudson, 1980), pp.16–20.

16. Gabriel, *The Culture of War*, p.34.

17. Ferrill, p.19.

18. Mellart, p.63.

19. Ibid., p.102.

20. For the history of the sling, see Manfred Korfmann, 'The Sling as a Weapon', *Scientific American* 229, no. 4 (October 1973), pp.34–42.

21. Ibid., p.39.

22. H. Turney-High, *Primitive War: Its Practice and Concepts*, 2nd ed. (Columbia, SC: University of South Carolina Press, 1971), pp.26–28.

23. These figures are calculated using Yigael Yadin's formula. See Yigael Yadin, *The Art of Warfare in Biblical Lands in Light of Archaeological Discovery* (New York: McGraw-Hill, 1964), vol. 2, p.20. Gwynne Dyer, *War* (New York: Crown, 1985), pp.15–16. Dyer draws on Mellaart's figures for his description.

24. Qunicy Wright, *A Study of War* (Chicago: University of Chicago Press, 1965), p.63.

Chapter 2: Armies of the Ancient World

1. Frank A. Kiernan and John K. Fairbank, *Chinese Ways in Warfare* (Cambridge, MA: Harvard Universty Press, 1974), p.2.

2. Edmund Balmforth, 'A Chinese Military Strategist of the Warring States: Sun Pin', (Ph.D. dissertation, Rutgers University, 1979), p.58.

3. Gwynne Dyer, *War* (New York: Crown Publishers, 1985), p.21, for an estimate of the size of Sargon's army.

4. Arther Ferrill, *The Origins of War* (London: Thames and Hudson, 1985), p.58.

5. The strength of the Egyptian army is based upon an extrapolation of the figures provided by Robert J. Wenke, *Patterns of Prehistory: Mankind's First Three Million Years* (New York: Oxford University Press, 1980), p.486.

6. Ferrill, p.58.

7. Ibid.

8. Ibid., p.70.

9. T.N. Dupuy, *The Evolution of Weapons and Warfare* (New York: Bobbs-Merrill, 1980), p.10.

10. Robert A. Laffont, *The Ancient Art of Warfare* (New York: Time–Life Books, 1966), vol. 1, p.45.

11. These figures are taken from Plato's account of the war and are considerably less than the numbers offered by Herodotus, who gives the size of the Persian army at 2,641,640 men.

12. See General Sir Percy Sykes, *A History of Persia* (London: Macmillan, 1985), vol. 1, pp.196–98.

13. Laffont, pp.38–39.

14. Major General Gurcharn Singh Sandhu, *A Millitary History of Ancient India* (Delhi, India: Vision Books, 2000), p.187.

15. J.F.C. Fuller, *Julius Caesar: Man, Soldier, Tyrant* (New York: DaCapo Press, 1965), p.95.

16. Richard A. Gabriel and Donald Boose Jr, *Great Battles of Antiquity* (Westport, CT: Greenwood Press, 1994), p.355.

17. Ibid., p.415; see also Walter Goffart, *Barbarians and Romans* (Princeton, NJ: Princeton University Press, 1980), for a more comprehensive examination of German tribal society.

18. Tim Newark, *The Barbarians* (London: Blandford Press, 1985), chap. 2; see also Hans Delbruck, *History of the Art of War: The Barbarian Invasions* (Lincoln, NB: University of Nebraska Press, 1990), vol. 2, p.307.

19. Sandhu, *A Military History of Ancient India*, p.199.

20. Ibid., p.223.

21. Thomas Day Seymour, *Life in the Homeric Age* (New York: Biblo and Tannen Publishers, 1965), pp.586–87.

22. Ibid., p.571.

23. Thucydides, Book 2: 13 (Pericles); see also Delbruck, vol. 1, p.39.

24. Ibid.

25. Ibid.

26. Jane C. Waldbaum, 'From Bronze To Iron: The Transition from the Bronze Age to the Iron Age in the Eastern Mediterranean', in *Studies in Mediterranean Archaeology* 54 (Goteborg, Sweden: 1978), p.39, Table IV.I.

Chapter 3: Life of the Common Soldier

1. James Mellaart, *The Neolithic of the Near East* (New York: Charles Scribner, 1975), p.132.

2. It is only since the age of antisepsis and vaccination, both dating only from the last third of the nineteenth century, that the death rate for children began to decline, and then only in the West.

3. Egypt, for example, is still plagued by epidemics of snail fever caused by parasites from a snail living in the irrigation canals.

4. Jonathan P. Roth, *The Logistics of the Roman Army at War: 264 BC–AD 235* (Boston: Brill, 1999), p.9.

5. Richard A. Gabriel, *The Great Armies of Antiquity* (Wesport, CT: Praeger, 2002), p.265.

6. Richard A. Gabriel, *The Great Captains of Antiquity* (Westport, CT: Praeger, 2001), pp.19–20.

7. Roth, p.9; see also Dio Cassius, *History of Rome* 75.2.4.

8. Roth, pp.9–10.

9. Richard A. Gabriel, *Warrior Pharaoh* (New York: Iuniverse, 2001), p.8. See also by the same author, *The Military History of Ancient Israel* (Westport, CT: Praeger, 2003), p.113.

10. For an analysis of a number of battles in the ancient period that demonstrate both the sophistication of battle tactics and the competence of the ancient soldier, see Richard A. Gabriel and Donald W. Boose Jr, *Great Battles of Antiquity* (Westport, CT: Greenwood Press, 1994); for a more recent and comprehensive treatment of the same subject, including the ancient armies of the non-Western world at that time, see Richard A. Gabriel, *Empires at War: A Chronological Encyclopedia of War in the Ancient World*, 3 vols (Westport, CT: Praeger, 2005).

11. Ibid.

12. Ibid., ch. 20, 'Charlemagne and the Empire of the Franks'.

13. John Dominic Crossan, *The Historical Jesus: The Life of a Mediterranean Jewish Peasant* (San Francisco: Harper Collins, 1992), p.141.

14. Sarva Daman Singh, *Ancient Indian Warfare* (Delhi: Motilal Banarsidass, 1977), ch. 8, 'Ethics of War'; see also V.R. Ramachandra Dikshitar, *War in Ancient India* (Delhi: Motilal Banarsidass, 1987), ch. 2, 'The Laws of War'.

15. James B. Pritchard, *Ancient Near Eastern Texts* (Princeton, NJ: Princeton University Press, 1955), 'The Soldier's Oath', pp.353–54; see in the same work, 'The Hittite Laws', pp.186–96; for an examination of Egyptian law, see Richard A. Gabriel, *Gods of Our Fathers: The Memory of Egypt in Judaism and Christianity* (Westport, CT: Greenwood Press, 2002), ch. 1, 'The Dawn of Conscience'.

16. Pritchard, 'The Soldier's Oath', p.354.

17. Ibid., p.476.

18. William Kelly Simpson (ed.), 'A Soldier's Lot', in *The Literature of Ancient Egypt* (New Haven, CT: Yale University Press, 1972), pp.216–17.

19. 'Horemheb Delivers The Poor From Oppression, 1315 BC', in Jon E. Lewis (ed.), *Ancient Egypt* (New York: Carroll and Graff, 2003), p.165.

20. Ibid., p.167.

21. Richard A. Gabriel and Donald W. Boose Jr, *Great Battles of Antiquity* (Westport, CT: Greenwood Press, 1994), p.82. For a more complete analysis of law, crime and

punishment in ancient Egypt, see Joyce Tyldesley, *Judgement of the Pharaoh: Crime and Punishment in Ancient Egypt* (New York: Peartree Publishers, 2002).

22. Dikshitar, *War in Ancient India*, p.79.
23. Xenophon, *The Persian Expedition* (London: Penguin, 1949), pp.256–58.
24. Ibid., p.92.
25. Ibid.
26. Peter Connolly, *Greece and Rome at War* (NJ: Prentice-Hall, 1981), p.139.
27. Titus Livius, *The War With Hannibal* (London: Penguin, 1972), 28, 30:29.
28. Richard A. Gabriel, *The Military History of Ancient Israel*, p.118.
29. Gabriel, *Empires at War*, vol. 1, ch. 14, 'Caesar's Wars and the End of the Roman Republic'.

Chapter 4: Killing Technology: Weapons and Armour in Antiquity

1. Gurcharn Singh Sandhu, *A Military History of Ancient India* (New Delhi: Vision Books, 2000), p.69.
2. Ibid.
3. Jane C. Waldbaum, 'From Bronze To Iron: The Transition from the Bronze Age to the Iron Age in the Eastern Mediterranean', in *Studies in Mediterranean Archaeology* 54 (Goteborg, 1978), p.39, Table IV.I.
4. Arther Ferrill, *The Origins of War* (London: Thames and Hudson, 1985), p.67.
5. Singh, p.102.
6. Quintus Curtius Rufus, *The History of Alexander* (London: Penguin, 2001), Book 9, 8:1.
7. Except for cannon which continued to be made mostly of bronze until at least the American Civil War, when rifled steel cannon made their first appearance.
8. Richard A. Gabriel and Karen S. Metz, *From Sumer to Rome: The Military Capabilities of Ancient Armies* (Westport, CT: Greenwood Press, 1991), p.57.
9. For a detailed examination of Egyptian military medicine in the ancient period, to include their skill in dealing with fractured skulls, see Richard A. Gabriel and Karen S. Metz, *The History of Military Medicine: From Ancient Times to the Middle Ages* vol. 1 (Westport, CT: Greenwood Press, 1992), Ch. 3.
10. Robert L. O'Connell, *Of Arms and Men* (New York: Oxford University Press, 1989), pp.34–35.
11. Thomas Day Seymour, *Life in the Homeric Age* (New York: Biblo and Tannenn, 1965), pp.578, 631–32.
12. Steven Weingartner, 'The Saga of Piyamaradu', *Military Heritage* (October, 2001), p.81, for a portrayal of the long spears of this period used by Mycenaean soldiers. Seymour suggests they were 16ft long.
13. Yigael Yadin, *The Art of Warfare In Biblical Lands in Light of Archaeology* vol. 1 (New York: McGraw-Hill, 1963), p.136.

14. Sandhu, p.69.

15. Gabriel and Metz, *From Sumer to Rome*, p.61.

16. Ibid.

17. Yadin, p.45.

18. Peter Connolly, *Greece and Rome at War* (Englewood Cliffs, NJ: Prentice-Hall, 1981), p.233.

19. O'Conell, p.38. For an excellent analysis of the *gladius*, see Steven Weingartner, 'The Gladius', *Military Heritage* (August, 2000), pp.10–15.

20. E. Stephen Gurdjian, 'The Treatment of Penetrating Head Wounds of the Brain Sustained in Warfare', *Journal of Neurosurgery* 39 (February, 1974), p.158.

21. This estimate provided by Richard Glantz, professional archer.

22. Yadin, vol. 2, p.348.

23. Fatigue estimates provided by Glantz.

24. Gabriel and Metz, *From Sumer to Rome*, pp.70–71.

25. Christopher Duffy, *The Military Experience in the Age of Reason* (New York: Atheneum, 1988), pp.207–08.

26. The definitive work on the military slinger is Manfred Korfmann, 'The Sling as a Weapon', *Scientific American* 229, no. 4 (October, 1973), pp.34–42.

27. Ibid.

28. G.R. Watson, *The Roman Soldier* (Ithaca, NY: Cornel University Press, 1969), p.60.

29. Yigael Yadin, *The Art of War in Biblical Lands in Light of Archaeology* vol. 1 (New York: Mc Graw-Hill, 1963), p.197.

30. Ibid., p.135.

31. Ibid., p.197.

32. The estimate as to weight was provided by Karl Netsch, professional blacksmith, and is based on the assumption that the iron armour was 2mm thick.

33. Peter Connolly, *Greece and Rome at War* (Englewood Cliffs, NJ: Prentice-Hall, 1981), p.58.

34. Ibid. For the history of linen armour, including its probable source in Egypt, see Gregory S. Aldrete, Scott Bartell and Alicia Aldrete, *Reconstructing Ancient Line Body Armor: Unraveling the Linothorax Mystery* (Baltimore, MD: Johns Hopkins University Press, 2013), pp.27–28.

35. Richard A. Gabriel and Donald W. Boose Jr, *Great Battles of Antiquity* (Westport, CT: Greenwood Press, 1994), p.188.

36. Richard A. Gabriel, *Empires At War* vol. 3 (Westport, CT: Praeger, 2005), Ch. 30, 'Empires of the Americas'.

37. Connolly, p.230.

38. Ibid., p.231.

39. Singh, p.98.

40. Sandhu, p.127.

41. Nigel Stillman and Nigel Tallis, *Armies of the Ancient Near East: 3000 to 539 BCE* (Sussex: Flexiprint, 1984), p.194; see also Thomas Day Seymour, *Life in The Homeric Age* (New York: Biblo and Tannen, 1965), pp.662–64.

42. Ibid., p.93.

43. Ibid., p.114.

44. Ibid.

45. Gabriel and Boose, p.179.

46. Richard A. Gabriel and Karen S. Metz, *From Sumer to Rome: The Military Capabilities of Ancient Armies* (Westport, CT: Greenwood Press, 1991), p.54.

47. Ibid.

48. Richard A. Gabriel, *The Culture of War: Invention and Early Development* (Westport, CT: Greenwood Press, 1990), p.87.

49. Connolly, pp.52–53.

50. Richard A. Gabriel, *The Culture of War*, p.87.

Chapter 5: Death, Wounds, Infection, Disease and Injury in Ancient Armies

1. Richard A. Gabriel and Karen S. Metz, *From Sumer to Rome: The Military Capabilities of Ancient Armies* (Westport, CT: Greenwood Press, 1991), p.85.

2. Livy, *The War With Hannibal*, Book 12, 49–50.

3. Gabriel and Metz, p.88.

4. Ibid., p.87.

5. Donald W. Engels, *Alexander the Great and the Logistics of the Macedonian Army* (Berkeley, CA: University of California Press, 1978), p.151.

6. Graham Webster, *The Roman Imperial Army of the First and Second Centuries AD* (New York: Barnes and Noble, 1979), pp.260–65.

7. H. Froelich, *Die Militarmedizin Homers* (Stuttgart, 1897), pp.56–60.

8. H.M. Frost, *Orthopedic Biomechanics* (Springfield, IL: Charles C. Thomas, 1973), p.198.

9. More technical information on the diseases and infections discussed herein can be found in *The Professional Guide to Disease* (Springfield, PA: Intermed Communications, 1982). As regards disease in antiquity, see Frederick F. Cartwright, *Disease and History* (New York: Barns and Noble, 1991) and R.S. Bray, *Armies of Pestilence* (New York: Barns and Noble, 1996).

10. Gabriel and Metz, p.97. For a detailed description of the medical techniques of military physicians in antiquity, see by the same authors, *A History of Military Medicine: Vol. 1 From Ancient Times to the Middle Ages* (Westport, CT: Greenwood Press, 1992).

11. *The Professional Guide to Disease*, pp.321–22.

12. Peter A. Aldea and William Shaw, 'The Evolution of Surgical Management of Severe Lower Extremity Trauma', *Clinics in Plastic Surgery* 13, no. 4 (October, 1986), p.561.

13. Ibid.

14. Gabriel and Metz, p.99.

15. Ibid.

16. Robert E. McGrew, *Encyclopedia of Medical History* (New York: McGraw-Hill, 1985), p.104.

17. Ibid., p.103.

18. Ibid., p.104.

19. *Historical Statistics of the United States* (Washington, DC: Department of the Census, 1975), p.1,140.

20. McGrew, p.348.

21. Ibid., p.349.

22. Ibid.

23. Ibid.

24. Ibid.

25. Ibid., p.352.

26. Ibid., p.313.

27. R.J. Doyle and Nancy C. Lee, 'Microbes, Religion, and Warfare', *Canadian Journal of Microbiology* 32, no. 3 (March, 1986), p.195.

28. McGrew, p.318.

29. Engels, p.54.

30. Ibid., pp.123–26.

31. S. Jarcho, 'A Roman Experience With Heatstroke in 24 BC', *Bulletin of the New York Academy of Medicine* 43, no. 8 (August, 1967), pp.767–68.

32. Morris Kerstein and Roger Hubbards, 'Heat Related Problems in the Desert: The Environment Can Become the Enemy', *Military Medicine* 149 (December, 1984), pp.650–56.

33. Ibid., p.653.

34. Ibid., p.659.

35. Ibid., p.656.

36. P. Byron Vaughan, 'Local Cold Injury: Menace to Military Operations', *Military Medicine* 145 (May, 1980), p.306. See also Alan Steinman, 'Adverse Effects of Heat and Cold on Military Operations', *Military Medicine* 152 (August, 1987).

Chapter 6: Logistics: The Invisible Art in Ancient Warfare

1. Donald W. Engels, *Alexander the Great and the Logistics of the Macedonian Army* (Berkeley, CA: University of California Press, 1978), Table 3, p.145.

2. Roth, pp.62–67.

3. Ibid., p.119; see also Richard A. Gabriel and Karen S. Metz, *From Sumer to Rome: The Military Capabilities of Ancient Armies* (Westport, CT: Greenwood Press, 1991), p.23.

4. As noted by Josephus, *The Jewish War*, 1.395.

5. Roth, p.83.

6. Ibid.

7. Erna Risch, *Quartermaster Support of the Army*, 2nd ed. (Washington, DC: Center of Military History, 1989), p.291.

8. Duncan K. Major and Roger S. Fitch, *Supply of Sherman's Army During the Atlanta Campaign* (Ft Leavenworth, KS: Army Services School Press, 1911), pp.10, 25.

9. U.P. Thapliyal, 'Military Organization in the Ancient Period', in S.N. Prasad, *Historical Perspectives of Warfare in India* (Delhi: Motilal Banarsidass, Centre for Studies in Civilizations, 2002), p.77.

10. Richard A. Gabriel, *The Culture of War: Invention and Early Development* (Westport, CT: Greenwood Press, 1990), p.73; see also Robert Laffont, *The Ancient Art of War* (New York: Time-Life Books, 1966), pp.38–39.

11. Gurcharn Singh Sandhu, *A Military History of Ancient India* (Delhi: Vision Books, 2000), pp.186–87.

12. James Huston, *Sinews of War: Army Logistics, 1775–1953* (Washington, DC: 1966), p.219.

13. Roth, p.125.

14. Ibid., p.128.

15. Livy, *History of Rome*, 27.12.7.

16. Ann Hyland, *Equus: The Horse in the Roman World* (New Haven: Yale University Press, 1990), p.92.

17. Yigael Yadin, *The Art of Warfare in Biblical Lands in Light of Archaeology* (New York: McGraw-Hill, 1963), vol. 1, p.89.

18. Arther Ferrill, *The Origins of War* (London: Thames and Hudson, 1985), p.72.

19. Xenophon, *Cyropaedia*, bk.6, 50–55; the weight is an extrapolation from Xenophon's statement that the number of talents carried by an ox was twenty-five. A talent never weighed less than 58lb.

20. Jonathan P. Roth, *The Logistics of the Roman Army at War: 264 BCE–CE 235* (Boston: Brill, 1999), p.87.

21. Thomas Day Seymour, *Life in the Homeric Age* (New York: Biblo and Tannen, 1965), p.590.

22. Roth, p.133.

23. Livy, *History of Rome*, 26.43.8.

24. Keith Hopkins, 'Taxes and Trade in the Roman Empire, 200 BCE to CE 400', *Journal of Roman Studies*, 70 (1980), p.86, Table 2.

25. Roth, p.182.

26. Ibid., p.187.

27. Thapliyal, pp.75–77, for an explanation of the Indian supply system.

28. Donald V. Sippel, 'Some Observations on the Means and Costs of the Transport of Bulk Commodities in the Late Republic and Early Empire', *Ancient World*, 16 (1987), p.37.

29. Gabriel and Metz, p.24.

30. *Animal Management* (London: British Army Veterinary Department, 1908), p.299.

31. Bernard S. Bachrach, 'Animals and Warfare in Early Medieval Europe', in Bernard S. Bachrach (ed.), *Armies and Politics in the Early Medieval West* (Aldershot, Hampshire: Variorum), p.717.

32. Ibid.

33. K.D. White, *Roman Farming* (Ithaca, NY: Cornell University Press, 1970), p.295.

34. Gabriel and Metz, p.25.

35. Ibid.

36. James D. Anderson, *Roman Military Supply in North East England* (Oxford: British Archaeological Reports, British Series, 224, 1992), p.15.

37. Hyland, pp.71–72.

38. White, p.132.

39. Emmett M. Essin, 'Mules, Packs, and Packtrains', *Southwestern Historical Quarterly*, 74/1 (1970), p.54.

40. Engels, Table 7, p.153.

41. Ibid., p.14.

42. Thapliyal, p.777.

43. Marcus Junkelmann, *Die Legionen des Augustus: Der romische Soldat im archaologisch Experiment* (Mainz, Germany: Philipp von Zabern, 1986), p.34.

44. Engles, Table 7, p.153.

45. Livy, *The Histories*, 11.16.7

46. Laffont, p.56.

47. Michael Grant, *History of Rome* (New York: Charles Scribner, 1978), p.264.

48. 'The Roman Empire and Military Airlift', *The Wall Street Journal*, December 9, 1987, A7.

49. H.W.F. Saggs, *The Might That Was Assyria* (London: Sidgwick and Jackson, 1984), p.255.

50. Richard A. Gabriel, *The Culture of War*, p.76.

51. Yaha Zoka, *The Imperial Iranian Army from Cyrus to Pahlavi* (Teheran: Ministry of Culture and Arts Press, 1970), pp.90–96, for the Persian navy.

52. Herodotus, bk 7, 89–97.

53. General Sir Percy Sykes, *A History of Persia* (London: Macmillan, 1985), pp.163–164.

54. Thapliyal, p.77.

55. Richard Gabriel and Karen Metz, p.28.

56. Roth, p.198.

Chapter 7: Siegecraft and Artillery

1. James Mellaart, *The Neolithic of the Near East* (New York: Charles Scribner, 1975), pp.50–58.
2. Gurcharn Singh Sandhu, *A Military History of Ancient India* (Delhi: Vision Books, 2000), p.58.
3. Ibid., pp.26, 58.
4. Majid Khadduri, *Encyclopedia Britannica*, 15th ed., sv. 'Sumerian Civilization'.
5. Leonard Cottrell, *The Warrior Pharaohs* (New York: Dutton, 1969), pp.45–48.
6. Sarva Daman Singh, *Ancient Indian Warfare* (Delhi: Motilal Banarsidass, 1965), pp.126–27.
7. Khadduri, p.906.
8. Ibid.
9. Yigael Yadin, *The Art of Warfare in Biblical Lands in Light of Archaeological Discovery* vol. 1 (New York: McGraw-Hill, 1963), p.16.
10. Ibid., p.18.
11. Richard A. Gabriel, *The Military History of Ancient Israel* (Westport, CT: Praeger, 2003), p.241.
12. Yadin, pp.19–20.
13. Gabriel, p.131.
14. Yadin, vol. 2, pp.313–28.
15. Ibid., vol. 1, pp.55, 147.
16. Ibid., vol. 2, pp.313–28.
17. Richard A. Gabriel and Donald W. Boose Jr, *The Great Battles of Antiquity* (Westport, CT: Greenwood Press, 1994), pp.310–11.
18. Richard A. Gabriel, *The Culture of War* (Westport, CT: Greenwood Press, 1990), pp.237–38.
19. Ibid.
20. Ibid.
21. A good account of Greek siege machinery can be found in J.K. Anderson, 'Wars and Military Science: Greece', in Michael Grant and Rachael Kitzinger (eds), *Civilization of the Ancient Mediterranean* vol. 1 (New York: Charles Scribner, 1988), pp.679–89.
22. Sandhu, p.233.
23. Ibid.
24. Ibid.
25. Ibid., p.154.
26. Gabriel and Boose, p.201.
27. Graham Webster, *The Roman Imperial Army of the First and Second Centuries AD* (New York: Barnes and Noble, 1979), pp.240–43.
28. Gabriel and Boose, pp.367–69.

29. T.N. Dupuy, *The Evolution of Weapons and Warfare* (New York: Bobbs-Merrill, 1980), p.29.
30. Ibid.
31. Ibid., p.30.
32. Ibid.
33. Ibid.
34. Josephus, *The Jewish War*, bk 5: 6.3.
35. Vegetius, ii, 25.
36. Dupuy, p.24.
37. Ibid., p.30.
38. Ibid.

Chapter 8: Iron Rations: The Soldier's Diet

1. Richard A. Gabriel, *Muhammad: Islam's First Great General* (Dulles, VA: Potomac Press, 2007), p.91.
2. Richard A. Gabriel, *Subotai the Valiant: Genghis Khan's Greatest General* (Norman, OK: Oklahoma University Press, 2006), p.36.
3. Richard A. Gabriel, *Hannibal: The Military Biography of Rome's Greatest Enemy* (Dulles, VA: Potomac Press, 2011), p.103.
4. Jane M. Renfrew, 'Vegetables in the Ancient Near Eastern Diet', *Civilizations of the Ancient Near East*, vol. 1, ed. Jack M. Sasson (Peabody, MA: Hendrickson Publishers, 1995), p.202.
5. Livy, 44.26.6.
6. Sarva Damn Singh, *Ancient Indian Warfare* (Delhi: Motilal Banarsidass, 1997), p.132.
7. Livy, 44.26.6.
8. Appian, *Celtic Wars*, 1.3.
9. Julius Caesar, *Gallic Wars*, 5.14.
10. Dio Cassius, 62.5.5–6.
11. Richard A. Gabriel, *Soldier's Lives Throughout History: Antiquity* (Westport, CT: Greenwood Press, 2007), p.37. See also Graham Webster, *The Roman Imperial Army of the First and Second Centuries AD*, 3rd ed. (Totowa, NJ: Barnes and Noble, 1985), p.263.
12. Thomas D. Seymour, *Life in the Homeric Age* (New York: Biblio and Tannen, 1963), p.232.
13. Ibid., p.233.
14. Ibid., p.214.
15. Jonathan P. Roth, *The Logistics of the Roman Army at War (265 BCE–235 CE)* (Boston: Brill Publishers, 1999), p.51. See also Renfrew, p.197.
16. Donald W. Engels, *Alexander the Great and the Logistics of the Macedonian Army* (Berkeley, CA: University of California Press, 1978), p.125.

17. Irma S. Rombauer and Marion Rombauer Becker, *The Joy of Cooking* (New York: Penguin, 1993), p.175.

18. J.I. Robertson, *Tenting Tonight: The Soldier's Life* (Alexandria, VA: Time-Life Books, 1984), p.85.

19. Roth, *Logistics of the Roman Army*, p.12. Perhaps the best work on the food supply of the Roman army is Paul Erdkamp, *Hunger and the Sword: Warfare and Food Supply in Roman Republican Wars* (Amsterdam: J.C. Gieben Publisher, 1998).

20. Ibid., p.8.

21. Napoleon was the first of the modern commanders to experiment with meat preserved in tins, followed closely by the British in the Crimean War. Northern forces in the Civil War had tinned beef. Very often the meat spoiled in the tin and was inedible. Other times, the meat developed bacteria such as botulism that was deadly if consumed.

22. Roth, *Logistics of the Roman Army*, p.185.

23. Robertson, *Tenting Tonight*, p.85.

24. Ibid.

25. H.W.F. Saggs, *The Might That Was Assyria* (London: Sidgwick and Jackson, 1984), p.166.

26. Roth, *Logistics of the Roman Army*, p.8.

27. Jane M. Renfrew, 'Vegetables in the Ancient Near Eastern Diet', p.201.

28. A.L. Basham, *The Wonder That Was India* (New York: Grove Press, 1954), p.195.

29. Thomas Day Seymour, *Life in the Homeric Age* (New York: Biblo and Tannen, 1965), p.216.

30. Victor W. von Hagen, *The Ancient Sun Kingdoms* (New York: The World Publishing Company, 1956), p.444.

31. Renfrew, 'Vegetables in the Ancient Near East Diet', p.193.

32. Ibid., p.192.

33. Brian Hesse, 'Animal Husbandry in the Human Diet in the Ancient Near East', in Jack Sasson (ed.), *Civilizations of the Ancient Near East* vol. 1 (Peabody, MA: Hendrickson Publishers, 1995), p.213.

34. Ibid., p.220.

35. Richard A. Gabriel, *Lion of the Sun* (New York: iuniverse, 2003), P.110.

36. Engels, *Alexander the Great and the Logistics of the Macedonian Army*, p.123.

37. Rombauer, *The Joy of Cooking*, p.175.

38. Robertson, *Tenting Tonight*, p.85.

39. Richard A. Gabriel and Karen Metz, *A History of Military Medicine: From Ancient Times to the Middle Ages* (Westport, CT: Greenwood Press, 1992), p.165.

Chapter 9: Medical Care in Ancient Armies

1. Richard A. Gabriel and Karen S. Metz. *From Sumer to Rome: The Military Capabilities of Ancient Armies* (Westport, CT: Greenwood Press, 1991), p.113. For

a detailed history of military medical care in the armies of the ancient world, see by the same authors, *A History of Military Medicine: From Ancient Times to the Middle Ages* vol. 1 (Westport, CT: Greenwood Press, 1992).

2. Guido Majno, *The Healing Hand* (Cambridge, MA: Harvard University Press, 1975), p.84. See also Fielding H. Garrison, *The History of Medicine* (London: W.B. Saunders, 1968), p.59; see the section entitled 'Identity of Forms of Ancient and Primitive Medicine', pp.17–24.

3. Garrison, p.54.

4. For the text of Hammurabi's code governing the medical profession of Babylon, see Majno, p.43.

5. Martin Levey, 'Some Objective Factors of Babylonian Medicine in Light of New Evidence', *Bulletin of the History of Medicine* 35 (January–February, 1961), p.65.

6. The text of the letter is available in Majno, p.66.

7. For a photograph of the Stele of Vultures depicting these events, see Yigael Yadin, *The Art of Warfare in Biblical Lands in Light of Archaeological Discovery* (New York: McGraw-Hill, 1963), p.135.

8. Majno, p.94.

9. Ibid., p.96.

10. Ibid., pp.111–15.

11. Ibid., pp.116–17.

12. Garrison, p.62.

13. Gabriel and Metz, *From Sumer to Rome*, p.129.

14. P.B. Adamson, 'The Military Surgeon: His Place in History', *Journal of the Royal Army Medical Corps* 128 (1982), p.44.

15. Xenophon, *The Persian Expedition*, Book 5, 3.

16. Donald W. Engels, *Alexander the Great and the Logistics of the Macedonian Army* (Berkeley, CA: University of California Press, 1978), pp.16–17.

17. For the development of psychiatry, including military psychiatry, in the ancient world, see Franze G. Alexander and Sheldon T. Selesnick, *The History of Psychiatry* (New York: New American Library, 1966), pp.49–76; see also Richard A. Gabriel, *No More Heroes: Madness and Psychiatry in War* (New York: Hill and Wang, 1987), pp.97–100.

18. Gabriel and Metz, *From Sumer to Rome*, p.140.

19. Vivian Nutton, 'Medicine and the Roman Army: A Further Reconsideration', *Medical History* 13 (1969), p.263.

20. Orville Oughtred, 'How the Romans Delivered Medical Care Along Hadrian's Wall Fortifications', *Michigan Medicine* (February, 1980), p.58.

21. Lieutenant Colonel A.M. Acharya, 'Military Medicine in Ancient India', *Bulletin of the Indian Institute of Medicine* 6 (1963), pp.50–57.

22. Gabriel and Metz, *A History of Military Medicine*, p.131; see also U.P. Thapliyal, 'Military Organization in the Ancient Period', in S.N. Prasad (ed.), *Historical Perspectives of Warfare in India* (Delhi: Centre for Studies in Civilization, 2002), p.92.

23. Acharya, p.52.

24. Ibid.

25. Ibid., p.56.

26. Ibid.

27. Majno, p.287.

28. Gabriel and Metz, *A History of Military Medicine*, p.138.

29. Thapliyal, p.92.

Chapter 10: War and Madness

1. David Grossman, *On Killing* (Boston: Back Bay Books, 1995), pp.121–29.

2. Grossman, pp.99–100.

3. Livy, *The War With Hannibal*, trans. Aubrey De Selincourt (London: Penguin Books, 1965), pp.151–52.

4. Richard A. Gabriel, *No More Heroes: Madness and Psychiatry in War* (New York: Hill and Wang, 1987), p.77.

5. Ibid., p.72.

6. Ibid., p.73.

7. Ibid.

8. Ibid., p.77

9. Ibid.

10. Ibid.

11. Gabriel, *No More Heroes*, p.98.

12. Richard A. Gabriel, *The Military History of Ancient Israel* (Westport, CT: Praeger, 2003), p.91.

13. For more on this point, see Richard A. Gabriel, *Military Psychiatry: A Comparative Perspective* (Westport, CT: Greenwood Press, 1986).

14. Richard A. Gabriel and Karen S. Metz, *Man and Wound in the Ancient World: A History of Military Medicine from Sumer to the Fall of Constantinople*, p.154.

15. Ibid.

16. Some scholars have argued, however, that Homer portrays Odysseus as suffering from psychiatric collapse. *Odyssey* 8.83.

17. Herodotus, 7.230, 232, for Aristodemus and Pantities respectively. Xenophon in the *Constitution of the Spartans* 9.3–6 tells of the difficulties faced by men in Sparta who failed to perform adequately in battle, including the difficulties their sisters faced in finding husbands.

18. Herodotus (9.71). See Lawrence A. Tritle, *From Melos to My Lai* (New York: Routledge, 2000).

19. See Lawrence A. Tritle, *From Melos to My Lai* (New York: Routledge), pp.75–76.

20. *The Complete Plays of Sophocles: Ajax*, trans. Sir Richard Claverhouse Jebb (London: Bantam, 1982), 9011.

21. Herodotus, 9.63.

22. Xenophon, *The Anabasis* book 3, chapter 1. 'I am sure that not numbers or strength bring victory in war; but whichever army goes into battle stronger in its soul.'

23. Max Hastings, *Military Anecdotes* (New York: Oxford University Press, 1985), p.18.

24. Richard A. Gabriel, *The Madness of Alexander the Great and the Myth of Military Genius* (Barnsley: Pen and Sword, 2015), Chapter 4.

25. On the Aesclepian temples as psychiatric treatment, see D. Kouretas, 'The Oracle of Trophonius: A Kind of Shock Treatment Associated with Sensory Deprivation in Greece', *British Journal of Psychiatry* 113, no. 505 (1979), pp.1,441–46; Jon Romano, 'Temples, Asylums, or Hospitals?', *Journal of the National Association of Private Psychiatric Hospitals* 9, no. 4 (Summer, 1978), pp.5–12; M.G. Papageorgiu, 'Incubation as a Form of Psychotherapy in the Care of Patients in Ancient Greece', *Psychotherapy* 26 (1975), pp.35–38.

26. For an analysis of the case studies found on the *stelae* at Epidaurus, see Lynn Li Donnici, *The Epidaurian Miracle Inscriptions: Text, Translations, and Commentary* (Atlanta, GA: Scholars Press, 1995).

27. Ibid., pp.115, 109 respectively.

28. Richard A.Gabriel, 'The Roman Military Medical Corps', *Military History*, (January, 2011), pp.39–44.

29. Richard A. Gabriel, *No More Heroes*, pp.109–13, for a description of the Russian contributions to military psychiatry.

30. Richard A. Gabriel, *Between Flesh and Steel: A History of Military Medicine from the Middle Ages to the War in Afghanistan* (Dulles, VA: Potomac Books, 2013), pp.176–79.

31. Richard A. Gabriel, 'War, Madness and Military Psychiatry', *Military History*, (Spring, 2014), pp.57–50.

32. Grossman, *On Killing*, Chapter 3.

33. Ibid.

34. Ibid.

35. Gabriel, *No More Heroes*, p.87.

36. Roy L. Swank and Walter E. Marchand, 'Combat Neuroses: The Development of Combat Exhaustion', *Archives of Neurology and Psychiatry*, vol. 55 (1946), p.244.

Chapter 12: Thutmose III of Egypt and the First Battle in Military History

1. David O'Connor, 'Thutmose III: An Enigmatic Pharaoh', in *Thutmose III: A New Biography*, ed. Eric Cline and David O'Connor (Ann Arbor: University of Michigan Press, 2008), pp.5–6.

2. Ibid.

3. Donald B. Redford, 'The Northern Wars of Thutmose III', in Cline and O'Connor, *Thutmose III: A New Biography*, p.325.

4. Arielle P. Kozloff, 'The Artistic Production of the Reign of Thutmose III', in Cline and O'Connor, *Thutmose III: A New Biography*, p.317.

5. Dennis Forbes, 'Menkheperre Djehutymes: Thutmose III, a Pharaoh's Pharaoh', *KMT* 9, no. 4 (Winter 1998–99), p.183.

6. Piotr Laskowski, 'Monumental Architecture and the Royal Building Program of Thutmose III', in Cline and O'Connor, *Thutmose III: A New Biography*, p.229.

7. Richard A. Gabriel, *Thutmose III: The Military Biography of Egypt's Greatest Warrior Pharaoh* (Dulles, VA: Potomac Books, 2009), p.9.

8. O'Connor, 'Thutmose III: An Enigmatic Pharaoh', p.5.

9. Gabriel, *Thutmose III: Military Biography*, p.19.

10. R.O. Faulkner, 'Egyptian Military Organization', *Journal of Egyptian Archaeology* 39 (1953), p.42.

11. Raymond W. Baker, *Encyclopedia Britannica*, 15th ed., s.v. 'History of Egyptian Civilization'.

12. Manfred Bietak, 'The Thutmosid Stronghold of Perunefer', *Egyptian Archaeology* 26 (Spring, 2005), pp.13–14.

13. Torgny Save-Soderbergh, *The Navy of the Eighteenth Egyptian Dynasty* (Uppsala, Sweden: Uppsala University Press, 1946), p.34.

14. Ibid. p.42.

15. Gabriel, *Thutmose III: Military Biography*, p.147.

16. Ibid., p.34

17. Ibid., p.84

18. R.O. Faulkner, 'The Battle of Megiddo', *Journal of Egyptian Archaeology* 28 (1942), p.2.

19. The name of the Eleutheros Valley is taken from Strabo, *Histories*, xvi, 2, 12, and was used throughout classical times. The name appears in the Bible (Maccabees 11:7 and 12:30), but we do not know by what name it was known to the Egyptians.

20. Gabriel, *Thutmose III: Military Biography*, p.87.

21. Ibid., p.96.

22. Ibid., pp.99–104.

23. Ibid., pp.106–12.

Chapter 13: Egyptian Shipbuilding and the Invention of Amphibious Warfare

1. Torgny Save-Soderbergh, *The Navy of the Eighteenth Egyptian Dynasty* (Uppsala, Sweden: Uppsala University Press, 1946), p.34.

2. R.O. Faulkner, 'Egyptian Seagoing Ships', *Journal of Egyptian Archaeology* 26 (February, 1941), p.3.

3. Richard A. Gabriel, *Scipio Africanus: Rome's Greatest General* (Dulles, VA: Potomac Books), p.152, for the shipping capacity of Roman transport ships being the same as that of early Egyptian ships. See also George W. Houston, 'Ports in Perspective: Some Comparative Material on Roman Merchant Ships and Ports', *American Journal of Archaeology* 92, no. 4 (1988), pp.553–64.

4. Faulkner, 'Egyptian Seagoing Ships', p.3.

5. Save-Soderbergh, p.34.

6. Anthony J. Salinger, *War in Ancient Egypt* (Malden, MA: Blackwell, 2005), p.6.

7. Manfred Bietak, 'The Thumoside Stronghold of Perunefer', *Egyptian Archaeology* 26 (Spring, 2005), pp.13–17.

8. Save-Soderbergh, p.90.

9. Ibid., p.37.

10. James Cornell, 'Naval Activity in the Days of Solomon and Ramses III', *Antiquity* 21 (1947), p.66.

11. Save-Soderbergh, p.46.

12. Faulkner, p.4; the dates are taken from Sir Alan Gardiner, *Egypt of the Pharaohs* (Oxford: Oxford University Press, 1961), pp.434–35.

13. William F. Edgerton, 'Ancient Egyptian Ships and Shipping', *American Journal of Semitic Languages and Literature* 39, no. 2 (January, 1923), pp.116–17.

14. Edgerton, 'Dimensions of Ancient Egyptian Ships', *American Journal of Semitic Languages and Literature* 46, no. 3 (April, 1930), p.146.

15. Faulkner, pp.7–8.

16. Edgerton, 'Ancient Egyptian Ships and Shipping', p.121.

17. Faulkner, p.4.

18. Edgerton, 'Dimensions of Ancient Egyptian Ships', p.121

19. Faulkner, pp.3–4.

20. Salinger, p.54

21. Faulkner, p.8.

22. Ibid.

23. Edgerton, 'Dimensions of Ancient Egyptian Ships', p.149.

24. William F. Edgerton, 'Ancient Egyptian Steering Gear', *American Journal of Semitic Languages and Literature* 43, no. 4 (July, 1927), pp.255–265.

25. Edgerton, 'Ancient Egyptian Ships and Shipping', p.116.

26. Faulkner, p.7.

27. Richard A. Gabriel, *Empires at War* vol. 1 (Westport, CT: Greenwood Press, 2005), p.88.

28. Lionel Casson, 'Seasons and Winds, Sailing, and Rowing Speed', in *Ships and Seamanship in the Ancient World* (Princeton, NJ: Princeton University Press, 1971), p.270.

29. Ibid. See also H. Koster, *Das antike Seewesen* (Berlin, 1923), p.125.

30. Koster, p.125; see also Connie Lambrou-Phillipson, 'Seafaring in the Bronze Age Mediterranean', *Aegaeum* 7 (1999), pp.11–19.

31. Avner Raban, 'Minoan and Canaanite Harbors', *Aegaeum* 7 (1991), pp.129–46; see also Houston, 'Ports in Perspective', p.559.

Chapter 14: The Exodus as Military History

1. Martin Buber, *Moses: The Revelation and the Covenant* (Amherst, NY: Humanity Books, 1998), pp.24–25.

2. Norman K. Gottwald, *The Tribes of Yahweh* (Maryknoll, NY: Orbis Books, 1979), pp.352–59.

3. William H.C. Propp, *Exodus 1–18: The Anchor Bible* (New York: Doubleday, 1998), p.487.

4. Ibid.

5. Quintius Curtius, *History of Alexander*, Book V, ii 7, trans. John C. Rolfe (Cambridge, MA: Harvard University Press, 1946), p.345.

6. Ibid.

7. Propp, *The Anchor Bible*, p.489.

8. Edouard Neville, 'The Geography of the Exodus', *Journal of Egyptian Archaeology* 10 (1924), p.24.

9. Chaim Herzog and Mordecai Gichon, *Battles of the Bible* (Jerusalem: Steimatzky's Agency, 1978), p.21; see also Diodorus Siculus, Book 1, 30.4.

10. Diodorus Siculus 1, 30.4.

11. In Manetho's account of the Egyptian high priest of On who wrote a history of Egypt for Ptolemy I, he tells of a group of 'heretics' led by one Osipah that was driven from Egypt because they were infected with a plague of tularemia. In his account, widely accepted at the time, Egyptian troops were sent after the Israelites not to prevent them from leaving Egypt, but to make certain that they did. See Richard A. Gabriel, *God's Generals* (Barnsley, South Yorkshire: Pen and Sword, 2016).

12. *Numbers*, 10:31.

13. The difference in combat capability was that the Amalekites were light infantry, mostly bowmen, while the later Arab cavalry infantry were heavy infantry that, when dismounted, could hold their own against rival heavy infantry.

14. George E. Mendenhall, 'The Census List of *Numbers* 1 and 26', *Journal of Biblical Literature* vol. 77 (1958), pp.54–64.

15. T.R. Hobbs, *A Time For War* (Wilmington, DE: Micael Glazer, 1989), p.78.

16. Yigael Yadin, *The Art of Warfare in Biblical Lands in Light of Archaeological Discovery* vol. 2 (New York: McGraw Hill, 1963), p.19.

17. Richard A. Gabriel, *The Military History of Ancient Israel* (Westport, CT: Praeger, 2003), pp.86–95, for a treatment of the size and combat composition of the Israelite army at Sinai.

18. Chaim Herzog and Mordecai Gichon, *Battles of the Bible* (Jerusalem: Steimatzky's Agency Ltd, 1978), p.30.

19. *1 Chronicles* 12:33.

20. Herzog and Gichron, *Battles of the Bible*, p.85.

21. *1 Chronicles* 12:34.

22. *1 Chronicles* 12:25.

23. *1 Chronicles* 12:9.

24. *1 Chronicles* 12:37.

25. *1 Chronicles* 12 1-2.

26. *1 Chronicles* 12:35.

27. Gottwald, *The Tribes of Yahweh*, p.426.

28. Extrapolating from earlier figures, one might conclude that the Israelite population that left Kadesh-Barnea was about 35,000 strong, allowing for a normal fertility rate. This number of people would permit an Israelite army of 8,000–9,000 men under Joshua on the eve of the invasion of Canaan.

Chapter 15: Joshua At Jericho: A Study in Special Ops

1. George E. Mendenhall, 'The Census Lists of *Numbers* 1 and 26', *Journal of Biblical Literature* 77 (1958), pp.52–66, for the original calculations as to the size of the Israelite army at Sinai.

2. Richard A. Gabriel, *The Military Hstory of Ancient Israel* (Westport, CT: Greenwood Press, 2003), p.113.

3. Ibid., p.114.

4. Robert G. Boling and G. Ernest Wright, *Joshua: The Anchor* Bible (New York: Doubleday, 1982), p.205.

5. Yigael Yadin, *The Art of Warfare in Biblical Lands in Light of Archaeological Discovery* vol. 2 (New York: McGraw-Hill, 1964), p.16; see also Abraham Malamat, 'Israeli Conduct of War in the Conquest of Canaan According to Biblical Tradition', in *Symposium Celebrating the 75th Anniversary of the Founding of the American Schools of Oriental Research*, ed. F.M. Cross (Cambridge, MA: American Schools of Oriental Research, 1979), p.37.

6. Gabriel, p.121; Yadin, p.52.

7. Malamat, p.46.

8. Gabriel, *Military History of Ancient Israel*, p.127.

9. Boling and Wright, p.170. One of these shallow fords is still used today and is located 12km south-east of Jericho. It is called *al Maghtas* by the local population.

10. Gabriel, p.129.

11. E.A. Wallis Budge, *Osiris and the Egyptian Resurrection* (New York: Dover Publications, 1973), pp.219–24, for origins of circumcision and its Egyptian connection.

12. Richard A. Gabriel, *Gods of Our Fathers: The Memory of Egypt in Judaism and Christianity* (Westport, CT: Greenwood Press, 2001), pp.73–74; see also James H. Breasted, *The Dawn of Conscience* (New York: Charles Scriber, 1947), pp.353–54.

13. The text is generally understood to mean that Joshua made his reconnaissance the night before the battle. See Boling and Wright, p.198.

14. Ibid., p.206.

15. E.V. Hulse, 'Joshua's Curse and the Abandonment of Ancient Jericho: Schistosomiasis and a Possible Medical Explanation', *Medical History* 15 (1971), p.376.

16. Ibid.

Chapter 16: The Catastrophe: The Violent End of the Bronze Age

1. Eric H. Cline, *1177 BC: The Year Civilization Collapsed* (Princeton, NJ: Princeton University Press, 2014), pp.1–3.

2. In the Hebrew *Bible*, see *Amos* 9:7 and *Jeremiah* 47:4, where Crete is referred to by its ancient name, Caphtor. Also, Cline, p.4.

3. Robert Drews, *The End of the Bronze Age: Changes in Warfare and the Catastrophe ca 1200 BC* (Princeton, NJ: Princeton University Press, 1993), p.1; see also Fernand Braudel, 'L'Aube', in Braudel (ed.), *La Mediterranee l'espace et l'histoire* (Paris: 1977), pp.82–86, for the comparison.

4. Cline, p.140.

5. It is generally accepted by the most recent scholarship that there were no Dorian invasions, and that the Mycenaean collapse was due to other reasons. Cline, p.149.

6. Cline, p.8.

7. Drews, pp.20–21.

8. Yigael Yadin, *The Art of Warfare in Biblical Lands in Light of Archaeological Discovery* (New York: McGraw Hill, 1964), vol. 2, p.20.

9. There are five ways to attack a city: (1) penetration from above, i.e., assault over the walls by scaling ladders or hooks; (2) penetration through the barrier walls, i.e., use of a battering ram or siege machinery; (3) penetration from below, i.e., mining or tunnelling; (4) penetration by ruse, i.e., entrance gained by some unguarded passageway; or (5) by deception and drawing the enemy out of the gates. Yadin, vol. 2, p.16; see also Abraham Malamat, 'Israelite Conduct of War in the Conquest of Canaan According to the Biblical Tradition', in *Symposium Celebrating the 75th Anniversary of the Founding of the American Schools of Oriental Research*, ed F. M. Cross (Cambridge, MA: American Schools of Oriental Research, 1979), p.50.

10. For estimating the average number of inhabitants living in an urban dwelling and the problems associated with such estimates, see Jeffrey R. Zorn, 'Estimating the Population Size of Ancient Settlements: Methods, Problems, Solutions, and a Case Study', *Bulletin of the American School of Oriental Research* (1994), pp.31–48.

11. Richard A. Gabriel, *The Military History of Ancient Israel* (Westport, CT: Praeger, 2003), p.121; see pp.113–14 for calculations regarding the size of Joshua's army.

12. While Joshua's army was more than ten times larger than the defending force, a reasonable guess might be that an attacking force would likely need to have at least a five or six to one advantage to have any chance of success of overcoming the fortifications.

13. The enclosed area and length of the walls of many ancient cities can be found in Aaron Alexander Burke, *The Architecture of Defense: Fortified Settlements of the Levant during the Middle Bronze Age* (Chicago, IL: University of Chicago, Ph.D. Dissertation, 2004).

14. The changes in warfare, especially the demise in chariot warfare and the increased use of 'swarming tactics' by greater numbers of infantry armed with new weapons, is the major thesis of Robert Drews' book, *The End of the Bronze Age*. While major changes in the conduct of war did take place, it seems to me that they took place mostly after the Catastrophe, in the Iron Age that followed it, not during or before the Catastrophe occurred.

15. Amihai Mazar, 'The Fortification of Cities in the Ancient Near East', in Jack M. Sasson (ed.), *Civilizations of the Ancient Near East* (Peabody, MA: Hendrickson Publishers, 1995), vol, 3, art. 7, p.1,529.

16. Ibid.

17. The cities of Megiddo and Hazor in Israel are exceptions in that they are constructed of stone and not mud brick.

18. Zorn, pp.31–48, for calculation of dwelling units relative to geographic size of the enclosed areas of cities.

19. Colonel D.H. Gordon, 'Fire and Sword: The Technique of Destruction', *Antiquity* (January 1, 1953), p.149.

20. Waziristan lies west and south-west of Peshawar in Pakistan. The region was an independent tribal territory until 1893, when it was incorporated into Pakistan and the British Empire. A tribal Pashtun region, it was a constant source of irritation to the British, who conducted frequent punitive expeditions into the area between 1860 and 1945. A revolt broke out in 1919–1920, forcing a large British military response in which Colonel Gordon took part.

21. Gordon, p.149.

22. Ibid.

23. Ibid.

24. Ibid.

25. Ibid.

26. Ibid.

27. Ibid., p.151. Gordon notes that dwellings fashioned of mud and wattle with thatch roofs burned easily.

28. Ibid.

29. Ibid.

30. It might strike some as peculiar to suggest that heavy rain might have caused the flat mud roofs of Late Bronze Age dwellings to collapse, given today's hot and dry climate in the eastern Mediterranean. However, even today, rainfall in the area is quite substantial. Gordon suggests that 'the monsoon probably spread at least to the Iranian border in the 3rd and 2nd millennia [BC]', with the result that more mud roofs 'collapse from rain than were ever destroyed by fire'. Gordon, p.151.

31. Ibid.

32. Scipio Africanus' attack on New Carthage happened in just this manner. Having breached the walls, the defenders withdrew to their citadel, where they held out for days. Scipio began to slaughter the civilian population, convincing the defenders to surrender or face a similar fate.

33. The few surviving records regarding the tiny size of the fleets of sea raiders suggest that the raiding parties were quite small.

34. Joshua burned Jericho and Ai after taking both cities by storm. The reason seems to have been that Joshua was conducting a war of extermination, to drive the Canaanites from the entire area, and not one of resettlement, at least not until he had driven off the Canaanites

35. The evidence of Sea People settlement is thin, consisting mostly of Mycenaean pottery finds. But the Mycenaeans were great traders, and the pottery might just as easily have reached the eastern Levant cities in normal economic intercourse.

Chapter 17: The Dawn of the Iron Age: The Iron Army of Assyria

1. Eric Cline, *1177 BC: The Year Civilization Collapsed* (Princeton, NJ: Princeton University Press, 2014), p.173.

2. James D. Muhly, 'Mining and Metal Work in Ancient Western Asia', in Jack M. Sasson (ed.), *Civilizations of the Ancient Near East* (Peabody, MA: Hendrickson Publishers, 1995), p.1,515.

3. Ibid.

4. Jane Waldbaum, 'From Bronze to Iron: The Transition from the Bronze Age to the Iron Age in the Eastern Mediterranean', *Studies in Mediterranean Archaeology*, vol. 54 (Goteborg, 1978).

5. Michael C. Astur, 'Overland Trade Routes in Ancient Western Asia', in Sasson, p.1,417.

6. A.T. Olmstead, *The History of Assyria* (Chicago: University of Chicago Press, 1951), p.64.

7. Sarah C. Melville, *The Campaigns of Sargon II of Assyria* (Norman, OK: Oklahoma University Press, 2016). See also *Encyclopedia Britannica*, vol. 21, 1985, p.927.

8. Olmstead, pp.607–08.

9. Ibid., pp.605–06, for size of Assyrian bureaucracy. See also *Encyclopedia Britannica*, Ibid.

10. Astur, 'Overland Trade Routes in Ancient Western Asia', p.1,417.

11. Olmstead, p.607.

12. Ibid., p.604.

13. Arthur Merrill, *The Origins of War* (London: Thames and Hudson, 1985), p.70. For more on the size of the Assyrian army, see W.F. Saggs, 'Assyrian Warfare in the Sargonid Period', *Iraq* 25, part 2 (Autumn, 1963), p.145.

14. Trevor N. Dupuy, *The Evolution of Warfare and Weapons* (New York: Bobbs-Merrill, 1980), p.10. An Assyrian field army of 50,000 was approximately two-and-a-half times the size of the 20,000-man, four-division army of Egypt at the height of its power in the Bronze Age.

15. Olmstead, p.603.

16. Robert Laffont, *The Ancient Art of Warfare* (New York: Time-Life Books, 1966), chap. 1, p.45. See also Georges Conteneau, *Everyday Life in Babylon and Assyria* (London: Edward Arnold, 1954), p.142.

17. Olmstead, p.603.

18. Saggs, p.145.

19. *Encyclopedia Britannica*, vol. 21, 1985, p.925.

20. Ibid.

21. The first Assyrian cavalry forces were comprised of two–man units, each upon a single mount. One horseman guided the reins of the second horse, upon which rode an archer. This initial development occurred under King Tukulti-Ninurta II (890–884 BC). It took fifty years for cavalry to evolve into the use of a single horseman mounted on a single mount at the Battle of QarQar in 853 BC.

22. Laffont, see chart on p.40.

23. Ferrill, p.67.

24. Laffont, p.45

25. Olmstead, p.604.

26. Dupuy, p.10.

27. Yigael Yadin, *The Art of Warfare in Biblical Lands in Light of Archaeological Study* (New York: McGraw-Hill, 1960), vol. 2., pp.94–95.

28. On the subject of boots, see Laffont, p.45, and Conteneau, p.144.

29. Hammered iron $\frac{1}{8}$in thick weighs 5lb per ft². Accordingly, a soldier in a full suit of Assyrian scale armour, helmet and iron-shinned boots, armed with a sword and carrying a shield and a spear, would carry a combat load of approximately 60lb, or about the same load as carried by a modern soldier.

30. This estimate regarding the increase of the rate of fire was provided by several archers who regularly engage in formal competition. It is, of course, only an estimate.

31. For an analysis of the Assyrian chariot, see Yadin, pp.297–300; as regards its manoeuvrability, especially in rough terrain, see Conteneau, p.145.
32. Yadin, pp.298–99.
33. *Encyclopedia Britannica*, vol. 21, 1985, p.923.
34. The definitive work on the subject of Assyrian horse supply remains J.N. Postgate, *Taxation and Conscription in the Assyrian Empire* (Rome: Biblical Institute Press, 1974); see also Merrill, pp.71–73.
35. Merrill, p.72.
36. Laffont, p.48.
37. Ibid.
38. Saggs, pp.146–46.
39. Ibid., p.151
40. Yadin, p.303.
41. Saggs, p.152.
42. Continueau, p.59.
43. *Encyclopedia Britannica*, vol. 21, 1985, pp.928–30.
44. *Numbers* 3:1–7.
45. Laffont, p.49.

Chapter 18: Animals In War

1. Jonathan P. Roth, *The Logistics of the Roman Army: 264 BC–235 AD* (Boston: Brill, 1999), p.83.
2. Ibid.
3. Erna Risch, *Quartermaster Support of the Army* 2nd ed. (Washington, DC: Center of Military History, 1989), p.291.
4. Duncan K. Major and Roger S. Fitch, *Supply of Sherman's Army during the Atlanta Campaign* (Ft Leavenworth, KS: Army Services School Press, 1911), pp.10, 25.
5. U.P. Thapliyal, 'Military Organization in the Ancient Period', in S.N. Prasad, *Historical Perspectives of Warfare in India* (Delhi: Motilal Banarsidass, Center for Studies in Civilizations, 2002), p.77.
6. Gurcharn Singh Sandhu, *A Military History of Ancient India* (Delhi: Vision Books, 2000), pp.186–87.
7. James Huston, *Sinews of War: Army Logistics, 1775–1953* (Washington, DC: 1966), p.219.
8. Roth, p.125.
9. Livy, *History of Rome*, 27.12.7.
10. This is probably the most logical reason for why the Persian commander, himself a cavalry commander who had transported 2,000 cavalry to Marathon and put them ashore, did not employ them in battle. See Richard A. Gabriel and Donald W. Boose Jr, *The Great Battles of Antiquity: A Strategic and Tactical Guide to Great*

Battles that Shaped the Development of War (Westport, CT: Greenwood Press, 1994), pp.145–47.

11. Rossel S. Marshall, 'Domestication of the Donkey: Timing, Process, and Indicators', *PNAS* 105 (10) (11 March 2008).

12. The donkey was also the symbol of Ra, the Egyptian Sun god, the highest deity in the Egyptian pantheon.

13. Sandra L. Olsen, *Horses Through Time* (Boulder, CO: Rinehart Publishers, 1995), p.32.

14. 'Training Donkeys', *Harts Horsemanship* (4 May 2015).

15. James D. Anderson, *Roman Military Supply in North East England* (Oxford: British Archaeological Reports, British Series, 224, 1992), p.15.

16. David Smith and Stephanie Wood, 'Donkey Nutrition', in Elisabeth Svendsen, James Duncan and David Hadrill, *The Professional Handbook of the Donkey* 4th ed. (Yatesbury: Whittet Books, 2008), p.10.

17. The source for this is the American Mule Museum. It makes sense in that the people of Paphlagonia and Nicaea live in a heavily wooded and mountainous region of Anatolia where the mule's sure-footedness and ability to carry heavy loads would have been to great advantage to the residents.

18. Muhammad commanded his troops atop his white mule at the Battle of Wadi Hunayn. See Richard A. Gabriel, *Muhammad: Islam's First Great General* (Norman, OK: University of Oklahoma Press, 2007), pp.184–85.

19. 'Mule', *Encyclopedia Britannica: A Dictionary of Arts, Sciences, and General* Vol. 18 (Henry G. Allen Company, 1988), p.342.

20. Roth, pp.62–67.

21. K.D. White, *Roman Farming* (Ithaca, NY: Cornell University Press, 1970), p.132.

22. Emmett M. Essin, 'Mules, Packs, and Packtrains', *Southwestern Historical Quarterly*, 74 (1970), p.54.

23. This compares with Hannibal's army during the Italian campaign that could move at 9 miles a day. His Gallic allies were 'eaters of meat and drinkers of milk' (Tacitus) and insisted that they bring their cow herds along with them on campaign. In addition, Gauls took their families with them in carts drawn by slow teams of oxen.

24. The Soviet-Afghanistan war lasted from 1979 to 1989.

25. Glen M. Schwartz, 'Pastoral Nomadism in Ancient Western Asia', in *Civilizations of the Ancient Near East*, ed. Jack M. Sasson (Peabody, MA: Hendrickson Publishers, 2000), p.256.

26. *The Fact Site: The Camel* (internet source), p.2.

27. Ibid., p.3.

28. Donald W. Engels, *Alexander the Great and the Logistics of the Macedonian Army* (Berkeley, CA: University of California Press, 1978), p.14.

29. *The Fact Site: The Camel*, p.3.

30. At the Battle of Badr (16 March AD 624), Muhammad was able to determine the strength of the enemy he faced by asking two prisoners how many camels the enemy slaughtered the night before to feed their troops. The prisoners answered 'nine or ten', from which Muhammad reckoned that at ninety men a camel, the enemy force was between 900 and 1,000 men. Gabriel, *Muhammad*, p.91.

31. Richard A. Gabriel, *The Military History of Ancient Israel* (Westport, CT: Praeger, 2003), pp.81–84.

32. Schwartz, p.256.

33. 'Camel Cavalry', *Wikepedia*, p.3; see also Jim Hicks, *The Persians* (NY: Time-Life Books, 1975), p.21.

34. Sir Percy Sykes, *A History of Persia* vol. 1 (London: Macmillan, 1985), p.146.

35. Richard A. Gabriel, 'Arab Armies', in *The Great Armies of Antiquity* (Westport, CT: Praeger, 2002), chap. 17, for an analysis of Arab armies and their use of the camel.

36. Sarva Daman Singh, *Ancient Indian Warfare* (Delhi: Motilal Banarsidass, 1997), p.74.

37. Ibid., p.73.

38. Ibid.

39. John M. Kistler, *War Elephants* (Westport, CT: Praeger, 2006), p.40.

40. Ibid., pp.54–77.

41. For the Battle of Zama, see Richard A. Gabriel, *Hannibal: The Military Biography of Rome's Greatest Enemy* (Dulles, VA: Potomac Books, 2011), pp.192–209.

42. William Gowers, 'The African Elephant in Warfare', *African Affairs*, vol. 46 no. 182 (2013), p.83.

43. Ibid. See also Philip Rance, 'Elephants in Warfare in Late Antiquity', *Acta Antiqua Academia Scientiarum Hungaricae* 43 (2003), pp.335–84.

44. Kistler, p.111.

45. The elephant's primitive alimentary system digests less than half the food eaten; the rest is defecated. An elephant urinates every two hours, producing 5–10 litres of urine each time. It defecates every 100 minutes, depositing five to seven faecal lumps each time. An elephant evacuates approximately 250lb of faecal waste a day. Alexander discovered this interesting fact when he ordered elephants chained outside his tent as a symbol of his prestige. Kistler, p.42.

46. O.R. Gurney, *The Hittites* (Baltimore, MD: Penguin, 1952), p.106.

47. Singh, *Ancient Indian Warfare*, pp.55–56.

48. Ibid., p.58.

49. Gabriel, *Military History of Ancient Israel*, pp.299–300.

50. Sandu, *A Military History of Ancient India*, p.100.

51. Nigel Stillman and Nigel Tallis, *Armies of the Ancient Near East: 3000 to 539 BC* (Sussex: Flexiprint, 1984), p.128.

52. Richard A. Gabriel, *Philip II of Macedonia: Greater Than Alexander* (Dulles, VA: Potomac Books, 2010), pp.72–82, for Philip's cavalry.

53. Gabriel and Boose, *Great Battles of Antiquity*, p.177.

54. Ibid., p.199.

55. Singh, *Ancient Indian Warfare*, p.70.

56. Ibid., p.63.

57. Jilly Cooper, *Animals in War* (UK: Corgi Books, 1983), pp.129–34.

Chapter 19: Buddha's Military Experience and PTSD

1. Richard A. Gabriel, *God's Generals: The Military Lives of Moses, The Buddha and Muhammad* (Barnsley,: Pen and Sword, 2016), pp.106–07.

2. The sources for the life of Buddha are a variety of different and often conflicting sources, none of which were composed during or even close to Buddha's lifetime. The earliest full biography, the *Buddhacarita*, is composed in poetic form, and dates from the second century BC, almost 500 years after Buddha's death. Other partial biographies, the *Lalitavistara* (third century BC) and the *Mahavastu* (fourth century BC), are no more reliable than the first. Thus the need to rely upon the Pali Canon, which was composed by Buddhist monks as a quasi-official canonical history, although they make no attempt at a formal biography.

3. The Ashvakas, Aspasians, Assakenoi and Asvayanas were four Aryan tribes that fought against Alexander in his Afghanistan campaign. See Richard A. Gabriel, *The Madness of Alexander the Great and the Myth of Military* Genius (Barnsley: Pen and Sword, 2015), pp.148–49. For the genetic evidence that Buddha was an Aryan with Aryan physical characteristics, see Michael Bamshad et. al., 'Genetic Evidence on the Origins of Indian Caste Populations', in *Genome Res.* 11 (6), pp.994–1,004; see also Sarah Grey Thompson and Terrence Kaufman, *Language, Contact, Creolization, and Genetic Linguistics* (Berkeley, CA: University of Californian Press, 1991).

4. H.S. Bhatia, *Vedic and Aryan India: Evolution of Political, Legal, and Military Systems* (New Delhi: Deep and Deep Publications, 2001), p.84.

5. Karen Armstrong, *Buddha* (New York: Viking Books, 2001), pp.20–22. Armstrong's view that the Sakya territory 'was so remote that Aryan culture had never taken root there, and they had no caste system' is simply wrong. The Sakya capital was known as the city that trained the best archers in India.

6. Richard A. Gabriel, 'Buddha: Enlightened Warrior', *Military History* (May, 2011), pp.40–41.

7. J.P. Dharma, *Republics in Ancient India: 1500–500 BC* (Leiden: E.J. Brill, 1968), p.182.

8. In ancient times, a tribal society could raise approximately 25 per cent of its population for military duty; in sieges, perhaps somewhat more.

9. Dharma, *Republics in Ancient India*, p.19.

10. A.L. Basham, *The Wonder That Was India* (New York: Grove Press, 1959), p.160.

11. Major General Gurcharn Singh Sandhu, *A Military History of Ancient India* (New Delhi: Vision Books, 2000), p.117.

12. V.R. Ramachandra Dikshitar, *War In Ancient India* (Delhi: Motilal Banarsidass, 1987), p.44.

13. Basham, *The Wonder That Was India*, pp.160–61.

14. Dikshitar, *War in Ancient India*, p.46.

15. Gabriel, *God's Heroes*, p.10.

16. Dikshitar, *War in Ancient India*, pp.54–55.

17. Ibid., pp.10–35, for a treatment of the psychological disposition of the *kshatriya* warrior.

18. Ibid.

19. The *sati* (or *suttee*) custom is very ancient indeed, and we find it among the earliest kings of Ur and the Scythians. Many ancient peoples cremated a man's widow, horses and other possessions so that he might have all he loved and required in the afterlife. The practice is mentioned in one of the oldest verses of the *Rig Veda*. The term *sati* means 'virtuous woman'.

20. Sharma, *Republics in Ancient India*, p.203.

21. http://www.jaibheem.com/B-page-7.htm

22. Gabriel, *God's Generals*, pp.115–21.

23. Ibid., pp.121–23.

24. Gabriel, *The Madness of Alexander the Great*, pp.132–36.

25. Devadatta first hired archers to shoot Buddha. When this failed, he tried rolling a boulder down a hill to crush his teacher. When this failed, he obtained a drunken elephant to trample Buddha.

26. The *Mahparinibbana Sutta* of the Pali Canon is probably the most reliable source for the details of Buddha's death.

27. Mettanando Bhikkhu and Oskar von Hinueber, 'The Cause of Buddha's Death', in *Journal of the Pali Text Society*, 26 (2000), pp.7–16, for the modern diagnosis as to the cause of Buddha's demise.

Chapter 20: Philip II of Macedon: Greater Than Alexander

1. N.G.L. Hammond, *The Macedonian State: Origins, Institutions, History* (Oxford: Clarendon Press, 1989), pp.49–50.

2. E.A. Fredericksmeyer, 'Alexander and Philip: Emulation and Resentment', *Classical Journal* 85, no. 4 (April–May, 1990), p.305.

3. Pierre Leveque, 'Philip's Personality', in *Philip of Macedon*, ed. by Miltiades B. Hatzopoulos and Louisa D. Loukopoulos (Athens: Ekdotike Athenon, 1980), p.187.

4. Richard A. Gabriel, *The Great Captains of Antiquity* (Westport, CT: Greenwood Press, 2001), p.81.

5. The basic original sources for Alexander are Diodorus, Plutarch, Justin and Arrian, with Arrian's records being the most valuable and complete.

6. See Peter Green, *Alexander of Macedon, 356–323: A Historical Biography* (Berkeley, CA: University of Californian Press, 1991), p.158, for the composition of Alexander's invasion army.

7. Except for the famous Immortals, who were heavily armoured and fought with long spears.

8. Robert E. Gaebel, *Cavalry Operations in the Ancient Greek World* (Norman, OK: University of Oklahoma Press, 2002), p.191

9. For Alexander's tactics, see A.R. Burn, 'The Generalship of Alexander the Great', *Greece and Rome* 12, no. 2 (October, 1965), pp.146–54; see also Gaebel, *Cavalry Operations in the Ancient Greek World*, pp.183–93. For more detail, see J.F.C. Fuller, *The Generalship of Alexander the Great* (New Brunswick, NJ: Rutgers University Press, 1960).

10. Lucius Flavius Arrianus (Arrian), *Anabasis of Alexander*, trans. P.A. Brunt and E. Cliff Robson (Cambridge, MA: Loeb Classical Library, 1948), 1.5–10. See also Gaebel, *Cavalry Operations in the Ancient World*, p.194, for other citations on the same subject.

11. See Burn, 'The Generalship of Alexander the Great', pp.142–43, for Alexander's debt to Philip's officers.

12. Guy MacLean Rogers, *Alexander: The Ambiguity of Greatness* (New York: Random House, 2004), p.222.

13. Ibid., p.229.

14. Alexander was wounded in the thigh at Issus; in the shoulder by an arrow at the siege of Gaza; in the leg by an arrow on the march to Maracanda; in the face and neck by a thrown stone at Cyropolis; in the shoulder by an arrow while en route to India; in the ankle at Massaga; and in the right breast by an arrow that drew blood, but did not puncture the lung at the citadel in territory of the Malli. He suffered seven wounds in all, with two being life-threatening.

15. George Cawkwell, *Philip of Macedon* (London: Faber and Faber, 1978), p.164.

16. Richard A. Gabriel, *Scipio Africanus: Rome's Greatest General* (Dulles, VA: Potomac Books, 2008), p.10. The anecdote is provided by Sextus Julius Frontinus in his *Strategemata* (LacusCurtius website, 2007).

Chapter 21: Stolen Valour: An Analysis of Alexander the Great's Wounds

1. For the experiment concerning the ability of the linothorax to resist penetration, see Rossella Lorenzi, 'Laminated Linen Protected Alexander the Great', paper delivered at the annual conference of the *Archaeological Institute of America*

(Anaheim, California, 10 January 2010). See also Gregory S. Aldrete, Scott Bartell and Alicia Alorete, *Reconstructing Ancient Linen Body Armor* (Baltimore, MD: Johns Hopkins University Press, 2013).

2. The helmet with rams' horns and vertical white feathers sometimes shown in later artists' works first appears on Egyptian coins sometime after Alexander left Egypt. It is by no means certain that it was a combat helmet or that Alexander wore it in battle. Most likely, it was a ceremonial helmet, the rams' horns being the symbol of the Egyptian god Ra.

3. Lucius Flavius Arrianus (Arrian), *The Campaigns of Alexander*, trans. Aubrey De Selincourt (London: Penguin Books, 1984), 1.14.6– 7.

4. Diodorus of Sicily, *Histories* (Harvard, MA: Harvard University Press, 1963), trans. C. Bradford Welles, 17.20.6–21.

5. Arrian, 1.16.

6. Quintius Curtius Rufus, *History of Alexander*, trans. John Yardley (London: Penguin Classics, 1984), 8.1.20.

7. Diodorus, 17.21.2.

8. Richard A. Gabriel and Karen S. Metz, *From Sumer to Rome: The Military Capabilities of Ancient Armies* (Westport, CT: Greenwood Press, 1991), p.63.

9. Curtius, 3.2.10.

10. N.G.L. Hammond, 'Casualties and Reinforcements of Citizen Soldiers in Greece and Macedonia', *Journal of Hellenic Studies* 109 (1989), p.60.

11. Curtius, 4.17.

12. Ibid.

13. Ibid.

14. Ibid., 4.19–20.

15. Arrian, 2.27.

16. Curtius, 4.17.

17. Ibid., 4.21–24.

18. Arrian 3.29–30.

19. Christine Salazar, *The Treatment of War Wounds in Graeco-Roman Antiquity* (Boston: Brill, 2000), p.198.

20. Curtius, 6.3.

21. Ibid., 6.10.

22. The danger of wound infection and disease in Afghanistan was clearly evident in the Soviet experience there. Of the 620,000 Soviet soldiers that served in Afghanistan, 469,685 were hospitalized for wounds or disease. Fully 75.7 per cent of the Soviet force was hospitalized, 11.4 per cent for wounds and 88.5 per cent for disease. The diseases that affected the Soviet force were hepatitis, plague, malaria, cholera, diphtheria, meningitis, infectious dysentery, amoebic dysentery, rheumatism, heat stroke, pneumonia, typhus and para-typhus, most of which were probably extant

during Alexander's time. The failure of the ancient sources to mention examples of infection or even inflammation of wounds in India or Afghanistan during Alexander's campaigns there is suspicious. See Richard A. Gabriel, 'Bugs, Bullets, and Bones: Death, Disease, Casualties, and Military Medicine in the Soviet War in Afghanistan', *Military History* (forthcoming).

23. Curtuis, 7.22.
24. John Lascaratos, 'The Wounding of Alexander the Great in Cyropolis: The First Reported Case of the Syndrome of Transient Cortical Blindness', *History of Ophthalmology* 42 (November–December, 1997), p.286.
25. Salazar, *Treatment of War Wounds*, p.199, citing Plutarch, *Moralia*, trans. P. Clement, VIII (London: 1969), 341 B.
26. Curtius, 7.5–6.
27. Ibid., 8.3.
28. We may take Curtius' account here as reliable. Hammond notes that this section of Curtius' work draws heavily upon Aristobulus, who was a staff officer with Alexander and is generally considered reliable. See N.G.L. Hammond, *Three Historians of Alexander the Great: The So-Called Vulgate Authors* (Cambridge: Cambridge University Press, 1983), whose work makes a bold attempt to assess the reliability of the sources.
29. Lascaratos, 'The Wounding of Alexander the Great in Cyropolis', pp.284–85.
30. I am indebted to my friend, John Cowan, former Chair of the Physiology Department of the Faculty of Medicine at the University of Ottawa, for much of the medical information in this section.
31. John M. O'Brien, 'The Enigma of Alexander: The Alcohol Factor', *Annals of Scholarship* 1 (1980), pp.31–46.
32. Arrian, 4.14.
33. Ibid., 4.26.
34. Curtius, 8.8.
35. Arrian, 6.10; Curtius, 9.5.9–11.
36. Ibid.
37. The average thickness of body tissue below the breast line ranges from approximately 1–1½in from top to bottom. Above the breast, average thickness is 3in. Alexander is described in the sources as 'muscular', and it is possible that the thickness of his upper breast was greater, perhaps almost 4in.

Chapter 22: Rome against Carthage: Why Hannibal Lost

1. Leonard Cottrell, *Hannibal: Enemy of Rome* (New York: Holt, Rinehart and Winston, 1960), p.218.
2. For the influence of Hellenism on Hannibal's strategic thinking, see B.D. Hoyes, 'Hannibal: What Kind of Genius?', *Greece and Rome* 30, no. 2 (October, 1983),

pp.176–77; for its influence on Hannibal's tactics, see Giovanni Brizzi, 'Hannibal: Punier and Hellenist', *Das Altertum* 37, no. 4, pp.201–10.

3. The importance of understanding the culture of one's enemy was thrown into sharp relief again during the American and North Vietnamese peace talks in Hanoi in an effort to end the Vietnam War. One of the participants, Colonel Harry Summers, remarked to his Vietnamese counterpart, 'Well, whatever the outcome, you never defeated us on the battlefield.' The North Vietnamese colonel smiled and said, 'That is true. But it is also irrelevant!'

4. On the nature and importance of Rome's colonies to its war effort and how they differed from Greek and Carthaginian colonies, especially with regard to their respective military functions, see Andrew Stephenson, *Public Lands and Agrarian Laws of the Roman Republic* (Baltimore: Johns Hopkins University Press, 1981); see also E.T. Salmon, *Roman Colonization under the Republic* (London: Thames and Hudson, 1969), ch. 6.

5. Titus Livius (Livy), *The War With Hannibal*, trans. Aubrey de Selincourt (London: Penguin, 1965), 30.20.

6. Adrian Goldsworthy, *Cannae: Hannibal's Greatest Victory* (London: Orion Books, 2007) p.56.

7. Livy, *The War With Hannibal*, 30.20

8. Polybius, *The Histories of Polybius*, trans. Evelyn S. Shuckburgh (Bloomington, IN: University of Indiana Press, 1962), 9.22

9. John Lazenby, *Hannibal's War: A Military History of the Second Punic War* (Warminster: Aris and Phillips, 1978), p.8.

10. Richard A. Gabriel, *Hannibal: The Military Biography of Rome's Greatest Enemy* (Dulles, VA: Potomac Books, 2011), pp.216–17.

11. See Polybius, *The Histories*, 3.41.2, and Livy, *The War With Hannibal*, 21.49.2–4, for a discussion of Carthaginian and Roman naval strength.

12. B.D. Hoyes, *Hannibal's Dynasty: Power and Politics in the Western Mediterranean, 247–183 BC* (London: Routledge, 2003), p.154.

13. Livy, *The War With Hannibal*, 30.43.

14. Paul Erdkamp, *Hunger and the Sword: Warfare and Food Supply in Roman Republican Wars, 264–30 BC* (Amsterdam: J.C. Gieben, 1998), pp.185–86.

15. Livy, *The War With Hannibal*, 23.13.

16. Albert A. Nofi, 'Roman Mobilization During the Second Punic War', *Military Chronicles*, (May–June, 2005), p.10.

Chapter 23: Marcus Agrippa: The Forgotten Genius behind the Roman Empire

1. The ancient sources upon which this study draws are: Cassius Dio, *Roman History*, available in translation in the Loeb Classics and Penguin Classics series; Appian,

The Civil Wars, trans. John Carter (New York: Penguin Classics, 1996); Pliny, *Natural History*, available in many volumes from Loeb Classics series; and Nicholas of Damaskos, *Life of Augustus*, trans. Clayton M. Hall (1923), available online. The only modern treatments of Agrippa's life can be found in Meyer Reinhold, *Marcus Agrippa*: A Biography (New York: Humphrey Press, 1933); J.M. Rodaz, *Marcus Agrippa* (Rome: Ecole Franchise de Rome, Palas Farnese, 1884); and Lindsay Powell, *Marcus Agrippa: Right-Hand Man of Caesar Augustus* (Barnsley: Pen and Sword, 2015). See also Richard A. Gabriel, 'Agrippa Takes Charge: Rome's Shadow Emperor', *Military History Quarterly* (Winter, 2016), pp.51–55.

2. Pliny, Natural History, 7.6.

3. Appian, *Civil War*, 3.9.

4. Appian, 5.66.

5. Pliny, *Natural History*, 7.48, who says Agrippa was with Octavius in the swamp and cared for him there.

6. Ibid., 5.31.

7. Dio, 48.49.3.

8. Ibid., 50.1–3.

9. As cited by Virgil, *Georgicon*, 2.161–64.

10. Lindsay Powell, *Marcus Agrippa: Right-Hand Man of Caesar Augustus* (Barnsley: Pen and Sword, 2015), p.50.

11. Richard A. Gabriel, 'The Roman Imperial Navy: Masters of the Mediterranean', *Military History* (December, 2007), pp.36–43.

12. Gabriel, 'Agrippa Takes Charge: Rome's Shadow Emperor', *Military History Quarterly* (Winter, 2016), p.56.

13. Appian, 56.117.

14. J.P. Mallory, *In Search of Indo-Europeans: Language, Archaeology, and Myth* (London: Thames and Hudson, 1989), pp.73–76.

15. Appian, *Illyrica*, 28; Dio, 49.35.1.

16. Meyer Reinhold, *Marcus Agrippa* (Geneva, NY: Humphrey Press, 1933), p.49, citing Pliny, 36.121.

17. Ibid, p.52.

18. Pliny, 36.24.

19. Dio, 49.43.1, as cited by Rehinhold, p.48.

20. Dio, 55.8.4.

21. Orosius, 6.19.6; see Powell, p.83.

22. Powell, p.85.

23. Dio, 50.16.2.

24. Richard A. Gabriel, *Great Captains of Antiquity* (Westport, CT: Greenwood Press, 2001), pp.183, 196–98.

25. Ibid., pp.200–01.

26. Ibid., pp.207–08.
27. Ibid., p.209.

Chapter 24: The Roman Navy: Rome's Other Military Arm

 1. W.L. Rogers, *Greek and Roman Naval Warfare* (Annapolis, MD: Naval Institute Press, 1937), pp.529–530.
 2. Lindsay Powell, *Marcus Agrippa* (Barnsley: Pen and Sword, 2015), p.95
 3. Rogers, p.534; see also Dio, 50.35.1–4.
 4. Chester G. Starr, *The Roman Imperial Navy* (Westport, CT: Greenwood Press, 1960), p.212.
 5. Richard A. Gabriel, 'The Roman Navy: Masters of the Mediterranean', *Military History* (December, 2007), p.42.
 6. Polybius, *The Histories*, Book 1, 23, trans. Evelyn S. Shuckburgh (Bloomington, IN: Indiana University Press, 1962).
 7. Polybius, Book 1, 62; Rogers, p.270.
 8. Polybius, Book 1, 3. This may have been the first use of 'simulators' to train combat troops in history.
 9. Rogers, p.306
10. Ibid.
11. Polybius, Book 1, pp.24–25.
12. Chester G. Starr, *The Influence of Sea Power on Ancient History* (New York: Oxford University Press, 1989), p.56.
13. Polybius, Book 1, 29.
14. Starr, *Influence of Sea Power*, p.56.
15. G.H. Tipps, 'The Battle of Ecnomus', *Historia* 34 (1985), pp.432–65.
16. Starr, *Influence of Sea Power*, p.57.
17. Polybius, Book 1, 71, says that Rome lost 700 ships and the Carthaginians 500. The number of crewmen and marines lost was enormous. Polybius' number of 400,000 Romans lost comes close to the 420,000 American soldiers who lost their lives during the Second World War.
18. J.H. Thief, *Studies in the History of Roman Sea-Power in Republican Times* (Amsterdam: 1946).
19. Rogers, p.302.
20. Richard A. Gabriel, *Scipio Africanus: Rome's Greatest General* (Dulles, VA: Potomac Books, 2008), p.152.
21. Ibid.
22. Ibid.
23. Ibid., p.153.
24. Starr, *Influence of Sea Power*, p.59.
25. Ibid., p.61.

26. Pliny, *Natural History*, 7.98; also Starr, *Influence of Sea Power*, pp.62–63, 96.

27. Rogers, pp.428–29.

28. Ibid.

29. Ibid.

30. Rogers, pp.514–16; see also Richard A. Gabriel, *Great Generals of the Ancient World* (Barnsley: Pen and Sword, 2017), p.222.

31. Rogers, pp.514–16.

32. Ibid.

33. Starr, p.68; *Roman Imperial Navy*, pp.17–24.

34. Ibid., p.96.

35. Starr, *Influence of Sea Power*, p.76.

36. Rogers, pp.514–16.

37. Ibid.

Chapter 25: Rome: The Death of a Superpower

1. One can obtain a more detailed account of the general events noted in this chapter by reading Adrian Goldsworthy, *How Rome Fell* (New Haven, CT: Yale University Press, 2009), and Peter Heather, *Empires and Barbarians: The Fall of Rome and the Birth of Europe* (New York: Oxford University Press, 2009), which incorporate much of the information found in this chapter. Of somewhat more limited use to the reader, but sufficiently interesting, is my own 'Rome: How Empires Fall', *Military History* (September, 2013), pp.36–46.

Chapter 26: Muhammad: Islam's First Great General

1. The basic works in English on Muhammad's life are W. Montgomery Watt, *Muhammad: Prophet and Statesman* (London: Oxford University Press, 1961); also by Watt, *Muhammad at Medina* (London: Oxford University Press, 1956); Muhammad Hamidullah, *The Battlefields of the Prophet* (Paris: Revue de Etudes Islamiques, 1939); Philip K. Hitti, *History of the Arabs* (Hampshire: Palgrave, 2002); Maxime Rodinson, *Muhammad* (New York: New Press, 2002); Ibn Ishaq, *The Life of Muhammad*, trans. A. Guillaume (Oxford: Oxford University Press, 1967). My own work, *Muhammad: Islam's First Great General* (Norman, OK: Oklahoma University Press, 2007) might also be consulted. On the specific point of the Muslim influence on Christian doctrines of war, see Richard A. Gabriel, *Empires at War* vol. 3 (Westport, CT: Greenwood Press, 2005), p.792.

2. Hitti, p.17.

3. Vo Nguyen Giap, *People's War, People's Army: The Viet Cong Insurrection Manual for Underdeveloped Countries* (New York: Bantam, 1968), for the methods required to organize and conduct an insurgency.

4. Watt, *Muhammad At Medina*, p.257.

5. Hamidullah, p.40.
6. Watt, p.257.
7. The best work on the military aspects of the *Riddah* remains Elias S. Shoufani, *Al-Riddah and the Muslim Conquest of Arabia* (Toronto: University Of Toronto Press, 1972).
8. V.J. Parry and M.E. Yapp, *War, Technology and Society in the Middle East* (London: Oxford University Press, 1975), p.32.
9. Hitti, p.173.
10. Ibid.
11. Hamidullah, p.139.
12. Ibid., p.140.
13. Ibid.

Chapter 27: Riddah: The Great Muslim Civil War

1. Philip K. Hitti, *History of the Arabs* (Hampshire: Palgrave, 2002), p.40.
2. In the same way in which Paul of Tarsus seems to have influenced Christian doctrine and brought about the spread and institutionalization of Christianity, so it appears that Abu Bakr influenced the doctrines of Islam on critical theological points. It is also the case that it was Abu Bakr, not Muhammad, who was ultimately responsible for the spread of Islam and its institutionalization as a formal religion.
3. Elias Shoufani, *Al-Riddah and the Muslim Conquest of Arabia* (Toronto: University of Toronto, Arab Institute for Research and Publishing, 1973), pp.71–73. For Western perspectives on the *Riddah* that challenge the religious perspective, see Julius Wellhausen, *Skizzen und Vorarbeiten* vol. VI (Berlin: 1884–1899), pp.7–8; Carl H. Becker, 'The Expansion of the Saracens', *The Cambridge Medieval History* vol. II (New York: 1913), pp.335–36; Leone Caetani, *Studi di Storia Orientale* vol. 3 (Milan: 1911–1914), pp.349–52; and Bernard Lewis, *The Arabs In History* (London: 1958), pp.51–52. My own view is that W. Montgomery Watt, *Muhammad At Medina* (Oxford: Oxford University Press, 1956), pp.147–48, is correct when he argues that the *Riddah* proceeded from a combination of religious, political and economic motives.
4. Shoufani, p.62, citing Ibn Abi al-Hadid, VI, p.23.
5. Ibid. Al-Hadid provides a list of these commanders.
6. My account of Abu Bakr's campaigns closely follows that of Muhammad ibn Jarir al-Tabari (AD 838–923), *Annales*, 15 volumes, trans. into German and edited by M.J. de Goeje (Leiden: 1879–1901), vol. I. Shoufani, who is the leading Arabic expert on the *Riddah* available in English, states that Tabari's account is the most complete and trustworthy.
7. Tabari's list of Abu Bakr's field commanders during the *Riddah* can be found in Shoufani, p.116.

8. Hatti, p.141.

9. Ibid.

10. Most Arabs during Muhammad's time were illiterate, and even the most basic writing materials had to be imported by Byzantium and Persia. Arab history was preserved in oral tales and tradition, passed from generation to generation. Following this practice, Muhammad's sayings were preserved only orally until perhaps twenty years later, when they were finally written down. Thus the concern that if the 'Quran Reciters' were killed, the entire Muslim history would have been lost.

11. Shoufani, p.118.

12. An example of the flexibility of Muslim armies under Abu Bakr is evident in the movements of Khalid al-Walid's army. Khalid marched from Dhu al-Qassah to al-Buzakhah, where he fought a major battle against a coalition of the tribes of Najad. After defeating the coalition, al-Walid pressed out in several directions until one of his columns engaged the enemy at Al-Butah against the Yarbu. Winning here, he was ordered to swing far to the south-east to rescue Ikrimah bin Abi Jahl, who had been twice routed by the tribes of Beni Hanifah. Al-Walid fought the largest battle of the *Riddah* at Aqraba, dealing the Beni Hanifah a devastating defeat. He then turned north-east, crossed the remaining desert and began raiding along the Persian border. Poised to cross the Euphrates, al-Walid was ordered by Abu Bakr to turn west, march across the Syrian desert and join the Muslim armies preparing to attack Palestine and Syria.

13. Reuven Firestone, *Jihad: The Origins of Holy War in Islam* (London: Oxford University Press, 1999), p.37.

14. Ibid., p.39.

15. Edward Lane, *An Arabic-English Lexicon*, book 1 (London: Williams and Norgate, 1865), part 2, p.473.

16. Firestone, p.50.

17. The elements of *jihad* described here are taken from Andrew Bostom, *The Legacy of Jihad: Islamic Holy War and the Fate of Non-Muslims* (Amherst, NY: Prometheus Books, 2005); David Cook, *Understanding Jihad* (Berkeley: University of California Press, 2005); and Rudolph Peters, *Jihad in Classical and Modern Islam* (Princeton, NJ: Marcus Wiener Publishers, 1996).

Chapter 28: Constantinople: The Most Fought Over City in History

1. Michael Angold, *The Byzantine Empire, 1025–1204* (Longman, 1997), p.211.

Index